HENRY VIII

A Neo-Latin Drama by Nicolaus Vernulaeus

HENRY VIII

A NEO-LATIN DRAMA BY NICOLAUS VERNULAEUS

Translated and Edited with a
History of the Louvain Academic Theater

by

LOUIS A. SCHUSTER, S.M.

UNIVERSITY OF TEXAS PRESS, AUSTIN

1964

Published with the assistance of a grant from the Ford Foundation under its program for the support of publications in the humanities and social sciences

for MILDRED and GEORGE

ACKNOWLEDGMENTS

The six years of part-time research represented by this study have enriched me with the friendship of many scholars who continue to merit my indebtedness. Initial gropings were given direction and constructive criticism by Leicester Bradner and Craig R. Thompson. Thereafter the cooperation of Marianist confreres George Montague, Joseph Verrier, Charles Dreisoerner, Charles Miller, and David Fleming proved indispensable in assembling first editions from European libraries and expediting translation. The final form of the book bears the impress of various professors at the University of Texas: Professors Thomas P. Harrison, Rudolph Willard, Leo Hughes, and Guy Steffan; the translation owes much to the painstaking care and critical acumen of Professor Harry J. Leon and his wife, Ernestine Leon. Finally the late Professor Henri de Vocht of the University of Louvain afforded me generous access to his prodigious learning and private library in an atmosphere of genial scholarship that will long be cherished.

Further indebtedness is expressed to the Trustees of Amherst College for granting a summer sabbatical at the Folger Shakespeare Library, where the venture was launched, and to the Southern Fellowships Fund for enabling me to consult primary source materials and complete the manuscript at the Library of the University of Louvain, Belgium. The staffs of these two libraries, as well as those of the Library of Congress, the British Museum, the Royal Library of the Hague, the Royal Library of Belgium, and other libraries here and abroad, have been unexceptionally gracious in their assistance.

L.A.S.

St. Mary's University
San Antonio, Texas

CONTENTS

INTRODUCTION

The preoccupation of scholars during the past century with the vernacular literatures of the Renaissance has not only relegated Neo-Latin literature to a position of comparative oblivion but has tended to make us forget that the vast corpus of Renaissance works written in Latin even exists. No thoroughgoing history of Renaissance Latin literature has as yet been attempted simply because such an undertaking would prove well nigh limitless. As Walter J. Ong reminds us, "It would cover all Europe and America and weave in and out of every vernacular literature from Portuguese to Hungarian, and from Italian to Icelandic, and be simply the history of the Western mind."[1]

Neo-Latin drama, like other areas of this Renaissance hinterland, remains still largely unexplored. Since the final decade of the nineteenth century, however, pioneers such as Paul Bahlmann, Johannes Bolte, Wilhelm Creizenach, Johannes Müller, F. S. Boas, Alfred Harbage, Paul O. Kristeller, Don Cameron Allen, Archer Taylor, Marvin T. Herrick, and Leicester Bradner have been surveying the terrain and drawing in its contours. The results of their trail blazing have enticed other scholar prospectors into the Neo-Latin wilderness, each of them intent on reclaiming a patch of territory, subjecting it to scrutiny, and reducing it to order.[2] Critical editions and translations of Neo-Latin drama though sporadic, have been on the increase over the past two decades; yet hundreds of plays, both in print and in manuscript, need to be investigated before the impact of the academic theater on vernacular drama and Renaissance culture can be assessed.[3]

---

[1] *Ramus, Method, and the Decay of Dialogue* (Cambridge, Mass.: Harvard University Press, 1958), p. 10. As the result of a proposal at the 1952 MLA Convention, a cooperative history of modern Latin literature (1400–1600), under the general editorship of James R. Naiden, was assigned to thirty-two scholars, each of whom was responsible for one aspect of the history. The projectors of the venture, it should be noted, were under no illusions that the finished history, however imposing, would be anything other than a cursory treatment.

[2] Information on the status of Neo-Latin studies, including recent dissertations and research in progress, is available in a number of periodicals, the most helpful of which is *Neo-Latin News,* published since 1954 as a supplement to *Seventeenth Century News.* Also useful are the Annual Bibliography of *PMLA* since 1932 (General Section, Heading V), the Annual Bibliography of *Studies in Philology* since 1922 (Recent Literature of the Renaissance), *Renaissance News* and *Studies in the Renaissance* since 1948 (both issued by The Renaissance Society of America).

[3] Since 1954 the Desiderata of Modern Latin Literature (a scholarly control center originating in the Neo-Latin Section of the MLA) together with panels devoted to Opportunities for Research in Renaissance Drama (likewise connected with MLA) has continued to stress the need for more translations of academic drama as well as research into the histories of individual college theaters of the Renaissance.

The present study is intended to help meet this need. It aims to contribute, however modestly, to a significant advance in the pioneering efforts of Neo-Latin scholarship by rescuing from neglect and making generally accessible to students of the drama one of the most interesting Neo-Latin tragedies of the late Renaissance. Since the play in question was informed by purposes and shaped by conventions peculiar to the academic theater, it seemed advisable to reconstruct its somewhat unfamiliar theatrical context with the hope of insuring a sympathetic reading and proper critical response.

This reconstruction led through untrodden ways in Renaissance country. The report of the adventure, involving the history of a particular college theater, a study of the life and works of its most celebrated playwright, together with an inquiry into the cultural exchange between England and the Netherlands which fertilized the play, is offered as a complementary contribution to Renaissance studies.

Thus the opening chapter is devoted to the life and works of the Louvain playwright Nicolaus Vernulaeus, an undertaking hitherto unattempted in English. The second chapter reaches back to the beginnings of the theater of the University of Louvain and traces for the first time the evolution of this theater against a background of shifting values, of political and religious realignments. The perspective afforded by this panoramic view invites, in the third chapter, a focus on the Vernulaeus theater itself, its purposes, its conventions, its integration with the academic life of the University, together with a critical survey of the Vernulaeus canon in which these principles find dramatic embodiment. This reconstruction of the historical, religious, and dramatic reference in which *Henricus Octavus* can be intelligently approached prepares for the immediate introduction to the play itself—the burden of Chapter IV. At this point a treatise on the English schism from Rome, by Nicholas Sander, a recusant Oxford don, is shown as the seed which, having lain dormant for two generations, grew to dramatic fruition under the hand of the Louvain playwright. The historical accuracy of Vernulaeus' source, the nature of his dramatic transmutation of it, the playwright's indebtedness to the classics, and finally a critical appraisal of *Henricus Octavus* are here introduced. The detailed examination of these elements, however, is reserved for the Explanatory Notes to *Henricus Octavus*, which follow the text of the play and its English translation.

PART ONE

Prolegomena to *Henricus Octavus*

Chapter I

THE LIFE AND WORKS OF NICOLAUS VERNULAEUS

When the faculty of the Catholic University of Louvain assembled in their collegiate church on January 8, 1649, to assist at the burial services of their former colleague, Nicolaus Vernulaeus, they realized that they were attending no mere grammarian's funeral. They had all lived with the renowned priest-professor and not a few of them had witnessed the burgeoning of his powers since his first days as an instructor of rhetoric at the Porc College. Promoted to Public Professor of Eloquence, later to the presidency of the College of Luxembourg, Vernulaeus was finally entrusted with the highest administrative position of the University of Louvain, that of rector, an office he held on three occasions. The chair of Latin Professor of the illustrious Trilingue College to which were added the titles of Royal Historiographer and Counselor of Philip IV and Ferdinand III, came as a crowning distinction of his lifework.[1]

During his forty years of teaching and administration, Vernulaeus continued to write and study. In characteristic Renaissance fashion he threw his net wide over the waters of rhetoric, moral philosophy, economics, political science, history, and literature. From his pen issued an unbroken flow of ideas that were welcomed by the Louvain presses. The works of Vernulaeus, frequently in waves of new editions, had soon spread beyond the Netherlands to other parts of Europe, carrying with them the fame of Louvain's dramatist and teacher of rhetoric, together with the achievements of his students.

Nicolas de Vernulz, son of Pierre de Vernulz and Marie de Merjay, was born on Easter Day, April 10, 1583, at Roblemont, a village near Virton in the Duchy of Luxembourg.[2] His father followed a military

[1] Henri de Vocht, "Vernulaeus," *Biographie Nationale de Belgique*, Vol. XXVI (1936–37), cols. 676–82.

[2] The principal primary sources for the life of Vernulaeus are: Valerius Andreas, *Fasti academici studii generalis Lovaniensis* (2d ed.), pp. 1, 10, 13, 48, 87, 144, 247–48, 281–82, 326, 330, 395–96, cited hereafter as *Fasti*; Valerius Andreas, *Bibliotheca belgica* (2d ed.), pp. 699–701; Antoine d'Ave, *Oratio in funere N. Vernulaei,* cited hereafter as *Oratio in funere*; *Vita et scripta Nicolai Vernulaei* (anonymous), prefacing Vol. II of *Tragoediae, in duos tomos distributae* (2d ed.), cited hereafter as *Vita et scripta*; Henri de Vocht, *Inventaire des archives de l'université de Louvain, 1426–1797, aux archives générales du royaume à Bruxelles,* No. 103 (*Liber dictatoris*); No. 710 (*Acta facultatis artium,* X), pp. 487, 491, 493–94, 543, 549; No. 711 (*idem.,* XI), pp. 19v, 28v, 31, 34r, 39v, 40, 61, 71, 89, 91, 460, 467, 473–75, 488,

career in the Spanish Netherlands, serving as a captain in the army of Alessandro Farnese, Duke of Parma and Regent of Philip II. Nicolas began his studies at Trèves, probably at the Jesuit college, and in his eighteenth year continued his philosophy courses at Cologne.[3] At the invitation of J. B. Gramaye, Professor of Eloquence at Louvain, Vernulaeus accepted the position of Instructor of Rhetoric at the Porc College in 1608.[4] A year later Vernulaeus had written and produced his first school play.[5] It was very probably the immediate success of his disciple as school dramatist and teacher of rhetoric that prompted Gramaye, on November 10, 1610, to resign the chair of Rhetor Publicus[6] as well as the canonry attached to this professorship and confer them both on Vernulaeus. This unprecedented maneuver caused a Town-Gown flurry that was to persist for more than a year.[7]

The reason for the dispute lay in the bilateral character of the chair of Rhetor Publicus to which Vernulaeus was named. Since the canonry appointment (the prebend of which financed the professorship) was controlled by the City authorities, the City virtually appointed the Rhetor

---

530–33, 547; (*idem.*, XII), pp. 3r–6v, 317r; No. 729 (*Index des Acta*), pp. 155–65, 178–82, 185; No. 762 (*Professeurs publics*); No. 4766 (*Controversies des professeurs littéraires*); No. 1442 (*Collège de Busleyden*); No. 3517 (*Collège de Milius*); No. 5061.

[3] "Nicolaus Roberti Montis Lutzenburgensis . . . et Johannes Montang Lotharings quia pauperes solverunt tantum pro pedellis," Stadtarchiv Köln, allgemeine Verwaltung der Universität Köln, No. 74: Fünfte Matrikel (1559–1627), fol. 197. The notice given by J. Bolte ("Vernuläus," *Allgemeine deutsche Biographie*, XXXIX, 628, as supplied by H. Keussen) is literally inexact, though not misleading.

[4] John Baptist Gramaye (1580–1635), native of Antwerp, received his master's degree at Louvain in 1596 and his licentiate in law in 1600. In addition to being Professor of Eloquence, he was a playwright, royal historiographer, and an antiquarian of some note. His *Historia Lutzenburgensis*, published at Cologne in 1605, may have necessitated a visit there and have been the occasion of his contact with the young Vernulaeus. See Henri de Vocht, *History of the Foundation and Rise of the Collegium Trilingue Lovaniense 1517–1550*, I, 74, n. 2, cited hereafter as *Collegium Trilingue*.

[5] *Gorcomienses sive fidei exilium tragoedia. Exhibita ludis encoenialibus Lovanii anno 1609 ab alumnis collegii Porcensis.*

[6] The Rhetor Publicus was likewise referred to as "Rhetor Lovaniensis," or "Rhetor Academicus." This chair was established by the Faculty of Arts in 1443, attesting already at that date the existence of literary studies complementing grammar. The Rhetor Publicus conducted classes in rhetoric on Tuesday and Friday mornings at 10 o'clock in the public auditorium of the Arts faculty. The canonship attached to this chair was honorary, involving neither presence in choir nor recitation of the breviary. See J. N. Paquot, *Mémoires pour servir à l'histoire littéraire des dix-sept provinces des Pays-Bas*, III, 429, cited hereafter as *Mémoires*; Léon van der Essen, *Une institution d'enseignement superieur sous l'ancien régime*, pp. 19, 99, cited hereafter as *Une institution*.

[7] Andreas, *Fasti*, pp. 247–48.

Publicus, although ordinarily it recognized only those candidates proposed by the Louvain Arts faculty. Vernulaeus was neither Louvain-trained nor a member of its Arts faculty. Consequently, when the City, by exception, recognized Vernulaeus as Gramaye's successor, the University authorities objected and refused to recognize the appointee they had not proposed. When the ensuing discussions between the City and the University terminated, Vernulaeus was retained as Public Professor of Eloquence.

Meanwhile the Arts faculty, like Daudet's papal mule, nursed its grudge and waited. When, soon afterward, Vernulaeus requested admission to the Faculty Council, he was informed that professors of philosophy alone were eligible.[8] Determined to make himself eligible, Vernulaeus began his theology studies at Louvain. Ironically enough, it was by virtue of his position as vice-regent of the Porc that he was admitted to the Faculty Council on July 10, 1617. On December 11 of the following year he obtained his licentiate, two days after the Council had ordered him to complete his thesis.[9]

The growing reputation of Vernulaeus as a teacher of rhetoric and the wide circulation of his student orations were indisputable accomplishments; yet neither the teachers of rhetoric nor the discipline they represented was given full academic recognition by the theologians and philosophers of Louvain. Already in 1612 Vernulaeus had begun a campaign to enhance departmental prestige: he applied for permission to use the public Arts auditorium several days a week for discussions in *universa philologia,* as he termed his courses in rhetoric, but even here he met opposition. Thus in 1614, being denied access to the auditorium, Vernulaeus was obliged to have the Rector intervene in his behalf.[10] At the same time, as spokesman for all the professors of rhetoric in the preparatory schools, he opened a controversy with the Faculty, claiming for his colleagues the same privileges accorded the philosophy professors. Undismayed by defeat, he renewed his struggle for recognition in 1622. So persuasively did he present his arguments before the Conseil Privé and University inspectors that he gained for his fellow-rhetoricians the prerogatives and departmental prestige hitherto denied them.[11] Equally progressive were his innovations in methodology. Openly denying the

[8] See *Archives of the University of Louvain,* No. 714, fols. 491, 492, 494, 502, 503, 540, 550; No. 715, fols. 20, 31, 61, 67, 72, 92, cited hereafter as *AUL.* For the summary of these archive materials, see de Vocht, "Vernulaeus," *Biographie Nationale de Belgique,* Vol. XXVI, cols. 676–77.

[9] *AUL,* No. 387, fols. 107, 92.

[10] See de Vocht, *Biographie Nationale de Belgique,* Vol. XXVI, col. 677.

[11] *Ibid.,* cols. 678–79.

efficacy of the medieval method of disputation, as the young Milton of the *Prolusiones* would also do some fifteen years later, Vernulaeus applied the scientific method to the study of Latin literature. Viewed in historical perspective, his reforms in the conception and methodology of literary studies in the beginning of the seventeenth century entitle him to a place in the vanguard of educational pioneers.[12]

The grueling apprenticeship of Vernulaeus, the subtle tyranny of administrational protocol, and the entrenched conservatism of the theologians and philosophers steadily challenged his energies and matured his powers. The Faculty's early suspicions of the newcomer with his persistence and zeal for innovation gradually dissolved before the man's quiet sincerity, his encyclopedic erudition, and his already brilliant record of publication. In 1619, when the Counts of Fugger opened the College of Luxembourg in Louvain, Vernulaeus was chosen as its first president,[13] a position he held until his death.[14]

One of the distinguished public appearances of Vernulaeus was occasioned by the celebration of the second centenary of the Studium Generale of Louvain in September, 1626. The fortnight of festivities reached a climax in an *opus publicum*, in which the most eloquent professors of the University paid homage to its achievements during the previous two centuries. Vernulaeus, Louvain's public orator, was chosen to represent the Arts faculty.[15] His address, delivered in the impressive Gothic college church of St. Peter, celebrated the generosity of the Dukes of Brabant toward the University.[16]

A more spirited, if less academic, occasion that roused Vernulaeus to public oratory was the celebration of the deliverance of the city of Louvain from the besieging armies of Louis XIII and the United Provinces. It is not difficult to imagine the pride which the rolling periods of their professor must have raised in the hearts of the Louvain students, most of

[12] *Ibid.*, col. 677.

[13] "Primus vero Praeses Collegio hujus an. MDCXIX ex voluntate Illust. Fuggerorum, constitutus fuit ab illius Provisoribus Nicolaus Vernulaeus S. Th. L. ex Ducatu Luxemb. oriundus." Andreas, *Fasti*, p. 281.

[14] Two of Vernulaeus' nephews boarded at the Luxembourg college: Jaspard Jupille (from September 22, 1648, to March 2, 1649) and Claude de Merjay (from April 16, 1647, to April 16, 1649). *AUL*, No. 3517, fols. 2, 13. His niece, Elisabeth de Vernulz, aided in the administration of the college. *Ibid.*, fol. 1.

[15] Two other discourses were pronounced, one by Petrus Castellanus, professor of Greek and Hebrew at the Trilingue, the other by Valerius Andreas, professor of civil law. See Henri de Vocht, "Les jubilés de l'université sous l'Ancien Régime, 1526, 1626, 1726," in *L'Université de Louvain à travers cinq siècles*, pp. 19–30.

[16] "De munificentia ducum Brabantiae in academiam lovaniensem, habita in aede D. Petri . . . cum academia lovaniensis secundum saeculare jubilaeum celebraret," *Elogia oratoria* (Cologne: 1635), pp. 413–37.

whom had manned the city walls shoulder to shoulder with the towns-people in a display of courage and heroic resistance that led to victory on July 4, 1635.[17] These occasional public appearances, however, were mere interludes in the life of Vernulaeus the teacher. Shortly after his stirring liberation address we find the public orator reminding his young soldier-students that the war is over, and that it is time they get back to their books.[18]

Vernulaeus' four decades of teaching at Louvain were signalized by a series of honorary offices and official titles awarded him in his role of priest and professor. Early in his career, before 1626, he was awarded a canonry at Renaix, another at St. Peter of Douay. A chaplaincy at Ivoix followed on April 5, 1631.[19] In 1644 and 1645 he was again chosen rector of the University of Louvain. The following year he was appointed to the chair of Latin in Trilingue College which Justus Lipsius and Erycius Puteanus had previously occupied. He also was named Royal Historiographer and Counselor of the Spanish kings and of German Emperor Ferdinand III.[20]

A cataloguing of Vernulaeus' academic struggles and administrative posts may leave an impression of bustling, almost furious activity. The fact is that Vernulaeus was regarded by his contemporaries as an unprepossessing, sweet-tempered man.[21] On the other hand, his industry seems to have been tremendous, even to the point of excess. Not content with classroom contact, Vernulaeus' students invaded his home at all hours of the day and night, seeking his guidance and instruction.[22] Vernulaeus made himself available to all of them. Particularly noteworthy was his influence over the sons of noble families of Poland, Bohemia, and Germany.[23]

Vernulaeus' lifelong dedication to youth was rooted in religious conviction. In the midst of academic duties, he found time for a strenuous

[17] *Triumphus lovaniensium, ob solutam urbis suae obsidionem, per recessum duorum potentissimorum exercituum christianissimi Franciae regis, & foederatorum Belgii ordinum.* For another contemporary account of the siege of Louvain, see the work of Vernulaeus' close friend Puteanus: *Historiae belgicae liber singularis de obsidione lovaniense anno 1635.*

[18] *Oratio ad juventutem cum Kal. Augusti 1635 post solutam urbis lovaniensis obsidionem studia resumerentur.*

[19] In June, 1647, Vernulaeus transferred the prebend of his Ivoix chaplaincy to his nephew Lambert de Vernulz, Curé of Chavancy St. Hubert, who as a boy played the role of Virgo in *Henricus Octavus. AUL,* Nos. 763, 5061.

[20] Andreas, *Fasti,* p. 281; Paquot, *Mémoires,* III, 430.

[21] *Vita et scripta,* n.p.; Paquot, *Mémoires,* III, 431; d'Ave, *Oratio in funere,* fols. A3r, C2r.

[22] *Vita et scripta;* see also d'Ave, *Oratio in funere,* fol. B2r.

[23] Stefan Rygiel, *Puteanus und die Polen,* pp. 23, 28–29, 38–39, 45.

prayer life. He celebrated Mass daily, frequented Sodality meetings, cultivated devotion to the Blessed Virgin, St. Nicholas, St. Anthony of Padua, the Blessed Sacrament, and daily recited the rosary and meditated with exemplary piety, as his students attested.[24] As a Catholic priest, he devoted himself unreservedly to the work of the church in the persons of his students. It was this same religious urgency that held him at his desk for forty years and called forth from his pen more than fifty volumes. The many eulogistic verse-tributes of his students bear witness to the esteem and loyalty he evoked as teacher and friend; the stirring funeral oration delivered by his former student Antoine d'Ave reveals the same profound admiration. That his reputation extended far beyond the classroom is evidenced by a remark of Archduke Leopold, who, on entering the Duchy of Luxembourg in 1647, immediately inquired after Vernulaeus' health. "That man," he affirmed, "was born for the common weal."[25]

Vernulaeus' career as a student, teacher, and writer was dominated by a single purpose: the training of youth for their dual responsibilities to church and state. He considered any deviation from this purpose a waste of time.[26] This preoccupation with the practical is the key to all his writings, a principle he admitted unequivocally: "I have always maintained that in dealing with youth the most important consideration is, 'Will it help them in future real-life situations?'"[27] Most of Vernulaeus' works are the direct product of his teaching, being either model orations, textbooks designed to present curriculum subjects in methodical fashion, or school dramas. His remaining publications are almost invariably dictated by his official positions as Rhetor Publicus, Rector of Louvain, or Royal Historiographer.[28]

The titles of Vernulaeus' first published orations reveal his lifelong interest in contemporary religious and political issues, Mariology, and the place of Latin studies in the Arts curriculum.[29] Concurrently with his own publications, he inaugurated a series of student orations written

[24] D'Ave, *Oratio in funere*, fol. Cv.
[25] Paquot, *Mémoires*, III, 432.
[26] D'Ave, *Oratio in funere*, fol. B2v.
[27] *Institutionum politicarum libri iv, qui omnia civilis doctrinae elementa continent*, fol. a4, cited hereafter as *Institutionum politicarum*. The eminently practical cast of Renaissance education is clearly demonstrated by Hardin Craig. See *The Enchanted Glass: The Elizabethan Mind in Literature*, pp. 87–95.
[28] A chronological list of Vernulaeus' writings is given in Appendix C.
[29] *Quis inter orbis monarchas potentissimus. Dissertatio politica* (1613); *De conceptione & visitatione Mariae, orationes duae. Accedit tertia de affinitate & cognatione eloquentiae cum caeteris scientiis* (1614).

under his supervision and intended as models of oratory.[30] Their appearance in 1614 created a demand that persisted for more than a century. The fifteen model orations had increased to forty-five in the third edition of 1630. By 1720, the series had gone through more than ten editions, each succeeding publication being augmented by new selections.[31]

The orations almost inevitably come to grips with vital issues of the day: Should heretics be constrained by force? Should a scholar desert his ivory tower for public life? Can an army officer profit by a liberal education? What are the duties of a general, a counselor? Should Bacchanalia be encouraged? Is control of the sea more crucial than control of the land?[32] To this day these student forensics retain their freshness and directness. Paquot says of these orations: "They are first-rate; their style is pure, melodious, flowing, lively, and consistently free of monotony; they progress smoothly, their imagery is pleasing, and the subject matter is well chosen; furthermore, they contain practical considerations, a wholesome moral tone, and often new ideas."[33]

A second series introduced a practical church-state problem: whether a state should tolerate the coexistence of different religious sects.[34] The conclusion tended to reject a diversified confessionalism by attempting to prove it a threat to national unity. Subsequent orations reveal the same timeliness of subject matter: the plausibility of a world federation; whether French or Spanish monarchs have been more loyal to the Roman Church; the reputation for military prowess as discussed by seven soldiers representing Spain, Belgium, Germany, France, Italy, Poland, and Hungary.[35]

[30] *Rhetorum collegii Porcensis inclytae academiae Lovaniensis orationes, sub Nic. Vernulaeo* . . . (1614). Later editions are: Louvain, 1633, 1645, 1649; Cologne, 1619, 1639, 1663–88; Antwerp, 1684.

[31] De Vocht, *Biographie nationale de Belgique,* Vol. XXVI, col. 679. The fourth edition (Cologne, 1639) groups the collected orations under the traditional genres of demonstrative, deliberative, and judicial, to which is added a series of religious orations.

[32] See *Rhetorum collegii Porcensis . . . orationes,* Pt. I, 1663; Pt. II, 1688 [both in Newberry Library]. The orations are equipped with marginal glosses pointing the rhetorical graces and artifices.

[33] *Mémoires,* III, 432.

[34] *Dissertatio politica de una & diversa religione, constans orationibus X, habita ab eloquentiae candidatis juvenibus in publica artium schola Lovanii sub D. Nic. Vernulaeo* (1618).

[35] *Disputatio politica, de universa republica . . . proposita a Nicolao Lahodowsky* (1621); *Certamen oratorium inter duos oratores, Francum et Hispanum: utri de ecclesia romana melius meriti sint, Franciae an Hispaniae reges?* . . . (1624); *Certamen oratorium de militari gloria, inter septem milites, hispanum, belgam, germanum, francum, italum, polonum, hungarum,* (1624).

The importance of these orations in the final assessment of Vernulaeus' dramatic work can hardly be overemphasized. Not only do the
school plays share with the rhetorical exercises their author's lifelong absorption in vital political and religious issues, but they likewise reveal in
their structural and stylistic patterns a constant dependence on rhetorical
devices.[36] It is true that the orations never exploit fully the dramatic potentialities of a situation. Yet their use of characters to personify nations,
their lively debate over opposing issues, and their persuasive character
lend them an unmistakably dramatic cast. The overlap of rhetorical and
dramatic disciplines in Vernulaeus is most apparent in such orations as
the complaint and acquittal of the sons of Herod before Augustus.[37]

In addition to his model orations and personal addresses, Vernulaeus
published a textbook on rhetoric in 1619. Its popularity is attested by six
editions in less than fifty years.[38] Ten further volumes deal with ethics,
political theory, and economics, the latter an omnium–gatherum of
sociology, domestic economy, child psychology, and marriage guidance.[39] They show Vernulaeus' desire to winnow from the experience of
the past those principles of conduct he thought eminently practical and
essential.[40] Especially germane to his dramatic work are his four volumes
on political questions. In them he takes a definite position on such pertinent issues as the problem of coexistence, the origin of authority, the
causes justifying rebellion, the prevention of war, the nature of tyranny,
the training of princes, legates, counselors, magistrates, courtiers, and
military officers—all of which issues recur frequently as themes in his
historical tragedies. If some of these subjects seem an unlikely choice
for a professor-priest, it should be borne in mind that Vernulaeus was
the son of an army officer and that he was writing during the harrowing
times of the Thirty Years' War (1618–48). The imbalance resulting from
this military preoccupation and its encroachment on academic life be-

[36] The rhetorical techniques most commonly employed by Vernulaeus are singled
out for illustration in the Explanatory Notes which accompany the text of *Henricus
Octavus.*

[37] See *Rhetorum collegii Porcensis . . . orationes*, Pt. III (1663), pp. 394–402. J.
Bolte finds Vernulaeus' practice of assigning various aspects of the same subject and
the appointment of student plaintiffs and advocates in complete conformity with the
Jesuit prescriptions in the *Ratio studiorum*. See his *Coligny, Gustaf Adolf, Wallenstein: drei zeitgenössische lateinische dramen von Rhodius, Narssius, Vernulaeus*,
p. xvii.

[38] *De arte dicendi libri tres; una cum praxi rhetoricae & duobus de inventione
libris* (1619). Also Louvain, 1631, 1637, 1667; Jena, 1631; Nuremberg, 1658.

[39] *Institutionum politicarum; Institutionum moralium libri iv* (1625); *Institutionum oeconomicarum libri duo . . .* (1626).

[40] *Institutionum politicarum* (1647), fol. a4.

came occasionally irritating: the sound of the Muses, Vernulaeus complains, is drowned in the clash of armor; students carry weapons instead of books; few Maecenases are at hand.[41]

In his official capacities as Royal Historiographer, Rhetor Publicus, and Rector of the University, Vernulaeus composed and published more than twelve volumes. None of these panegyrics, funeral orations, or celebrations of military victories have immediate relevance to his dramatic work.[42] They do, however, exhibit Vernulaeus' unswerving loyalty to both the Spanish and Austrian branches of the Habsburg dynasty and so help delineate the politico-religious matrix in which his plays are cast.

Between 1609 and 1648 Vernulaeus wrote fourteen historical tragedies. All his plays were printed and all of them, apparently, were acted at Louvain by his students.[43] The majority of them deal with major conflicts in which spiritual authority, usually in the person of an ecclesiastic, clashes with temporal power in the person of a king or military leader. Thus Abbot Picus of Gorkum is pitted against Sea-beggar Admiral de la Marck (*Gorcomienses*); the Roman soldier-convert Eustace, against the Emperor Hadrian (*Eustachius*); Pope John, Symmachus, and Boethius, against East Gothic King Theodoric (*Theodoricus*). Similarly, Bishop Lambert opposes Frankish King Pepin (*Lambertus*); Thomas Becket, King Henry II of England (*Thomas Cantuariensis*); More and Fisher, King Henry VIII (*Henricus Octavus*); and Bishop Stanislas of Cracow, King Boleslav of Poland (*Stanislaus*). The persecution of the Catholic faith by the Arian West Goths is the theme of *Hermenigildus*; *Crispus*, on the other hand, re-enacts the Phaedra saga in a Christian setting.

[41] See the Dedicatory Letter to *Tragoediae decem* (1631).

[42] Typical official writings include a series of orations commemorating the victories of Spinola, elegies on Archduke Albert and Isabella, defenses of the Habsburg dynasty, a manual on the University of Louvain, and an address of welcome to Ferdinand III.

[43] Eight of the fourteen dramas were published as separate titles: *Gorcomienses* (Cologne, 1610); *Divus Eustachius* (Louvain, 1612); *Theodoricus* (Louvain, 1623); *Henricus Octavus* (Louvain, 1624); *Ottocarus* (Louvain, 1626); *Joanna Darcia* (Louvain, 1629); *Maximus* (Louvain, 1630); *Fritlandus* (Louvain, 1637). Two others were published jointly: *Conradinus* and *Crispus* (Louvain, 1628). With the exception of *Maximus*, all the plays published separately before 1630 were collected and reissued in *Tragoediae decem* (Louvain, 1631); this collection included two hitherto unpublished plays: *Stanislaus* and *Thomas Cantuariensis*. All the tragedies of Vernulaeus were reprinted collectively in a posthumous edition, *Tragoediae, in duos tomos distributae* (Louvain, 1656), the previously unpublished *Lambertus* and *Hermenigildus* being included. References on title pages, in dedicatory letters, and in appended poems indicate that nine of the plays were acted in September or in October (*Ludis remigialibus*) or during the first week of the New Year (*Ludis encoenialibus*).

Conradinus and *Joanna Darcia* are political tragedies in which the champions of freedom and justice succumb to superior forces but gain moral triumph in their defeat. Finally in the three rebellion plays—*Maximus, Ottocarus,* and *Fritlandus* (Wallenstein)—insurrection against lawfully constituted authority brings eventual ruin to the instigators.

A survey of the life and works of Vernulaeus establishes his position as a Catholic Humanist of the late Renaissance; furthermore, it clearly outlines the specific characteristics of that position. The earlier Christian Humanists had envisioned a form of Christianity compatible with classical ideals, with liberty of thought, and with scientific objectivity. The religious wars that followed in the wake of the Reformation, however, had exposed their illusions and rendered a choice of confessions imperative.[44]

Vernulaeus' enlistment in the camp of Rome and his subsequent career of consecrated partisanship are the ultimate unifying principle of his lifework. To his role of *miles Catholicus*, in turn, he enlisted the support of those human forces of Renaissance education and culture which were his heritage. Of these human values, the Renaissance ideal of rhetoric became his most abiding inspiration. As an instrument in the service of religion, rhetoric could operate on the reason and passions of men to bolster a Rome-Habsburg dyarchy to which Vernulaeus wholeheartedly subscribed.[45] In addition, Vernulaeus capitalized on the Renaissance tendency to simplify, to explain, to interpret, and to apply: his scholarship was directed to the gleaning and dissemination of truth as he saw it, rather than to an extension of its horizons.[46] No less characteristic of the man and his age was a preoccupation with the practical aspects of education, as well as a considerable intellectual versatility.

It is not surprising that Antoine d'Ave, Professor of Ethics, when searching for an appropriate image to immortalize his teacher's memory, selected the metaphor of oratory to summarize Vernulaeus' life and work:

As the good orator you have always been, you brought your life's oration to a successful conclusion: by your lifelong integrity and honesty, by your sanctity and manifold wisdom, you persuaded not men alone, but God Himself. Indeed you were that kind of orator whose tongue was eloquent, whose pen was more eloquent, and whose life was eloquence itself.[47]

[44] See Henri Pirenne, *Histoire de Belgique,* IV, 448.

[45] In this connection, Craig suggests that possibly the greatest interest of the Renaissance was oratory and its principles as applied to politics and theology (*The Enchanted Glass,* p. 161).

[46] *Ibid.,* p. 143.

[47] D'Ave, *Oratio in funere,* fol. C2.

Like the majority of playwrights, Vernulaeus worked within a living dramatic tradition. In his case, the tradition was that of Neo-Latin school drama, long since abandoned, but once of widespread cultivation and significance in Renaissance education and culture. To understand Vernulaeus' position as a late-Renaissance school dramatist, it will be helpful to reconstruct the centuries-old dramatic tradition of the University of Louvain in which he worked. The perspective afforded by this reconstruction in the pages that follow will enable us to return with fresh insight to the nature of the Vernulaeus theater in general and to the place of *Henricus Octavus* as one of its major achievements.

Chapter II

RISE AND GROWTH OF THE LOUVAIN
ACADEMIC THEATER

The academic theater of Louvain took root and flourished in the preparatory schools of the University. Toward the middle of the fifteenth
century, four of these schools—the Lily, the Porc, the Castle, and the
Falcon—had been granted instructional monopolies by the University
authorities.[1] Within their halls the trivial and quadrivial subjects were
taught to teen-agers not yet sufficiently advanced for University studies.
Since all lectures, debates, and academic functions of the University
were carried on exclusively in Latin, each preparatory school conducted
classes ranging from rudimentary instruction in Latin to the stage of
mastery required for University attendance.

It was in the Porc preparatory school that Vernulaeus began his teaching career. Like many other instructors of grammar and rhetoric, Vernulaeus quickened the interest of his students by having them deliver orations and act out plays which he composed. With the staging of his first
play at the University of Louvain in 1609, he became associated with a
theatrical tradition that had been evolving for well over a hundred
years.[2]

The first stirrings of the Louvain academic drama can be traced to
the Lily preparatory school. There, on February 23, 1481, before an audience of dignitaries, faculty members, and fellow-students, several aspiring lawyers performed the *Declamatio*, a debate engendered by discontent with current disciplinary regulations of the Lily.[3] Speaking for his
fellows, a Junior plaintiff accuses the Fiscalis of overinquisitiveness and
severity and proceeds to unleash a string of complaints. Obligatory at-

[1] See Andreas, *Fasti*, p. 9.

[2] The complete history of the Louvain academic theater, like the histories of most
other college theaters of the Renaissance, remains unwritten. The great losses
suffered by the Library of the University of Louvain in the two world wars increase
the difficulty of reconstructing its theatrical history. It is principally through the
long and painstaking research of the late Professor Henri de Vocht of Louvain that
the surviving source materials have been recovered; in the present study they are
organized chronologically for the first time.

[3] The beginning of the text is cited in de Vocht, *Collegium Trilingue*, I, 218, n. 5.
See also M. Louis Polain, *Catalogue des livres imprimés au quinzième siècle des
bibliothèques de Belgique*, II, 1248.

tendance at the newly inaugurated lectures on poetics, for example, is frowned upon because the topic is considered impractical. Regulations about public feasts and dances, gambling, immodesty in dress and behavior are questioned. Authority itself is challenged.[4] Successive rejoinders of the defendant establish the dialogue pattern of the two characters and thus create a basically dramatic composition. Noteworthy is the fact that the debate began in the public Arts auditorium and later, after the principal meal, was resumed in the Lily by an alternate Fiscalis and another Junior.[5]

No evidence of any further dramatic activity at Louvain during the last quarter of the fifteenth century has survived. That a tradition was maintained, however, seems undeniable when we compare the *Declamatio* of 1481 with the *Dialogus* written and produced in the Lily by Martin van Dorp in 1509. To acquire perspective for understanding the beginnings of this theatrical tradition it is necessary to reconstruct briefly the academic situation which helped shape the dramatic work of Dorp.

As teacher of Latin in the Lily, this illustrious Humanist was not content to limit his instruction to the mechanics of the language, but supplemented his teaching with explications. So enthusiastic was his explanation of Plautus that a public presentation of the *Aulularia* was given in the Lily on September 3, 1508.[6] Dorp supplied a prologue, fitting the circumstances of production to the Louvain Fair audience attending it. In addition he solved the problem involved in staging the unfinished *Aulularia* by appending a catastrophe of his own.[7] Six months later the students of the Lily performed the *Miles Gloriosus*, to which a similar Dorpian prologue had been affixed.[8] The success of Dorp's presentations of these two comedies of Plautus spread to the Low Countries, inspiring

---

[4] De Vocht, *Collegium Trilingue*, I, 219.

[5] *Ibid.*, n. 1.

[6] *Ibid.*, I, 187, 216.

[7] The *Tomus*, as Dorp called his catastrophe, is stylistically and metrically Plautine and adheres closely to the plot sketched in the *Argumentum* of the *Aulularia*. Thomas More found Dorp's addition very creditable: "As regards elegance of language or sallies of wit—and they are Plautine indeed—no part of Dorp's comedy seems inferior to the work of Plautus" (*Thomae Mori Angliae ornamenti eximii, lucubrationes, ab innumeris mendis repurgatae*, p. 423). The structural superiority and stylistic inferiority of Dorp's *Tomus* to the addition supplied by Antony Urceo Codrus have been observed. See Wilhelm Creizenach, *Geschichte des neueren Dramas*, II, 55–56. See also de Vocht, *Collegium Trilingue*, I, 216.

[8] The *Miles* was staged in the Lily on a "Bacchico Die," probably Shrove Tuesday, February 20, 1509. See Corn. Franc. de Nelis, *Sylloge* [of literary documents connected with the University of Louvain] (Louvain: University Press, 1704–69), pp. 88–93 (cited in de Vocht, *Collegium Trilingue*, I, 216).

other schoolmasters and creating a demand that printers readily supplied.[9]

At the height of his prestige as teacher and producer of Plautus, Dorp abandoned the staging of classical plays as a method of educational training. It is impossible to ascertain the reasons for his theatrical about-face. Perhaps the radical impropriety of having Plautine innuendoes drilled daily into the memories of his students and issuing publicly from their lips before a Christian audience confronted Dorp with a dilemma steadily faced by most Renaissance schoolmen. Furthermore, he may have concluded that even the most persuasively Christian prologue and epilogue could do little to counteract the pagan atmosphere of the classics they buttressed. There is no documentary evidence to support such a conjecture, but regardless of motive he did substitute in their stead a composition of his own, a dramatic colloquy in which youth is warned against philandering and laziness, and urged to embrace a life of virtuous industry.[10] It should again be mentioned that a precedent for Dorp's *Dialogus* had been established in the Lily twenty-eight years earlier by the *Declamatio*, in which student complaints had been dramatized in the form of a debate. Dorp amplified the simple form of the *Declamatio* by distributing his argument among four allegorical characters. In their mythological setting, a majestic Virtus and a stern Hercules parry the thrusts of a coaxing Venus and an impulsive Cupid.[11] Though uniformly moral in aim and tone, the *Dialogus* operates within a framework of purely human values: reason and worldly advantage alone are proposed as argument for virtuous conduct. Dorp's prose dialogue was performed before an illustrious audience in the Lily in 1510 and enjoyed spectacular success.[12] Its influence on the academic drama of Louvain and the Netherlands was, as we shall observe, immense.

[9] Between 1512 and 1540, for example, there were eight printings of the *Aulularia* in Antwerp and Deventer alone. See W. Nijhoff and M. E. Kronenberg, *Nederlandsche Bibliographie van 1500 tot 1540*, I, 1731–33; II, 3737–42, cited hereafter as *Nederlandsche Bibliographie*. See also de Vocht, *Collegium Trilingue*, I, 217, n. 4.

[10] *Dialogus: in quo Venus & Cupido omnes adhibent versutias: ut Herculem animi ancipitem in suam militiam invita virtute perpellant* (Louvain: Thierry Martens, 1513). No copy of the first edition has yet been located. The *Dialogus* was reprinted by Martens, along with the *Tomus Aulularia*. See Nijhoff and Kronenberg, *Nederlandsche Bibliographie*, I, 737. See also de Vocht, *Monumenta Humanistica Lovaniensia*, pp. 331–33, 366–67, cited hereafter as *Monumenta*.

[11] In a letter written in November, 1513, Jerome de Busleyden expressed his admiration for Dorp's use of dialogue to individualize character. See de Vocht, *Jerome de Busleyden, Founder of the Collegium Trilingue, His Life and Writings*, pp. 446–47, cited hereafter as *Jerome de Busleyden*.

[12] The *Dialogus* was immediately transcribed and circulated. In the Dedication of the first edition (November, 1513), Dorp admitted to John de Nève that the text

Dorp's two productions of Plautus, together with his original *Dialogus,* comprise his total contribution to the Louvain theater. Shortly after the production of the *Dialogus,* he abandoned his profession of rhetorician-playwright, devoting his energies thereafter to theology. However brief his career as a school dramatist, it is noteworthy that between 1508 and 1512 Dorp established the main directions which Louvain playwrights were to follow during the remainder of the sixteenth century: namely, the revival of ancient classical drama on the one hand and, on the other, the production of original plays by schoolmasters, who drew heavily on biblical subjects and the tradition of the morality play and adapted that tradition to the educational milieu. For his pioneering work in classical productions and dramatic composition as well as for the influence he exerted on later school dramatists, Martin van Dorp of the Lily merits the distinction of being the progenitor of the Louvain academic theater.

The first playwright indebted to the *Dialogus* was Remacle d'Ardennes, court poet of Margaret of Austria and friend of Dorp.[13] His *Palamedes* appeared in 1512.[14] In it Remacle transfers the Venus-Virtue antithesis of Dorp's dialogue from the world of mythology to the slave market, where Palamedes is forced to choose between wisdom and wealth in the persons of two slaves, Sophia and Chrysus. A friend, Philotas, finally persuades the youth to purchase Sophia; she, in turn, teaches Palamedes how to manage the wealthy Chrysus as a docile servant. Although there is no evidence that Remacle d'Ardennes' play was acted at Louvain, the indebtedness of its author to Dorp and his Humanist circle establishes the *Palamedes* as one of the early fruits of the Louvain theater.

The alternate path pioneered by Martin van Dorp in his productions of Plautus did not long remain untraveled. Within five years after the production of the *Miles Gloriosus* in the Lily, Adrian Barlandus, colleague of Dorp and Latin teacher at the Porc preparatory school, repeated the success of the adapted *Aulularia* at Arras College, staging it in one of the

---

needed a thorough revision but that its wide circulation in manuscript restrained him from emending it. See de Vocht, *Monumenta,* pp. 128–29, 307, 326–35, 366–67, 402–03.

[13] Both Remacle d'Ardennes and Dorp shared the patronage of George of Halewyn (Halluin, Haloinus). See de Vocht, *Collegium Trilingue,* I, 207, n. 5.

[14] *Remacli Arduenne florenatis Palamedes* (Paris: Giles de Gourmont, 1512). The play was completed on January 1, 1512, in London, where Remacle was teaching. It was reissued in London by Richard Pynson the same year. This Pynson edition, now at the Folger Shakespeare Library, may well be the first stage play printed in England. Part of Act IV is in verse, the rest of the play in prose.

rooms of the college on Quinquagesima Sunday, February 26, 1514.[15] Barlandus retained Dorp's catastrophe (*Tomus*), but supplied his own prologue. In the following September the Porc players produced in their own school the *Hecuba* of Euripides in Erasmus' Latin translation, introducing the play with a dialogue of Barlandus. By 1524 the classic repertoire of the Porc included the *Andria*, the *Eunuchus*, the *Adelphi*, and the *Hecyra* of Terence, the majority of them bolstered by Barlandus' prologues and epilogues.[16]

We have no record of the audience reaction to these plays, but the impression made on the student actors, as one might expect, seems to have been indelible. A typical illustration of this fact is a letter written from Fez on April 12, 1541, in which Nicolas Clenardus recalls to Abbot Streyters of Tongerloo their student roles in the *Andria* and the *Eunuchus*.[17] On the other hand, there is no doubt that the example of classical productions at Louvain was widely imitated, especially by the schoolmasters who had witnessed the performances in the Lily or the Porc. Gerald Bachusius, for example, produced the *Adelphi* in 1524, and in 1525 the *Aulularia* in the refectory of the Chapter of St. Donatian at Bruges. His successor, Adrian Chilius, blazed new trails on the academic stage with his translation of Aristophanes' *Plutus* and Lucian's *Auction of Philosophers*.[18]

These three pioneer dramatists, Martin van Dorp, Remacle d'Ardennes, and Adrian Barlandus, were members of a Louvain literary circle that included Jerome de Busleyden and the renowned Erasmus. Enthusiasm for the ideals of Christian Humanism had served to draw them together in a common interest. Their zeal for the New Learning was to cause a general realignment of intellectual forces, a reshaping of the aims and attitudes of scholarship, and a consequent revolution in educational methods.[19] Thus the dramatic activity at Louvain during the first two

---

[15] De Vocht, *Collegium Trilingue*, I, 217.

[16] Etienne Daxhelet, *Adrien Barlandus, humaniste belge, 1486–1538, sa vie, son oeuvre, sa personnalité*, pp. 208–20, cited hereafter as *Adrien Barlandus*; L. Massebieau, *Les colloques scolaires du seizième siècle et leurs auteurs, 1480–1570*, pp. 131–57; A. Bömer, *Die lateinische Schülergespräche der Humanisten*, II, 113–27; Paul Dittrich, *Plautus und Terenz in Pädagogik und Schulwesen der deutschen Humanisten*, p. 13. See also Creizenach, *Geschichte des neueren Dramas*, II, 56.

[17] Alphonse Roersch (ed.), *Correspondance de Nicolas Clénard*, I, 182; II, 137, cited in de Vocht, *Collegium Trilingue*, I, 218. See also *Nic. Clenardi epistolarum libri duo* (Antwerp: Chr. Plantin, 1566), pp. 60–61.

[18] A. C. de Schrevel, *Histoire du séminaire de Bruges*, I, 134–35.

[19] Henri de Vocht's four-volume *Collegium Trilingue* provides an exhaustive documentation of the origin and growth of Humanism at Louvain.

decades of the sixteenth century was merely one of the minor extensions of this new Christian Humanist ideal.

Through the foresight and generosity of Jerome de Busleyden and the administrative brilliance of Erasmus, the Humanist ideals of the Louvain circle were institutionalized and perpetuated in the Busleyden Institute, more commonly known as the Collegium Trilingue Lovaniense. Just as the roots of the Louvain theater drew sustenance from this Humanist coterie, so the subsequent growth of academic drama in the Netherlands was shaped principally by the great Latin professors and students of the new foundation.

Adrian Barlandus inaugurated the Latin lectures at the Trilingue on September 1, 1518.[20] One of his students, Peter Nanning (Nannius), soon came to share his teacher's enthusiasm for classical literature.[21] Shortly after graduation, Nannius drew on his thorough knowledge of Terence and Plautus by reorganizing their staple plot devices into a witty comedy entitled *Vinctus*.[22] The play sparkles with action and life; not the least of its merits is a most felicitous blending of its two Latin models.[23] In addition to the *Vinctus* written at Gouda, Nannius composed five dramatic soliloquies at the Trilingue. Strongly Senecan in inspiration and anticipating the *Imaginary Conversations* of Walter Savage Landor and the dramatic monologues of Robert Browning, these brief psychological dramas develop the inner tensions and resolutions of Lucrece, Susanna, Judith, Agnes, and Camma, respectively.[24] Although these rhetorical-dramatic creations of Nannius represent a mere fragment of his literary work, they remain his most original compositions.

[20] De Vocht, *Collegium Trilingue*, III, 530.

[21] Petrus Nannius, native of Alkmaar, enrolled at Louvain in 1518 and remained there two years. Ordination to the priesthood followed and later the directorship of the School of Gouda in 1521. See A. Polet, *Petrus Nannius, 1500–57*, p. 5.

[22] *Vinctus* was printed in Antwerp by Simon Cock and Gerard Nicolas and published on July 21, 1522. See Nijhoff and Kronenberg, *Nederlandsche Bibliographie*, I, 1584. The play seems to have escaped the notice of Bahlmann, Creizenach, Bradner, and other historians of Renaissance academic drama.

[23] De Vocht draws attention to the masterly climax of Act III, scene ii: referring to similar classical imitations by Reuchlin in his *Henno* and *Sergius*, he finds the latter inferior to the *Vinctus*. See *Collegium Trilingue*, II, 178. For an analysis of Reuchlin's plays, see Paul Bahlmann, *Die lateinischen Dramen von Wimphelings Stylpho bis zur Mitte des sechzehnten Jahrhunderts, 1480–1550*, pp. 18, 20, cited hereafter as *Die lateinischen Dramen*; Creizenach, *Geschichte des neueren Dramas*, II, 44 ff.; Marvin T. Herrick, *Tragicomedy, Its Origin and Development in Italy, France, and England*, p. 19, cited hereafter as *Tragicomedy*.

[24] *Dialogismi heroinarum* (Louvain: Barth. Gravius, 1541). A French translation by John Millet was published in 1550: *Dialogismes, ou délibérations de cinq nobles dames*. See Paquot, *Mémoires*, XIV, 65.

As Latin professor of the Trilingue (1539–57), Nannius continued the tradition of great teaching established by his predecessors Barlandus (1518–19) and Goclenius (1519–39). His explication of classical texts was directed toward the moral, intellectual, and literary development of his hearers. For example, his lectures on the *Aeneid* were introduced by an *Oratio de amore*, in which he distinguished the various concepts of love in classical literature, taking pains to warn his students of the baneful results of Astarte and inciting them to virtue.[25] This Christian interpretation of the moral aspects of the classics figures prominently in the aims of Renaissance school drama.

The example of Nannius and the intellectual ferment created by the provocative lectures of the Trilingue soon gave rise to a cluster of Louvain student-dramatists: Zovitius, Philicinus, Schöpperus, and Brechtanus.

James Zovitius (Friescharius) received his early education from a Louvain-trained scholar.[26] Before the age of twenty, Zovitius had already completed his formal training at the Trilingue and had written and produced *Ruth*, a drama in five acts.[27] To lighten the biblical story he introduced a pair of vagabonds; he further insured the tragicomic effect by alternating sententious Senecan soliloquies with homespun dialogue.[28] During the following year as schoolmaster at Breda, Zovitius composed the *Didascalus*.[29] Written during the quiet hours of evening, this play re-creates, in debate form, the plight of the overworked schoolmaster who is at the mercy of his fiendish charges and their exasperating parents. The complaints against Didascalus (the teacher) are advanced by Demus (a pupil), whereupon Jupiter sends Mercury to convene a court at Breda. At great length the character Colacoglottus pleads for Demus while Alethia, in turn, defends the teacher. The judge terminates the hearing by pronouncing the complaints of Demus to be slanderous.[30]

---

[25] De Vocht, *Collegium Trilingue*, IV, 97.

[26] William de Zaghere, teacher of Zovitius, studied under Barlandus and received his master's degree from Louvain in 1512. See Daxhelet, *Adrien Barlandus*, p. 300, cited in de Vocht, *Collegium Trilingue*, III, 265, n. 6.

[27] *Ruth* (Antwerp: Michael Hillen, 1533). See Nijhoff and Kronenberg, *Nederlandsche Bibliographie*, II, 4106.

[28] See Bahlmann, *Die lateinischen Dramen*, p. 50; Creizenach, *Geschichte des neuren Dramas*, II, 118; Herrick, *Tragicomedy*, p. 22, n. 13.

[29] *Didascalus, comoedia ut doctissima, ita ut lepidissima* (Antwerp: Giles Coppens for Ant. Dumaeus, 1540), See Nijhoff and Kronenberg, *Nederlandsche Bibliographie*, II, 4105. Paquot (*Mémoires*, XIV, 198) refers to an edition by John Steels, Antwerp, 1534. A copy of the 1541 Cologne edition is in the Folger Library.

[30] Bahlmann, *Die lateinischen Dramen*, p. 50; Creizenach, *Geschichte des neueren Dramas*, II, 168–69. The similarity of Zovitius' *Didascalus* to the *Declamatio* per-

The striking originality of the *Didascalus* was quickly recognized: a new dramatic vein had been opened and was soon exploited by other playwrights.[31] With the third and last play, *Ovis perdita,* the career of Zovitius came to full flower. The parable of the lost sheep, enriched and enlivened by allegorical characters, was soon to become a favorite in Continental school theaters.[32]

Strongly contrasting with the short and brilliant career of Zovitius is that of his contemporary Peter Campson (Philicinus). A product of the Trilingue, Philicinus made his debut as school dramatist in 1543 with a dialogue on the sacrificing of Isaac.[33] The soliloquies of God, Abraham, and Isaac are inflated and tedious; in contrast, the speaking role of each of the two servant boys is limited to a single line.[34] The work is further marred by endless digressions, empty rhetoric, and mysticism.[35] Philicinus' second attempt, a tragicomedy based on the Resurrection, is a more competent performance.[36] Its highly unconventional Mary Magdalen greets the risen Christ with characteristic homeliness of speech: "I am no Esther or Susanna, I know, that thou shouldst hear my prayers, but the storehouse and workshop of all foul faults."[37] Philicinus arranges the incidents of the gospel narrative into five acts, allowing the expectation of the Resurrection to foreshadow the joyous climax.[38] The tragedy *Esther* was the last of Philicinus' attempts at school drama.[39] Composed in 1544, it lay ignored by the author until 1563, when its publication could serve as a tribute to a newly appointed dignitary.[40]

---

formed in the Lily in 1481 helps one understand the viability of a dramatic tradition in the schools.

[31] The *Studentes* of Stymmelius appeared in 1549; the *Archilocus* of Frachaeus in 1550. Both plays show obvious indebtedness to the *Didascalus.* See Creizenach, *Geschichte des neueren Dramas,* II, 169 ff.

[32] Bahlmann, *Die lateinischen Dramen,* p. 50; Creizenach, *Geschichte des neueren Dramas,* II, 127–28.

[33] *Dialogus de Isaaci immolatione, ad puerilem captum accomodatus* (Antwerp: John Steels, 1544). See Paquot, *Mémoires,* IX, 244. This dialogue was the model for Schöpperus' *Abrahamus tentatus,* 1551. See Bahlmann, *Die lateinischen Dramen,* p. 96; A. Baumgartner, *Die lateinische und griechische Literatur der christlichen Völker,* p. 613.

[34] Bahlmann, *Die lateinischen Dramen,* p. 92.

[35] Creizenach, *Geschichte des neueren Dramas,* II, 99.

[36] *Comoedia tragica, quae inscribitur Magdalena evangelica.*

[37] Herrick, *Tragicomedy,* p. 59.

[38] In the dedicatory letter (dated from Binche, January 10, 1544) to *Magdalena,* Philicinus credits Brechtanus for his assistance in the plotting of the play. The original form of the Magdalen story appears to have been a poem written by Philicinus in iambic dimeters.

[39] *Tragoedia Esther* (Antwerp: J. Steels, 1563).

[40] Creizenach, *Geschichte des neueren Dramas,* II, 120.

As a dramatist, Philicinus was mediocre. His modicum of success, however, attests the genuine vitality of the dramatic tradition of Louvain and the urgency it created in its disciples to realize their full teaching potentialities.

Associated with Zovitius and Philicinus was a student from Germany, James Schoepper (Jacobus Schöpperus), who studied at Louvain and returned to his native Dortmund as priest and playwright.[41] Schöpperus' imitation of Philicinus' *Isaac* in his *Abrahamus tentatus*, together with his adaptation of Zovitius' *Ovis perdita* in a play published under the same name (1553), suggests the common acquaintance of the three trilingual students. In addition to the two plays already mentioned, Schöpperus composed four other school dramas for his pupils.[42] Although his plays have been described by one critic as bungling work, the *Joannes decollatus* maintains a rather high level of inspiration and interest.[43] Its theatrical impact is assured by a series of dramatic devices previously unknown to the academic stage. Creizenach for instance, illustrates Schöpperus' originality, by singling out the involuntary babbling of the truth by a scheming fool.[44]

During the third and fourth decades of the sixteenth century, the twelve school dramas of Zovitius, Philicinus, and Schöpperus illustrate the living tradition of the Louvain theater. The production of Roman comedies inaugurated earlier in the century by Dorp, enthusiastically continued by Barlandus and artfully rearranged by Nannius, was in turn succeeded by schoolmaster dramatizations of biblical subjects drawn equally from the Old and New Testaments. This emergence of Christian dramatic material as an educational instrument reached its climax in the work of Brechtanus.[45] Thoroughly acquainted with the achievement of his predecessors, this young Franciscan drew on the most abiding ele-

---

[41] Baumgartner, *Die . . . Literatur der christlichen Völker*, p. 613.

[42] *Voluptatis ac virtutis pugna* (Cologne, 1546), *Ectrachelistis, sive Joannes decollatus* (Cologne, 1546), *Monomachia Davidis et Goliae* (Dortmund, 1550), *Euphemus* (Basel, 1553).

[43] The adverse criticism is Creizenach's (see *Geschichte des neueren Dramas*, II, 129–30). It should be remarked that however "bungling" Schöpperus' work may seem today, it was not unpopular in the sixteenth century. The *Abrahamus* enjoyed three printings; three other plays were also reprinted. In addition the collected plays of Schöpperus—*Comoediae et tragoediae sacrae* (Dortmund, 1552)—were reissued at Cologne in 1562 and again in 1564. See Leicester Bradner, "The Latin Drama of the Renaissance (1340–1640)," *Studies in the Renaissance*, IV (1957), 67, cited hereafter as "The Latin Drama."

[44] Creizenach, *Geschichte des neueren Dramas*, II, 129–30.

[45] Livinus of Brecht (Brechtanus) *ca.* 1510–88, native of Antwerp, attended the Trilingue, received his master's degree and then joined the Franciscan Minorite Convent at Louvain. See de Vocht, *Collegium Trilingue*, IV, 107.

ments of the Louvain dramatic heritage and extended that tradition into a new dimension by his *Euripus*.[46]

The play is a moral tragedy involving the struggles of young Euripus with the forces of good and evil.[47] These two forces are clearly delineated on the stage by means of two paths, the one arduous, the other easy.[48] In the opening act Euripus ascends the rugged path in the company of Tempus Gratiae and Timor Dei, the former a winged youth, the latter a priestly sage with a white beard. Euripus resists the daytime enticements of Venus and Cupid on the path below, but during his evening sleep he is swayed by sensuous music and wounded by Cupid's shaft. The Chorus concludes the act with a sapphic hymn on the fear of God.

Euripus wavers in the second act, descends to join the attractive pair who straightway doff his Pauline armor and helmet of salvation and fit him out with gay attire and a feathered hat. At the youth's request, Tempus Gratiae promises to remain as long as God permits.

The third act introduces a love scene. At the height of his involvement with Venus, Euripus descries a brood of deformed shapes hitherto concealed by her skirts. The list of deformities includes: adultery, rape, foulness, folly, incest, lewdness, scurrility, the sin of Gomorrah, seminal emission, contention, brawling, murder, envy, jealousy, gluttony, drunkenness, insolence. Venus assures Euripus that the shapes, though horrid when first beheld, gradually grow attractive with the experience of love. In consternation, he scrambles back to his high road with Tempus Gratiae. Before long Cupid coaxes him down again. Venus now demands unswerving fidelity, insisting that he surrender his sapphire ring. Euripus hesitates but finally concedes.

The tragic fall ensues in the fourth act. Two dreadful women appear: Pestis Inguinaria (Syphilis), armed with bow and arrow, and Mors (Death), brandishing a javelin. Pestis Inguinaria wounds the sleeping Euripus, covers his body with loathsome sores, and leaves Tempus Gratiae to mourn over Euripus' loss of his wedding garment. The

---

[46] *Euripus: tragoedia christiana, autore F. Livino Brechto Antuerpiensi, e familia Franciscana Lovaniensia*. The dedicatory letter to Prince George of Austria is dated 1549. The supplement provides a list of appropriate religious maxims. I have used the Folger Library copy of the second edition.

[47] The waverer Euripus possibly derives from the "Euripus homo" of Erasmus. See *Erasmi collectanea adagiorum veterum* in *Desiderii Erasmi Roterodami opera omnia*, Vol. II, col. 357, No. LXII.

[48] The motif of the two paths had already been used by Bartholomew Palau at Salamanca in his *Farsa llamada Custodia*. See Creizenach, *Geschichte des neueren Dramas*, III, 149. John Heros employed the device, probably in imitation of Brechtanus, in his *Egistos* (1562). *Ibid.*, pp. 376, 406.

stricken waverer continues to hope for a cure until Mors deals the death
blow with her spear.

In the final act the blackened, repulsive spirit of Euripus appears,
bound with ropes, in the antechamber of hell. There Venus, Cupid, and
a pack of devils pommel and deride the victim, taunting him with the
prospect of endless torture. A final grim warning against juvenile vice
closes the play.

The *Euripus* reveals Brechtanus' acquaintance with earlier Louvain
dramatists.[49] His exceptional dramatic talent, on the other hand, pre-
cluded any form of slavish imitation. With unerring instinct he drew on
his dramatic heritage, singling out ends and means which he transformed
and fused into an intensely personal idiom. Never before had allegorical
characters of such vitality walked the academic stage; age-old symbols,
such as the wedding garment, the helmet of salvation, and the sapphire
ring, became visually and dramatically effective embodiments of religious themes. Furthermore the vice-virtue antithesis, previously elaborated in the merely rhetorical convention of the debate, was now
projected dramatically on the stage by the symbol of the two paths. Finally the vivid re-enactment of the inner struggles of the protagonist,
from early vacillation to unforgettable doom, helped make Brechtanus'
only play the most popular tragedy of the Louvain theater and one of
the classics of Neo-Latin drama.[50]

The turbulence of war which rocked Europe and the Netherlands during the second half of the sixteenth century continually disrupted the
academic life of the University. In 1542 the Louvain students repulsed
the attack of mercenary soldiers led by Martin van Rossum. During several months of 1566 they helped guard the city ramparts. William of
Orange in person laid siege to Louvain in 1572; the plague which followed on his heels found students quitting the town wholesale. One after
another, schools closed. From 1578 on, a royal garrison of Walloons,

---

[49] The influence of Dorp's *Dialogus de Hercule, Venere et virtute* (1513) has
been observed in Brechtanus' graphic depiction of a soul hesitating between virtue
and vice. See de Vocht, *Monumenta*, pp. 129, 331–33. The latter acts of *Euripus*
show evident influence of Nannius' *Oratio de amore* (1543) and especially his
second *Somnium, sive paralipomena Virgilii* (1545), which Brechtanus undoubtedly
heard in the Trilingue lecture hall or read in manuscript. See Polet, *Petrus Nannius*,
pp. 62–64, 68, 196. See also de Vocht, *Collegium Trilingue*, IV, 108–09.

[50] The stage history of *Euripus* is impressive. It was produced not only in Louvain
and the Netherlands, but in such cities as Vienna, Munich, Innsbruck, Trèves, Dillingen, and Prague. Its popularity in the newly founded Jesuit schools is documented
by Johannes Müller (*Das Jesuitendrama* . . . , II, 43–46, 107). Paul Hoffaeus of
Prague translated the *Euripus* into German prose, producing his version in 1560. In
1582, Cleophas Distelmayer of Dillingen rendered it in German verse. See de Vocht,
Collegium Trilingue, IV, 109.

Germans, Italians, and Bourgignons was stationed at Louvain to protect it against the Orangists; ironically, these mercenaries increased the havoc, holding the local inhabitants in terror by incessant brutality, pillage, and rape. In 1582, the Duc d'Alençon attacked Louvain and was repulsed. The following year Van dem Tympel, lieutenant of William of Orange, renewed the attack. It was only with the arrival of Archduke Albert and Isabella at the close of the century that a respite was gained.[51] The effect of the war on the Louvain theater was no less shattering than on the city and the University. Although it seems improbable that the theater of Louvain was completely neglected during this period of transition, there is no evidence that any plays were written or produced in the preparatory schools until the turn of the sixteenth century.[52]

When Vernulaeus was chosen by J. B. Gramaye as his successor at Porc in 1608, Gramaye had already achieved a prolific record of dramatic writing and production.[53] He showed a predilection for biblical subjects, saints' lives, mythology, and historical personages. Since none of his plays survive, we have no way of determining the precise nature or merit of his contribution to the Louvain dramatic tradition. It seems very probable, however, that Gramaye revitalized a heritage that had languished during the half-century of political and religious strife.

Between 1608 and 1648 Vernulaeus restored the former splendor of the Louvain theater singlehandedly by his fourteen historical tragedies, all of which were written and produced by him at Louvain. During the same period Andreas Catullus, Latin poet and playwright of the College

[51] Van der Essen, *Une institution*, pp. 29–32.

[52] It has been impossible to ascertain whether any of the four plays of Andreas Fabricius were written or staged at Louvain: *Religio patiens* (Cologne, 1566); *Samson* (Cologne, 1569); *Evangelicus fluctuans* (Cologne, 1569); *Jeroboam rebellans* (Ingolstadt, 1585). Fabricius was called to Louvain by Philippe de Hofden, abbot of St. Gertrude, around 1553 and remained there possibly eight years. See Paquot, *Mémoires*, VIII, 433–34.

[53] In his article on Vernulaeus in *Allgemeine deutsche Biographie* (XXXIX [1895], 630), Johannes Bolte refers to the *Specimen litterarum et linguarum* (1622), in which Gramaye lists sixteen pieces he composed and produced at Louvain: *Abraham und Maria* [sic], *Elias, Salomon, Susanna Alexius, Briseis, Heraclius, Susanna* (!) [sic], *Gertrudis, Isaias, Catherina, Barbara, Mauritius, Bajazetes, Justinianus, Pyramus und Thisbe*. In addition to these, Gramaye's *Andromeda Belgica*, printed at Louvain in 1600, was acted before Albert and Isabella. (See *Excerpta ex actis facultatis artium universitatis Lovaniensis, 1427–1797*, p. 149, cited in de Vocht, *Collegium Trilingue*, I, 74, n. 2.) According to E. Van Cauwenbergh, librarian of the University of Louvain, the unique copy of *Specimen litterarum et linguarum* was destroyed in the fire of May, 1940. For a discussion of Gramaye's work as geographer and philologist, see Félix Nève, *La renaissance des lettres . . . en Belgique*, pp. 319–42.

de Vaulx, produced his drama *Prometheus* in 1613,[54] an occasional composition designed as a plea for his tottering school. Catullus praises the administration of City and University but regrets, through the mouth of Apollo, that the liberal arts have not nobler housing facilities and a richer dowry. The city administration is urged to vote an annual subsidy for the college.[55] A more gripping drama based on sensational intrigues of the wife of Emperor Otto III came from the pen of an Augustinian priest, Theodorus Wallaeus, in 1631.[56] Its dramatization of an actual historical crisis for purposes of moral instruction utilizes the dramatic formula which Vernulaeus by this time was steadily exploiting.[57]

It was principally through the enthusiastic teaching and writing of Vernulaeus that the Porc preparatory school monopolized the rhetorical training at Louvain during the first half of the seventeenth century.[58] Latin lessons in the Lily were discontinued already in 1613, and when Vernulaeus edited his *Academia* in 1627, the Porc alone taught Latin. "It is regrettable," he observes, "that the most distinguished university in the whole world should be so greatly handicapped in this area."[59] The abandonment of Latin at the Porc in 1657 cut off the wellsprings that had fed the Louvain theater for more than a century and a half.

For that period there is record of twelve schoolmasters who were engaged in writing Latin plays to make better Latinists and better citizens of their students. Of the fifty-five plays composed by the Louvain dramatists, the *Euripus* of Brechtanus remains the most remarkable, both for its originality and striking impact as well as for its long history of production and influence. The contribution of Vernulaeus as the crowning achievement of the Louvain academic tradition will be discussed in the next two chapters.

[54] Félix Nève, *Mémoire historique et littéraire sur le collège des Trois-Langues à l'université de Louvain,* pp. 375–405.

[55] De Vocht, *Collegium Trilingue,* I ,75, n. 6. For a detailed analysis of *Prometheus,* see Nève, *Renaissance des lettres . . . en Belgique,* pp. 390–402.

[56] *Divinae iustitiae theatrum sive Maria Othonis III imp. uxor tragoedia, autore R. P. Theodore Wallaeo Augustiniano* (Louvain: Philip Dormalius, 1631).

[57] Wallaeus' play was staged in the Porc. Among the spectators was Erycius Puteanus, illustrious Latin professor of the Trilingue and lifelong friend of Vernulaeus. Puteanus' evaluation of its style, moral content, and historicity is appended to the 1631 edition, a copy of which is in the library of the University of Chicago.

[58] De Vocht, *Collegium Trilingue,* I, 73–74.

[59] *Nicolai Vernulaei academia lovaniensis,* pp. 130, 123.

Chapter III

THE DRAMATIC ART OF VERNULAEUS

The twofold purpose of Neo-Latin drama was succinctly stated by Erasmus in the dedicatory letter to the 1524 edition of his *Colloquies*. "This book," he averred, "makes better Latinists and better persons."[1]

Ends and Means of the Vernulaeus Theater

The pedagogical function of the academic theater as a major complement to rhetorical studies persisted throughout the Renaissance. College theatricals developed "better Latinists" by allowing schoolboys periodically to step from their classrooms onto the stage. Here, in simulated life situations, student actors and audience witnessed how classroom drills in language and rhetoric could serve as forceful communication. Not only did the college theater enhance the value of rhetoric and lend prestige to the rhetorician-playwright: it regularly trained the memories of student actors, improved their delivery, and developed their intelligence and taste—thus preparing them to walk confidently from the academic stage to the theater of public life.

The didactic role of the Louvain theater, on the other hand, was gradually modified by the increasingly confessional cast of education as the Renaissance progressed. For early Christian Humanist playwrights such as Dorp and Nannius, the making of "better persons" had been inspired and controlled by a cosmopolitan-Christian ideal in which both classical and Christian elements found a place. The pressures of the Reformation and the eventual entrenchment of Louvain in an ultramontane position gradually modified the Humanist concept.[2] In the new mirror for princes of the midsixteenth century, current religious and political urgencies sprang into a sharpness of focus that narrowed the tolerant perspective

---

[1] Cited by Craig Thompson (trans.), *Ten Colloquies of Erasmus*, p. xxviii.

[2] The first authoritative and solemn condemnation of Luther's doctrine was the *Condemnatio* of the Louvain Faculty of Divinity, read aloud in conclave on November 7, 1519, and published the following February. *Epistola . . . Cardinalis Dertrusensis ad facultatem theologiae lovaniensem. Eiusdem facultatis doctrinalis condemnatio qua condemnatur doctrina Martini Lutheri . . . condemnatio facultatis theologiae coloniensis* (Louvain: Th. Martens, February, 1520). See H. de Jongh (R. Roger and F. Chernoviz, eds.), *L'ancienne faculté de théologie de Louvain au premier siècle de son existence, 1432–1540*, pp. 213–22.

of the earlier Renaissance. We have already observed how this reshaping of educational ideals left its impress on the academic drama of Zovitius, Philicinus, Schöpperus, and Brechtanus.

During the second half of the sixteenth century the consolidation of the University of Louvain as a bulwark of the Catholic Reformation continued.[3] With the official promulgation of new statutes in 1617, every effort had been made to immunize the faculty against heresy and provide an intellectual citadel for a confessional state.[4] From this militant, authoritatively imposed order, the rhetorical and dramatic work of Vernulaeus received its inspiration and direction.

The pedagogic purpose of his drama adhered to the traditional formula of making better Latinists. "It was my intention," he states, "to form our young men by training them in public speaking and deportment—not to court prestige presumptuously."[5] Its didactic purpose, on the other hand, was largely determined by Vernulaeus' belief that the religious unity of the Netherlands could be regained only by the dominance of the Throne-Altar dyarchy to which he subscribed. To train students in their future responsibilities to this dyarchy was Vernulaeus' ultimate purpose; this, in turn, prompted his selection of historical tragedy as a genre and predisposed his concentration on church-state conflicts.

Vernulaeus' choice of historical tragedy as the dramatic medium consonant with his purpose was quite deliberate. Tragedy, he maintained, was intimately related to moral and political philosophy because of its power to dramatize the nature of the human condition no less than the vacillations of political life. Through its use of characters and scene it could represent every possible change of fortune, from the downfall of princes to the disastrous consequences of haphazard policy. In so doing, it could afford a regimen for princes and expose the pitfalls of leadership. For these reasons, Vernulaeus concluded, tragedy deserved to be called the instructress of prudence.[6]

The didactic function of tragedy, he further believed, was shared by

---

[3] See Pirenne, *Histoire de Belgique,* IV, 450.

[4] *Ibid.,* pp. 450–51. By "confessional state" is here meant a type of religio-political organization in which (in the case of Belgium) the population is predominantly Catholic, wherein Catholicism is legally recognized as "the religion of the state," and wherein it is considered logical as well as politically necessary that legal restrictions be imposed on other religions, notably on their propaganda. See John Courtney Murray, "Contemporary Orientations of Catholic Thought on Church and State in the Light of History," *Theological Studies,* X (June, 1949), 183.

[5] *Gorcomienses,* p. 19.

[6] See his *Ottocarus, fols.* 2ᵛᵒ–3ʳᵒ.

history. Any candidate for public office was urged by Vernulaeus to ex-
plore the records of the past. Chronicles could unfold the story of social
upheavals, fraud, and intrigue, thereby apprising the aspiring magistrate
of abuses he would one day face. Within the pages of history the reader
could daily take his place in the council chamber and hear the advice of
statesmen; battles could be fought again and made to yield their lessons
of military tactics; the whole world could be traversed and its diverse
institutions, mores, and customs reviewed.[7]

Vernulaeus' choice of historical tragedy enabled him to harness the
teaching functions of both history and tragedy. His fourteen tragedies
constitute his chief contribution to the Louvain dramatic tradition.
While adhering to the time-honored pedagogic purpose of making "better Latinists," Vernulaeus considerably modified the concept of making
"better persons." It is in the light of this change of didactic purpose that
the Vernulaeus theater must finally be assessed: the "better person" he
envisaged was not the Christian Humanist ideal of Dorp and Nannius,
but the influential citizen of a confessional state.

Vernulaeus' selection of historical tragedy as the most effective medium for training militant Catholic statesmen led, in turn, to a choice of
subject and theme most consonant with his purpose. Thus seven of his
fourteen plays re-enact church-state conflicts.[8] Three others dramatize
the evils of unlawful rebellion.[9] The remaining four are largely concerned
with religious and political issues.[10]

Major themes of individual plays are occasionally indicated by alternative titles. The title page of Vernulaeus' first play reads: *"The Martyrs
of Gorkum or Faith's Exile."* The subtitle of *Divus Eustachius* is *"The
Triumph of Faith and Patience,"* and that of *Maximus, "Rebellion against
Emperor Gratian and Its Punishment."* Dedicatory letters, addresses to
the reader, and arguments prefacing the various editions supply more
explicit thematic information. The dedicatory letter of *Theodoricus,* for
example, indicates the author's use of the protagonist to illustrate the
reprehensible nature of overweening ambition, rashness, improper
motivation, and bribery.[11] Similarly, Conradin and Crispus are offered as

---

[7] See his *Institutionum politicarum,* Chap. VI, "Proemium in institutiones politicas."
[8] *Gorcomienses* (1610), *Theodoricus* (1623), *Henricus Octavus* (1624), *Thomas
Cantuariensis* (1631), *Stanislaus* (1631), *Lambertus* (1656), and *Hermenigildus*
(1656).
[9] *Ottocarus* (1626), *Maximus* (1630), *Fritlandus* (1637).
[10] *Divus Eustachius* (1612), *Conradinus* (1628), *Crispus* (1628), *Joanna Darcia*
(1629).
[11] *Theodoricus,* p. 4.

models of invincible fortitude and righteous aggressiveness, while their fate serves to document the waywardness of Fortune.[12]

Connected with the major themes of each play are patterns of supporting themes which elaborate Vernulaeus' concept of the ideal prince, magistrate, military officer, counselor, and cleric, and at the same time crystallize the accumulated wisdom of the human race. Among the themes that recur most frequently are the following: great kings are prudent and merciful; no king should be governed by a woman; kings are custodians of divine law, not interpreters; the prince acts out his life on a stage with the world as audience; the vices of princes are invariably imitated by their subjects; tyranny is always short-lived; no force can bend a tyrant's will; ruling always entails grief; the prosperous man is seldom wise; Fortune does not necessarily favor the just cause; courts breed every form of vice; Venus is cooled by Martian exploits; only a just war brings glory to the victors; flight conquers lust more effectively than reason; a murderer is inevitably haunted by the vision of his victim; conscience is the severest torturer of malefactors; a woman's tears are formidable artillery; religious diversity wreaks havoc; the common herd is fickle and unappreciative; justice cannot exist without religious sanction.

Through careful selection of dramatic genre, subject, and theme, Vernulaeus fashioned the academic theater into an instrument for teaching the lessons of history with dramatic vividness. His concern for the truth of history, as he saw it, was primary. Thus when forced to choose between historical truth and dramatic propriety, he inevitably sacrificed the latter when a compromise was unavailable, though not without reluctance. For example, many of the Gorkum episodes, Vernulaeus realized, should have been reported, not acted, on stage. His concession to history rather than to art is carefully defended:

"I admit I did not strive for tragic grandeur in this slight production, being more mindful perhaps of historical accuracy and truth than of art; and hence many things which should have been reported are acted out, and many things which should have been omitted are given voice—my reason being that the ear should not be denied what the eye had been presented. Nevertheless, my decision was not without precedent and authority. . . . I wished to praise the martyrs by presenting their own deeds, not mine; and thus my preoccupation was truth."

Later a compromise is observable in Vernulaeus' retention of multiple martyr characters on stage to satisfy the demand of historical accuracy

---

[12] See *Conradinus et Crispus tragoediae*, fol. iiij.

and his curtailment of speaking roles, on the other hand, to satisfy the demand of dramatic art:

"There were indeed more martyrs in the Gorkum arena than on our stage, but the number of speaking roles would have exceeded the proper limit. And so I reduced the martyrs to silence, but I did not eliminate them."[13]

Just as the dramatic materials of the Vernulaeus theater were largely determined by its didactic purpose, so its expressive features received their major orientation from the rhetorical tradition of academic tragedy.[14] When Vernulaeus wrote his first play in 1609, the tradition of Neo-Latin tragedy in which he worked was already three centuries old. The earliest surviving Neo-Latin play clearly illustrates that the *"eloquentia latina"* of the schools had already been fertilized by Senecan drama.[15] The practice of dramatizing legend or history in Senecan fashion was continued by early Renaissance school dramatists, a few examples being Antonius Luschus, *Achilleis* (*ca.* 1390), Gregorius Corarius, *Progne* (*ca.* 1428), and Leonardus Dathus, *Hiempsal* (1442).[16] The thoroughly medieval use of such allegorical figures as Ambition, Envy, and Discord in the otherwise-Senecan *Hiempsal* attests the early absorption of non-classical elements by the Senecan-rhetorical school of Latin drama. Thus it is clear that already in the fifteenth century an amalgamation of rhetorical, Senecan, and medieval elements resulted in a distinctive tragic

[13] *Gorcomienses,* pp. 20–21.

[14] The present pioneering stage of Neo-Latin scholarship, especially in drama, precludes any thoroughgoing assessment of the manifold influences at work in the evolution of the Neo-Latin academic theater. However, it seems quite probable that by the end of the sixteenth century the structural forms of the Roman drama, together with the viable forms of medieval moralities, mysteries, and farces, had been absorbed by academic playwrights and imposed on Christian materials. The blending of Terentian and medieval patterns, for example, is observable in the evolution of the Christian Terence plays, while the fusion of Senecan and Terentian techniques can be traced in the *tragedia mista* of Giraldi Cinthio. See Herrick, *Tragicomedy,* pp. 16–92.

[15] The *Ecerinis* (1314) of Albertinus Mussatus, earliest-known Senecan imitation, dramatizes the tyrannical career of Ezzelino, lieutenant of Frederick II. In his Preface, Mussatus relates how the wickedness of Ezzelino and that of Atreus and Medea reminded him of Seneca and evoked his imitation. It is noteworthy that this earliest-known Latin tragedy re-enacts a recent local historical crisis for a didactic purpose—as the plays of Vernulaeus would do later. The fact that it was written for public recitation, not stage production, helps explain its rhetorical apparatus. Finally, the introduction of Satan, as well as the neglect of the unities of time and place, reveals the influence of medieval drama. See Bradner, "The Latin Drama," pp. 31–32; Irving Ribner, *The English History Play in the Age of Shakespeare,* pp. 43–44. I have used the second edition of *Ecerinis* (Venice, 1636), a copy of which is available at the Folger Library.

[16] See Bradner, "The Latin Drama," p. 32.

genre, with history (*res gestae*) accepted as the proper basis. The preponderance of historical subjects that were strictly religious, together with the gradual emergence of a Christian tragic principle informing them, gave rise to a new dramatic genre which might be designated the Christian Seneca.[17] It is within this Christian Senecan tradition of academic drama that the dramaturgy of Vernulaeus finds its reference.

Already in his first play Vernulaeus had decided upon the structural matrix in which all fourteen of his dramatic subjects were to be shaped. The Senecan elements of this matrix are the five-act structure, chorus, stichomythic dialogue, sententious utterances, set speeches, extended metaphors, expository prologue, and occasional use of the narrating messenger and spectral apparatus. Vernulaeus' use of Senecan mechanism, however, was in no way a slavish imitation. Functioning side by side with it are techniques inherited from the Christian medieval tradition: allegorical figures mingle with other characters and communicate freely with them; the number of characters far exceeds the classical limit; seven speaking roles in one scene are not uncommon; scenes in any one act may range in number from one to twelve; both the Christian God and pagan gods are invoked; unities of time and place are consistently ignored; scenic effects are occasionally sketched by a few deft verses; long soliloquies are regularly interrupted by an old man who stands apart and interjects choric commentary; processional movements across the stage are not infrequent; finally, eschatological subjects are dramatized in their proper locales.

This blend of classical and native forms on the technical level is paralleled by the Christian transmutation of Senecan motives on the thematic level. The "notable moralitie" of Seneca which attracted Sidney is easily oriented to a Christian reference.[18] In like manner the Stoic con-

---

[17] The term "Christian Seneca" is not currently used in Neo-Latin scholarship. There seem to be grounds for adopting this term, however, because of its analogy with the term "Christian Terence," now widely used. Like the Christian Terence, the Christian Senecan tradition endeavored to forge a new kind of sacred drama by blending the best of both classical and Christian traditions. (See Herrick, *Tragicomedy*, pp. 61–62.) The term "Christian Seneca" seems to have been coined by Johannes Bolte, a famous Neo-Latin scholar who used it to characterize the work of Vernulaeus: "Hat der Haarlemer Schulmeister Schonäus seine gesammelten dramatischen Werke unter dem Titel eines *Terentius christianus* erscheinen lassen, so könnte man seinen um vierzig Jahre jüngeren Löwener Collegen [Vernulaeus] als den *Seneca christianus* bezeichnen." "Vernuläus," *Allgemeine deutsche Biographie*, Vol. XXXIX, col. 630.

[18] The amalgamation of Senecan and other classical systems of morality with Christianity represents an unbroken tradition of more than a thousand years. For a summary documentation of this tradition, see Ralph Graham Palmer, *Seneca's* DE REMEDIIS FORTUITORUM *and the Elizabethans*, pp. 7–20.

victions of the brevity of life, the capriciousness of Fortune, the opportunity afforded virtue by calamity, and the primacy of rationality combine in the Christian alembic of Vernulaeus' art.[19] Finally, the horrible and sensational aspects of Senecan drama find generous acceptance in the Vernulaeus theater, where they serve to intensify the lurid cravings of a tyrant, the death spasms of a criminal maniac, or the terrors of everlasting torture.

A recapitulation of the technical and thematic features of Vernulaeus' dramaturgy reveals, therefore, an indebtedness to both native and classic traditions. Future studies in Neo-Latin drama will undoubtedly show that a fairly regular pattern of Christian Seneca conventions had already crystallized in the academic theater by the end of the sixteenth century. The exploitation of these conventions may, to some extent, account for Vernulaeus' early competence in this genre.[20]

In conclusion, it has been shown that the pedagogic and moral-didactic purposes of the Vernulaeus theater dictated the playwright's choice of historical tragedy as the medium for training students in their future sacral and secular responsibilities; furthermore, that Vernulaeus' work in this genre was animated, directed, and sustained by a living tradition of Christian Senecan drama which, in the course of centuries, had wrought a fusion of classic and native dramatic elements, both formal and material.

[19] It should be noted that the Vernulaean theater flourished in the context of late sixteenth-century Neo-Stoicism which climaxed the anti-Ciceronian movement prevalent in England and on the Continent. See Leontine Zanta, *La renaissance du stoïcisme au xvie siècle*, pp. 2–26. The nature of the anti-Ciceronian movement is masterly described by Morris W. Croll in a series of three articles: "Attic Prose in the Seventeenth Century." (*Studies in Philology*, XVIII [April, 1921], 79–128) relates the movement to classical models and authorities; "Muret and the History of 'Attic' Prose" (*PMLA*, XXXIX [June, 1924], 254–309) describes its relations to the ideas of its age; "Attic Prose: Lipsius, Montaigne, Bacon," (*Schelling Anniversary Papers* [New York, 1923], pp. 117–50) carries the history of the movement into the generation following Muret. Justus Lipsius, founder of Neo-Stoicism, preceded Puteanus and Vernulaeus as Latin professor of the Trilingue. Although Lipsius died before Vernulaeus arrived at Louvain, his treatises on Stoicism, and especially his attempts to demonstrate the compatibility of Stoic doctrine to Catholic theology, must have been familiar to Vernulaeus.

[20] "An Introduction to the Jesuit Theatre," unpublished doctoral dissertation of the late William H. McCabe, S.J., suggests a strong Jesuit influence at work in the Vernulaeus theater. Father McCabe's concentration on the tragedies of Joseph Simons, St. Omers playwright and contemporary of Vernulaeus, reveals definite parallels in dramatic handling between Simons and Vernulaeus, thus implying a living Christian Seneca tradition. The Jesuits Bidermann and Caussin have left a series of tragedies that also fit into this tradition. Unfortunately, few of the Jesuit plays were published. The present revisional stage of Father McCabe's work prohibits further documentation in this study.

To understand more exactly the nature and development of Vernu-laeus' dramatic art within this living tradition, it will be necessary to survey the fourteen historical tragedies which, written over a period of forty years, comprise Vernulaeus' contribution to the Louvain academic theater and ultimately determine his position as a Neo-Latin playwright.

Survey of the Dramatic Canon of Vernulaeus

It has already been pointed out that the plots of all the Vernulaean plays were predetermined by the sequence of historical events which they dramatized. Vernulaeus' abiding respect for historical truth did not prevent him from rearranging and relating these historical incidents in an order of dramatic effectiveness that would render the action as mean-ingful as possible. The moral significance of history in public and private life was his primary concern. Dramatic structure, in turn, contributed to the maximum expression of this significance. A chronological reading of Vernulaeus' first four plays reveals an initial groping for effective plotting and characterization that is gradually rewarded by a sureness of design which seldom thereafter falters.

Vernulaeus made his dramatic debut in 1609 with *Gorcomienses*, a dramatization of the martyrdom of nineteen Catholic clerics of Gorkum, Holland, who were hanged on July 9, 1572, by the Sea-beggars. Possess-ing many of the ingredients of a Vernulaean production—a restless, tyrannical protagonist (Baron la Marck), an adamant ecclesiastical ad-versary (Nicolaus Picus), bloodthirsty allegorical figures, choruses of exiles, rhetorical apostrophes, stychomythic forensics, mythological al-lusions, and sundry atrocities—the play is nevertheless a hodgepodge. The young professor had yet to learn that allegorical characters cannot sustain an entire act of four scenes; that a structure of loosely connected, unmotivated postponements of vengeance on the part of the protagonist is ramshackle; that the position of the catastrophe in the fourth act is pre-mature; and that a fifth act offering nothing but a series of lamentations is ineffectual. On the other hand, the play provided rhetorical exercise for Vernulaeus' pupils; its spectacle pleased the students; its political and religious import impressed the attending academic and civil authori-ties. Finally, it remained a successful tribute to Catholic Belgium and the Spanish dynasty.

Divus Eustachius, performed three years later (1612), evinces little improvement in structural design, a defect attributable largely to the episodic nature of the Eustachius legend it strove to re-enact. Its ram-bling structure and improbable coincidences are best suggested by a summary of its action as arranged by Vernulaeus. Converted by the sight of a cross-crowned deer, Roman officer Eustace endures a Job-like series of trials. A plague exterminates his livestock and drives the Eustace family from Rome. Happening upon a sea captain, Eustace arranges a voyage. The captain discovers that Eustace is penniless and capitalizes on the situation by abducting Eustace's attractive wife. Stranded with his two sons, Eustace fords a stream and deposits his younger son on the bank. Meanwhile the older son, momentarily left behind, is attacked by a wolf. Eustace rushes back across the stream to the rescue, thus temporarily abandoning the younger son who, in turn, is assaulted by a lion. The end of the second act finds Eustace wifeless and childless.

The scene shifts to Parthia where Eustace has been summoned by Trajan to quell a rebellion. Among his victorious troops are his two sons, unknown to each other and to their father. The eventual recognition of father and sons is climaxed by the appearance of the abducted wife in the Parthian camp. Upon returning to Rome, the reunited family is discovered to be Christian and is condemned *en masse*. Together they face a ravenous lion that suddenly turns innocuous and even frolicsome. The punishment of the brass bull is next imposed. The canticles of the Eustace family rise with the heat of the blast furnace, then gradually subside. When the lifeless bodies are found unscorched and radiant, the enraged Emperor has them thrown to the hounds.

Despite the plethora of incidents and the improbability of the plot, Vernulaeus does develop the theme of loss and recovery with considerable conviction, the affection of Eustace for his wife and children has moments of freshness and tenderness, the battle songs are rousing, and the climax of martyrdom is correctly timed. Structurally, Vernulaeus' first two plays show extremes of experimentation: where *Gorcomienses* suffers from inanition of incident, *Eustachius* reveals a surfeit.

The decade of dramatic inactivity that followed the appearance of *Eustachius* found Vernulaeus preoccupied with publishing editions of student orations and his own volumes on rhetoric, with licentiate studies in theology, and with administrational duties as subregent of the Porc and president of the College of Luxembourg.

The appearance of *Theodoricus* in 1623 marks a striking advance in Vernulaeus' dramatic art that can be explained only by his indebtedness to a more experienced craftsman.[21] No play in the Vernulaeus canon is

---

[21] A scene-by-scene comparison of Vernulaeus' *Theodoricus* with the similarly entitled play of Jesuit Nicholas Caussin, published with Caussin's four other dramas in *Tragoediae sacrae* (1629), reveals a close, but unslavish, adherence to the plot line of Caussin's play. It is obvious that the structural effectiveness of the Louvainist's per-

more crowded with Senecan horrors and melodramatic incident. Theodoric (d. 526), king of the Ostrogoths in Italy, is furiously dedicated to
the propagation of Arianism. Finding Pope John I, Boethius, and Symmachus opposed to his program, he assassinates them and is in turn
haunted by their shades. Theodoric's Macbeth-like hallucinations reach
their climax during a banquet scene. Where his guests see only a huge
fish on the table, the King gapes at the frothing jaws and teeth of the
murdered Symmachus, who suddenly seems to spring from the platter
and rend his murderer piecemeal. The subsequent horrendous deathbed
scene of the tyrant, the sentence of damnation pronounced by his victims, and the expulsion of Theodoric's damned soul to eternal hellfire
bring the play to a gasping finale.

Vernulaeus improves on Caussin's structure by placing the banquet
scene at the end of the fourth act instead of in the middle of it. On the
other hand, he out-Caussins Caussin, and Seneca, especially in the scene
where Boethius' wife receives her husband's gory head from the gloating
Arian monarch. When one compares the final impression made by *Theodoricus* with that of the earlier plays, he realizes that Vernulaeus' adaptation of the Jesuit dramatist's work marks a distinct progress in his artistic
growth. Not only has the Louvain playwright acquired experience in the
distribution of incident and complication of action: he has likewise
learned to depict psychological tensions more vividly and credibly.

A detailed examination of Vernulaeus' fourth published play, *Henricus
Octavus*, written the following year, will demonstrate the playwright's
new grasp of structural form and characterization.[22] Instead of a maniacal

---

formance is largely due to its model. That the indebtedness does not end here can be
gathered from the juxtaposition of set speeches, the verbal parallels of which suggest
that Vernulaeus had Caussin's text before him as he composed. Compare, for example, the following passages:

> Regum quadrigis scandere astrorum globos
> Calcare coelum pedibus, atque inter sacros
> Stellarum honores figere hac palmas manu
> (Caussin, I, iii)

> . . . ut ipsos sedis aethereae globos
> Haec arma fraenent, pedibus & calcans polos
> Media inter astra laureas figam meas.
> (Vernulaeus, I, i)

I quote from the Folger copy of the third edition of Caussin's *Tragoediae sacrae*
(Paris, 1629). In his study of Caussin's drama, Hocking fails to mention Vernulaeus'
indebtedness to Caussin's *Theodoricus*, but does point to the influence of the Jesuit's
Hermengildus on Vernulaeus' play of the same title. See George Drew Hocking, *A
Study of the* TRAGOEDIAE SACRAE *of Father Caussin (1583–1651)*.
[22] See Chapter IV and Explanatory Notes.

protagonist vulcanized against every humane influence and mature in vice at his first appearance, we are shown a magnanimous person whose gradual disintegration of character is set forth so convincingly that we never lose sympathy for his plight as a human being under the strain of decision.

Vernulaeus' most productive dramatic period extends from 1623 to 1631. Although the surviving evidence of printed plays and records of performance during this period does not enable us to establish a definitive chronological sequence of composition and production, it is highly probable that Vernulaeus wrote a new play each year for nine consecutive annual holiday performances.[23] Before reviewing these nine plays, it may be instructive to furnish a more detailed analysis of Vernulaeus' dramatic art as illustrated by *Thomas Cantuariensis*, one of the early plays of this middle period.

The first act of *Thomas Cantuariensis* fulfills its expository function in characteristically straightforward fashion. The opening soliloquy of King Henry II of England establishes the context of divine-right sovereignty and introduces the monarch's ambition to gain renown by securing a just tribunal. This general statement of the theme is particularized in the following scene by the resolution of King and counselors to curtail the power of ecclesiastical courts. Nigellus, confessor to the King, challenges Henry in the third scene. Their clash clarifies the church-state conflict and reveals the opposing principles underlying it. Vernulaeus next objectifies the struggle between Henry and Becket by having the King draft the Clarendon Constitutions onstage and demand that Becket subscribe to them.

Future lines of action are prepared for, at the same time, by the unambiguous characterization of the principal contenders. The rashly ambitious Henry is pitted against the adamantine Archbishop; in addition, the King's mental turmoil is intensified by contrast with Thomas' un-

---

[23] The years 1623 and 1624 are represented, respectively, by individual publications and performances of *Theodoricus* and *Henricus Octavus*. The year 1625 has left no evidence of activity; however, the parallelism of the religio-political crisis involving two King Henrys of England (Henry II and Henry VIII) and two Thomases who were chancellors and saints (Thomas Becket and Thomas More) suggests 1625 as the date for *Thomas Cantuariensis*. The Becket play was not printed as a separate title, but appeared in the collected edition *Tragoediae decem*, 1631. *Ottocarus* was published in 1626. The following year, seemingly fallow, is represented by the twin publication of *Conradinus* and *Crispus* in 1628. *Joanna Darcia* appeared in 1629, *Maximus* in 1630. The year 1631 is possibly the date to be assigned to *Stanislaus*, which, like *Thomas Cantuariensis*, was first printed in the collected edition of *Tragoediae decem* of that year.

divided soul. This alignment of forces is continued in the arrangement of four counselors and four bishops to form contrasting blocs, the one obsequious, the other vacillating and pusillanimous.

The exposition of the problem and situation by means of characters in action is summarized by the Chorus at the close of Act I.[24] Furthermore, the direction to be taken by the ensuing complication is pointed by the critical question: Will the state in the person of King Henry overcome the resistance of the church in the person of Thomas?

The next three acts of *Thomas Cantuariensis* reveal a complication of incident that reaches two climactic stages before mounting to the main climax of Act IV. The disposition of incident along this trajectory is causally sequential: each scene advances the action to a position that leads logically to the next situation. Thus in Act II the Catholic Church in the form of a maiden catechizes Archbishop Thomas and is assured of his unqualified support. In the following interview between Henry and Thomas, the audience witnesses the Archbishop's disdain of royal flattery and his immunity to threat. It is thus prepared for Thomas' inflexible stand during the public hearing that climaxes the act.

The resulting stalemate leads, in the third act, to a countermovement of the counselors, who alienate the four bishops from Thomas. The realignment of forces resulting from this stratagem finds Henry, the counselors, and the acquiescent bishops united in their opposition to the Archbishop. At this point the carefully articulated action rises to an impressive climax. Shouldering his episcopal cross, Thomas enters the council chamber, opposes the proposed legislation with devastating incisiveness, refuses to affix his seal of approval, and is ejected from the assembly. The temporary deadlock prompts a second countermovement by the counselors: the King is advised to demand a complete fiscal account of Thomas' previous expenditures as chancellor—an impossible exaction which will force Thomas' arraignment by the King's tribunal. This final stratagem is the result of a brain-storming session and is arrived at only after previous alternatives have been aired and discarded. (It should be noted, in passing, that the practice of dramatizing the formulation of policy from tentative beginnings to final resolution is a favorite and effective technique of the Vernulaeus theater.) Thomas' inability to meet the exaction will incur guilt of *lèse majesté* and the

---

[24] The Chorus in the Vernulaeus theater is invariably Janus-like in attitude: it reviews previous action and anticipates future developments, thus functioning structurally as a bridge between formal act divisions. Its primary function, however, is didactic. One might say that it serves as a pulpit to the stage through its preoccupation with the moral significance of history in its dramatic re-enactment.

sentence of banishment. In the outer lobby Thomas resists the specious arguments and imprecations of the departing bishops.[25] With the exile of the Archbishop and his kin at the close of Act III, the progress of the King's cause reaches its zenith.

The final two acts evince a similar competence in structure. The patched-up truce between Thomas and Henry at the climax of Act IV is prepared for by a dovetailed succession of events that swing from the papal headquarters of Alexander III in Rome to the French court of King Louis VII. The seeds of disaster, carefully planted in the foregoing acts, now reach full growth in the final act and bear their baneful fruit in the murder of the Archbishop.[26] Vernulaeus preserves the unity of impression during these final scenes by restricting his attention to the actual martyrdom and its spiritual significance. The effect of Thomas' death on Henry, on the murderers, and on the church-state issue, is completely ignored. It should be noted that Vernulaeus regularly uses the negative principle of omission as a means of dramatic economy. Nevertheless, it is difficult to ascertain, in the present instance, whether the dramatic vividness of the martyrdom compensates sufficiently for the loss of unity involved in the uncollected loose ends. There is no doubt, however, that the blend of tragic catastrophe and spiritual illumination attained in the death of Thomas is effective theater.

As a representative play of the Vernulaeus canon, *Thomas Cantuariensis* exhibits a carefully plotted action with recognizable beginning, middle, and end. Its structure is characterized by a simplicity of line that tends to be monolithic in its exclusion of varied incident and supporting detail. As would be expected, this structural simplicity is likewise marked by the absence of subplot: the use of plot and character to express the heterogeneous complexity of the human condition is foreign

---

[25] Vernulaeus frequently subjects his heroes at critical moments to a barrage of *eloquentia dissuasoria* from near kin or intimates: Abbot Picus is beleaguered by his blood brothers (*Gorcomienses*, III, v); Boethius by his wife, Elpidia (*Theodoricus*, II, vi); Thomas More by his wife and daughter (*Henricus Octavus*, V, iv); Thomas Becket by his relatives (*Thomas Cantuariensis*, III, vi); Conradinus by his mother, Elizabeth (*Conradinus*, I, v); and Hermenigildus by his brother Recaredus (*Hermenigildus*, V, ii).

[26] The opposition of the counselors to ecclesiastical jurisdiction (I, ii) and their antipapal attitude (I, iv) come to a white-hot focus in Act III, scene i. Thomas is already seen as the sole obstacle to the King's peace program, and the thought of doing him violence is already made vocal. The instrumental cause of the murder is planted in Act IV, scene ii, when the Pope commissions Thomas to enjoin the penalty of excommunication on the wayward bishops and demand a period of expiation, without granting Thomas, however, the powers of absolution. Finally, King Henry's public expression of disgust with his craven court menials incites the fury of his counselors, who attempt to prove their allegiance by murdering the Archbishop.

not only to the Vernulaeus theater but to academic drama in general.

A chronological reading of the subsequent plays of Vernulaeus' middle period reveals mediocre achievement in *Ottocarus* (1626) and *Conradinus* (1627?), followed by a consistently high level of artistry in *Crispus* (1628), *Joanna Darcia* (1629), *Maximus* (1630), and *Stanislaus* (1631). *Ottocarus,* Vernulaeus' first rebellion play, re-creates the thirteenth-century Polish king's military revolt against Emperor Rudolf I, founder of the Austrian dynasty. Fomented late in the first act, the rebellion is subsequently launched in the second act, only to be averted by Ottokar's peace treaty with Rudolf, which climaxes Act III. Returning home, Ottokar is lashed into a renewal of the rebellion by the tongue of Queen Kunegundis and is eventually overwhelmed by the Emperor.

In spite of the play's basic weakness in the characterization of the protagonist—Ottokar's submission to Rudolf (III, vii) is inconsistent with his proud nature—there are individual, if minor, successes. Kunegundis emerges as a fiercely vengeful woman, indomitable in spirit and potent in reprisal. She is the first of Vernulaeus' defiant women. The role of the *senex* is more thoroughly integrated with the action than previously.[27] His wry commentary pricks monomaniacal statements as they rise from the tongue and challenges heretical remarks by timely aphorisms.

Conradinus, the least-inspired play of Vernulaeus' middle period, reveals merely a competent surface organization of conflict. Upon reaching the age of fifteen, Conradin, medieval Duke of Swabia and Franconia, disregards the pleas of his mother and nurse and sets out with Frederick, Duke of Austria, to regain Sicily from Charles, Duke of Anjou. The young idealists are no match for the veteran warrior and tyrant. Their ultimate defeat is postponed by flight, but they are eventually captured, tried, and put to the sword. The final impression of the play is a sobering one, however illuminated by the Christian gallantry of the victims. One puts down the play wondering whether gallantry in any form can excuse the rashness attending it.

There is nothing morally ambiguous about the companion play, *Crispus,* a recasting of the Phaedra saga in a Christian mold. Returning from a victorious war in the Rhineland, the son of Emperor Constantine

---

[27] The heightened role of the *senex* in *Ottocarus, Conradinus, Crispus, Joanna Darcia, Stanislaus, Lambertus,* and *Hermenigildus* is undoubtedly explained by the absence of allegorical characters in these plays. In *Maximus* the choric function of the old-man commentator is likewise pervasive, abetted only slightly by the late appearance of *Iustitia Divina.* On the other hand, in *Gorcomienses, Theodoricus,* and *Fritlandus* we find the *senex* sharing his choric duties with allegorical figures. The remaining three plays of the canon—*Eustachius, Thomas Cantuariensis,* and *Henricus Octavus*—have allegories but no *senex.*

is given a Roman ovation, and a royal triumph is decreed by the Senate. As preparations for a public celebration get under way, the domestic tragedy is set in motion by Empress Fausta, stepmother of Crispus. In a sequence characterized by psychological subtlety and irony, she discloses her anxieties to Crispus, who, not suspecting her intent, attempts to console her. When Fausta's import is suddenly revealed, Crispus recoils in horror and rejects his stepmother's advances. The enraged Empress retaliates by throwing herself at her husband's feet where she sobs out a contrived story of Crispus' attack on her person. Constantine is wracked by the scandal and summons his son to the tribunal. The trial scene is deeply moving. Unable to pass sentence on Crispus, Constantine breaks down and commits the decision to a subordinate. Crispus, who cannot bring himself to disclose his stepmother's wantonness in open court, is found guilty and thereby condemned to death. From this point the play moves swiftly and relentlessly to its tragic conclusion. Fausta's guilt is bared, the order of execution is countermanded; but Crispus, surrounded by his admiring officers, has already faced death. A chorus of soldiers sings out the courage of Crispus as his body is carried in triumph before the weeping Emperor.

Crispus is one of Vernulaeus' most artistic achievements. The domestic action is compressed, gaining dramatic intensity through the preparations for the hero's royal triumph. The resulting contrast between the private intrigue and the pending public celebration produces an irony of situation that is artfully exploited. No less satisfying is the balance between spectacle and psychological nuance. No allegorical figures assist in projecting the conflict of wills and the delicately poised tensions that invade the family circle and eventually disrupt it. Instead we are shown a filament spun out of a woman's passionate desire that gradually enmeshes the principal characters in a web of tragic circumstance they cannot escape without a surrender of their individual natures. Because of its skillful portrayal of character, its carefully wrought interplay of emotions, its articulation of incident, and its unity of conception, *Crispus* attains high rank in the history of academic drama.[28]

Vernulaeus' depiction of women characters attains maturity in his next play, *Joanna Darcia*.[29] In *Crispus*, the hero of German battlefields is

[28] The *Crispus* of Jesuit Bernardus Stephonius (Rome, 1601), reprinted in *Selectae PP. Soc. Iesu tragoediae*, is less intense than Vernulaeus' play, principally because the seduction scenes are narrated, not dramatized. There seems to be no significant influence of Stephonius on Vernulaeus.

[29] Vernulaeus' *Joanna Darcia* seems to be the first of the long series of plays with Joan in the lead role. A French translation by Antoine de Latour was published late in the nineteenth century (see *Jeanne D'Arc, tragédie latine par Nicolas de Vernulz*

overwhelmed on his own hearth; in *Joanna Darcia,* the heroine forsakes
her pastoral village for the arena of international wars and there meets a
like fate. This change of emphasis from private to public issues is central
to the drama of Joan. Each act dramatizes one of the five major divisions
of the plot: the desperate situation of France under English siege, the
appearance of the savior of France in the person of Joan, the liberation of
Orléans, the coronation of Charles VII at Rheims, and the capture and
martyrdom of the Maid.

This well-proportioned structure is dominated by the eighteen-year-
old heroine, who, unlike Shakespeare's creation, is seen as a human instrument wholly inspired by divine grace. Like other Vernulaean martyrs, Joan faces opposition with no sign of inner perturbation. It is this
lack of tension within the protagonist that prompts one to label *Joanna
Darcia* a drama of religious beatitude rather than a tragedy. Technically,
her triumphant death coincides with her tragic catastrophe as protagonist, but the coincidence, in this case, does not involve an identification.
In quality of organization as well as in the successful depiction of the
martyr-protagonist, *Joanna Darcia* is matched by other works of the
canon, yet there are features which make this play unique. The scene of
the anointing and crowning of Charles at Rheims (III, vi), for instance,
is made impressive by Vernulaeus' use of music and liturgical detail. Precise directions (the chanting of the *Veni, Creator,* group genuflection,
the vesting of the bishop, and dismissal) regulate the protocol of the
scene—one of the few surviving stage directions in the Vernulaeus
theater. Joan's final farewell, not her torture, concludes the play.

Finally, the general tone of the poetry is characterized by a sense of
immediacy that suggests the dramatist's projection of personal experience. A visit to Vernulaeus' native village, Roblemont, Belgium, provides
a fresh context for reappraising several passages in *Joanna Darcia.* For
example, Joan's farewell to Domremy is strikingly vivid in its imagery.
Its pictures of shadowed hillsides, thick forests, swift streams, the crook
Joan used for prodding sheep, fording rivers, and pulling down apples,
have a ring of authenticity not easily adapted from Roman poets. With
its medieval atmosphere, its environment of rolling hills speckled with

---

[Orléans: H. Herluison, 1880]). Its influence on Schiller's play was advanced (not
very convincingly) by a German scholar earlier in the century (see *C. Goettlingii
Commentariolum de Nicolao Vernulaeo Schilleri antecessore in tragoediis viraginis
Aurelianensis et Wallenstenii* [Jena: Libraria Braniana, 1862]). Finally, on the occasion of the glorification of Joan of Arc in the Cathedral of Orléans, May 8, 1921, a
eulogy of Vernulaeus, describing his dramatic tribute to the Maid of Orléans, was
delivered by Georges Goyau, member of the French Academy. A copy of his speech
is in the parish archives of Roblemont, Belgium.

sheep, its forests and streams, modern Roblemont remains the kind of village Joan could have forsaken. No other play of the Louvain professor bears this spirit of nostalgia for the scenes of his boyhood.

Maximus (1630), Vernulaeus' second rebellion play, shows considerable advance in artistry over *Ottocarus* (1626), the author's original attempt in this genre. Fourth-century Roman Emperor Gratian chooses Theodosius to share his throne, a decision which incites Maximus, commander of the legions in Britain, to rebel. During an initial military maneuver, Gratian is treacherously slain. The sight of the stricken Emperor sends the rebel into a spasm of grief and remorse, but he clings to his ambition of world conquest. At the request of Empress Constantia, Ambrose, Bishop of Milan, requests of Maximus the body of Gratian and sues for peace. Maximus refuses, and in reprisal, sets out to devastate Italy and kill Gratian's son, Valentinian. Ambrose sends the royal family to Greece to seek refuge and aid from Theodosius; meanwhile the Bishop rallies the Milanese to withstand the advance of Maximus. The fourth act shifts to the Grecian court of Theodosius, where the importunities of the Roman Empress are frustrated by peace overtures made by the legates of Maximus. Theodosius' hesitancy to engage rashly in a war of revenge is dissolved by the pleas of Galla, his fiancée. Soon after his marriage, Theodosius sails for Italy and vanquishes the rebel mercenaries. Maximus and his son are captured, brought to trial, and executed onstage in the final moments of the play.

A summary of the action of *Maximus* suggests the extent of its complication, the variety of incident and its fullness of cast, the successive climaxes, and the vastness of the world issues it brings to the academic stage. Furthermore its protagonist has a sufficient mixture of good and evil motives to prevent his emergence as a mere monster.

The final play of Vernulaeus' middle period, *Stanislaus* (1631), is strongly reminiscent of the dramatist's previous manipulation of materials taken from English history. Like Henry VIII, King Boleslaus II of Poland grows tyrannical under the sway of an illicit passion and is roundly denounced by Stanislaus, Bishop of Cracow. Stanislaus, like Thomas of Canterbury, is slain in church. The main action of the play is centered in King Boleslaus, who, in an effort to maintain his adulterous union with Christina, wife of Count Miceslaus, forces Stanislaus to a trial rigged with suborned witnesses. The Bishop, accused of swindling the nobleman Petriscus and his heirs of an estate, finds himself reduced to extremity by the death of the nobleman. Finding no other witnesses available, Stanislaus goes to the grave of Petriscus, removes the burial stone, and calls the nobleman back to life. The trial scene reaches an

eerie and sobering climax with the appearance of the resurrected Petriscus, who exonerates the Bishop and wins his acquittal. Stung to reprisal
by Stanislaus' sentence of excommunication, Boleslaus assaults the
Bishop while he is saying mass. After the royal henchmen crumple at
the Bishop's feet, Boleslaus himself advances and puts Stanislaus to the
sword. This sacrilege causes a general uprising. Finally, anticipating his
subjects' intentions to kill him, Boleslaus takes his own life.

The play exploits typical Vernulaean themes of church-state conflict,
of lust leading to tyranny, and of the responsibility of princes in the temporal order.[30] The clash of wills involved in these themes is implemented
by a complete range of rhetorical artillery: meditative monologue, impassioned soliloquy, formal debates, staccato exchanges, high- and low-
styled dialogue, and set speeches of declamation, both deliberative and
judicial. In its pleasing variation of these forms of *eloquentia latina* issuing naturally from the developments of plot and character, in its vividness of characterization and firmness of structure, this last play of the
middle period is representative of Vernulaeus' superior work in academic
drama.

The final period of Vernulaeus' dramatic activity is represented by a
trio of plays, *Fritlandus, Lambertus,* and *Hermenigildus,* the latter two
published posthumously.[31] The subject matter of the first play needed no
introduction, as Vernulaeus remarked in its *argumentum,* since the
name of Albert Wallenstein was on everyone's lips and his treachery and
fate well known even to children. *Fritlandus* is the playwright's final
attempt in the dramatization of contemporary history: it was played in
the Louvain theater in August, 1636, scarcely two years after the actual
death of its protagonist, murdered at Eger on February 25, 1634. The
playwright sees Wallenstein as a seventeenth-century Sejanus, whose
soaring ambition spurred by evil counsel merited just retribution. The
ignominy of the former darling of Fortune served clearly as a documentary and cautionary lesson to his age and a vindication of the providen-
tial role of the Habsburg dynasty.[32]

For all its timeliness of subject, *Fritlandus* is not one of Vernulaeus'
most artistic achievements.[33] The allegorical figures representing Ger-

---

[30] Vernulaeus' choice of one of the stirring crises in the history of medieval Poland
was no doubt intended as a tribute to the Polish students then attending Louvain,
many of whom profited by his personal attention.

[31] They were included in *Tragoediae, in duos tomos distributae.*

[32] See *Fritlandus,* dedicatory letter, fol. *3ʳ, *3ᵛ, *4ʳ.

[33] J. Bolte edited the play, along with two other Neo-Latin dramas that re-enact
the careers of Coligny and Gustavus Adolphus. See *Coligny, Gustaf Adolf, Wallenstein: drei zeitgenössische lateinische Dramen von Rhodius, Narssius, Vernulaeus.* For

many (Germania) and the guardian spirit of the Austrian dynasty (Genius Austriacus) state and define the significance of the issues; yet in contrast to *Theodoricus,* for example, in which Revenge, the devil, and the ghosts are structurally functional in frightening the protagonist on his deathbed and later in passing judgment on his soul, they are not integrated in the dramatic design and so remain quite meaningless to the plot. A more striking deficiency of the Wallenstein tragedy is its lack of complication. Lalgus, the flattering parasite who prods the protagonist into rebellion, is seemingly snatched out of thin air and given little motivation for his action.[34] Furthermore, the use of Piccolomini as a foil to the protagonist, while effective as a contrasting device, fails to complicate the intrigue. As a result the narrative of the play is a straightforward presentation of a rebellious prince's ambition, the discovery of his treachery, and the retribution meted out to him. It is this radical flaw of oversimplicity in plotting which relegates *Fritlandus* to a secondary position in the Vernulaeus canon.

In this connection, a comparison with Glapthorne's *Wallenstein* (1639) is instructive. The Englishman's play offers a wide variety of incident taken from the same materials available to Vernulaeus. Wallenstein's two sons are involved with Isabella and their affair is qualified by the broad ribaldry of Colonel Newman. Wallenstein offers Isabella to his son Albert, provided he kills her the day after the wedding. Accused, meanwhile, of stealing the Duchess' jewelry, Isabella is sentenced by Wallenstein to be hanged. When a guard seizes his fiancée, Albert kills him and is in turn stabbed fatally by Wallenstein, who soon after kills his page, thinking him the ghost of his murdered son. Thus Wallenstein's downfall during the famous banquet scene is made to issue from a complex web of crime and intrigue expertly woven across the first four acts. Glapthorne's play, which was performed at the Globe, illustrates the strong contrast between the dramatic components of the public theater in England and those of the academic stage here represented in Vernulaeus.[35]

Lambertus,[36] on the other hand, is one of Vernulaeus' most effective

---

a brief analysis of *Fritlandus,* see also Theodor Vetter, *Wallenstein in der dramatischen Dichtung des Jahrzehntes seines Todes* (Frankfurt, 1894), pp. 20 ff.

[34] The inadequacy of Lalgus' role becomes more striking when one compares the similar role assigned to Baroness Terzky in Schiller's *Wallenstein.*

[35] See Henry Glapthorne, *The Tragedy of Albertus Wallenstein, Late Duke of Friedland, and General to the Emperor Ferdinand the Second. The Scene Egers. Acted, with good allowance, at the Globe on the Bankside, by His Majesty's Servants.* See also above, Chap. III, n. 29.

[36] *Tragoediae, in duos tomos distributae* (1656), pp. 865–903.

dramas. As patron of the diocese of nearby Liège, St. Lambert would not be totally unfamiliar to the Louvain students, some of whom had undoubtedly visited the tomb of this seventh-century saint at Liège. Like Henry VIII and Boleslaus II, Frankish Prince Pepin is wracked by the opposing tensions of illicit love and moral duty. Fettered by the charms of Alpais, Pepin is denounced by Bishop Lambert, who insists on the dismissal of the mistress and the reinstatement of the wife. After a series of partial victories on either side, Alpais summons her brother Dodo, Duke of Ardennes, who somewhat reluctantly kills the Bishop and his nephews. The murdered victim, in turn, gains a posthumous victory: his death paralyzes the Prince with grief, spiritually rejuvenates the murderous Duke, and precipitates the rejection of Alpais.

The banquet scene climaxing Act III, as well as the murder sequence, is developed with remarkable vigor. In the former, host Pepin seats the Bishop, the knights, and the ladies at table, the *senex* grumbling meanwhile at being neglected. The banquet then proceeds against a background of music. Upon request, Bishop Lambert blesses each goblet of wine, including that proffered by Alpais. Before she drinks, however, the Bishop commits a breach of etiquette by addressing her as whore, and demands that she forsake the court after the banquet. The dinner is disrupted, of course, by the outburst that ensues.

The murder sequence, unlike Vernulaeus' previous practice, is approached gradually and enveloped in layers of descriptive poetry. The Bishop and his nephews are huddled about the spent fire in their home at midnight. As they wait in ominous uncertainty, their minds stray from the room to the stillness outside, where the full moon travels the sky and the stars look down over the vast sea, where every tree is hushed and dwellings are buried in slumber, where the city noises have yielded to the quiet breathings of universal nature.[37] Through this stillness the murderers advance in the following scene, calling upon the moon to witness the immolation of the victims singled out by Alpais. The hushed atmosphere is suddenly broken by the clash of weapons outside the house, the calls of alarm from within, and the furious slaughter that follows. As the victims fall in death, the song of angelic choirs rises offstage.

A final remarkable innovation found in *Lambertus* is the interchange

---

[37] Iam luna medium plena decurrit polum,/Et prona vastum sydera aspiciunt mare./Silet omnis arbor, stabula tranquillo silent/ Sepulta somno, totus in cineres abit/Consumptus ignis; urbium clamor jacet/Tantum quietem cuncta respirant suam. /Servemus horam, somnio indultum satis/Etiamque somno, Coelitum scandat domos/Animus precando. *Lambertus*, V, i, 1–9.

between Pepin and the *senex*, in which the former catalogues his woes while, in litany fashion, the latter adds the response (I, iii, 15–21):

Pep. My fighting arm droops in battle.	*Sen.* Because of Alpais.
Pep. I cannot subdue beasts of prey.	*Sen.* Because of Alpais.
Pep. I avoid the rigors of a soldier.	*Sen.* Because of Alpais.
Pep. My will struggles within me.	*Sen.* Because of Alpais.
Pep. Sleep visits not my eyes.	*Sen.* Because of Alpais.
Pep. My soul is sorely wounded.	*Sen.* Because of Alpais.
Pep. And hither and yon am I hurled.	*Sen.* Because of Alpais.

Hermenigildus,[38] the fourteenth and final performance of Vernulaeus, is a competent play whose action is sprung by a rancorous and ineluctable stepmother. Issuing upon the academic stage from sixth-century Spain are the impetuous Levigildus, Arian king of the Goths, and his Arian queen Gosuinda, the stepmother; two royal sons, Hermenigildus and his younger brother Recaredus, together with various princes, soldiers, intriguers, and royal attendants. The play re-enacts the return of the Catholic Hermenigildus to the court of his estranged father. There his stepmother, capitalizing on the opposed Arian and Catholic beliefs of father and son, has Hermenigildus imprisoned on trumped-up charges. Before Levigildus discovers the treachery of his queen, Hermenigildus has been executed. Prostrate with remorse, the King views the body of his son as it lies bathed in wondrous light and attended by heavenly music. He renounces Arianism and buries Hermenigildus in funereal splendor.

Noteworthy is the characterization of Hermenigildus' friend and knight, Adolphus, who stands by his master through success and peril like another Horatio. Recaredus, brother of the martyr, is equally convincing in his loyalty as he draws his poniard to expiate his father's injustice. The theme of the play is aptly summed up in the words of the *senex*: any strong man can overcome the furies; a few can even overcome an ordinary woman; but none can ever vanquish a stepmother: she is the world's worst evil (I, iii, 38–40).

This summary survey of Vernulaeus' fourteen plays gives rise to several general conclusions about his dramaturgy. In regard to structure, we have observed that the early plays show a period of trial and error in which the apprenticeship gropings are succeeded by competent craftsmanship. Thus the plays of the middle and final periods, however uneven in inspiration, are solidly constructed: the main crisis invariably occurs

[38] *Tragoediae, in duos tomos distributae* (1656), pp. 904–68.

at the end of Act III; thereafter the opposing forces gather strength and lead to the climax and catastrophe late in the final act. Although there are notable exceptions, the plot in Vernulaeus tends to be simple, sometimes to the point of baldness. The resulting singleness of focus is usually directed to the moral significance of the action.

In characterization, Vernulaeus is less concerned with the individual than with the type. The pedagogic purpose of his drama demanded strong contrasts of vice and virtue rather than psychological subtlety of character. As a result, one finds little variation between the tyrannical mania of Theodoricus and Ottokar, between the carnal vagrancies of Henry VIII or Pepin, between the spiritual fortitude of Becket or Boethius, of Lambert or Stanislaus. Driven by vices and virtues that are basically unchanging and therefore typical, these stock characters voice their inner compulsions and convictions in predictable pattern and phrase. The Vernulaean martyr-hero is untroubled by inner tension. He faces death with stoic detachment, alternating with joyous acceptance. The villain-hero, on the other hand, is invariably subjected to soul torture that projects itself in convulsions, nightmares, and physical prostrations. Unlike their static counterparts, these villains advance gradually in vice, their retrogression from virtue being occasionally interrupted by sincere, if temporary, intentions to amend their ways.

Of the many themes which the playwright sought to dramatize, none seems to have quickened his imagination more intensely than that of illicit passion. In his best plays—*Henricus Octavus, Crispus, Stanislaus,* and *Lambertus*—the conflict between flesh and spirit is the central struggle. Vernulaeus was able to sympathize with its urgency and never suggested that its remedy could easily be applied. Equally remarkable is his success in courtroom scenes, in lingering deathbed agonies, in the depiction of defiant women, and in the portrayal of masculine friendship.

Most of Vernulaeus' dramatic powers are already maturely at work in *Henricus Octavus*, the fourth play of his career. This and the previous chapters have sought to provide the context in which this play can be viewed in perspective. Our attention can now be limited to the play itself, its sources and their manipulation, the nature of the artistry at work in its making.

Chapter IV

AN INTRODUCTION TO *HENRICUS OCTAVUS*

That a drama about Henry VIII of England was written by a Belgian professor less than a century after the King's death is interesting but hardly remarkable. But that the same Louvain professor should base his play on a book written by a former Oxford don and later Regius professor of the University of Louvain, who died in Ireland during a fruitless attempt to overthrow Queen Elizabeth, forms indeed a remarkable example of literary influence.[1]

Description of the Source

The origins of the English schism from Rome had involved the Tudor and the Habsburg dynasties in a somewhat personal way, since Catherine, wife of Henry VIII, was the aunt of Emperor Charles V. There were hopes that Philip II, only son of Charles V, might permanently repair this breach when, as husband of Mary Tudor, he himself bore the title of King of England. However, his responsibilities to his new role in English affairs, together with his preoccupation with a similar role bequeathed to him in the Spanish Netherlands, proved the wrong kind of challenge for his peculiar talents. The death of Mary Tudor and the subsequent accession of Elizabeth on November 17, 1558, marked a turning point in the fortunes of English Catholics that included those of a young lecturer in canon law at the University of Oxford, Nicholas Sander.[2]

The life story of Dr. Nicholas Sander is one of the colorful strands

---

[1] It is customary for Vernulaeus to indicate toward the close of the *argumenta* of his plays the sources on which he relied. Thus in the *Argumentum* to *Henricus Octavus*, he states that he is principally indebted to Nicholas Sander's work on the English schism, titled *De origine ac progressu schismatis anglicani*. The first edition of this work (Cologne, 1585) was translated with an Introduction and Notes by David Lewis in 1877 under the title *Rise and Growth of the Anglican Schism*. For the sake of brevity this English translation of Sander by Lewis will be cited hereafter simply as S-L.

[2] In 1551, Sander (1530?–1581) had been promoted bachelor of laws and soon after was nominated "shagling" lecturer, or, according to Sander, "tamquam regius professor iuris canonici." *De visibili monarchia ecclesiae*, p. 682, cited hereafter as *Monarchia*. "The shagling or shagglyng lectures were such as were extraordinary or temporary, allowed either by public authority, common consent or recommendations." A. Wood, *Athenae Oxonienses* (3d ed.), Vol. I, col. 43, n. 2.

woven into the fabric of sixteenth-century English history. Its quiet emergence in a Surrey homestead yields to the discipline of Winchester and Oxford and then, crossing the Channel, catches the public splendors of Rome, Trent, and Madrid. Crisscrossing the continent in a series of diplomatic missions and ecclesiastical visitations in Prussia, Poland, and Austria, then pausing studiously in various cities of Flanders, the trail of his life finally ends in Ireland amid the atrocities of a barbarous war. At present we must limit our attention to those circumstances in his career which illuminate his position as the author of a work on the English Reformation.[3]

The Act of Supremacy and Act of Uniformity passed by Elizabeth's first Parliament in January, 1559, affected the sister universities of Oxford and Cambridge, many of whose professors and students sought refuge abroad.[4] Among this group of learned refugees was Nicholas Sander. Arriving at Rome in October, 1559, Sander was befriended by Cardinal Morone, Protector of England, and thereafter came under the notice of Cardinal Stanislaus Hosius, Prince-Bishop of Ermland.[5] Hosius was so favorably impressed by the talents of Dr. Sander that when on March 10, 1561, the Cardinal was appointed one of the five legates who were to preside over the fresh sessions of the Council of Trent, he took

---

[3] The best summary treatment of Sander is the contribution of Thomas Graves Law in the *Dictionary of National Biography*, Vol. XVII, cols. 748–51. J. H. Pollen's article, "Dr. Nicholas Sander" (*English Historical Review*, VI [January, 1891], 36–47), casts new light on Sander's polemical work, especially his book on the English schism. John B. Wainewright fills in several lacunae of Sander's final years by his careful edition of "Some Letters and Papers of Nicolas Sander, 1562–1580" (*Miscellanea XIII* [Publications of the Catholic Record Society], XXVI, 1–57). The most thorough study available is that of Thomas McNevin Veech, *Dr. Nicholas Sanders and the English Reformation, 1530–1581*, referred to hereafter as *Sanders and the Reformation*.

[4] "Parliament will rise this week, the two Houses having enacted that all the convents and monasteries of friars, monks, nuns, and Hospitallers of St. John of Jerusalem are to be suppressed as heretofore, and all these religious to be expelled. Such of them who will take the oath against the Pontifical authority, and approve the new laws, abjuring their own professions, are to receive pensions for their maintenance; but the greater part of them have left the kingdom in order not to take such oath." Il Schifanoya to the Castellan of Mantua, London, May 2, 1599, *Calendar of State Papers and Manuscripts relating to English Affairs, existing in the Archives and Collections of Venice, and in other libraries of northern Italy*, VII, 68, cited hereafter as *Ven. Cal.* Note also the letter of John Jewel to Henry Bullinger, May 22, 1559: "Our universities are so depressed and ruined that at Oxford there are scarcely two individuals who think with us; and even they are so dejected and broken in spirit that they can do nothing." *Zurich Letters*, Ser. I, p. 33, quoted in Veech, *Sanders and the Reformation*, pp. 21–22, n. 7. See also *S-L*, p. 261.

[5] In Rome, Sander was ordained priest by a fellow-countryman, Thomas Goldwell, exiled Bishop of St. Asaph (*Monarchia*, p. 686). Shortly afterward he took the degree of S.T.D. and was thereafter known as Dr. Sander.

Sander to the Council as one of his theologians. After the close of the Council, December 4, 1563, Sander accompanied Cardinal Hosius to Ermland, where he gained the friendship of Monsignor Commendone, legate at the court of King Sigismund Augustus of Poland.[6] Apart from occasional missions with Hosius and Commendone to the King of Poland and other German princes, Dr. Sander spent the next seven years devoting his full energies to the cause nearest his heart.

Louvain, the Catholic Oxford from 1559 until the founding of the English College at Douay in 1568, was the intellectual and political hub of activity for the English refugees who had settled in Spanish Flanders and northern France. There Sander joined his Oxford colleagues and soon became one of the more brilliant of the Louvain school of English Catholic apologists.[7] In addition to his duties as professor in the Faculty of Theology, Sander engaged in a war of books with Jewel, Nowell, and other Protestant divines that had been launched by Thomas Harding in 1563 and supported by fellow-"Louvainists."[8] Sander's Louvain works are characterized by close reasoning and painstaking research.[9] His crowning achievement, *De visibili monarchia ecclesiae*, comprises a vast number of testimonies from the church fathers, doctors, and councils, ar-

---

[6] In the Preface to one of his later publications, Sander recalls the hospitality and generosity of his patron Hosius. See *Nicolai Sanderi sacrae theologiae professoris tres orationes in scholis publicis Lovanii habitae, 14 cal. ianuarii, A.D. 1565*, fols. A2v.–A3.

[7] On July 28, 1565, Sander and two other Wykehamists, John Marshall and Thomas Stapleton, took in their own names a three-year lease of a house in the Rue Neuve (Bax, *Historia Universitatis Lovaniensis* [Brussels: Royal Library MS. 22172], II, 149, quoted by Henri de Vocht, "Thomas Harding," *English Historical Review*, XXXV [April, 1920], 236, n. 4). The building rented by the three Oxonians also provided a home for Oxford students enrolled in the faculty of Theology at Louvain. See Veech, *Sanders and the Reformation*, p. 54.

[8] It should be noted, however, that Sander did not arrive at Louvain until the end of 1564, when the religious controversy was already in full vigor. Of the eighteen English Catholic writers who rallied behind Harding at this time with books of their own, ten were Winchester men: Thomas Dorman (3 books), John Fenn (1), Nicholas Harpsfield (1), John Martial (2), Robert Poyntz (1), John Rastell (5), Nicholas Sander (6), Thomas Stapleton (6). To these should be added John Fowler, the printer, who also wrote one book. Thomas Harding himself contributed five volumes. The other writers were William (afterward Cardinal) Allen (2), George Bullock (1), Alan Cope (1), Louis Evans (afterward apostatized) (2), Thomas Hoskins (1), Robert Johnson (Henry Joliffe) (1), Richard Shacklock (1), Laurence Vaux (1). See J. H. Pollen, *The English Catholics in the Reign of Queen Elizabeth*, p. 107, n 1.

[9] One of Sander's most distinguished contemporaries at the University of Louvain was the future Cardinal Bellarmine. The Louvain method of controversy, which interested him deeply, influenced considerably his *Controversies*. His debt of gratitude to the English theologians, and in particular to Nicholas Sander, was acknowledged by him in his later works. See Veech, *Sanders and the Reformation*, p. 70.

ranged chronologically, on the subjects then most controverted in Europe.[10] The merits of its author attracted the notice of Pius V, and he summoned Sander to Rome in January, 1572. The Louvainists, who had elected Sander as their procurator, were confident that he would be created cardinal. The Pope, however, died shortly after Sander's arrival, and his plans for the English theologian were never known. During his year and a half sojourn in Rome, apparently as adviser on English affairs, Sander began the shortest yet most famous of his works, *De origine ac progressu schismatis anglicani.*

In November, 1573, Sander arrived in Madrid and appears to have remained there the next five years, presumably negotiating with the Spanish Treasury in regard to the pensions assigned to the English Catholics in the Low Countries.[11] Doubtless, too, he urged Philip to undertake the overthrow of the Protestant government of England by force of arms.[12] "The state of Christendom," Sander wrote to William Allen, president of the seminary of Douay, "dependeth upon the stout assailing of England."[13] Philip, however, was unfavorable to the proposition. The king was as fearful of war, Sander told Allen, as a child of fire.[14] Meanwhile Sir James Fitzmaurice and Sir Thomas Stukely had persuaded Gregory XIII to allow them to execute in Ireland the sentence of deprivation against Elizabeth. On June 20, 1579, Fitzmaurice, disregarding Philip's prohibition, set sail for Ireland.[15] Dr. Sander, under order of Pope Gregory, accompanied him as papal agent.[16]

[10] The seventh book of the *Monarchia* is a vigorous and deadly attack on the English Reformation and its leaders. The circulation of the book in England alarmed Burleigh, who took special measures to have it suppressed and counteracted. For a detailed account of its genesis, its secret printing, and the repercussions it caused in England, see Veech, *Sanders and the Reformation,* pp. 86, 89–99, 112–97.

[11] The arrival of Sander in Madrid did not escape the notice of the English envoys, who reported to Burleigh that "Doctor Sanders cam from Rom to Madred in November yn 1573; the Keng gave hem at his ferst comeng 300 Doketts, and sens 20 Doketts, and ther as yet remanethe." *A Collection of State Papers Relating to Affairs in the Reign of Queen Elizabeth from 1571–1596* (William Murdin, ed.), p. 243.

[12] In May, 1574, Burleigh heard from a French source the rumors of an invasion of Ireland and of Sander's doings. The "Advertisements from France Concerning Ireland" are endorsed by Burleigh. See *Calendar of State Papers, Domestic Series, Elizabeth, addenda, 1566–1579* (Mary Anne Everett Green, ed.), p. 462.

[13] Sander to Allen from Madrid, March 6, 1577. See T. F. Knox, *The Letters and Memorials of William Cardinal Allen* (Records of the English Catholics), II, p. 38.

[14] Pollen, "Dr. Nicholas Sander," p. 37.

[15] Stukely, together with Sebastian, king of Portugal, perished in the Battle of Alcazar on August 4, 1578.

[16] Veech surmises that Sander's hopes for the success of the expedition were none too sanguine, that his departure was dictated largely by obedience and gratitude to Gregory. After all, the two vessels of sixty tons, sparsely manned, were a mockery of the "stout assailing" Sander had advocated. Certainly Sander's friends were out-

The last two years of Sander's life comprise a story of almost incredible hardship and disaster met with unflagging courage. The temporary victories and reversals of the rebellious party reached a climax in the capitulation of its commander Sebastian de San Josepho and his unconditional surrender of the Fort del Oro of Smerwick (St. Mary Wick) to Deputy Lord Grey on November 9, 1580. Edmund Spenser, secretary to Lord Grey, was present at the taking of the fort and justified the atrocities that followed the surrender.[17] The English troops, led by Walter Raleigh, penetrated the fort and, under Grey's order, slew every man, woman, and child found in the enclosure with the exception of San Josepho and his twenty or thirty officers, who were spared and held for ransom.[18] The sacrifice of eight hundred lives that forenoon was followed two days later by the barbarous execution of Oliver Plunkett and William Walsh, Sander's servant. Refusing the oath of allegiance, and supremacy, they were led to a forge, where their arms and legs were broken. After a night of agony they were hanged, drawn, and quartered.[19] Fortunately for himself, Sander was not in the fort at the time of its capture. With a price on his head, the papal agent spent the winter months with a friendly herdsman and died, somewhat suddenly, from an attack of dysentery in April, 1581.[20]

The final years of Sander's life cast a lurid light on much that may seem obscure in its previous course and enable one to savor more fully the issues that drove his pen as a controversialist. A noted English scholar describes this urgency of Sander with sympathetic penetration:

In times of peace it is hard to conceive of the horrors of war, and so we may easily fail to bring home to ourselves the reality of the struggles amid which Sander's lot was cast. But the massacre of Smerwick and the inhuman cruelties done to his servant show us unmistakably how real and ruthless were the foes against whom Sander strove. These excesses were but extreme forms of the persecution which had wrecked his home and driven him from his native

---

spoken in their discontent: "Why does the pope send Sander to Ireland? We value him more highly than the whole of Ireland." Froude, *History of England from the Fall of Wolsey to the Defeat of the Spanish Armada*, XI, 212, 230, from *Simancas MS.*, quoted in Pollen, "Dr. Nicholas Sander," p. 38.

[17] *A View of the Present State of Ireland* in *Works* (London: Globe Edition, 1879), pp. 655–56. For the MSS. and edition of Spenser's account, written in 1596 and first printed as an appendix by J. Ware, *The Historie of Ireland* (Dublin, 1633), see *Dictionary of National Biography*, XVIII, 805. For Spenser's career in Ireland, see *ibid.*, pp. 797–98.

[18] See *Calendar of State Papers, Ireland, 1574–1585*, p. 267, under Entry 27: Report to Walsingham.

[19] *Ibid.*, pp. 267 (Entry 27), 268 (Entry 38).

[20] St. Leger to Burleigh from Cork, June 3, 1581. "Dr. Saunders dead of an Irish ague two months since." *Ibid.*, p. 306 (Entry 38).

land. Thenceforward his life had been devoted to combating with act, word, and pen the movement which finally overwhelmed him, and accordingly there come to be sayings and doings of his which cannot be understood except by those who bear this contest in mind.[21]

In reviewing those features of Sander's life which affect his credibility as a historian, we find several that are definitely favorable and none which clearly excludes a favorable opinion. He was esteemed by his colleagues as a scholar thoroughly trained at Oxford, Rome, and Louvain; furthermore, he enjoyed in his day the confidence of popes, cardinals, and great rulers. Even more remarkable, perhaps, is the fact that so divided a party as that of the English refugees should have chosen him as their arbitrator at Rome and Madrid. Today there is no longer any doubt that his official positions at the Vatican and Madrid enabled him to acquire information unknown to generations of historians until the latter half of the nineteenth century, when the great volumes of state papers and official documents began their appearance.[22] Nor is there any doubt, on the other hand, that his influence on the misdirection of papal policy is seen today as unfortunate; that his involving the Irish in a disastrous revolt and the traitorous stigma left by his political venture that was to be borne by his fellow-exiles are responsibilities not easily shrugged off in the name of sincerity and unwavering heroism. We may now turn our attention from the author to his book *De origine ac progressu schismatis anglicani,* which is the source of Vernulaeus' play on Henry VIII.

Perhaps the most striking feature of Sander's work was its popularity on the Continent. In its time no other book about England enjoyed there a larger circulation. Within the first decade of its publication in 1585, there were fifteen editions; the total number in later years more than doubled this.[23] No less remarkable is the consensus of writers who have accepted it as an authority. Pollen asserts that practically all writers on the Catholic side, from Bellarmine and Suárez down to Benedict XIV, refer to Sander's name as a sufficient warrant for the accuracy of state-

[21] Pollen, "Dr. Nicholas Sander," p. 40.

[22] A detailed assessment of Sander's credibility as historian of the English Reformation in the light of official documents will be found in the Explanatory Notes to *Henricus Octavus.*

[23] In Germany it appeared nine times; in France, seven; in Spain, six; in Italy, four. There were other editions in Holland, Poland, and Portugal. These publications were in Latin, French, German, Spanish, Italian, Portuguese, and Polish. All but two modern translations were printed on the Continent. These statistics, compiled from the *British Museum Catalogue* and De Backer, *Bibliothèque des écrivains de la comp. de Jésus,* sub voce *P. Ribadeneyra,* n. 5, are cited by Pollen, "Dr. Nicholas Sander," p. 41.

ments to be found in his work, and the continuator of Baronius is often content to reproduce him at length when English affairs are to be described.[24] There is no doubt that Sander was the standard authority for his party until the appearance of John Lingard. Equally remarkable is the abuse it provoked from its adversaries. Finally it must be emphasized that Sander's work stood alone in its time as the complete *ex professo* published book on the English schism.[25]

The history of the volume had its beginnings, as we have seen, in Rome about the year 1572. Unfinished as it was, it soon circulated in manuscript copies, one of which was secured by Edward Rishton, a Douay priest, who prepared it for the press at the urging of one Dr. Jodocus Skarnkert of Cologne.[26] Rishton's task of editing the first three sections of Sander's manuscript was an easy one. They dealt with the reigns of Henry VIII, Edward VI, and Mary Tudor in straightforward narrative that needed little correction. The last part, which treated the reign of Elizabeth, however, was now twelve years behind date and would need extensive alteration. Rishton therefore put Sander's last section aside and wrote a fresh history for himself, prefixing a "synop-

---

[24] *Ibid.* On the other hand, it is interesting to note that Bossuet resented the idea that his English opponents should imagine that he was relying on Sander for his account of the English Reformation: "Le docteur Gilbert Burnet, qui en est l'auteur, nous reproche dans sa préface, et dans toute la suite de son histoire, d'avoir tiré beaucoup d'advantage de la conduite de Henri VIII. . . . Il se plaint surtout de Sanderus, historien catholique, qu'il accusa d'avoir inventé des faits atroces, afin de rendre odieuse la réformation anglicane. . . . Nous n'avons pas besoin d'un Sanderus; M. Burnet nous suffit pour bien entendre ce que c'est que cet ouvrage de lumière." J. B. Bossuet, *Histoire des variations des églises protestantes* (Lyons, 1827), II, 3–4, quoted in Veech, *Sanders and the Reformation*, p. 238, n 1.

[25] There were other Catholics, of course, who dared express their real thoughts during the second half of the sixteenth century, but their writings circulated only in, manuscript copies. George Cavendish's *The Life and Death of Cardinal Wolsey* (cited hereafter as *Life of Wolsey*) is a typical example. Written between 1554 and 1558, it remained in manuscript until 1641. The printing of Sander's work was hence a daredevil feat of its first publisher.

[26] *S-L*, pp. cxlii–cxliii. In his Letter to the Reader, cited in *S-L*, Edward Rishton does not identify Skarnkert, saying merely that Skarnkert was an old friend he had known at Rome. Veech claims that "Skarnkert" was a pseudonym adopted by Robert Persons, but gives no proof (*Sanders and the Reformation*, p. 234, n. 3). Pollen, on the other hand, does not commit himself: "Who Dr. Jodocus Skarnkert was, who finally saw the book through the press, we know not" (Pollen, "Dr. Nicholas Sander," p. 42). Edward Rishton, native of Lancashire, entered Brasenose College, Oxford, in 1568, began his theological studies at Douay in 1573, and four years later was ordained priest at Cambrai. After some time in Rome he returned to England as a missionary priest, was arrested, and condemned to death. The sentence, however, was not carried out; Rishton remained a prisoner in the Tower until January, 1585, when he was banished. He died of the plague at Ste Ménéhould on June 30, 1585. See *S-L*, pp. xiv–xvi.

sis" to explain what he had done and why.[27] The first edition of Sander's work appeared at Cologne with the following title:

Doctissimi viri Nicolai Sanderi, de Origine ac Progressu Schismatis Anglicani, Liber. Continens historiam maxime Ecclesiasticam, annorum circiter sexaginta, lectu dignissimam: nimirum, ab anno 21. regni Henrici 8, quo primum cogitare coepit de repudianda legitima uxore serenissima Catherina, usque ad hunc vigesimum septimum Elizabethae, quae ultima est ejusdem Henrici soboles. Editus & auctus per Edouardum Rishtonum. Praecipua capita totius operis post praefationem authoris continentur. Coloniae Agrippinae, Anno Domini 1585.

This edition is divided into four parts. The first treats of the origin and causes of the schism under Henry VIII; the second deals with the progress of the schism and the introduction of Zwinglian doctrines during the reign of Edward VI; the third section presents a summary of the return to Catholic unity under Mary, and the fourth records Elizabeth's repudiation of Catholic doctrine in favor of Calvinism. It is the first section alone which formed the quarry from which Vernulaeus mined his dramatic materials.

Having sketched the relevant features of Sander's career, as well as the genesis and outline of his book, we may now question by what authority he wrote a history of the English Reformation. Sander tells us in his Preface that he gathered his materials "from public records, from the testimony, oral and written, of men of the greatest consideration, or at least from my own knowledge and observation."[28] It is generally held that Sander was born in 1530; he was, therefore, seventeen when Henry VIII died. Accordingly, for the momentous events which concern us in this study, he had little personal knowledge.[29] Unlike his customary practice, Sander rarely indicates in this work the source from which he is quoting. Today, however, largely as a result of the painstaking documentation of the first edition by translator David Lewis, we are well informed of the written authorities on whom Sander drew. The principal ones are Cardinal Pole, Nicholas Harpsfield, George Cavendish, William Rastell, Polydore Vergil, William Roper, William Tyndale, Edward Hall, John Sleidan, and John Foxe.[30]

[27] Sander, *De origine ac progressu schismatis anglicani*, fols. 142–45 (cited hereafter as *De schismate anglicano*).

[28] *S-L*, p. cxlvii. The original reads: "Secundum ea quae vel ex publicis monumentis excerpimus, vel ex gravissimorum hominum tam scriptis quam verbis hausimus, vel saltem ipsi cognovimus & observavimus, bona fide iam exponemus."

[29] During the reign of Edward VI and Mary Tudor, Sander was at Oxford and was thus able to form his own ideas about contemporary events.

[30] For the documentation of the above sources, the reader is referred, *passim*, to the Explanatory Notes to *Henricus Octavus*.

There can be no doubt that Sander's extended sojourn at Louvain and Rome enabled him to acquire considerable information from the "testimony, oral and written, of men of the greatest consideration," such as Thomas Harding, Thomas Stapleton, William Allen, John Martial, and Thomas Goldwell. Furthermore, his access to official correspondence at the Vatican and later at Madrid seems to offer the only explanation we have for the accuracy of those parts of his history which have since been verified by the publication of relevant archive materials.[31]

Before giving a more detailed account of Sander's treatment of the reign of Henry VIII (the first section of his work and the one to which Vernulaeus is principally indebted), it seems fitting to survey briefly the adverse criticisms of Sander as a historian.

We have already noticed the great favor shown Sander by those of his party; the disfavor expressed by his antagonists is no less emphatic. In February, 1572, Dr. Cox, tutor to Edward VI, referred to Sander's book as one written by a "mercenary employed by certain Cardinals . . . and decked out like Aesop's jackdaw."[32] Heylin labeled the author "Dr. Slanders"; Strype, whose knowledge might have been thought to lend objectivity, called him "a most profligate fellow, a very slave to the Roman See, and a sworn enemy to his own country"; Francis Mason estimated that in Sander's "libel," "the number of lies may seem to vie with the multitude of lines"; Camden, admitting Sander's learning, declared that he was "more credulous than becomes a man of exact judgment."[33] Dr. Gilbert Burnet, after insisting that Sander could not restrain "that malice which boiled in his breast, and often fermented out too palpably in his pen," cited 123 instances of error in the work.[34] He likewise admonished

---

[31] For example, *Römische Dokumente zur Geschichte der Ehescheidung Heinrichs VIII. von England, 1527–1534* (cited hereafter as *Römische Dokumente*), published by Stephan Ehses, which appeared too late to be included in the Calendar publications, gives daily accounts of the divorce trial by Campeggio, which Sander must have either seen or been apprised of. Again, the *Saturday Review* (XXI [March, 1866], 290; XXVI [July, 1868], 82; [October, 1868], 464; XLIV [September, 1877], 398) commends Sander's accuracy, particularly in respect to information derived from Roman sources (cited by T. G. Law, "Nicholas Sander," *DNB*). See also, *passim*, Explanatory Notes to *Henricus Octavus*.

[32] *Zurich Letters*, Ser. I, No. 167 (ed. Parker Society), quoted in Introduction to S-L, p. xxi. Cox's verdict was given, strangely enough, before he had seen Sander's book. *Ibid.*

[33] For these and other such opinions, with references indicated, see *ibid.*, pp. xxii–xxiv.

[34] "An Appendix Concerning Some of the Errors and Falsehoods in Sander's Book of the English Schism," *The History of the Reformation of the Church of England by Gilbert Burnet*, Nicholas Pocock (ed.), IV, 543–85, cited hereafter as Burnet-Pocock, *History*. In 1688, Joachim Le Grand answered the attacks that Burnet had made on the historical probity of Sander by including a defense of Sander in his history of the

Oxford antiquarian Anthony Wood for his leniency toward "that scandalous writer."[35] J. A. Froude, the most vehement of nineteenth-century opponents, represents a landmark in Sanderphobia:

In a history of 'The English Schism' he collected into a focus every charge which malignity had imagined against Henry VIII and his ministers; and so skilful was his workmanship that Nicholas Sanders, in the teeth of Statute and State Paper, in direct contradiction to every contemporary document which can claim authority,—except the invectives of Pole, which he appropriated and exaggerated—has had the shaping of the historic representation of the Anglican Reformation. Sanders' 'On the Origin and Progress of the English Schism' has governed the impressions of millions, who have least believed that they were under his influence. Not a scandalous story was current at the time of the revolt from the Papacy but Sanders took possession of it and used it—used it so adroitly that he produced a book which eclipsed Buchanan's 'Detectio,' and made Mary Stuart's doings appear pale and innocent beside the picture of rapine, lust, and murder, which he held up before the eyes of Europe.[36]

The "teeth of Statute and State Paper" have been less cruel on Sander's reputation as a historian than Froude anticipated. Nicholas Pocock, editor of the divorce records and of Harpsfield's *Pretended Divorce*, speaks of the fashion, ever since the appearance of Burnet's attacks, to disparage Sander as "eminently untrustworthy . . . At one time I was of the same opinion," Pocock continues, "but the more intimately acquainted I became with Sanders' work, the more reason I found to change my judgment about him."[37] Earlier, Pocock stated his opinion at greater length: "Many facts, which have been disbelieved because he was the only narrator of them, have been proved to be true by recent publications of contemporary documents . . . Sanders, though very prejudiced, was not dis-

---

divorce of Henry VIII: *Histoire du divorce de Henri VIII, roy d'Angleterre et de Catherine d'Aragon, avec la défense de Sanderus, la réfutation des deux premiers livres de l'Histoire de la réformation de M. Burnet, et les preuves*, cited hereafter as *Histoire du divorce*. For a critical view of Burnet's work, see E. Fueter, *Histoire de l'historiographie moderne* (trans. E. Jeanmaire), pp. 219–21.

[35] Quoted in Veech, *Sanders and the Reformation*, p. 257. Wood countered by saying that his judgment of Sander was based on a comparison of the information given in the *De origine ac progressu schismatis anglicani* with the records of the University of Oxford which the antiquarian had consulted. Wood added, "And if our religion hath had its original, or base, on lust, blood, ruin and desolation, . . . why should it be hidden away, seeing it is so obvious to all searchers into record." A. Wood to Burnet, July, 1679. *Ibid.*

[36] J. A. Froude, *History of England from the Fall of Wolsey to the Defeat of the Spanish Armada*, XI, 204.

[37] Nicholas Harpsfield, *A Treatise on the Pretended Divorce between Henry VIII. and Catherine of Aragon* (ed. N. Pocock), Preface, p. 1, cited hereafter as *Pretended Divorce*.

honest; he believed what he wrote, and, upon the whole, is tolerably correct in his facts."[38] In his article on Sander in the *Dictionary of National Biography*, Thomas Graves Law likewise reflects the shift in attitude of modern scholars in favor of Sander: "Recent historians have, however, shown that notwithstanding his animus and the violence of his language, his narrative of facts is remarkably truthful. In almost every disputed point he has proved right and Burnet wrong."[39] Even A. F. Pollard, in recalling the author's nickname, "Dr. Slanders," adds, "But later research has shaken that calumny, and his books are now accepted as worthy to be ranked with those of his best antagonists."[40]

A survey of the evolution of critical opinion concerning the historical validity of Sander's work indicates a gradual return to the position of eminence he once enjoyed among his fellow-exiles. There can be no doubt that Vernulaeus likewise accepted the veracity of the former Louvain professor's history of the schism, and saw in its clear outlines not only a challenge for his dramatic talents but an abiding lesson that could be vitalized on the academic stage.

When he began reading Sander's book, he must have felt at once the energy at work on each page. Here was not just another theological tract, but a dramatic story involving historical characters who came alive before his eyes; a narrative spiced with concrete detail, court gossip, anecdote, and charged with understatement and irony.

Sander begins by recalling the promising forward look of Europe at the opening of the sixteenth century. After describing the marriage of Henry and Catherine and their first happy years together, he paints full-length portraits of the pious queen and the dissolute monarch, lingers over Henry's gradual disenchantment with his wife, then relates the beginning, middle, and end of the royal divorce with its international repercussions and the personages drawn into its current: principally, Wolsey, Longland, the Bishop of Tarbes, Anne Boleyn, More, Fisher, Campeggio, Ridley, Pole, Warham, and Cranmer. The marriage with Anne, the despoliation of church property, the martyrdoms of Fisher and More, the death of Catherine, and the execution of Anne Boleyn are offered in striking tableaux that prepare for Henry's disintegration and his eventual death of despair.

---

[38] Introduction to *Records of the Reformation*, I, xlii, cited hereafter as *Records*.
[39] P. 750, col. 1. See also Fueter, *Histoire de l'historiographie moderne*, p. 205: "Nicholas Sander's work on the English schism fits squarely in the category of partisan polemics. His assumptions rest upon better sources than Protestant apologists claimed; but, nevertheless, it remains a bitterly partisan work."
[40] *The History of England, 1547–1603* (Vol. VI of *The Political History of England*), p. 369.

Reading the narrative, one realizes that the scope and shape of the story call out for dramatic handling. The simple revolution of Fortune's wheel rises to weal and sinks to woe in characteristic medieval tragic direction; the thrusts and counterthrusts that drama thrives on and the tensions they produce are ready for manipulation; the events have magnitude; the court scenes telescope within the walls of Blackfriars the wide-ranging and perennial conflict of church and state. The materials, in other words, lie midway between potency and act, waiting for selection, condensation, interpretation.

The real villain of the piece, in Sander's eyes, was Wolsey, whose ambition set him scrambling from lowly circumstances to the chancellorship, from which eminence he grasped repeatedly for the papal tiara. Crossed by Charles V's sudden indifference to him in two papal elections, Wolsey sought to retaliate by promoting a marriage between Henry VIII and a French princess. To secure this proposed Anglo-French alliance, Wolsey resurrected the issue of the validity of Henry's marriage to Catherine, aunt of Charles V and widow of Henry's brother. The thwarted ambitions of Wolsey, together with the wayward affections of Henry and the calculated resistance of Anne to royal concubinage without benefit of crown are seen, by Sander, as the origins of the separation. The divorce itself, and the subsequent schism, rapidly developed from these origins.[41]

Sander's preoccupation with the divorce led him to devote considerable attention to Anne Boleyn and her family. Not content with attacking her morals (in which he was justified), he gave wider currency to the idle story that she was the daughter of Lady Boleyn and Henry VIII. It was this slander which contributed most to making Sander's book a *succès de scandale* and prepared the role of Jesuitical fox assigned him later by Charles Kingsley in *Westward Ho!*[42]

Vernulaeus' Use of His Source

A reading of *Henricus Octavus* against the first section of Sander's *De schismate anglicano* affords an interesting disclosure of the art of

---

[41] The term "divorce," used in speaking of Henry's repudiation of Catherine, is inaccurate, though commonly used. Neither side admitted a divorce. Henry claimed that the marriage was null and void from its inception, while the Catholic party regarded it as a valid marriage which could not be broken in any manner. Thus Nicholas Harpsfield entitled his book *A Treatise on the Pretended Divorce between Henry VIII and Catherine of Aragon.*

[42] See especially Chaps. V and XI.

dramatic transmutation as well as the craftsmanship of a particular Continental school-dramatist. The action of the play is distributed effectively over five acts. In the first act we see four evil allegorical figures— Heresy, Tyranny, Lust, and Impiety—emerging from Hell, hatching their plans, and clustering like witches around the tormented Henry. Anne enters, exhibiting at once her pose as determined but reluctant virgin, and unnerving Henry utterly. Crafty Wolsey plots the undoing of Catherine, opens the question of invalid marriage to Henry, and leaves him in turmoil, wrangling with the good allegories who now surround him.

The second act introduces Catherine, More, Fisher, Campeggio, and members of Parliament in scenes of private confidence and public court hearings, climaxed by Catherine's dramatic appeal to the Pope and Henry's momentary acquiescence. More court hearings follow in Act III, in which Ridley and Warham plead eloquently the Queen's cause. Campeggio stalls the process by proroguing the court, More and Fisher reject the tendered oath. Finally, Henry breaks the deadlock by suddenly marrying Anne. The act ends with the protagonist and the newly crowned queen at the top of Fortune's wheel, as holiday shouts fill the stage.

Acts IV and V show the wheel dipping in a series of rapid calamities. The Pope repudiates the new queen, Wolsey is dismissed; Henry demands allegiance as king and pope, causing the martyrdoms of Fisher, More, and others; Catherine dies in banishment, Anne is found guilty of various infidelities and is executed; finally, Henry, swollen with disease, dies in despair.[43]

Vernulaeus achieved the concentration needed by introducing Henry at the height of his infatuation with Anne Boleyn and, avoiding what he regarded as the anticlimax of subsequent wives, has him die onstage soon after Anne's execution. He preserved the multifariousness of his source by crowding the stage with fourteen historical characters, eight allegorical ones plus an angel, three councilors, together with two choruses of English maidens and Catholic exiles. The world reverberations are kept awake by messengers from Rome, by well-spaced allusions to Spain and France, by comings and goings across the Channel, and by reports about the reactions of the English to the proposed divorce. Contemporary accounts attest the profound impression made by the play on dignitaries,

---

[43] A review of *Henricus Octavus,* including a running commentary interspersed with excerpts from the play, was written by J. Mitford for *The Gentleman's Magazine,* XXIII (May, 1845), 501–04.

professors, and students who witnessed its performance.[44] Since such an impression cannot be achieved at a profound level merely by effective plotting, it will be instructive to examine briefly the kind of organization worked out below the surface.[45]

Vernulaeus conceived the visible conflict of church and state, and the national destinies involved therein, as extensions of the conflict within the mind of the protagonist. The didactic purpose of the play (to educate future statesmen in the responsibility of choice by showing the evil effects of improper choice) depends for its fulfillment on how vividly the essential conflict is projected.

To objectify the dilemma of the protagonist, Vernulaeus relied heavily on allegorical figures to function as visible correlatives of Henry's inner struggles. The four allegories representing his good side and the other four, his bad, keep the issues clearly patterned before the audience. The four evil allegories, in turn, are made typical partners in crime, destructive lust initiating a chain reaction that explodes into heresy, tyranny, and general lawlessness.[46]

A second device, reinforcing allegory, is the soliloquy. Henry's first speech makes excellent use of his royal accouterments to contrast his outer magnificence with his inner destitution:

This scepter in my hand gleams and glistens; this purple I wear hangs rich and splendid; on my anointed brow the royal diadem sparkles. So it is that Fortune clothes kings deceitfully; so it is that glory entangles them treacherously. How splendidly does this crown blaze on my royal head! But within this tortured breast anxieties groan aloud. Splendor shines on my forehead, but anguish whips the heart within me. Whatever adorns, presses down; whatever gleams, corrupts; whatever glitters, bites with sharp grief and finally kills. One woman is the cause of all this grief and that woman is Anne Boleyn (I, ii, 1–12).

A later soliloquy connects the inner conflict with its larger issues:

The same turmoil all over again and the same anxieties tearing at my heart with scourges. I hesitate and I doubt; no one is at hand to advise me. The Pope drags my mind one way; Anne drags it back. I swing back and forth between certainty and doubt. I do not want something, and still I want it anyway. What I want I like; what I do not want is still the right thing to do. All England crouches over and hangs on my shoulders. The whole world keeps watching what my next move will be (IV, iv, 1472–80).

[44] See, for example, the reaction of the Reverend Desbois mentioned in the dedicatory letter to *Henricus Octavus*.

[45] For more detailed analysis of the artistic features of the play, see the introductions to individual scenes given in the Explanatory Notes.

[46] A modern adaptation of this morality device is found in T. S. Eliot's *Murder in the Cathedral*, where the four tempters have a somewhat similar function.

Another problem Vernulaeus faced was to create an Anne for whom Henry would think the world well lost: the creature of Sander would never do:

She was rather tall of stature, with black hair and an oval face of sallow complexion, as if troubled with jaundice. She had a projecting tooth under the upper lip and on her right hand six fingers. There was a large wen under her chin and therefore to hide its ugliness she wore a high dress covering her throat. She was handsome to look at, with a pretty mouth, amusing in her ways, playing well on the lute, and was a good dancer.[47]

Vernulaeus solved this problem simply by adjusting the point of view, by having us first see Anne through the eyes of Henry:

She slays me with her enchantment; her laughter and alluring figure, her inviting mouth and springtime beauty burn right through this breast of mine and feed its fire. Her eyes slay me with a single glance, her hair imprisons my soul with its soft fetters of love. Unnumbered people all around are subject to my powerful rule; I am subject to Anne alone. I am King and at the same moment an abject slave (I, ii, 83–91).

The following scene confirms this infatuation with the appearance of Anne. So convincingly does she maneuver the King that we no longer doubt her ability to hold ground with the Pope or Catherine in a tug of war over Henry's allegiance.

By the end of Act I Vernulaeus has defined the inner conflict; he has introduced the contenders for Henry's choice. Meanwhile the virtuous and the vicious allegories have demonstrated the opposed directions suggested to Henry's will. From these *données* the line of action zigzags forward to the climax of Act III. The progress of this action is swelled by new contenders in the struggle, who align themselves behind Anne or Catherine. At the same time the complexity of the inner conflict is developed by the increasingly subtle dialectic of the allegories. Henry is seen at the center of these tensions, pulled now to the left, now to the right and back again in sudden reversals that characterize his wavering will and impetuous spirit. Strongly contrasting with Henry's vacillation are the forthright decisions and consequent deaths of Fisher and More in Acts IV and V.

In spite of this fundamentally theatrical handling of issues, at times the play bogs down for the modern reader. The choruses incline to be prolix and occasionally annoying in their glib righteousness; the rhetorical invocations to deities and the solar system sound inflated; finally,

[47] S-L, p. 25.

emotions such as grief and horror are not infrequently wrung out to the point of tediousness.[48]

In spite of its rhetorical cast, Vernulaeus' art maintains an appeal to this day. The evocation of the tragedy of choice, its prodding insistence, and the havoc left in its wake are powerfully realized. Furthermore, the battle Henry faces in choosing between Anne and Rome is never falsified by a removal from its arena of flesh and spirit. The pull of passion is never allowed to slacken; its urgency is never canceled by facile moralizing.

As a pedagogical instrument, *Henricus Octavus* was designed to impress the future citizens of Belgium, Germany, Poland, and Bohemia with the divine judgment on heresy provoked by lust. In addition, it served to remind them clearly that though Henry's decision was the wrong one and its consequences irrevocable, it nevertheless remained the kind of decision that no syllogism or pat formula could solve. The irreversibility of human choice is driven home, but the question mark of tragedy is not removed. It is largely this refusal to seek refuge in easy moralizing that lifts the play above the level of dramatic sermonizing and made it not only an apt instrument for the training of princes but a dramatic organism with an integrity of its own. Art is not wrenched into the service of truth; it preserves its autonomy as a handmaid in that service.

Language, Style, and Versification

We have observed in the preceding chapter that the expressive features of the Vernulaeus theater were oriented by a rhetorical tradition of academic drama in which the influence of Seneca was observable in the mechanics of structure as well as in thematic development. Passing from these larger aspects of organization to those involving language itself, we may learn more of Vernulaeus' art by ascertaining what principles governed his selection of words, and what rhetorical and metrical patterns helped control their arrangement.

---

[48] I am aware that dramatic technique is successful when it succeeds in expression. Hence an opinion concerning the success or failure of any one technique of Vernulaeus involves a critical judgment informed by the conventions of the Renaissance academic stage. Thus it seems quite likely that the Louvain schoolboys and teachers savored fully the rhetorical excellence of the set speeches, the classical allusions, and the precise rendering of the metrical sweeps of the chorus. Furthermore, the elegiac quality of Vernulaeus' play seems to have been characteristic of early seventeenth-century literature, and not restricted to Neo-Latin drama. For its presence in French drama, for example, see Lancaster E. Dabney, *French Dramatic Literature in the Reign of Henry IV*, pp. 447–48.

At this point it is well to recall that the principal pedagogic purpose of school drama was to afford teen-age students the opportunity to speak good Latin in public.[49] Latin was the core subject of the preparatory schools. Without a thorough command of the language, including ability to communicate orally and in writing, the candidate for higher studies would face an impasse, since all subjects of the curriculum were taught in Latin. It seems very likely that the major principle operative in Vernulaeus' selection of language was the pedagogic situation in which he worked. He wrote the kind of Latin that would be within the grasp of his pupils, though definitely above the level of student performance; a language that combined simplicity with elegance and forcefulness.[50]

For all its simplicity, the language of *Henricus Octavus* reveals the author's familiarity with a wide range of classical authors: Plautus, Terence, Lucretius, Catullus, Cicero, Vergil, Horace, Ovid, Seneca, Lucan, Pliny, and Juvenal. Foremost among these is Lucius Annaeus Seneca. As an arts major at Trèves and Cologne, Vernulaeus had become familiar with Senecan tragedy; later, as professor at Louvain, he nurtured his students on the same diet. Even a cursory reading of *Henricus Octavus* suggests the playwright's predilection for Senecan vocabulary, especially adjectival forms.[51] Typical verbs which contribute to the physiognomy of Seneca's language are likewise reproduced in the play.[52] Mention may also be made of a number of substantives that seem to be Senecan favorites.[53] Even more indicative of the pervasive Senecan influence over the

---

[49] The disputation method had no place in the Trilingue from its very beginnings in 1518. This pioneering method of education, with its insistence on objective inquiry and abandonment of discussion, gradually spread to other colleges of Louvain and, by Vernulaeus' time, had left its mark. One of the purposes of school drama was to fill the gap advantageously. See de Vocht, *Collegium Trilingue*, IV, 449–53.

[50] One has only to read the impressive collection of Neo-Latin plays at the Folger Library to be impressed by Vernulaeus' superiority over most of his fellow-tragedians, not only in dramatic power but also in command of language and versification. In general, it can be said that the language of academic drama, though more demanding of one's concentration than medieval Latin, is far less sinewy than a page of Erasmus, Vives, or More.

[51] For example, *dirus* (vv. 13, 25, 60, 386, 453, 737, 1183, 1298, 1654), *efferatus* (63), *efferus* (14, 62), *fulminandus* (2072), *foedus* (332, 631, 650, 1759), *impotens* (1097), *peremptus* (1918, 2064), *perustus* (44), *tenellus* (499, 876, 914), *tumefactus* (334), *tumidus* (1402, 2185).

[52] See, for example, *consumere* (v. 386), *compescere* (1458, 1941), *illucescere* (2020), *lancinare* (828), *micare* (80), *pavescere* (623), *perure* (86, 337), *saevire* (846, 1769, 1847), *sitire* (60), *titubare* (999), *torpescere* (1104).

[53] *Affatus* (vv. 547, 573), *chaos* (2), *globus* (625, 2150), *iubar* (72, 144, 152, 536, 929, 975, 1456, 1919, 2059, 2181), *medullae* (533, 957, 1433), *praecordia* (623), *planctus* (1688), *solamen* (746), *torus* (46, 100, 230, 311, 435, 507, 653, 826, 849, 880, 908, 936, 1148, 1294, 1386, 1453, 1465, 2116, 2127). *Tonans,* Seneca's

language of Vernulaeus is the considerable number of phrases that are carved from the Roman tragedian's work and fitted, many without trimming, into the new structure. Further examination of Vernulaeus' language suggests that whereas the more violent themes evoke a strong Senecan coloring of word and phrase, passages of grandeur and tenderness reflect the influence of Vergil, whose works were likewise staples in the seventeenth-century curriculum.[54] Words and phrases that one associates with the *Aeneid* first come to mind.[55] In addition, there are "poetic" expressions which Vergil was fond of that find their way into the play.[56] Finally, Vernulaeus sprinkles his text with Vergilian archaisms.[57] Although Seneca and Vergil exert the strongest influences on the playwright's vocabulary, there are verbal echoes of Horace[58] as well as of Plautus and Terence.[59] As one might expect, the Christian subject matter of Vernulaeus' plays made demands on postclassical coinages and Christian adaptations with which he was familiar as a student of philosophy and theology, and later as a priest.[60]

A review of the main influences that controlled Vernulaeus' choice of language makes it clear that Latin, both in its natural and artificial phases of evolution, has left its varied impact on the playwright's vocabulary. Like stripes on a flag, these influences account, in large measure, for the

---

usual appellation for the deity, is frequently used by Vernulaeus (49, 221, 281, 333, 422, and *passim* from here forward).

[54] See J. C. Scaliger, *Poetices libri septem*, p. 228.

[55] Typical examples are *Martis opus* (v. 180); *Phoebus* (147, 424, 430, 574, 617, 929, 2045); *unda* (6) and *aequor* (548, 1710, 1748) for "sea"; designation of parenthood by *genitor* (744, 1054, 1089, 1337, 1344, 1750, 2014), *genitrix* (3, 1344), and *parens* (3, 424, 682, 1337, 1345, 2073); of "home" by *lares* (1058) and *fores* (8, 70); of "souls of the deceased" by *manes* (126, 1169, 1716, 1769, 2067) and *umbrae* (1230).

[56] A complete list would include *lumina* (v. 87), *genae* (455, 782, 1455), *bis deni* (729, 1910, 1911), *bis seni* (877), *lacer* (1689), *aetherius* (536, 2003, 2148), and *exanimis* (2162).

[57] *Ast* [for *at*] (vv. 517, 618); *repostum* [for *repositum*] (138).

[58] *Caballus* (v. 6), *Notus*, "south wind" (159), *vices* (420, 757, 1495, 1925), *cythara* (160), *curru soluto* (617), *immane quantum* (1795).

[59] *Plaustrum* (v. 39), *actutum* (69, 292, 603, 1418), *applaudere* (729), *enecare* (1968), *bene alicui velle* (1981–82), *vixit* for *mortuus est* (2098, 2103, 2104, 2105), *eccum* (715), and *vah* (2201).

[60] The following expressions in *Henricus* were undoubtedly meant to be interpreted in their Christian context: *antistes* (v. 1995), *cathedra* (1280), *catholicus* (1285), *Christianus* (663, 1180, 1181, 1184, 1521, 1687, 1705, 1706, 1767, 1805, 1826, 2034, 2083), *cenobius* (1774, 1887), *dilectio* (681), *haeresis* (4, 30, 1171, 1242, 1249, 1261, 2080), *idolum* (45, 183, 1106, 2129), *martyr* (2088), *monarcha* (116, 317, 2195), *papa* (902, 1541, 1550, 1684, 1881, 2101), *sacer* (23, 47, 73, 408, 517, 967, 1688, 1823), *sacerdos* (1196), *secta* (664, 980), *schisma* (980).

coloring of Vernulaeus' language, though they may fail to reveal its proper texture.

Contemporary assessments of Vernulaeus' art throw little light on his reputation as a manipulator of language. The numerous commendatory verses of students and fellow-professors appended to his published works are straightforwardly eulogistic, not critically illuminating. Perhaps the single exception is the account of a fellow-rhetorician, Bernard Heymbach, who described Vernulaeus' language as invariably colored by a certain freshness of figure that never lapsed into luxuriance; he likewise praised his sententious expressions that lend sparkle to the page.[61] On the other hand, contemporaries who seem to have been informed of Vernulaeus' habits of composition were amazed at his facility in redaction. Antoine d'Ave, student of Vernulaeus and later professor of rhetoric at Porc College, testified that his master composed *Henricus Octavus* in eight days: "I speak as an eyewitness: the meter and style you see here, Reader, is the work of eight days; the true spring of the Muses bubbles up like that and wells forth, whereas the vicious Siren does not."[62] In his funeral oration of Vernulaeus, Professor d'Ave elaborated on this remarkable trait of the playwright, pointing out that Vernulaeus never rewrote or deleted a line, that his pen set down quickly what had been premeditated and ordered in the author's mind.[63] Heymbach made the same observation, refuting those who seem to have reacted unfavorably to Vernulaeus' speed of composition and clarity: "There seems little reason to apologize for writing clearly," he maintains. "It is better to send away an audience fully informed of the issues of a play by allowing them to see things in broad daylight, rather than leaving them in a fog of obscure impressions."[64] Vernulaeus himself admitted that his plays were not "elephantine labors brought forth after ten years of gestation"; neither was he another Tages sprung from the soil in poetic maturity. His inspiration, however, could be an overnight process and his actual composition a matter of days.[65]

Having seen the influences at work on Vernulaeus' use of words, together with contemporary assessments of his facility in composition, we may pass to the rhetorical patterns in which his language was ordered.

---

[61] See *Otium itinerarium*, appended to *Tragoediae, in duos tomos distributae*, unnumbered page 15.

[62] Lines 26–28 of thirty-eight hexameters appended to the first edition of *Henricus Octavus*, following immediately after the *Finis tragoediae*.

[63] See d'Ave, *Oratio in funere*, fol. B3v.

[64] See *Otium itinerarium, loc. cit.*, pp. 15–16.

[65] See dedicatory letter to *Divus Eustachius*, p. 4.

It is hardly necessary to recall, in this connection, that Vernulaeus' artistic ideals were informed by the Renaissance predilection for formal beauty, elegance of phrase, and rhetorical ornament.[66] As a schoolmaster who had dedicated many years to the study of rhetoric, as author of a textbook on the art of discourse, and as Public Professor of Rhetoric at the University of Louvain, Vernulaeus was a master of the many techniques for securing emphasis, vividness, and clarity. An analysis of *Henricus Octavus* shows his command of metaphor, simile, periphrasis, and personification; of epanadiplosis, epanalepsis, epanastrophe, and epanorthosis; of prolepsis and hyperbaton, of hypallage and hysteron-proteron; of chiasmus, anaphora, asyndeton, polysyndeton, parataxis, and other unlovely-sounding figures.[67] Repetition in various forms seems to be his favorite device for securing emphasis; personification is drawn upon steadily for insuring concreteness. Most endearing of his techniques for the modern reader, perhaps, is his fondness for punning.[68]

At this point it may be well to keep in mind that much of the pleasure the play afforded by its parade of recognizable patterns or figures, its variations on basic turns of expression, its rhetorical gymnastics, has been muted by the disappearance of a rhetorically oriented culture. One can point to its existence and estimate, somewhat vaguely, the impact of this rhetorical splendor on the audience of *Henricus Octavus*. On the other hand, a complete re-creation of a climate of taste that has alienated itself is manifestly impossible, even for the serious student of the Renaissance. One can but register the rhetorical niceties as they appear and presume that the pleasure they undoubtedly afforded were major ingredients of a literary appreciation that has since become artificial, and to that extent, unreal.

We may conclude our introduction to *Henricus Octavus* by reviewing those features of the playwright's versification which reveal his artistry. Except for the choruses, the play is written throughout in iambic trimeters, or senarii, the favorite meter of Roman tragedy and comedy. A representative sampling of lines from the play discloses an adherence to the metrical demands of the senarius line that is stricter than that usually associated with Roman dramatic practice.[69] Vernulaeus generally retains

---

[66] For a contemporary assessment of the Renaissance concept of formal elegance in composition, see, for example, Scaliger, *Poetices libri septem*, pp. 399–491.

[67] What purports to be a fairly representative list of Vernulaeus' rhetorical devices may be examined in the Explanatory Notes.

[68] For examples of Vernulaeus' puns, see Explanatory Notes to vv. 71, 85, 534, 826, 1009, 1223, 1614.

[69] Ordinarily, all feet in the senarius but the last are replaceable by a spondee, anapest, tribrach, dactyl, or proceleusmatic.

the iamb in the even feet (the sixth foot, of course, may be pyrrhic), occasionally substituting a tribrach in the second or fourth. The uneven feet show a preference for the spondee as a substitution, although the anapest, dactyl, or tribrach may be employed. The anapest, when used, is generally substituted in the fifth foot, in accordance with the precedent of Seneca. The caesura, in turn, almost invariably occupies the semiquinarial position.

Within this fairly rigid matrix Vernulaeus cast the speaking roles of his fourteen tragedies, exhibiting in each a thorough command of metrical composition. As producer and director of his own plays, he drilled his student actors in their lines, taking care that they reproduced *viva voce* the nuances of quantity and stress intended.[70]

The four choric movements provide a variety of metrical patterns: anapestic dimeter, iambic dimeter and trimeter, dactylic hexameter, and a sapphic strophe.[71] The anapestic dimeter occurs frequently in Roman tragedy, notably in Seneca, as a vehicle for elegiac expression. It may be observed in *Henricus Octavus* that each anapest is replaceable by a spondee.[72] The dactyl appears as a substitution in the uneven feet and is generally followed by a spondee.[73] The exceptions to this sequence are relatively few.[74]

The second chorus is composed entirely of iambic dimeters; the other three choruses show sprinklings of the same pattern. Vernulaeus' practice in this metrical form allows considerable freedom of substitution in the uneven feet, especially in the first, where the iamb may be replaced by a spondee or one of its quantitative equivalents.[75] Only very oc-

[70] Félix Nève remarks (*La renaissance des lettres . . . en Belgique*, p. 379) that the university audience was accustomed to these metrical dramas declaimed "with a certain briskness, thanks to the regular and harmonious rhythm of the iambic verses in which the texts were usually composed."

[71] For identification of the meters used in individual verses of the choruses, see the Explanatory Notes.

[72] There seem to be no completely regular anapestic verses in the play, nor pure spondaic verses.

[73] Verse 378, "Quid tot *pectoris acuis* motus," seems to be the only exception: here the dactyl occurs in the second foot and is followed by an anapest.

[74] The sequence of dactyl in the *first foot* followed by an anapest occurs in v. 403, "*Unaque patriam* foemina pudet"; 405, "*Foemina validos* perdidit Anglos"; 1675, "*Linquere patrias* certum est sedes"; 1680, "*Has tibi lachrymas*, has tibi lachrymas"; 1734, "*Imbibe lachrymas;* non sine lachrymis"; and 1737, "*Dicere quoties* cupient animi." The sequence of a dactyl in the third foot and an anapest in the fourth can be seen in v. 1680, "Has tibi lachrymas, *has tibi lachrymas*" and in 1699, "Undique luctus, *undique lachrymae*." Finally, a dactyl in the third foot followed by a tribrach is found in v. 399, "Totum meretrix *possidet animum*" and in 413, "Postea saevo *vulnere perimet*."

[75] An example of an anapest in the introductory foot may be seen in v. 806, "*Ani-*

casionally does Vernulaeus set down perfectly regular iambic dimeters.[76]

We have already seen Vernulaeus' practice in iambic trimeter verse; his handling of the dactylic hexameter, furthermore, shows no remarkable departure from the accepted classical norm. The single remaining curiosity of the playwright's versification is the appearance of a sapphic strophe on the lips of Impiety, the only instance of this form in the play. Perfect regularity is observable in the first three lines of the stanza: the terminal trochaic dipodies enclose a dactyl; the caesura falls after the fifth syllable in each.[77] The Adonic verse which concludes the strophe is equally regular, composed as it is of a dactyl followed by a trochee.[78]

Our inquiry into the language, style, and versification of *Henricus Octavus* reveals Vernulaeus' formal indebtedness to the ancient Roman poets. In characteristic Humanist fashion he poured new wine into old bottles, seemingly convinced that the ancient receptacles were worthy to receive the draught he prepared for them. Foremost of these influences was Seneca, not only in the broad structural lines of playmaking, but in the minute techniques of language and metrics. Vergil and Horace, and other Roman writers in lesser degree, left their marks on the play as well. Through these varied influences the personality of Vernulaeus insinuates itself steadily, adapting and shaping the materials of history into a form that would illuminate their meaning and make of its student actors and audience better Latinists and better persons.

The foregoing chapters have sought to reconstruct the cultural context and literary tradition in which a particular late-Renaissance school dramatist worked. There remains the task of fitting the keystone to this structure: the play itself. To approach *Henricus Octavus* sympathetically, one must imaginatively reconstruct the theatrical situation of its first performance.

The actors are Louvain University undergraduates. For a fortnight they have been rehearsing their parts under the direction of their

---

*mum*que movit intimum." Although a dactyl is not substituted in the third foot, an anapest may be employed, as in v. 1281, "Firmabis im*perium* tuum." Finally, the second foot may be filled by a tribrach: v. 1267, "Oble*ctat ani*mum & dexteram."

[76] For example, v. 373, "Placere semper alteri"; 847, "Thronum Bolena regium," and 849, "Torum Bolena regium."

[77] It will be noticed that Vernulaeus follows Horace's predilection for using a spondee in the second foot. The sapphic strophe (vv. 1249–1252) in question, reads:

Alteram taedam manus ista vibret
Haeresis per me tua regna surgunt,
Dumque Rex Romae pia iura temnit
          Nasceris ipsa.

[78] The precedent for employing sapphic strophes within the chorus can be found in Seneca.

playwright-professor and priest, Nicolaus Vernulaeus. Of an afternoon in the first week of January, 1624, the hall of Porc College fills with a select audience of students, professors, and parents, many of whom have attended previous Vernulaean productions in the same hall. Since actors, audience, and author-producer are on friendly terms as fellow-members of a close-knit academic community, the attitude of the audience is benevolent and congenial rather than aloofly critical.

The majority of the spectators will understand the Latin verses and relish the rhetorical patterns in which the language is arranged. Fewer, however, will detect the many classical allusions and echoes. On the other hand, the impact of the play, its powerful depiction of the disintegration of the English monarch who is betrayed by lust into tyranny and heresy and subsequently arraigned before the final tribunal, will be lost on none of them.

PART TWO

HENRY VIII in Translation
Text of *HENRICUS OCTAVUS*
Explanatory Notes

NICOLAI VERNVLÆI

HENRICVS

OCTAVVS

SEV

SCHISMA

ANGLICANVM

TRAGOEDIA,

Exhibita Ludis Encenialibus
Louanij in Collegio
PORCENSI.

LOVANII,
Typis Philippi Dormalij.
cIↃ. IↃc. XXIV.
Cum Priuilegio.

NOTE: Asterisks are used within the English and Latin texts to direct the reader to the Explanatory Notes that follow the play. In the poetry, line numbering is marginal; in the Latin prose and in the translation (choruses excepted) it is internal. Line references in the Explanatory Notes are to the Latin text. In both the Latin prose and in the translation, a bracketed small Roman numeral precedes the line it indicates.

DEDICATORY LETTER

To the Very Reverend Lord D. Engelbert Desbois,*
Provost of the Distinguished Church of St. Peter of Lille.

Very Reverend Lord, there is no one who is not shocked and filled with grief over the defection of the renowned kingdom of England from the Catholic faith, which it had initially received, according to tradition, from Joseph of Arimathea.* In an effort to bear witness to my own grief, [v] as others have done, I recently laced on the buskin and presented a play in the Louvain public theater.* Onto the stage strode King Henry VIII who, in the throes of passionate love, proscribed the faith of his forefathers—the faith he had hitherto championed with sword and pen.* There were many better-than-average individuals, mortal men well deserving of immortality, [x] who longed to hold fast to the faith they found slipping away. Finding this impossible, they poured out their lifeblood in its embrace. The memory of More cannot be wiped away; and even after his own death the Bishop of Rochester lives on. Both of them as they died elicited tears from their distraught King; but their disapproval of his love affair and their refusal to recognize him as pope [xv] cost them their lives. Many others, reddened with their blood beneath the fatal headsman's axe, preferred to die for God's sake rather than live on for the King's. And so it was that the King-Pope, in his furious desire to assert his authority over the English church, made martyrs

Reverendo Admodum Domino D. Engelberto Desbois,*
Insignis Ecclesiae D. Petri Insulensis Praeposito D.C.Q.

Nobilissimum Britanniae Regnum, *Admodum Reverende Domine*, a Catholica Religione, quam, ut testes sunt Historiae, a *Iosepho ab Arimathia* primum acceperat,* defecisse, nemo est qui perculsus non doleat. Dolorem meum ut inter [v] alios testarer, cothurnos nuper indui, & in publico Lovanii theatro* Scenam aperui. Prodiit in proscenium *Henricus Octavus* Rex, & Maiorum Religionem, quam gladio styloque asseruerat,* amore saucius proscripsit. Multae non e vulgo Animae, viri mortales immortalitate dignissimi, abeuntem [x] illam retinere voluerunt; cum non possent, in eius amplexu sanguinem & vitam effuderunt. Obliterari *Mori* memoria non potest, & post cineres suos vivit *Roffensis Antistes*. Ambo suo sanguine lachrymas male sano Regi elicuerunt, sed quia amorem non probant, & Pontificem eum non agnoscebant, [xv] vixerunt. Plures alii sub feralis securis ictu suo cruore purpurati Deo maluerunt mori, quam Regi vivere. Ita Regius Pontifex dum authoritatem in Ecclesia Anglicana saeviendo quaerit, Martyres fecit. Illa

of them. Indeed, the most virtuous Queen Catherine became more renowned when she yielded her rights to a harlot; and when [xx] she for-
sook her kingdom she seemed to be exalted above any royal power. By
her stalwart character, to which her own tears added luster, she brought
tears to everyone's eyes—except her royal husband's. It is true that the
King was grieved (such is the power of conscience), but he did not
yield. Fate eventually forced him to yield. All this you saw, Very Reverend Lord, and [xxv] you yourself witnessed it here as a spectator. It
was at the performance that you frankly admitted how deeply your soul
had been stirred and your heart had been stricken with anguish. For
since your heart could hardly withstand some expression of grief, tears
came to your eyes.* However, since these joyless episodes were nevertheless a source of enjoyment, behold I here reopen the theater and with
you as patron reintroduce [xxx] this tragic monarch to the public stage.
May others read what you have witnessed;* under your patronage the
play will afford even more enjoyment. For your character is well known,
as Rome bears witness—to say nothing of our Belgium. Your learning,
deservedly crowned with laurel, is also recognized. [xxxv] As you enthusiastically paced the sacred halls of the University,* Louvain looked on
and loved you. From here you went to Rome* in order to learn in that
international theater and center of learning whatever can be learned
anywhere. Accompanying you at that time was the extremely upright
and accomplished Nicolas Michaut,* whose flawless character [xl] provided the grounds of a profitable friendship. In Rome you conducted

vero piissima Regina *Catharina* dum Scorto cessit maior facta est; & dum
regnum [xx] reliquit, omni regno excelsior est visa. Omnium ipsa oculos,
praeterquam Regis mariti, constanti virtute, quam lachrymae decorabant,
permovit. Ingemuit equidem ille (ea vis est conscientiae) sed victus non est.
Vicit tandem fatum. Haec vidisti, *Admodum Reverende Domine*, & [xxv]
praesens ipse spectasti. Perturbatum animi tui sensum, & perculsum dolore
affectum ingenue tum ibidem es fassus. Cum enim esse sine gemitu aliquo
cor tuum non posset, oculi maduerunt.* Sed quoniam placuit quicquid
tamen displicebat, ecce Tibi clausam tum Scenam iterum aperio, & [xxx]
cothurnatum hunc Regem tuo sub patrocinio in publicam lucem adduco.
Legant alii quae vidisti;* te certe Patrono amplius placebunt. Nota quippe
tua illa virtus est, cuius etiam testis est, ut nihil de Belgio nostro dicam, Roma.
Nota Doctrina est, quam emerita Laurus coronavit. Vidit [xxxv] te Lovanium
in sacris Academiae Spatiis* magno animo decurrentem, & amavit. Hinc
Romam, ut in illo Orbis compendio & Theatro disceres, quicquid disci ubique
potest, abivisti.* Comes tum ibi integerrimus & Ornatissimus Vir fuit *Nicolaus Michaut*,* in quo cum nulla virtus desideraretur, [xl] eius consuetudine
crevisti. In Urbe tanquam in templo aliquo aut Schola, ut cum virtute pru-

yourself as if you were in some kind of temple or school, so that you might develop a sense of prudence to match your native gifts of character.* Nothing that could be learned was able to escape your industry; even from those very ruins that remain as witnesses of learned antiquity, your inquiring mind discovered something to be learned. [xlv] Already then you were a favorite of the Roman bishops, of the Colonna, Farnese, and Madruzzo families;* even the royal legates and other important Rome dignitaries loved you. Indeed, they saw in you a native talent in full readiness and destined for glorious achievement, and this adorned by a character which matured with each day. There is no doubt that the sure guide to prudence [1] is the patterning of one's life and thought on the example of industrious men.* And to what degree you succeeded in patterning your life while in Rome is attested by the metropolitan See of Cambrai.* There it was your lot for many years to serve as Archdeacon so efficiently that you administered with consummate prudence that part of the Church committed to your care [lv] and thus afforded everyone an opportunity to judge how eminently fitted you were for a higher position. Influenced by your reputation, the Most Serene Princes of the Belgians took it upon themselves to summon you as Provost of the Church of Lille,* where your life and activity, as Envy herself attests, merit a still higher post.* Such is the power of innate character, of breeding, [lx] of education and industry. Your stock and lineage furnish illustrious models which even today the Belgians acknowledge. First of all, your uncle Louis Verreycken* so won the hearts of kings and princes by his worth that even though he was the unique embellishment of our

dentiam comparares,* versatus es. Nihil effugere industriam tuam potuit, sciri quod posset; & in ipsis ruderibus doctae istius Antiquitatis testibus curiosa mente, quod disceres, invenisti. [xlv] Gratus iam tum eras purpuratis illis Patribus, & te *Columnae, Farnesii, Madrutii;** ipsi etiam Regum Legati, & quicunque Romae magni, amabant. Erectam quippe Indolem, & Gloriae natam in te videbant, quam crescens quotidie Virtus exornabat. Nimirum haec certa est ad prudentiam via, [1] virorum illustrium exemplo animum suum & vitam conformare.* Quantus vero sis ibi formatus, testis est Metropolitana Cameracensis Ecclesia,* in qua pluribus annis ita Archdiaconum egisti, ut commissam tibi Ecclesiae istius partem summa prudentia administrares, & dignissimum te maiori [lv] dignitate consentiens omnium opinio iudicaret. Ea moti fama Serenissimi Belgarum Principes ad Insulensis Ecclesiae Praepositiuram* ultro evocaverunt; in qua ita vivis agisque, ut vel ipsa Invidia teste Decus tibi maius debeatur.* Tanta vis est innatae virtutis, tanta Generis, [lx] educationis, industriae. Illustria in illo Genere tuo ac stirpe sunt exempla, quae etiamnum Belgae suspiciunt. Tuus ille imprimis Avunculus *Ludovicus Verreickius,** ita Reges & Principes suis meritis sibi devinxit ut cum esset singulare Belgii nostri ornamentum, tum incredibili fide, [lxv]

Belgium, [lxv] he fulfilled the office of *Audientiarius** entrusted to him
with incredible trustworthiness, conscientiousness, and prudence. I do
not wish to recall all his accomplishments with my pen, since he has
already received every tribute to his deserts with a singular modesty
that is to be admired. Even after his death he lives on in the hearts of
Belgians, and we behold his image in his son and your cousin.* [lxx]
Ever since princes wanted this man to succeed in his father's position,
he never ceases to grow daily in the qualities his father possessed; and
insofar as he is a man of judicious industry and character, he proves
himself most deserving of greater dignities from the King. Your family
may indeed take pride in possessing those qualities of which [lxxv]
Belgians cannot be unmindful—that character which kings and princes
will never cease rewarding. Since indeed it is easier to admire this magnificence of yours than attempt its celebration, allow me, Very Reverend
Lord, to desist in my praises of you so that I might come and offer this
tragedy which I have dedicated in your name. This indeed [lxxx] is the
pledge of my esteem for you. I trust that you may receive it with your
wonted grace and affectionately embrace its donor.

Written at Louvain, November 22, 1624.
The devoted servant of Your Reverence,
Nicolaus Vernulaeus.

prudentia, sinceritate commissum sibi Audientiarii* munus obivit. Nolo ad
calamum ea revocare, quae gessit, cum omnem meritorum suorum laudem
uno modestiae admirandae sinu exceperit. Vivit ipse etiam post fata in Belgarum pectoribus, & eius in *Filio* Cognato tuo* imaginem videmus. [lxx]
Quem virum cum in patris loco Principes esse voluerint, tum patris meritis in
dies adhuc crescit; & qua est prudenti industria virtuteque maioribus se Regis
beneficiis dignissimum ostendit. Glorietur sane vestra Familia; in illa enim
ea merita sunt, quorum oblivisci [lxxv] Belgium non potest; ea Virtus, quam
ornare nunquam Principes Regesque desinent. Quoniam vero splendorem
illum vestrum satius est admirari, quam extollere conari, permitte, *Admodum
Reverende Domine*, ut de te silendo Tragoediam hanc tuo Nomini inscriptam
oblatum veniam. Ea enim [lxxx] est observantiae in te meae pignus, quam
ut solita tua Humanitate excipias, & tuo amore offerentem complectaris ob-
testor. Lovanii, x Calend. Decembris, MDCXXIV.

Reverentiae Tuae Obsequio Devotus
Nicolaus Vernulaeus.

To the Reader: THE SUBJECT MATTER OF THE TRAGEDY*

In this tragedy, dear reader, I offer you no fairy tales or flights of fancy,* but history in capsule form. Arthur, the elder brother of Henry VIII, married Catherine, the daughter of the Catholic sovereigns of Spain. Poor in health, [v] he died in youth without ever having lived with his wife. To consolidate peaceful relations between Spain and England, Henry VIII married Catherine with special permission from the Sovereign Pontiff. From this marriage were born three sons and two daughters (of whom Mary was the sole survivor of both parents). After twenty years [x] of married life Henry VIII put away Catherine, his reason allegedly a religious one, since Catherine had been his brother's wife. However, the truth of the matter was that he wanted to replace Catherine by Anne Boleyn, with whom he was deeply infatuated. After the Roman Pontiff had refused to approve the second marriage as well as the King's divorce of Catherine, [xv] Henry invested himself as Primate of the Church of England and confirmed his position by executing those subjects who refused to acknowledge his spiritual primacy. There followed the many martyrs in England and Ireland as well as the defection of these two kingdoms from Catholicism. And so by this single turn of events and by this alone did heresy filter into England, until then the tributary province of the Church of Rome. May God so ordain that [xx] England someday come to her senses and return to the fold. In addition to other sources,* allow me to refer you to Nicholas Sander's book titled *The Origin and Growth of the English Schism.*

AD LECTOREM: TRAGOEDIAE ARGUMENTUM

Nulla fabula aut figmentum* in hac Tragoedia est, Lector, en Historiam compendio tibi do. Arthurus natu maior Henrici Octavi frater cum Catharinam Catholicorum Hispaniae Regum filiam uxorem duxisset, ea ob infirmam [v] tenerae aetatis valetudinem minime cognita satis concessit. Illam de Pontificis Summi venia, ut inter Hispanos Anglosque pax confirmaretur, Henricus Octavus uxorem accepit, & ex ea filios tres, duasque filias, (ex quibus sola Maria, utrique parenti superstes fuit) genuit. Annis in hoc [x] matrimonio viginti consumptis, Henricus Octavus Catharinam, religione, ut prae se ferebat, motus, quod uxor fratris sui fuisset, re autem vera, ut Annam Bolenam, quam deperibat eius loco supponeret, repudiavit. Approbare cum has nuptias Romanus Pontifex Catharinaeque repudium non vellet, [xv] Henricus in Ecclesia Anglicana Primatum sibi arrogavit, & eorum qui voluntati suae obsequi nolebant, sanguine sancivit. Inde illi tot in Anglia Hiberniaque Martyres, & istorum a Catholica Religione regnorum defectio. Una enim & hac sola occasione in Angliam, tributariam olim Romanae [xx] Ecclesiae Provinciam Haeresis irrepsit. Faxit Deus, ut aliquando sapiat, & redeat. Vide praeter alios* Nicolaum Sanderum in *Libro de Origine ac Progressu Schismatis Anglicani.*

CAST OF CHARACTERS

King Henry   Alice, wife of Thomas More
Queen Catherine   Margaret, daughter of More
Mary, daughter of Catherine   [First Servant]
Thomas More   [Second Servant]
Fisher, Bishop of Rochester   Heresy
Campeggio   Lust
Wolsey   Impiety
Longland   Tyranny
Cranmer   The Catholic Religion
Brian   Reason
Warham [Queen's Procurator]   Piety
[Dr. Ridley]   Clemency
The King's Councilors   An Angel
Anne Boleyn   Chorus of Maidens
                Chorus of Catholic Exiles

OFFICE OF CENSOR

This tragedy, worthy of being printed, shows clearly how
truly the Philosopher spoke when he said, *Given one mistake, the rest follows.*

William Fabricius
Apostolic and Royal
Censor of books.

PERSONAE TRAGOEDIAE

Henricus Rex   Brianus   Impietas
Catharina Regina   Varramus   Tyrannis
Maria Filia Catharinae Senatores Regni   Religio Catholica
Thomas Morus   Anna Bolena   Ratio
Roffensis Episcopus   Aloysia Mori uxor   Pietas
Campegius   Margareta Mori filia   Clementia
Volsaeus   Haeresis   Angelus
Longlandus   Luxuria   Chorus Virginum
Granmerus

            Chorus Exulum Catholicorum

CENSURA

Tragoedia haec praelo digna evidenter ostendit quam vere
a Philosopho dictum sit, *Uno absurdo dato, caetera consequi.*

Guil. Fabricius
Apostolicus ac Regius
Librorum Censor.

ACT I, scene i*

Heresy, Lust, Impiety, Tyranny*

Her. The buried world, the dwellings bereft of light, and the lower regions foul with darkness* do I now forsake—I, Heresy, the loathsome spawner of treachery and the begetter of dire cruelty. Titan, [5] hide your countenance, turn your flaming steeds toward the western waves, let dawn fail to spread the day; yea, let a dark shroud cover even those tiny stars of evening. I have burst through the Tartarean gates and have clothed myself in the blackness of unending night. [10] Behold, this very world now shudders in terror and the shaken earth quails at my footfall. All this augurs well for me. I am pleased, I am more than satisfied. May any wickedness I conceive come to pass,* be it cruel, novel, strange, sorrowful, frightful, savage*—any evil at all [15] that an Englishman is unprepared for. I swear by this snaky head of mine,* by you my sisters, by the lord of hell,* and by Phlegethon* that beats upon the abode of sorrow with dread sound of weeping, that England, already racked with torment, will expose her body to disaster and at this very moment inhales the deadly pestilence. [20] O land of Britain, till now you have held your

ACTUS PRIMUS, scena i

Haeresis, Luxuria, Impietas, Tyrannis

Haer. Orbem sepultum, lucis immunes domos,
Tetrumque linquo noctis infernae chaos*
Genitrix nefanda fraudium, & saevae parens
Crudelitatis, Haeresis. Titan tuos
5 Absconde vultus, flammei occiduas petant
Undas caballi, nulla lux spargat diem,
Et ipsa noctis parvula obscurum tegat
Velamen astra. Tartari rupi fores,
Caliginemque noctis aeternae indui.
10 En horret ipse Mundus, & passu meo
Concussa Tellus trepidat: Hoc omen mihi est.
Bene est, abunde est, fiat hoc, fiat scelus,*
Quodcunque mente molior, dirum, novum,
Inusitatum, triste, terribile, efferum,*
15 Et quod Britannus nescit. Anguineum hoc caput,*
Et vos, Sorores, testor, & stygis Arbitrum,*
Et qui tremendam flebili tundit domum
Horrore Phlegeton,* versa iam, versa Anglia
Latus in ruinam flectet, & pestem trahit.
20 Britanna Tellus, hactenus celsum caput,

head proudly and have raised your noble hands to heaven. But enough attention has already been given to the Roman Catholic faith* and to Rome's holy precepts. Let him who thunders from the Tarpeian Rock* now lose his jurisdiction over you. [25] Let him who in the past controlled England now begin to tally the deaths and cruel executions* of his adherents; the few supporters of Rome will here meet their doomsday in blood. This land belongs to me, the lust of King Henry will establish my kingdom and render it inviolable. For this fact is certain: [30] wherever Heresy springs up, lawlessness rises with it. We are always born from the womb of wickedness; whoever madly rebels against God is guilty of a heinous offense. Now the prospects of victory are assured: the King, smoldering with passion, is completely infatuated with his darling beloved. She is his own daughter, [35] whom he sired in wicked incest;* and now he wishes to marry her. In vain, O Father of Roman Catholics, will your dawdling hand hurl the thunderbolt of excommunication from the Eternal City.* Venus all by herself will accomplish more than many wagonloads of threats could do. Now then, [40] my sisters, to the work at hand. First of all, Lust, make this your task: feed the King's love with devouring flames; parch his liver* and let him burst into flames as he nurtures the wound.

> Et extulisti Nobiles coelo manus.
> Fidei Quiritum* iam sit indultum satis,
> Romaeque sacris. Ille Tarpeia tonans
> E rupe Rector* Angliae quondam suae
> 25 Nunc iura perdat, funera & diras neces*
> Numeret suorum; ferre qui Romam queunt,
> Pauci hic cruento finient fato diem.
> Mea ista Tellus; Regis Henrici meum
> Libido regnum sanciet; nempe hoc ratum est,
> 30 Ubicunque surgit Haeresis, surgit nefas.
> E scelere semper nascimur; quisquis Deo
> Amens rebellat, sceleris infandi est reus.
> Sed certa iam sunt auspicia; Venerem suam
> Rex ustulatus deperit; natam suam,
> 35 Et quam nefando genuit incestu Pater,*
> Habere iam vult coniugem. Frustra tuum
> Ab Urbe lenta fulmen excuties manu
> Pater Quiritum;* sola plus poterit Venus
> Quam tot minarum plaustra. Iam tandem meae
> 40 Tandem Sorores pergite. Hic partes tuae
> Luxuria primae sunto, foecundis ales
> Flammis amorem; torreas Regis iecur,*
> Et intus alto vulnere in flammas eat.

Lust. Our flames already burn through his body so that he is utterly mad.* [45] The King's only idol is Anne; he has made up his mind to marry her and so violate the primal laws of marriage, or else refuse obedience to the sacred decrees of holy Rome.

Her. The second stage of crime consists in defying the Thunderer's wrath, the threats of human law, [50] and whatever that Prince of the spiritual order thunders down from the seven hills. Impiety, it is your task to undermine the King's loyalties: let him either marry Anne in sheer frenzy or else boldly repudiate the jurisdiction of the Tarpeian Father.

Imp. The King is nursing this idea. [55] And while his heart continues to swell with the pleasure his mistress affords, his interest in Heaven wanes. Venus imprisons him in her arms so that he now worships only one goddess, and that goddess is Venus.

Her. She is the only goddess I mean. [60] However, since a voluptuous person thirsts for blood and savage killings, your assistance, Tyranny, will be needed next. Make his mind wild, therefore, and his hands brutal; let banishments, executions, and flowing blood be the things he craves.

Tyr. I will transform the King into a savage and ruthless monarch with a godless mind. While the madman [65] shall hold Anne fast in his arms,

      Lux. Nostris perustus ignibus totus furit.*
45 Unum est Bolena Regis Idolum; vel hanc
    Sociare mens est coniugem, & primas thori
    Violare leges, vel piae Romae sacras
    Non ferre leges.
    Haer.   Alter est sceleris gradus,
    Tonantis iras, legis humanae minas,
50 Et quicquid ille montibus septem tonat
    Princeps sacrorum, temnere. Impietas tuum est
    Mutare Regis pectus; aut ducat suam
    Demens Bolenam, aut iura Tarpei patris
    Contemnat audax.
    Imp.   Regis hoc animo sedet;
55 Et dum voluptas pellicis pandit sinum,
    Coeli recedit cura. Quem captum Venus
    Amplexa stringit, unicum Numen colit,
    Venerisque Numen.
    Haer.   Numen hoc unum volo.
60 At cum cruorem sitiat, & diras neces,
    Quicunque mollis, nunc tuae partes erunt
    Tyrannis. Igitur effera mentem & manum,
    Exilia, caedes, sanguinem effusum velit.
    Tyr. Et efferatum & mente crudelem impia
    Agitabo Regem; dum suo demens sinu
65 Stringet Bolenam, Regios pascet cruor

the royal gaze shall feast on running gore. With one edict shall he strew the ground with more than a thousand slaughtered victims; the streets shall stream with blood, and corpses shall be stacked up in great heaps. *Her.* Look! Here he comes. Go at once, all together, and hem the King in. [70] Press round him, pommel on the doors of his lovesick heart. Let him be madly in love* and no longer his own master.*

ACT I, scene ii

King Henry, Lust, Impiety, Tyranny

Hen. This scepter in my hand gleams and glistens;* this purple* I wear hangs rich and splendid; on my anointed brow the royal diadem sparkles.* So it is that [75] Fortune clothes kings deceitfully; so it is that glory entangles them treacherously. How splendidly does this crown blaze on my royal head! But within this tortured breast anxieties groan aloud. Splendor shines on my forehead but anguish whips the heart within me.* Whatever adorns, presses down; [80] whatever gleams, corrupts; whatever glitters, bites with sharp grief and finally kills. One woman is the cause of all this grief and that woman is Anne Boleyn. She slays me with her enchantment;* her laughter and alluring figure, [85]

> Effusus oculos. Unico edicto neces
> Plus mille sparget; sanguine undabunt viae,
> Cadaverumque longa docetur strues.
> *Haer.* En ipse; Regem cingite actutum simul;
> 70 Instate circum, saucii cordis fores
> Pulsate, amans amensque* sit, nec sit suus.*

ACTUS PRIMUS, scena ii

Henricus Rex, Luxuria, Impietas, Tyrannis

> *Hen.* Equidem serenum fulget e sceptro iubar,*
> Et ista splendet purpura,* et sacrae micat
> Diadema frontis.* Nempe sic fuco tegit
> 75 Fortuna Reges, sic dolo innectit decus.
> Decus istud alti verticis quantum nitet?
> At intus arcti pectoris curae gemunt.
> Frontem serenat fulgor, at pectus dolor
> Intus flagellat.* Quicquid exornat, premit;
> 80 Quicquid serenat, inficit; quicquid micat
> Acri dolore mordet, & tandem necat.
> Una est dolorem quae mihi tantum facit,
> Una est Bolena; fascino nam me suo
> Occidit illa;* risus & formae lepos,

her inviting mouth and springtime beauty* burn right through this breast of mine and feed its fire. Her eyes slay me with a single glance, her hair imprisons my soul* with its soft fetters of love. Unnumbered people all around are subject to my powerful rule; [90] I am subject to Anne alone. I am King and at the same moment an abject slave.

Lust. Go forward with your plans, Your Majesty. After all, this is what it means to be a ruler; namely, to will whatever you please.* A man whose heart burns with love finds servility unendurable. With one stroke [95] he bursts the fetters of authority and law. The splendor of the royal countenance, the virile manhood* which is yours, a life of ease, of feasting and repose demand something which is foreign to your innate sense of decency.

Hen. Would it were allowed! This is no trifling urgency that flogs my sad spirit.* New passions overwhelm me [100] while my high-minded wife occupies the royal bed. But it is Anne who now sways my heart and my mind. Yet till now I have been content with the Queen.*

Lust. And will she for that reason prolong the torture and sorrow in your heart? You are by no means a new soldier of Venus marching forth to battle.* If Anne Boleyn alone [105] satisfies the King, let her satisfy him

---

85 Et oris illa gratia, & vernus decor,*
     Istud perurunt pectus, & flammas alunt.
     Uno trucidant lumina aspectu comae
     Animum hunc amoris vinculo blando ligant.*
     Tot his & illis impero populis potens,
90 Uni Bolenae servio; Rex sum & miser
     Sum servus idem.
     Lux.   Perge Rex, hoc scilicet
     Regnare tandem est, velle quod mentem iuvet.*
     Quicunque amore pectus accensum gerit,
     Servire nescit; iuris & legum simul
95 Nexum resolvit. Regii vultus decor,
     Virilis aetas,* otium, mensae, quies
     Aliquid requirunt, quod tuus nescit pudor.
     Hen. Utinam liceret! Cura non animum levis
     Tristem flagellat;* ignibus carpor novis,
100 Impletque celsa regios Coniux toros.
     At hoc Bolena pectus, hanc mentem trahit.
     Regina placuit.*
     Lux.   Languidum & moestum trahet
     Idcirco pectus? Veneris haud miles novus
     In arma prodis:* una si forsan placet
105 Bolena Regi, placeat, & thalamum impleat;

and occupy his bedchamber. Her mother did,* and so did her sister.*
Hen. Would it might be done! But she whom I find so delightful has no
desire to please the King in this way. She sets herself in opposition to my
wife. "I do not wish to love you as your mistress," she says, "but as your
wife."* [110] She insists on the seal of marriage vows. Meanwhile she
allows me no means of alleviating my lovesick heart.* This is the
wretched luck of the King; this is my wound, a wound that keeps throb-
bing with pain.
Imp. So you are in love and yet do nothing about it? Love has no laws;
[115] this false shame of a cowardly heart must be got rid of. You have
no idea how many things are permissible to kings. Are you going to keep
feeding the living flame in your wounded heart? And will the madness of
your burning breast keep raging while you drag out the day with sighs
and prayers? [120] Seek counsel and lay hold of any suggestion you find
attractive. Destroy whatever gets in your way; a king can do anything he
pleases.
Hen. She alone pleases me. I fear uprisings. The Emperor and other sovereigns* will be aware of any move I make, and perhaps my own [125]
English subjects will not be wholly favorable. Meanwhile I perish miserably—I burn alive and carry around my own ashes. Oh, Anne, Anne,

       Implevit illum mater,* implevit soror.*
       Hen. Utinam liceret! quae placet, non sic cupit
       Placere Regi; coniugem opponit meam.
       Amare pellex non volo, coniux volo,*
110 Sic, inquit illa; nuptiarum vult fidem.
       Lenimen aegro pectori nullum facit.*
       Haec misera sors est Regis, hoc vulnus meum,
       Et usque & usque vulnus excrucians meum.
       Imp. Et amas, & haeres? non habet leges amor;
115 Solvendus iste cordis imbellis pudor.
       Etiam Monarchis multa, quae nescis, licent.
       Alesne vivam pectoris laesi facem?
       Et aestuabit cordis accensi furor
       Suspiriosis dum trahis votis diem?
120 Consilia quaere, & quod placet votum occupa.
       Dissolve quicquid impedit; Regi licet,
       Regi placere quod potest.
       Hen.   Una haec placet.
       Vereor tumultus; Caesar & Regis* scient
       Si quid movebo; nec satis forsan meus
125 Probabit Anglus; interim occumbo miser,
       Vivensque & ardens iam meas Manes fero.

where are you dragging me?

Tyr. Alas! How sluggish your passion is! Reach out and seize whatever you want. Kings know nothing of sorrow; no bold man [130] who can force others to his will ever spends his time grieving. The homes of private citizens grieve but palaces of kings do not lament.* Others can only live in hope, but kings command. If anyone disapproves of your wishes, whatever they be, brandish your sword. Blows and threats and slaughter [135] will coerce the mob. Royal favor will win over some of the noblemen to your side; terror will force all the others into your way of thinking.

Hen. I have the blood of heroes in my veins and my strength is that of a god.* There lies hidden in my heart* a thing that will make the world shudder. It is scandalous for a king to burn with unholy passion.* [140] Look! Here she comes! My whole being is on fire with her. The very sight of her makes me ache with desire. One nod of her head stabs through my heart, she unnerves me completely.*

ACT I, scene iii

Anne, Henry, Brian

Anne. What is wrong, Your Majesty?* Why do you look at me so sadly and of late keep your troubles locked tight in your heart? You should

      Bolena, quo me? quo Bolena me trahis?
      Tyr. Heu lentus ardor! occupa votum manu,
      Dolere Reges non sciunt: quisquis potest
130 Alios severus cogere, hic nunquam dolet.
      Privata languent tecta, non Aulae gemunt.*
      Optare possunt caeteri, at Reges iubent.
      Si quis probare non volet quicquid voles,
      Ostende ferrum; verbera, & minae, & neces
135 Vulgus coercent. Nobiles quosdam favor,
      Alios in istud quod voles terror trahet.
      Hen. Herois in me est sanguis, & Divus vigor.*
      Manet hoc repostum corde,* quod Mundus tremat.
      Est turpe Regem pectoris flammam pati,*
140 En illa; mediis aestuor praecordiis;
      Ut video, ut aeger occido; nutu meum
      Hoc pectus uno sauciat, mihi me abstrahit.*

ACTUS PRIMUS, scena iii

Bolena, Henricus, Brianus

Bol. Quid Rex?* quid isto moestus obtutu novos
Animo dolores claudis? emergat iubar

radiate the joy [145] of a carefree spirit; no one but Your Majesty appears downcast, sorrowful, languishing and weighted with cares. Look how Phoebus shines and shows the world his beaming countenance, how he gilds the dancing troops of the great sky with his golden rays. But you, Your Majesty, [150] keep centered on yourself. Clear away whatever it is that clouds your mind.

Hen. Only when you alone are present does our beclouded soul admit its former radiance. You are our constant preoccupation, you are the strength of our spirit.

Anne. Put aside your worries; a life of ease is good for kings. [155] They are wont to have leisure—sometimes for sports and other times for love.

Hen. You alone possess our love. Allow this one preoccupation. I am wounded with love and bear it for your sake.

Anne. You are troubled over me? Be happy for your own sake, Your Majesty. I am happy, I have thrown my cares to the swift winds. [160] A happy disposition calls out for zithers and pleasant jests and graceful dancing. When you wish I will offer you my hand. *

Hen. May you offer me your love as well; you live deep in my heart, you are first in my thoughts. Believe me when I say, for I swear it is true, that you are grieving me sorely by your drawn-out cautious love, [165] that it

145 Mentis serenae; sola Maiestas iacet
     Deiecta, moesta, languida, & curis gravis.
     En cerne Phoebum, fulget, & clarum caput
     Ostendit orbi, & aetheris magni choros
     Radiis serenat aureis, tu Rex tibi
150 Incumbis ipsi; discute hoc quicquid tuum
     Obnubit animum.
        Hen.   Sola cum praesens ades,
     Mens nubilata pristinum admittit iubar.
     Tu cura nostra es, mentis & nostrae vigor.
        Bol. Depone curas, otium Reges beat;
155 Vacare ludis tunc solent & tunc suos
     Habent amores.
        Hen.   Sola tu nostros habes.
     Admitte curam, saucius pro te hanc gero.
        Bol. Pro mene curam? Vive Rex laetus tibi,
     Ego laeta rapidis tradidi curas notis.
160 Mens laeta cytharas poscit, & suaves iocos,
     Mollesque saltus; cum voles, iungo manum;
        Hen. Animumque iungas; * magna pars cordis mei es,
     Et magna curae. Crede iuratus loquar,
     Amore pectus vulneras lento meum,

is you alone who feed the flames of my heart. Give heed to my desires as you may.

Anne. Forgive me, Your Majesty, but there is one promise I have sworn: no one shall pluck my rose of virginity unless he first marry me.*

Hen. Consider me as your husband.

Anne. [170] He becomes my husband who takes an oath first and leads me as his bride in marriage. Your Majesty, you already have a wife; the Queen has been made the consort of your chamber.

Hen. Once you surrender yourself to the King* I will love you as my wife, if that is your wish. Let it suffice that you please me. [175] Let it suffice that you cause my heart to ache with pain. You will always be first in my love and in my vows.

Anne. Forbear, Your Majesty. I wish to have a holy wedding as a virgin. My mind is settled on this point. Gladly will I accept the royal love, but only as a virgin. Suppress these worries of yours. [180] Peace has come to your kingdom,* the work of Mars is at an end; you should not despise the blessings of your good fortune. Let your mind relax. It is only proper.

Hen. The proper way for me to relax, Anne, is to possess you. You are the goddess of my heart; you see here before you a king overwhelmed by your love.

165 Et sola nostri pectoris flammas alis.
     Coniunge votis dum licet animum meis.
     Bol. Ignosce Rex, iurata mens haec est mihi.
     Hanc castitatis nemo decerpet rosam,
     Nisi sit maritus.*
     Hen.   Crede me sponsum tibi;
170 *Bol.* Fit sponsus ille, qui prius iurat fidem,
     Sponsamque ducit; coniugem iam Rex habes;
     Regina thalami facta consors est tui.
     Hen. Tu iuncta Regi* cum voles coniux meo
     Amore fies: sit satis quando places.
175 Et vulnus istud pectoris quando facis.
     Amore prima semper & votis eris.
     Bol. Rex parce, virgo nuptias sacras volo.
     Haec certa mens est, regium patiar libens,
     Sed virgo amorem: discute has curas tuas.
180 Pax parta regno est,* Martius cessat labor,
     Felicitatis dona ne temnas tuae.
     Recreare mentem fas sit.
     Hen.   At per te mihi
     Bolena fas sit: cordis idolum mei es,
     Amore victum iam tuo Regem vides.

Anne. [185] If you are overwhelmed by my love, marry me. I can love only one who is my husband. But let us leave these matters; a wound grows worse with delay and the pains of love bite more sharply when one finds pleasure in them. How I wish your desires could be fulfilled! Now while you are still your own master, [190] it would be entirely wrong to squander that glory of your manhood. It is now you should lighten your melancholy spirit with jests.* Kings are not wont to worry about things they find disagreeable; they always look back on their sad years with loathing. Make the royal court ring out with song; [195] the present time of peace calls out for new dances and soft words of endearment.

Hen. Let us go; approach the hall joyfully in our company.

Bri. Just look how the King's love glows! Like a torch he burns. Anne is the sole darling of the inflamed King. He is quite overcome by her love, yes, quite undone. [200] He is completely infatuated with her. The sin is sweet to his palate; the shipwrecked victim seeks his own ruin. And just to think that this so-called virgin, in angling so cunningly for a husband, is actually determined to occupy the royal bedchamber. It is quite impossible that any evil could be worse than a crafty woman. [205] She cripples his heart with her words and wounds it with her eyes. She beguiles him ever with oaths, she slays him with an embrace. But look, un-

185 *Bol.* Amore vinctus coniugem fac me tuam.
     Amare tantum coniugem possum meum.
     Sed ista linque; vulnus augescit mora,
     Et cura mordet acrius quando placet.
     Utinam liceret, quod cupis. Nunc dum licet,
190 Aetatis istud perdere haud fas sit decus.
     Levare moestam iam decet mentem iocis,*
     Curare Reges non solent quod non placet;
     Annosque tristes semper oderunt suos.
     Fac Aula cantu personet; saltus novos,
195 Alloquia blanda tempus hoc pacis petit.
     Hen. Eamus, Aulam laeta tu mecum subi.
     Bri. En ille Regis ardor, en Regis faces.
     Una est Bolena Regis incensi Venus.
     Amore totus vincitur, totus perit.
200 Et totus illam deperit. Dulce est malum;
     Calamitatem naufragus quaerit suam,
     Et illa virgo scilicet, cauto virum
     Dum quaerit astu, regium poscit torum.
     Muliere cauta peius haud ullum est malum.
205 Sermone pectus laedit, atque oculis nocet.
     Iurando semper fallit, amplexu necat.
     Sed en, nec erro, cerno Volsaeum, gravis

less I am mistaken, I see Wolsey approaching. Some weighty problem is
on his mind; he seems very worried.

ACT I, scene iv

Wolsey, Longland, Brian

Wol. Longland, the King's spiritual welfare lies in your charge; [210]
just look how he is burning from head to toe with so extraordinary a
passion. Anyone who harbors a passion like this within himself knows no
peace of mind. When love cannot be possessed, the result is madness.
You know yourself that great kings want to be free to do what they
please.
Long. Most kings act [215] solely on impulse; any wish of theirs is a
command. When their blood is roused, they know how to yield to absolutely no one. Their will is law.
Wol. True, they will not be thwarted in anything that they can possibly
want; and yet there should be a limit to what they want. It is your duty
to concern yourself with the King's spiritual welfare [220] and I shall in-
struct you how to do it. Believe me, for I speak with God and Heaven
as witness, the Thunderer sees into this heart of ours and discerns the
preoccupations of our soul. I long for one thing only—that the eternal
salvation of the King be assured. I would prefer to be silent about this;

Res agitur intus, cura sollicitum tenet.

ACTUS PRIMUS, scena iv

Volsaeus, Longlandus, Brianus

Vol. Longlande, Regis in tua est manu salus,
210 Ut ecce amore totus insolito furit?
 Nescit quietem, quisquis hanc flammam gerit.
 Amor potiri cum nequit, tunc fit furor,
 Scis ipse, magni quod volunt Reges, sibi
 Licere cupiunt.
Long.   Impetu Reges agunt
215 Plerumque tantum; quod volunt, idem iubent.
 Cum fervet aetas cedere haud cuiquam sciunt.
 Lex est, voluntas.
Vol.   Irritum nunquam volunt
 Quod velle possunt; sit tamen votis modus.
 Regis salutem quaerere, hoc munus tuum est,
220 Modum docebo. Crede, nam coelo loquor
 Deoque teste; pectus hoc nostrum Tonans
 Animique curas cernit; hoc unum volo,
 Aeterna nostri certa sit Regis salus.

still I must speak out. [225] You know the secrets of the King; now learn this secret as well. No learned person will approve the marriage of the King and consider it valid*—you can be certain of this. Catherine married the King but such a marriage was legally impossible. A brother cannot marry his own brother's wife. [230] Even though she is worthy to be the consort of his wedding chamber, still the law forbids it. It is always immoral to represent as lawful what the law forbids. It is only proper that you advise the King; in fact your office requires it of you. Go, counsel him and explain the gist of my thought; right reason informs us of the nature of the case [235] and Faith reveals it.

Long. I shall take measures concerning the King's spiritual welfare at the opportune time and mention this observation of yours as well as your misgivings.

Wol. Approach him and he will be grateful to you. This is the only way one can serve the King's passion and his conscience at the same time.

Long. I shall see to it. Remain here close at hand [240] until the King summons me.

Bri. There is nothing that absorbs His Majesty more than this tremendous passion of his; whoever succeeds in finding a way of satisfying it will be doing the King a great service. He finds it all but impossible to keep this

      Silere vellem quod tamen cogor loqui.
225 Arcana nosti Regis, arcanum hoc quoque
      Iam nosce tandem. Nuptias Regis ratas
      Nemo probabit doctus,* haec certa est fides:
      Catharina Regi nupsit, haud potuit tamen.
      Accipere fratris coniugem frater nequit.
230 Digna illa consors est tori, sed lex vetat.
      Simulare semper est nefas quod lex vetat.
      Monere regem convenit; partes tuae
      Etiam hoc requirunt: I mone, & sensum meae
      Expone mentis, certa rem ratio docet,
235 Fides revelat.
      Long.   Consulam, quando hoc decet,
      Regis saluti, mentis hunc sensum tuae
      Curasque promam.
      Vol.   Gratus accedes, modus
      Hic solus esse Regio ardori potest,
      Etiam saluti.
      Long.   Pergo, tu praesto hic mane,
240 Dum Rex vocabit.
      Bri.   Gratius Regi nihil
      Amore tanto est; quisquis inveniet modum
      Regem obligabit; ferre vix tantam potest

smoldering emotion banked up inside his heart; his burning eagerness grows stronger as Anne keeps denying it any alleviation. It is always thrilling [245] to enjoy forbidden fruit.

Wol. The King's salvation must be attended to always and by everyone; when the head of the kingdom is safe and sound, the welfare of the members is assured. Brian, pay reverence to the reputation and good name of the King.

Bri. I stand up for the King's good name. Furthermore we should be ready [250] to die for our King. May his great yearning find relief.

Wol. There is one sure way of relief if he wishes to take it.

Bri. Look, the King himself is walking this way excitedly.*

ACT I, scene v

King Henry, Wolsey, Longland

Hen. Wolsey, if you can help solve my problems, do so. I keep rushing about, my heart is muddled [255] and my soul gives way and flounders. This way and that am I twisted round in terror and then spun back again in my perplexity. I am like the inconstant current of the Pontic Sea,* unable to control its own movements. I am turned and driven along and then borne off without resistance.

    Sub corde flammam; crescit ardor dum sui
    Negat Bolena copiam: semper placet
245 Habere quod quis non potest.
    Vol.   Regis salus
    Curanda semper omnibus; regni hoc caput
    Incolume quando est, certa membrorum est salus.
    Briane famam Regis & nomen cole.
    Bri. Defendo famam: Rege pro nostro mori
250 Etiam est decorum; faxit, ut tantus modum
    Inveniat ardor.
    Vol.   Certus est, si vult, modus.
    Bri. En concitato properat ipse Rex gradu.*

ACTUS PRIMUS, scena v

Henricus Rex, Volsaeus, Longlandus

    Hen. Volsaee, si quam rebus apportas opem,
    Expone mentem; corde confuso ruo,
255 Mens lapsa retro cedit, huc volvor tremens,
    Illuc revolver dubius; ac Ponti velut
    Incerta motus unda* non capit suos,
    Sic flector, & sic agitor, & languens feror.

Wol. One thing must be kept uppermost in our discussion: namely, the King's spiritual welfare. [260] Your Royal Highness, it is your salvation alone that I am concerned with. Thus my freedom springs from necessity. Allow me to counsel you. It is poor policy for great potentates to remain uninformed about anything whatsoever; indeed, many people fear princes who steadily exercise wide control through accurate and trustworthy advice. [265] It is God's will that you kings rule the people and administer justice to your subjects; it is not his will, in my opinion, that kings fall into error; for when princes sin they teach their subjects to sin by their open example.

Hen. Do you think perhaps I am falling into error?

Wol. Yes, I do, [270] but you yourself are not aware of it; your error is not clearly perceived. Catherine is not, as you suppose, your wife. Your Majesty, the woman who was formerly the wife of your brother Arthur can never be your wife. If you demand the infallible authority of divine testimony, [275] the sacred scriptures speak out.* Learned men in every part of the world teach that such is the case. It is time that the King should realize this fact, even though it is late; but even at this late date the error must be rectified.

Hen. But the case was judged.* I warn you, be careful about starting this trouble all over again. The Pope issued a decree; [280] he himself

       Vol. Haec lex loquendi certa sit, Regis salus.
260 Tuam salutem, Magne Rex, solam peto.
      Necessitatis inde libertas mea est
      Patere admonentem. Non decet quicquam Duces
      Nescire magnos; quippe quos multi timent,
      Qui regere certo multa consilio solent.
265 Praesse populis vos Deus Reges cupit,
      Et iura ferre subditis; non est, reor
      Errare Regum; namque dum peccant Duces
      Peccare certo vulgus exemplo docent.
      Hen. Errare forsan me putas?
      Vol.   Equidem puto,
270 At ipse nescis; error incertus tibi est;
      Catharina non est, quam putas, coniux tua.
      Quaeque ante coniux fratris Arthuri fuit,
      Rex, esse coniux non potest unquam tua.
      Oraculorum si fidem certam petis,
275 Sacrae loquuntur paginae;* toto docent
      In orbe Docti; sapere Rex tandem decet,
      Sero, sed error sero ponendus tamen.
      Hen. At iudicata res fuit;* quicquam hic cave
      Movere rursum. Pontifex legem dedit,

allowed me to marry Catherine.

Wol. But yet I must confess that he was in error. Even the Pope cannot allow something forbidden by the Eternal Lawgiver of the world.

Hen. Show me what should be done. If I have committed any error whatsoever, it must be corrected. Heaven will pardon it—it was youthful ignorance. [285] Princes are often misled by bad counsel.

Wol. Your putative wife must leave your bedchamber—this is the only way. Let another wife succeed her in your palace. The Pope will give a ruling and permit it whenever you wish. But first [290] the error should be called to his attention. No one responsible for the salvation of all kings can condone something unlawful.

Hen. Longland, take action immediately,* whatever the case demands. Write to Rome; my error should be brought to their attention. Let the Supreme Judge appoint a judge for my case.

Long. [295] I shall carry out your orders. Your Sacred Majesty should also decree that any doubts or undisclosed matters be resolved by Englishmen, for this is a serious matter.

Hen. See to this also. As king I want to make certain that I have a lawful wife. If the law deny Catherine to be my lawful wife, I must marry someone else.

280 Permisit idem.
      Vol.   Fatear, erravit tamen,
      Aeternus ille quod vetat mundi Tonans
      Permittere ipse non potest.
      Hen.   Doceas modum;
      Tollatur error si quis est error meus.
      Ignoscet Aether, error aetatis fuit.
285 Consilia saepe prava decipiunt Duces.
      Vol. Putata thalamum deserat Coniux tuum,
      Modus unus iste est; alia succedat tuam
      Coniux in Aulam. Pontifex legem dabit,
      Permittet idem cum voles; error prius
290 Sit notus illi; nemo delicto favet,
      Cui certa curae est omnium Regum salus.
      Hen. Longlande, quod res poscit,* actutum expedi.
      Perscribe Romam, notus error sit meus.
      Dicatque summus Iudicem Iudex meum.
295 *Long.* Curabo iussa: Sacra Maiestas tua
      Etiam per Anglos discuti hoc quicquid latet,
      Nam magna res est, iubeat.
      Hen.   Hoc cura simul.
      Habere certam coniugem iam Rex volo.
      Ducatur alia, Iura si ductam negant.

Wol. [300] That someone else might be the sister of the powerful King of France.* She is worthy of a king, and furthermore she is of royal blood.

Hen. I shall see to that when it is time: let no word of this be mentioned.*

Wol. I will take whatever steps are necessary for the King's spiritual welfare.

ACT I, scene vi

King Henry, Reason, Piety, Clemency

Hen. Now my future is certain;* I have found a way out of my predicament. [305] Let her go away! Let her withdraw! She cannot possibly be my wife. My first duty is my own salvation and after that the care of my kingdom. My wife Catherine, whom I am ashamed to have taken, cannot be kept; I disown her, I abjure her, I refuse to recognize her.* Anne will be my wife and bear me sons. [310] This is my heart's desire; she is the wife I wish.

Rea. What! Your wife Catherine forsake your royal couch? She should go away? She withdraw? Are you going to reverse the laws of nature?

Hen. I am obeying the laws of nature; it is impossible for her to be my wife, I say completely impossible.

Rea. [315] If it was possible for her to be your lawful bride, what pre-

300   *Vol.* Sit alia magni Galliae Regis soror,*
        Est digna Rege, Regius sanguis simul.
        Hen. Istud videbo, quod petit tempus, sile.*
        Vol. Curabo quicquid postulat Regis salus.

ACTUS PRIMUS, scena vi

Henricus Rex, Ratio, Pietas, Clementia

        Hen. Iam certa sors est,* sortis inveni modum.
305 Abeat, recedat, esse quae Coniux nequit.
        Prima est salutis cura, regnorum altera.
        Catharina Coniux, cuius acceptae pudet,
        Retinenda non est; abdico, eiuro, abnuo.*
        Mihi Bolena liberos coniux dabit.
310 Votum hoc amoris est mei; haec Coniux placet.
        Rat. Catharina linquat Regium Coniux torum?
        Abeat? recedat? Iura Naturae dabis
        Sic versa retro?
        Hen.   Iura Naturae sequor,
        Haec esse coniux non potest; non, non potest.
315 *Rat.* Quae lege duci potuit, esse quid vetat?

vents her from being your wife? The law ordains that you hold fast to your wedded wife; the Monarch of Heaven decrees it.

Hen. Shall I hold fast to the wife of my brother? It is unlawful.*

Rea. Whatever the Pope determines as lawful is lawful for you. He gave a decision, [320] he even declared that no law stood in the way of your marriage. You must believe the Father of the spiritual order.

Hen. I am concerned about my salvation; the present situation dissatisfies me.

Rea. You say you are dissatisfied with such a virtuous wife?* She who graces the English with her manners? The holy lady who through her own merits [325] gains God's favor for the English people? She, the famous offspring of rulers and the blood of kings?

Hen. I am dissatisfied. I am worried about my salvation.

Pie. You have good reason to be worried*—when you spurn the divine decrees and the Pope's abrogation.

Hen. I care nothing about this. [330] The Pope himself has erred and it is up to me to wipe out that error.

Pie. Piety is your motive indeed!* The fact is that loathsome Venus kindles your heart with her flames. You should fear Heaven; the Al-

---

       Retinere ductam coniugem leges volunt,
       Mandat Monarcha Coelitum.
       Hen.   Sponsam mei
       Retinebo fratris? Non licet.*
       Rat.   Fas est tibi,
       Fas esse quod vult Pontifex: legem dedit,
320 Edixit idem nuptiis nullam tuis
       Obstare legem. Crede Sacrorum Patri.
       Hen. Amo salutem; non placet.
       Rat.   Tibi non placet
       Tam sancta coniux,* moribus quae iam suis
       Ornat Britannos, sancta quae meritis Deum
325 Conciliat Anglis, clara quae proles Ducum
       Regumque Sanguis?
       Hen.   Non placet, curam meae
       Gero salutis.
       Pie.   Scilicet curam tuae
       Geris salutis,* iura cum spernis sacra,
       Et quod refixit Pontifex.
       Hen.   Nil hoc moror;
330 Erravit ille Pontifex, sed nunc mihi est
       Tollendus error.
       Pie.   Nempe te pietas movet.*
       Cum foeda flammis pectus incendit Venus.
       Vereare Coelum, corda scrutatur Tonans

mighty searches the pride-swollen hearts of kings. Impiety can no longer play its game [335] when Revenge raises up its undeniable torches.

Hen. God Himself makes known the reason behind our misdeeds; even He will favor my course of action.

Pie. Oh, yes! The Almighty will favor your lust* when as a godless husband you drive off your wife, when you find pleasure in [340] this lewd monstrosity of your manhood, this plague of the kingdom. Oh, abominable disgrace of our age!*

Rea. Even though Reason has no influence over you as king, still you should fear for your reputation.

Hen. As king I am concerned about my reputation while a wife of dubious status occupies my bedchamber. [345] And the question of reputation should put a stamp of approval on my present wishes as king. The way to establish any policy firmly is by using the sword as sanction.

Clem. The sword does not befit a benevolent monarch. You should establish your reputation by the law of kindness. When raging ferocity sits on the throne, its reign is short.

Hen. [350] I have made up my mind to carry out what I decided previously.

         Tumefacta Regum; ludere Impietas nequit
335   Vindicta certas quando molitur faces;
         Hen. Deus ipse, nostris aperit hunc sensum malis,
         Etiam favebit.
         Pie.   Scilicet Veneri tuae
         Tonans favebit;* Coniugem quando tuam
         Coniux repellis impius; quando placet
340   Aetatis illud, & tuae patriae lues,
         Monstrum impudicum, infame, saecli* dedecus.
         Rat. Etiamne ratio nulla te Regem movet,
         Vereare famam.
         Hen.   Fama me Regem movet,
         Incerta thalamos dum meos Coniux tenet.
345   Probare debet fama, quod iam Rex volo.
         Sancire ferro quicquid est, fixum sedet.
         Clem. Ferrum benignos non decet Reges; tuam
         Benignitatis iure famam sancies.
         Ubi saeva regnat ira, non regnat diu.
350   *Hen.* Peragere mens est quicquid optavi prius.

CHORUS

Of English Maidens

O cruel Love, how many evils do you stir up
When you assail the heart of a king!
Fewer ears of grain on Gargara* bend,
Fewer the surging currents that Euripus* drives,
355 Fewer the tiny pebbles tossed up by the sea.
O cruel Love! You torture the wretched
When you scorch their hearts with fire,
Ceaselessly prolonging their cares and woes,
Their griefs in an endless chain of misery.
360 Anyone who harbors lust in his heart
Gloomily counts the tiresome hours;
He forsakes the boredom of his lovesick bed
And loathes the pleasures of a hearty meal.
In his troubled soul he enjoys no peace.
365 A slow-burning fire steadily devours him.
True, he may shimmer in Tyrian purple,*
He may even frame laws for many lands;
Yet if his heart smolders with illicit love,

CHORUS

Virginum Anglicanarum

Crudelis Amor, quot mala misces
Animum Regis quando fatigas?
Non tot gravidos Gargara* culmos,
Non tot motus Euripus* agit
355 Non tot minimas pontus arenas.
Crudelis Amor! miseros torques,
Pectora flammis quando peruris
Usque catena longa curas,
Usque dolores luctusque trahens.
360 Quisquis venerem pectore claudit,
Numerat longas tetricus horas,
Deserit aegri taedia lecti,
Temnit lautae gaudia mensae.
Nescit laeso corde quietem
365 Et lento consumitur igne.
Tyrio quanquam fulgeat ostro*
Multis quanquam det iura plagis;
Vetito pectus si ardet amore,

He is a wretch shackled forever by its fetter.
370 He becomes a victim of loathsome Venus
And the devoted slave of his darling passion.
This slavery every lover knows:
In his struggle to keep on pleasing the other,
He ceaselessly grieves and ceaselessly quails;
375 He hopes for everything, everything he fears;*
While shivering he burns; while panting, is benumbed.*
Why do you persecute yourself, King Henry?
Why do you fan so many flames in your heart?
Whatever it is you are grieving about,
380 Something pernicious torments you miserably;*
Something that loving can never assuage.
Alas, what has become of your regimen of life?
Of the moral training you received in your youth?
Oh, where is the courage of the Christian soul?
385 The steadfast heart ineluctably armed?
A pernicious love devours your whole substance,
Keeps gnawing inside you with loathsome decay.
The King, alas, finds his sole solace in Anne,
The King, alas, finds his sole solace in lust.

Miser aeterna est compede victus.
370 Et fit foedae victima Veneri,
Tantumque suo servit Amori.
Amantium haec est servitus
Placere semper alteri
Semper moeret, semper & horret,
375 Quidvis sperat, metuit quidvis,*
Aestuat horrens, torpet anhelans.*
Quid te exagitas Rex Henrice,
Quid tot pectoris acuis motus?
Dirum est aliquid quodcunque doles,
380 Quod te miserum misere* inflammat,
Quod nec amando lenire queas.
Heu te, ubi docta regula vitae,
Et primae doctrina iuventae?
Heu te ubi, sacri virtus animi
385 Constans validis pectus in armis?
Omnia dirus consumit amor,
Et te misera tabe peredit.
Placet heu Regi sola Bolena,
Placet heu Regi sola libido;

390 And as he keeps struggling through Scylla and Charybdis,*
 He knows not the losses suffered therein.
 A man who languishes in lust, dies;
 He is not his own master*—a lover like this.
 He will recognize his crimes but only too late,
395 For his kingdom he will have already destroyed.
 The chaste Queen no longer interests the King;
 He yearns for the bed of a vile concubine.
 Integrity no longer has any appeal,
 Over all his being the harlot holds sway.
400 What groans, O England, O England, what groans
 Will you release from your sorrow-choked bosom!
 This love of the King spells inevitable doom;
 One woman unaided will ruin the nation.
 Many a time our descendants will say:
405 A mere woman crushed the powerful English;
 A woman converted the English to weaklings.
 And the King, while a slave to illicit love,
 Discarded our ancestors' holiest heritage.
 Alas, the mournful day! The mournful day!
410 Tears for ages to come await us,

390 Et sua nescit damna laborans,
 Inter Scyllas atque Charybdes.*
 Nam sic perit, qui deperit,
 Non est suus* qui sic amat,
 Sero sapiet cum mala noscet,
395 Et cum patriam fregerit omnem.
 Non casta placet Regina viro;
 Spurcae thalamum pellicis ardet;
 Non ulla placet probitas morum
 Totum meretrix possidet animum.
400 Anglia quos nunc, Anglia quos nunc
 Tristi mittes pectore luctus?
 Hic Regis amor certa ruina est;
 Unaque patriam foemina perdet;
 Dicent nostri saepe Nepotes,
405 Foemina validos perdidit Anglos;
 Foemina molles reddidit Anglos;
 Dum Rex turpi servit amori
 Optima Patrum sacra reliquit.
 Heu flenda dies, heu flenda dies!
410 Longae nobis lachrymae restant,

And our fathers' cruel fate leaves us in terror.
This love, now tickling with pleasant sensation,
Will someday slay with its raging wound.
This is the end of a love such as this:
415 To pine away endlessly, but never expire.

Et saeva Patrum fata timentur.
Amor hic blando vulnere laedens,
Postea saevo vulnere perimet.
Amoris iste finis est,
415 Perire semper, nec mori.

ACT II, scene i

Queen Catherine, Thomas More, Servants

Cath. O Blessed Ruler of the universe,* You who rule all things by an eternal decree, You who are the life and law of all creation, whose sacred majesty moves the quiet heavens by law eternally ordained, [420] restrains the power of kings and controls the destiny of the world by that same law! Can it be that human affairs flow in aimless succession?* Do You pay no heed to the earth, O God? Are the destinies of nations settled by mere hazard? O golden sun, great father of the ages [425] and lord of light;* O moon, you who nightly rule* your wandering retinues of stars, you who preside over the evening with your wavering light, will you two forever look down on these oppressive sorrows and storms? There is no night or day that fails to witness my steep [430] torrent of tears. The setting sun sees, and so does the new-born sun, that my life's only labor and preoccupation is weeping. How far, O God, will You allow this to go on and on! Will You permit this outrage to continue forever before your wrath is aroused? Can it be that [435] I who obey your laws and safeguard the vows of my royal marriage, that I whose honor

ACTUS SECUNDUS, scena i

Catharina Regina, Thomas Morus, Pedisequae

    Cath. Beate rerum Rector,* aeterno regis
    Qui cuncta nutu, vitaque & lex omnium:
    Cuius serenos sancta Maiestas polos
    Aeternitatis lege fatali movet,
420 Regumque Sceptra fraenat, & mundi vices
    Eadem gubernat. Ergone incerto fluunt
    Humana casu,* despicis terras Tonans,
    Et fata rerum sorte volvuntur sua?*
    Aurate Phoebe, Magne saeclorum Parens,
425 Lucisque Rector;* tuque quae noctu vagas
    Regis* cohortes syderum, & noctem face
    Dubia gubernas semper hos luctus gravis,
    Cernetis imbres? nulla nox, nullus dies,
    Quin effluentes cernat abrupto meas
430 Torrente lachrymas. Occidens Phoebus videt,
    Videt & renascens, unus est nostrae labor
    Et cura vitae, flere. Quo tandem Deus,
    Et usque & usque pateris, & lenta nefas
    Permittis ira! Scilicet quando tuas
435 Observo leges, regii quando tori

was never stained by an improper action should be driven from the royal palace as an unworthy wife? My royal husband has already broken the marriage oath he swore; he has pledged his word to a concubine, [440] and the shameless prostitute now plans to defile the royal bed. Am I to blame for this? I have always loved my husband with perfect fidelity and I have reverenced him as king. The entire English nation has ever lavished praise on me as queen in a way never accorded another. [445] And now this obscene blot on the royal throne; and now this concubine in the royal embrace; and now* this infamy attached to the royal household. Shall I be forced to see myself driven out as a vagrant, and repudiated, and banished,* and driven into exile?* [450] The tears I shed are innocent tears, undeserved tears, but still they are real. Gush forth, O tears!* My husband has been stricken with a diseased love, he has thrust me out of his heart. Oh, how cruel and deceitful, how fickle is the loyalty of rulers!

Thom. Your Majesty, why do you torture your [455] innocent mind with such grief? Why have your cheeks lost their wonted flush and beauty? If some evil is looming ahead, face it courageously; if some sorrow is tormenting you, feel free to confide in me.

        Intacta servo iura, nec pravo fides
        Violata motu est, regis expellar domo
        Non digna Coniux? iam datam solvit fidem
        Rex & Maritus; pellici adstringit fidem,
440 Et impudicum Regios scortum toros
        Maculare tentat. Culpa quae tandem est mea?
        Semper maritum casta dilexi meum,
        Coluique Regem, tota Reginam Anglia
        Non usitatis me extulit semper modis.
445 Et nunc, & istud regio in solio probrum,
        Et nunc, & istud regio scortum in sinu,
        Et nunc,* & istam regiae labem domus.
        Expulsa, & abdicata & eiecta, & vaga*
        Videre cogar exul, atque exul pati?*
450 O immerentes! immerentes sed tamen
        O ite lachrymae!* Periit insano meus
        Amore Coniux, corde me extrusit suo.
        O dira, falsa, incerta regnorum fides!
        Thom. Regina, tanto quid tuum luctu quatis
455 Animum immerentem? Solitus excedit genis
        Rubor decorque? Si quod insurgit malum,
        Oppone pectus; si quis excruciat dolor,
        Aperi dolorem.

Cath. Everyone knows the anguish that scourges my soul. [460] The infatuation of my royal husband—that is my misery.

Thom. You weep for things the future may bring; uncertainty causes such profound anguish. We must adjust ourselves to the times and never despair. This infatuation will dash itself to pieces by its own force.* The King, by temperament, [465] cannot stand being enslaved for any length of time.

Cath. Love does not follow rules. Unless the King becomes jaded, he will never want to relinquish this attachment. Once bewitched he will plunge headlong into infidelity.

Thom. The English people will not tolerate this crime.*

Cath. Many of them will, and wicked counselors will win the King over to their side.*

Thom. [470] You will live to see better times.

Cath. Oh, yes, to be sure—when I shall be deprived of palace, kingdom, and throne! As far as I can see, this is all the future holds for me.

Thom. Put away this foreboding! Our England will never reject her Queen.

Cath. The King's salvation is the point of dispute here; he himself finds fault with our marriage and denies its validity. [475] He can bring no

    Cath.   Quisquis est nostrum dolor
    Animum flagellans, notus est cunctis dolor.
460 Amor ille regis coniugis, meus est dolor.
    Thom. Ventura luges; tantus incerta dolor
    Causa creatur; tempori aptari decet,
    Sperare semper: impetu sese suo
    Amor iste franget;* indoles Regis diu
465 Servire nescit.
    Cath.   Non capit leges amor
    Nisi se fatiget, cedere haud unquam volet.
    Et fascinatus in nefas praeceps ruet.
    Thom. Scelus istud Anglus non feret.*
    Cath.   Multi ferent
    Et prava Regem Consilia secum auferent.*
470 *Thom.* Meliora cernes.
    Cath.   Nempe cum expellar domo,
    Regno, throno; restat hoc unum, reor.
    Thom. Tolle omen istud, nostra Reginam Anglia
    Nunquam repellet.
    Cath.   Regis hic agitur salus;
    Accusat ipse nuptias, negat ratas.
475 Obiicere crimen non potest; pellex placet,

accusation against me; his mistress pleases him, his chaste wife does not.
Thom. Passionate love is always short-lived; she who now gratifies the
King will soon incur his displeasure.*

Cath. I know not. A horrible fear engulfs my mind, a chill crawls through
my body, [480] and the dubious evidence of nightly dreams* tortures my
breast. Fallen into fitful slumber, I saw the royal crown snatched from
my head and the scepter slip from my grasp. I jumped up shuddering,
standing there stunned, but nevertheless later I find myself being driven
from the royal palace.

Thom. [485] That dream-filled night is deceptive; its evidence is unre-
liable and sleep gives rise to groundless grief. The truth is that your heart
can hardly be untroubled by some kind of anxiety: the strength of a
noble nature finds so many unjust affronts unendurable. [490] But there
is still good reason for hope. The English, the Pope, the Emperor, your
own country of Spain will defend your cause; I myself shall do whatever
is possible in your behalf, even if I must expose myself to the sword.

Cath. I am grateful for your devotedness. When you approach the King,
[495] Thomas, defend my cause. Servants, come with me; your grief is
proof of your love.

      Et casta Coniux displicet.
      Thom.   Brevis est furor
      Ab amore semper; illa quae Regi placet,
      Mox displicebit.*
      Cath.   Nescio, mentem timor
      Percellit atrox, serpit in corpus gelu,
480 Et dubia noctis pectus excruciat fides.*
      Vidi soporem membra cum caperent levem
      Diadema raptum vertici, & sceptrum meas
      Liquisse dextras; horrui, exilui, steti
      Attonita, sed mox Regia avellor domo.
485 *Thom.* Nox ista fallit, fluxa noctis est fides,
      Umbratilique somnus imponit dolo.
      Equidem dolore vix potest aliquo tuum
      Carere pectus; indolis magnae vigor
      Iniuriarum ferre tot fraudes nequit.
490 Sperare liceat attamen: Causam tuam
      Defendet Anglus, Pontifex, Caesar, tua
      Ibera Tellus; pectus hoc siquid potest,
      Etiam patebit ultimae pro te neci.
      Cath. Grata est voluntas ista; si Regem petas.
495 Defende causam More. Vos mecum meae
      Venite Famulae, vester in nostro est dolor
      Amore.

1 Ser. Your grief makes us sad. As long as the heart of Your Highness keeps beating with anguish, your delicate body can find no repose.

Cath. [500] It is my nature to fear any evil that threatens.

2 Ser. Nothing unfortunate can happen to the Queen without making my heart tremble with renewed pain.

Cath. Come with me; let God dispose of everything.

ACT II, scene ii

King Henry, Brian, Anne

Hen. Tell me, Brian,* what is the latest rumor about your King?

Bri. [505] That the King is solicitous about his spiritual welfare. After all, one's personal salvation, in itself, is more important than a whole kingdom.

Hen. What do they say about Anne?

Bri. A woman worthy of the royal bed, a virgin worthy of the scepter, and a companion worthy of your love.

Hen. [510] And my nobles? And Parliament? What is their reaction?

Bri. Whatever pleases the King pleases them; one's peace of soul, they say, must always be one's first concern.

Hen. Still, we fear them.

       Ped. I Noster in tuo est luctu dolor,
       Et dum dolore Regium pectus fremit,
       Artus tenellos nulla pertentat quies.
500 *Cath.* Meum est timere quicquid impendet mali.
       Ped. II Nihil evenire triste Reginae potest,
       Quin hoc ruinis terreat pectus novis.
       Cath. Venite mecum; cuncta disponat Tonans.

ACTUS SECUNDUS, scena ii

Henricus Rex, Brianus, Bolena

       Hen. Briane,* dic quae fama iam Regis tui est?
505 *Bri.* Regem salutis esse sollicitum suae.
       Namque una toto potior est regno salus.
       Hen. Quid de Bolena?
       Bri.   Regio dignam toro,
       Dignamque sceptro virginem, dignam tuo
       Amore amicam.
510 *Hen.*   Nobiles ecquid mei?
       Ecquid Senatus?
       Bri.   Quod placet Regi, placet;
       Curanda semper, inquiunt, primum est salus.
       Hen. Istos veremur attamen.

Bri. A few of them are troubled with certain fears, but exactly why, they do not know. No king worries about the opinions of his subjects. [515] Nobles follow a king when he favors them. The hope of promotion binds them fast. No one should pass judgment on his own sovereign.

Hen. But* the clerics, what do they think of me?

Bri. They keep complaining and search out reasons. Divided sympathies already cause many views. [520] Many refuse to approve; but more do approve.

Hen. And you, Brian, what is your opinion?

Bri. Whatever kings find agreeable is lawful,* for laws do not bind kings. The things they like are good things and hence permissible to rulers. It is the pleasure of kings to love what they want, in the first place, [525] and then to enjoy it; toil is meant for their subjects.

Hen. Excellent! This lady is a pleasure to me; she is my heart, my hope. Anne, pay no more heed to pale-faced fear,* let your gnawing scruples be banished. You will find rapture in the arms of your King.

Anne. [530] You will be free to enjoy my love whenever you wish, but on this condition: you will marry a modest virgin, one chaste and virtuous. I have kept myself inviolate. As for me, your love already per-

      Bri.   Paucos timor
      Invasit aliquis, causa quae sit, haud sciunt.
      Iudicia populi nemo Rex curat sui.
515 Regem sequuntur Nobiles quando favet.
      Spes dignitatis allicit; Iudex sui
      Nemo esse Regis debet.
      Hen.   Ast* ordo sacer.
      Quid ille de me?
      Bri.   Murmurat, causas petit,
      Divisa partes studia iam multas habent.
520 Probare multi non volunt, plures probant.
      Hen. Quid tu Briane?
      Bri.   Regibus quicquid lubet
      Istud licet:* nam Iura Reges non ligant.
      Quae grata sunt, sunt licita regnanti bona.
      Amare primum quod volunt, dein frui,
525 Regum est voluptas; subditos decet labor.
      Hen. Agedum voluptas haec mea est; hoc cor meum,
      Haec spes; Bolena, pallidum excutias metum,*
      Et mordicantes exulent curae procul.
      Fies beata Regis amplexu tui.
530 *Bol.* Isto licebit, cum voles, tantum modo.
      Duces pudicam, virginem, castam, probam.
      Fides pudoris integra est. Equidem tuus

vades my heart and innermost being,* the very sight of your face wounds* me with love. Yet never—I swear by [535] the jeweled roofs of heaven, by the homes of gods, by the radiance of ethereal light itself— never shall the cloister of my maidenhood be unlocked except in the bond of marriage.

Hen. Will you still reject the entreaties of the King?

Anne. Let the entreaties be made with modesty.

Hen. [540] They are made with love.

Anne. Entreaties will not overcome a chaste maiden, nor will love.

Hen. The truth is that you know not how to love your King.

Anne. I reverence you as my king; if you so desire, I will love you as my husband. You know how my breast is flaming with ardor. But modesty is my choice.

Hen. [545] Brian, see to it that nothing is wanting to my lady. Repair to the hall, both of you. I shall pause and reflect awhile.

Bri. Here comes Longland; he wishes to speak with the King.

        Mihi iam medullas* tangit, & fibras amor,
        Tuoque vultu vulneror,* nunquam tamen,
535 (Gemmata Coeli tecta, Divorum Domos
        Ipsumque testor lucis aethereae iubar)
        Nunquam pudoris claustra solventur mei
        Nisi nuptiarum vinculo.
        Hen.   Regis preces
        Etiam repelles?
        Bol.   Cum pudore sint preces.
540 *Hen.* Cum amore sunt.
        Bol.   Nec virginem solvent preces
        Nec amor pudicam.
        Hen.   Nempe tu nescis tuum
        Amare Regem.
        Bol.   Te meum Regem colo:
        Si vis amabo coniugem. Nosti meum
        Quo flagret igne pectus, at pudor placet.
545 *Hen.* Briane, cura ne quid huic desit meae.
        Subite in Aulam, consilia volvam hic mea.
        Bri. Longlandus ecce, Regis affatum petit.

ACT II, scene iii
King Henry, Longland

Hen. As the sea driven steadily by the angry south wind falls this way or that as the waves buckle,* [550] so runs the life of kings. One flood of troubles sweeps in and another flood follows in its wake; there are no calm seas for men who rule. If a prince finds anything at all to his liking, the mob is set against it. Furthermore, they all want to pass judgment on a prince; he cannot enjoy himself freely. Even so, I swear [555] by the majesty of the shining heavens that either I will get what I want or turn everything topsy-turvy. No rebellion against a king is justified.* Let them accuse me, let them condemn me, let them rage!* Anne shall assume the scepter and the royal throne.* This is my pleasure, this is what I want. [560] Longland, what have you to say?

Long. I have obeyed your orders; your cause has utterly failed. The decision you crave is not sufficiently justified by law. Everyone regards your marriage as valid; only a few people have any doubts on the question. Take this law also to heart: follow what the learned wish. [565] Believe me, Your Highness, there is only one way to insure your salvation. Do not alter what the Father of bishops* has unequivocally validated by law.

ACTUS SECUNDUS, scena iii
Henricus Rex, Longlandus

Hen. Ut semper aequor turbido impulsum noto
Vel huc vel illuc fluctibus fractis* cadit;
550 Sic vita Regum; turba curarum influit
Et turba rursum; nulla regnantum est quies.
Si arridet aliquid Principi, haud vulgo placet.
Et iudicare principem cuncti volunt.
Nunquam voluptas libera est. Testor tamen
555 Radiantis Aethrae numen, aut votum assequar,
Aut cuncta vertam. Nullus in Regem est satis
Iustus tumultus;* arguant, damnent, fremant,*
Sceptrum Bolena capiet, & Regis thronum.*
Haec est voluptas, & voluntas est mea.
560 Longlande, quid tu?
    Long.   Parui iussis tuis;
Discussa res est tota; nec certi satis
Iuris quod optas. Nuptias cuncti probant;
Dubitare pauci vix queunt. Menti tuae
Hanc adde legem; quod volunt docti, sequi.
565 Una est salutis, crede Rex, certae via,
Quod lege certa Praesulum sanxit Pater*
Mutare nolle.

Hen. Once more you drag my soul into doubt and confusion.

Long. All England loves the Queen and is solicitous for her; they admire the holiness of her life, [570] her unimpeachable conduct, her
modesty, her piety and faith. Virtue itself cannot provide a loftier ideal.

Hen. I must admit that she possesses all the graces of a virtuous life. So
holy, so modest, so thoughtful in her discourse! Her virtue radiates more
brightly than sunlight. [575] And so, what is to be done? Shall I, the
King, give up what I desire? What I love? That which lies hidden in this
heart? Shall I pluck out my heart? Is there anything at all I should fear?

Long. Perhaps Your Highness should fear the Emperor,* for [580] he
regards the Queen's cause as his own. Believe me, Your Majesty, the
House of Burgundy is distraught about this; so royal a lineage cannot
bear disgrace. It allows its grief to cumulate, then suddenly in one
stride launches out and mercilessly takes vengeance upon whatever
displeases it.

Hen. Again you throw [585] my mind into confusion. The Emperor is
indeed valiant in war and intimidates the whole world with his powerful
army. At this very moment he may be on the verge of attacking my kingdom. Why, alas, why do I speak like a maniac whose mind is jangled!

       Hen.   Rursus in dubios trahis
       Animum tumultus.
       Long.   Tota Reginam Anglia
       Amat, petitque; sanctitas vitae placet,
570 Castique mores, & pudor, pietas, fides.
       Reperire virtus ipsa maiorem nequit.
       Hen. Decus omne, fateor, integrae vitae tulit.
       Tam sancta, tam pudica, tam affatu gravis.
       Virtute radiat, iubare quam Phoebus magis.
575 Quid fiet ergo? deseram quod Rex volo?
       Quod amo? quod isto pectore occlusum latet?
       Meum revellam cor mihi? Nunquid mihi
       Quicquam est timendum?
       Long.   Forsitan Caesar tibi
       Rex, est timendus;* namque Reginae suam
580 Putat esse causam. Crede Rex Burgundica
       Domus hic laborat; dedecus nescit pati
       Regalis ille sanguis, iras colligit,
       Subitoque motu saevit, & quod non cupit
       Severitate vindicat.
       Hen.   Rursum abripis
585 Mentem in tumultus, Caesar est armis potens,
       Validaque totum territat mundum manu:
       Et imminere iam meis regnis potest.
       Quid heu? quid amens corde turbato loquor?

Shall I fear this Emperor? Or wield my scepter? [590] Shall I, a ruler,
obey the Emperor more than I have to? I will get what I want. How I
wish the Pope would look favorably on my predicament! He is greatly
indebted to me;* I came to his aid when he summoned me, I have given
him everything he wanted. Let him repay a favor to one who deserves it.
Long. Rome is [595] already aware of your problem;* the Pope is greatly
disturbed and he grieves over it. He would like to favor you: your deserving qualities affect him deeply. But in order to work out some way of
deciding this difficult case, he is sending a judge from Rome.
Hen. Who is he? Speak out!
Long. Campeggio, one of the cardinals. [600] At the same time Wolsey
has been added as a second judge.*
Hen. Splendid! Now my heart is unfettered, I can consider myself a free
man. Once the case is heard, many false charges will be wiped out. I
shall never object to the judge: let him come to my shores at once.
Long. He is presently arriving at the port of England [605] and entering
the kingdom.*
Hen. Do whatever remains to be done; I commit this to your charge.
Make arrangements for whatever the time demands.
Long. But look! The members of Parliament approach the royal throne.

       Istum verebor Caesarem, & sceptrum geram?
590 Parebo regnans Caesari? Plusquam est satis?
       Fiet, quod opto. Pontifex utinam meos
       Probet dolores! Debet hic multum mihi;*
       Iuvi vocatus, quicquid optavit, dedi.
       Meritis rependat gratiam.
       Long.   Novit tuam
595 Iam Roma causam,* Pontifex motus dolet,
       Favere vellet: merita commotum trahunt.
       At statuat aliquem ut arduae causae modum
       Ab urbe mittit Iudicem.
       Hen.   Quem? edissere.
       Long. E purpuratis Patribus Campegium.
600 Volsaeus alter iunctus est Iudex simul.*
       Hen. Bene est, soluto corde iam liber feror.
       Audita multos causa dissolvet dolos.
       Nunquam recuso Iudicem: actutum meas
       Subeat in oras.
       Long.   Angliae portum tenet,
605 Subitque regnum.*
       Hen.   Perge quod superest, tuis
       Hoc mando curis; quod petit tempus, para.
       Long. Sed en Senatus, Regium accedit thronum.

ACT II, scene iv

King Henry, Members of Parliament,

among them Bishop Fisher, Thomas More, and others

Fish. May Heaven grace your scepter, Great King. You behold here the members of Parliament distressed over the problem [610] of your salvation. We all beseech you to take counsel both for your own sake and for the sake of your country. England extends her hands* and in humble supplication offers the King her tears. Do not ever abandon your wife; she is upright, she is holy, she is a peerless model of resplendent chastity. [615] Mighty is the power of monarchs. Whatever rising sea-bathed Phoebus illumines with his golden torch, whatever on setting he touches when relaxing his reins: all this is the demesne of kings. Earth's people look up to kings with trembling and awe; they reverence kings as people chosen to wield the scepter of the very God. [620] But this Great Being is the Sovereign of kings, the God of kings. Before his majesty the thundering heavens quake and the shades of hell cower* in fear. Before this God, kings too ought ever to stand in awe. If an arrogant monarch angers Heaven by some unspeakable offense, [625] the Almighty hurls his flaming thunderbolts unerringly from a shaken sky. He strikes the proud

ACTUS SECUNDUS, scena iv

Senatus, Henricus Rex,

in Senatu Roffensis Episcopus, Thomas Morus, & Alii

 Rof. Fortunet Aether, Magne Rex, sceptrum hoc tuum.
 Vides Senatum, causa commotum trahit
610 Tuae salutis, consule & regne, & tibi;
 Precamur omnes; Anglia expandit manus*
 Supplexque Regi lachrymas offert suas.
 Nunquam repelle coniugem, sanctam, piam,
 Et castitatis inclytae exemplar novum.
615 Vis magna Regum est; aurea quicquid face
 Surgens ab undis lustrat, aut tegit cadens
 Curru soluto Phoebus; hoc Reges habent.
 Submissa Tellus, ceu vices magni gerant
 Tonantis, illos suspicit, tremit, colit.
620 At ipse Regum Rector, & Regum est Deus,
 Cuius tonantes Numen horrescunt poli,
 Timentque Manes; Hunc decet Reges Deum
 Semper pavescant:* si quis irritet polos
 Superbientis error infandus throni,
625 Frustra haud coruscos aethere incusso globos
 Molitur, altos vertices Regum quatit,

heads of kings, He overthrows entire realms and crushes their peoples. Beware this scourge of God! Beware lest one calamity overwhelm the entire kingdom. He will not tolerate, He will never tolerate,* [630] the impious deed you stubbornly insist on carrying out—of rejecting your wedded wife and dishonoring your sacred marriage bed with a shameful stigma. There is no room for doubt: you are overthrowing a decision established by law, you are denying its validity. Kings' crimes cannot long be kept secret: [635] the news has already spread. This disgusting passion turns kings awry. When sensual pleasure creeps into one's soul, reason is banished from her rightful throne and Venus becomes the heart's absolute monarch. Let this suffice, Your Majesty. Give ear to your councilors: hold fast to your wife [640] and pay no heed to the promptings of illicit passion.

Hen. This discourse on love, Your Excellency, bespeaks your great love for me. You are worried about our salvation and we thank you for your solicitude. But let there be no more fear or anxiety on your part. Have no misgivings about me. I swear by the living God [645] that I yearn, from the very depths of my heart, to save my soul. It is not a question of lust. Until now I have been permitted to spend my days with a holy wife, an illustrious lady of royal lineage and of charming aspect. Until now she has pleased me; but she can do so no longer.

         Et regna vertit integra, & plebem opprimit,
         Istud verendum est, una ne totum premat
         Ruina regnum. Non feret, nunquam feret*
     630 Quod obstinata mente moliris nefas.
         Eiicere ductam coniugem, & foeda sacrum
         Polluere thalamum labe. Non dubio est locus,
         Rem iudicatam solvis, & certam negas.
         Latere Regum scelera non possunt diu,
     635 Iam fama sparsit. Ista transversos agit
         Cupido Reges; cordis imperium Venus
         Exercet omne, ratio deiecta est loco,
         Animum voluptas cum subit. Sit Rex satis,
         Audi monentes, coniugem serva tuam;
     640 Et pone quicquid impius suadet furor.
         Hen. Amoris iste sermo, quem Praesul facis,
         Amoris in me est; nostra tibi curae est salus.
         Gratum est: vereri sed tamen iam sit satis.
         Nihil hic timete, conscium testor Deum,
     645 Amor hoc salutis corde sub nostro latet,
         Non est libido, coniugem sanctam hactenus
         Habere licuit, Regia excelsam domo,
         Vultu Venustam; placuit, ast ultra nequit.

Thom. It is always a wise practice [650] for great kings and princes to show some regard for public opinion. When princes lead scandalous lives, their subjects in turn try to fling off their sacred ties. Your Majesty, assume for the moment that Anne will ascend the royal throne. Imagine her wedded to the King and sharing his royal bed. What will the people say?* The commoners think her disreputable [655] and shameless,* a loose woman who has lost her honor by promiscuous habits. Nearby France is a witness: she was a harlot there.* And our own England is a witness; it was here that the virgin first lost her honor.* Her immorality is the common talk of the people. [660] To think that she, as consort of the King, would touch your scepters with unclean hands! Great King, pay heed to your reputation, for reputation, once injured, seldom returns. Besides, should a heretical woman wed a Christian king? She follows the sect of Luther* and its morals as well. [665] Even the common people are aware of this. Now that you are distinguished with a new title and known as Defender of the Church,* you should maintain your dignity. Rome will never look favorably on this shocking proposal; Rome will condemn it.

Hen. Thomas, your loyalty to the King has already been proven. [670] We are grateful for your opinion. But do not croak out these things again, these remarks of the mob. What you have just said is untrue: Anne is a

       Thom. Consulere famae maximos semper decet
650 Reges, Ducesque; vita cum foeda est Ducum
      Excutere sacrum subditi tentant iugum.
      Age Rex, Bolena regium ascendet thronum?
      Coniuncta Regi regium implebit torum?
      Quid Fama dicet?* Vulgus infamem putat
655 Et impudicam,* prostituto quae suum
      Pudore passim perdita extinxit decus.
      Vicina testis Gallia est, scortum hic fuit;*
      Et nostra testis Anglia est; virgo hic prius
      Fregit pudorem:* fabula & vulgi probrum est.
660 Ut nempe consors Regis impura manu
      Tua sceptra tractet? Magne Rex, famae tuae
      Meminisse debes, laesa vix unquam redit.
      Et Christiano nuberet Regi impia?
      Sectam Lutheri sequitur,* & mores simul.
665 Ea fama vulgi est. Tu tuum serva decus,
      Titulo superbus iam novo, dum Ecclesiae
      Defensor* audis. Roma nam nunquam hoc nefas
      Amica cernet, ipsa damnabit nefas.
      Hen. Probata More iam tua est Regi fides;
670 Grata est voluntas. Ista ne rursum occinas,
      Commenta vulgi; ficta sunt quae iam refers;

virgin; the rumors are unfounded and false. But so it often happens that the common crowd tear even the best people to shreds. Anne despises gossip, her conduct [675] is clothed in virtue. Let this suffice. Now, since there is no time for delay, be first to receive and welcome the judge delegated by Rome. I see him now approaching.

ACT II, scene v

Campeggio, King Henry, Wolsey

Cam. He who rules the city and the world with his sacred authority, the favorable arbiter of kings, [680] bids your kingdom bring you joy.* He embraces his son with holy affection and regards him as his own.

Hen. Long live the Holy Father, the Father of monarchs and the Lord of all things.

Cam. You see before you the judge of the case; the Holy Father has sent me. It is his will that [685] Cardinal Wolsey assist me as judge in the matter.

Hen. May it so be, this is my wish. Let him decide fairly the cause of the error.

Cam. Definite rumors have already swept across Europe. The Pope him-

     Bolena Virgo est, fama mentitur levis,
     Sic saepe lacerat optimos vulgus viros.
     Famam Bolena temnit, involvit suos
675 Virtute mores. Sit satis; nunc dum est opus,
     Quem Roma mittit Iudicem, occursu prius
     Excipite vestro, cerno, namque ad nos subit.

ACTUS SECUNDUS, scena v

Campegius, Henricus Rex, Volsaeus

     Cam. Urbemque & Orbem qui sacra fraenat manu
     Regum secundus Arbiter felix tibi
680 Iubet esse Regnum:* filium amplexu sacrae
     Dilectionis stringit, & retinet suum.
     Hen. Vivat beatus Pontifex, Regum parens,
     Dominusque rerum.
     Cam.   Iudicem causae hic vides;
     Me misit ille, mandat ut causae Arbiter
685 Volsaeus adsit.
     Hen.   Sit licet, votum hoc meum est,
     Decernat aequum quicquid errorem facit.
     Cam. Iam certa totum fama pervasit solum.
     Miratur ipse Pontifex, urget graves

self is dismayed, the Holy Roman Emperor is daily complaining more
bitterly. There is no doubt that everyone is gravely concerned. [690] If
the case could be settled by our own arbitration, the whole world would
rejoice.*

Hen. It is my wish too that you settle the matter. The time has come
when my spiritual welfare must be ruled by your judgment.

Cam. Would it were possible to carry out what justice demands without
raising a controversy.

Wol. It may be possible. We must first [695] encourage the Queen to find
peace of soul, since I feel sure she will so desire. She is modest and holy
and will want a quiet place to live alone.

Cam. Then we must first acquaint ourselves with the Queen's wishes. If
she wants to live by herself, the case is quite settled; if she wishes us to
act as judges, [700] let her be summoned at once to the tribunal.

Hen. Let this be determined immediately. I wish no delay. Wolsey, inform the Queen. Let us go into the Council Chamber; new plans shall
not be wanting.

       Caesar querelas, omnium est certus dolor.
690 Si causa nostro caperet arbitrio modum,
       Gauderet Orbis.*
       Hen.   Opto, vos finem date.
       Regenda vestro iam mea arbitrio est salus.
       Cam. Utinam liceret lite non mota exequi
       Quod poscit aequum.
       Vol.   Forte, Reginae prius
695 Suadenda pax est; ut reor, pacem volet.
       Modesta, sancta est, pacis optabit locum
       Ut sola vivat.
       Cam.   Ergo Reginae prius
       Tentetur animus; sola si vitam expetat;
       Res acta tota est; Iudices si nos volet,
700 Praesto ad tribunal adsit.
       Hen.   Hoc iam sit ratum.
       Nihil moror, Volsaee Reginam mone.
       Subeamus Aulam, consilia non deerunt nova.

ACT II, scene vi

Catherine, Wolsey, Warham

Cath. What is this I hear?* Is it true that the Holy Father has sent judges from Rome to hear my case?

War. [705] Yes, Your Majesty. The Cardinal legate is here from Rome. One must acknowledge him as judge.

Cath. Is this the way the King's stubborn temper mocks me? Does this lust so master the King, now that he is a victim of its blind assault? O Great Father of Heaven, [710] You who see the recesses of hearts and the very fibers of our being, who know the depths and hollows of our breasts, will You allow these things to go on? This criminal folly of the senseless King?

War. Do not let yourself become so agitated. God will direct your cause. [715] Wolsey is approaching.* Perhaps he bears a message.

Wol. Long live the Queen.

Cath. That title sounds strange on your lips.*

Wol. And until this very moment do I pay you reverence.

War. Until this very moment? What do you mean? What are you intimating?

ACTUS SECUNDUS, scena vi

Catharina, Volsaeus, Varamus

  Cath. Quis iste rumor?* Iudices ergo meae
  Ab urbe causae Pontifex Magnus dedit?
705 *Var.* Regina, sic est, purpuratus hic Pater
  Adest ab urbe, Iudicem hunc fas est pati.
  Cath. Ergo obstinatus, Regis insultat furor?
  Et ista coeco corripit victum impetu
  Libido regem? Magne Coelorum Tonans,
710 O qui recessus cordium & fibras vides,
  Imosque scrutans pectorum nosti sinus,
  Et ista pateris? Istud amentis nefas
  Facinusque Regis?
  Var.   Tanta tempestas tuum
  Ne turbet animum, diriget causam Tonans,
715 Volsaeus eccum;* forte mandatum feret.
  Vol. Regina vive;
  Cath.   Nempe, Reginam vocas.*
  Vol. Etiamque veneror hactenus.
  Var.   Nempe hactenus?
  Quid est? Quid urges?

Wol. I bring news of peace, if peace is welcome.

Cath. Peace is welcome, if [720] you leave me peace.

Wol. As you wish. Rome has just sent a judge to investigate your marriage with the King. He may dissolve it or he may ratify it. He has this authority.

Cath. Did you say "to investigate" my marriage with the King?* Before we were married the Pope [725] gave his sanction, his approval, and consent; two great kings joined our hands and ratified our contract; children were born to me and the King; all England rejoiced and the world applauded. Bear in mind that [730] we have lived together these twenty years* and never have even the most honorable men entertained any doubt of the legality of our marriage. Will you now stir up fresh controversy over a matter already settled?* Wolsey, you alone are the one* who is causing this outrage. You are destroying the King. Just because you [735] are overambitious and my nephew the Emperor can no longer support you, you seize upon me. This is why you spew out vile insults and seek to ruin me.

Wol. I am here to encourage a peaceful settlement, if peace is what you wish. If you refuse, the tribunal awaits you.

     Vol.   Nuntium pacis fero
     Si grata pax est.
     Cath.   Grata pax est, si mihi
720 Pacem relinquas.
     Vol.   Si voles, iam Iudicem
     Huc Roma misit, ipse connubium ut tuum
     Cum Rege noscat; solvat, aut ratum probet.
     Haec est potestas.
     Cath.   Nempe connubium ut meum
     Cum Rege noscat?* Pontifex istud prius
725 Sanxit, probavit, annuit; magni duo
     Iunxere Reges dexteras, foedus ratum
     Fecere nostrum, nata proles est mihi
     Regique, tota gratulata est Anglia,
     Applausit Orbis. Ecce bis denos simul
730 Habitamus annos,* certa connubii fides
     Dubios reliquit optimos nunquam viros.
     Quid nunc? & actam rursus agere rem cupis?*
     Volsaee tanti causa tu solus mali es,*
     Perdisque Regem. Scilicet quando tua
735 Gravis est libido, nec tibi Nepos meus
     Favere Caesar iam potest, in me irruis.
     Et dira fundis odia, & exitium ingeris.
     Vol. Suadere pacem venio, si pacem voles;
     Praesto est tribunal si negas.

Cath. Leave the room, go! [740] I will come to the tribunal; my cause emboldens me. O Fate! Will you keep tormenting me endlessly with your reverses of fortune? And shall some fault-finding judge destroy the validity of my marriage? Eternal Father, You see these tears I shed,* [745] You behold my soul's anguish. Oh, grant me some solace from on high!

*Proc.** My Lady, do not vex your heart with such weeping. Look, the King is coming to the tribunal; the judges are likewise present.

ACT II, scene vii

Campeggio, Wolsey, King Henry, Queen Catherine, Brian, Warham

Cam. A peaceful settlement would have been a desirable solution for genuine peace, [750] but there is no hope for that now.* The case demands a judgment, so now we sit as judges. The Supreme Prince and Pontiff of the spiritual realm so ordains. Read the commission so that our official authority and the manner of conducting the suit may be clearly understood.

(*The papal commission is read aloud.*)*

Cath.	Cede hinc, abi,

740 Veniam ad tribunal, causa me audacem facit.
O sors! & usque & usque me iactas tuis
Adversa fatis? Ergo Connubii mei
Quisquam revellet improbans Iudex fidem?
Aeterne Genitor, cernis hos fletus meos*
745 Animi dolores cernis, o aliquod mihi
Solamen a te!
*Proc.**   Domina, ne tanto tuum
Confunde luctu pectus, en Regem vides,
Venit ad Tribunal, Iudices adsunt simul.

ACTUS SECUNDUS, scena vii

Campegius, Volsaeus, Henricus Rex, Catharina Regina, Brianus, Varamus

Cam. Optanda fuerat optimae pacis quies;
750 Spes ista non est;* causa Iudicium petit.
Et nunc sedemus Iudices. Summus iubet
Princeps sacrorum Pontifex. Tabulas lege,
Nostra ut potestas constet, & causae modus.

(*Recitatur Pontificis Mandatum.*)*

Wol. Now the case must be pleaded. Let the King be first, [755] then the Queen. Their Majesties must accept the judges on both sides.

Cam. Brian, speak first for the King; then whoever wishes shall plead the Queen's cause. Order rules the court.

Bri. Since His Majesty so commands, [760] I shall commence the case for the King.*

War. Wait! It is not yet time for that. You must first demand our approval of the two judges.*

Bri. The Pope appointed both judges, for so the commission read; there is no need for delay, their authority is beyond dispute.

War. In spite of the commission, [765] the Queen refuses to consent. Just any judge you please should not and cannot be offered the defendant.

Bri. The commission is definitive, as long as it has not been revoked. Otherwise show the new commission. I shall begin again.

Proc. She appeals to a higher court; you must not yet plead the case. [770] The Queen refuses to acknowledge either the judges or the present location of the trial.

Cath. I appeal to a higher court. Let my judge be the Pope himself.

      Vol. Dicenda nunc est causa, Rex adsit prior,
755 Regina deinde. Ferre Maiestas suos
      Utrimque debet Iudices.
      Cam.   Nunc tu prior
      Pro Rege loquere, deinde Reginae vices
      Quisquis subibit, Ordo Iudicium regit.
      Bri. Pro Rege causam, quando Maiestas iubet
760 Aggrediar.*
      Var.   Agedum postulat nondum hoc locus.
      In hunc & istum Iudicem assensum prius
      Require nostrum.*
      Bri.   Iudices ambos dedit,
      (Recitata lex est) Pontifex; nulla est mora;
      Certa est potestas.
      Var.   Lex sit, assensum negat
765 Regina, quivis non dari Iudex reae
      Debet, potestque.
      Bri.   Certa lex est, quamdiu
      Revocata non est, aut novam legem doce.
      Aggrediar iterum.
      Proc.   Provocat, nondum tibi
      Dicenda causa est: nec locum, nec Iudices
770 Regina patitur.
      Cath.   Provoco, appello; meus
      Sit ipse Iudex Pontifex.

Cam. Why are you not in favor of this tribunal? We are the duly author-ized judges. Produce your rescript;* I myself will be the first to with-draw.

Cath. Neither the location of the trial nor the judges [775] are favorable to my complaint.* The originator of the lawsuit is seated here, the King himself who rules all the territories of England. I am a foreigner. The King knows both judges are obligated to him and his hopes are set on them. He elevated both prelates to office. I call God to witness [780] that no fear about this legal dispute besets my heart.* This case is ours; I appeal to a higher tribunal.

Wol. It is useless, unless you produce a rescript.

Hen. Why do you drench your cheeks with so much weeping, O Queen?* My thoughts certainly are not filled with hatred, but I cannot live with [785] a mind that is aware of its guilt nor these fears of a troubled con-science. I am worried about my salvation. Let the case be pleaded. I so will. Come to a decision, judges, and let there be no more delay.

Cath. Will the judges pay no heed to a case that has been appealed?*

Wol. Your appeal is neither lawful nor just; your case must be pleaded.

Cath. [790] O My King, by these tears,* if you still retain any love for me, behold your wife on her knees before you. Even if you reject me, you

     Cam.   Quid te movet
In hoc Tribunal? Iudices aequi sumus.
Mandata promas,* ipse discendam prior.
     Cath. Nec iste Iudicii locus; nec Iudices
775 Favent querelae.* Litis author hic sedet
Rex ipse cunctas Angliae fraenans plagas;
Ego peregrina. Iudices ambos sibi
Rex obligatos novit, & sperat suos.
Utrumque fecit Praesulem. Testor Deum
780 Pro lite nullus pectus infestat timor;*
Haec causa nostra est, provoco.
     Vol.   Frustra, novam
Vel prome legem.
     Hen.   Quid tuas tanto genas
Regina fletu spargis?* haud odio meus
Animus laborat, conscium pectus pati
785 Istosque dubiae mentis haud possum metus.
Cura est salutis; causa dicatur, volo.
Pronuntiate Iudices, nec sit mora.
     Cath. Nil provocatae Iudices causae dabunt?*
     Vol. Nec fas, nec aequum est, causa dicenda est tibi.
790 *Cath.* O Rex, per istas lachrymas,* si quid mei
Amoris in te est, supplicem cernis tibi,

do behold your own wife, your loving wife. By these hands, by these knees, by your scepter, I beg you, [795] for the sake of my daughter and yours, I implore you. Return some favor for my tears. Grant the wishes of your former beloved wife that the Supreme Pontiff hear and judge your cause and mine.

Hen. Rise, My Queen, I am willing to concede to your wishes.

CHORUS

Of English Maidens

800 Every lover can be swayed
    And is capable of kindness.
    Lust succumbs when the heart
    Trembles with true love.
    The King cannot withstand
805 The tears of his chaste wife.
    The face of this shining star
    Has moved the depths of his soul.
    But Venus cannot long endure
    A check to her bold emprises.
810 He will revert to his evil ways,

    Licet ipse nolis, Coniugem, cernis tuam
    Tuique amantem Coniugem, per has manus,
    Per ista genua, per tuum sceptrum, precor,
795 Per hanc meam, per hanc tuam natam, precor,
    Concede lachrymis aliquid, & quondam tuae
    Concede charae coniugi, Iudex tuam
    Meamque summus Pontifex litem audiat.
    Hen. Regina, surge, quod petis, fiat volo.

CHORUS

Virginum Anglicanarum

800 Quicunque amat flecti potest,
    Humanitatis est capax.
    Libido succumbit sibi,
    Cum pectus affectu tremit.
    Rex ferre non potest suae
805 Lachrymas pudicae coniugis.
    Animumque movit intimum,
    Vultus nitentis syderis.
    Sed ferre non potest diu,
    Venus quod obstat ausibus.
810 Iterum redibit ad nefas,

Once more will his passions flame forth.
Kings are skilled in false pretense,
Apparently conquered, they conquer still.
With no more than a few nods of her head
815 Anne will stir up a raging flame.
Love possesses this great urge:
To endure nothing which chokes its fire.
This is the stubborn force of a woman:
To gain her ends with promises.
820 Conqueror, resist while you are able
For that conqueress besieges,
Anne now claims the King.
She nourishes the fire but refuses her person,
And as she refuses, she fans the flame.
825 She is now his constant damnable companion,
She drags in talk of banquets and bedrooms,
Beguiling the King by drawing him on,
Mangling the King by drawing him on. *
This use of love to hoodwink a victim
830 Is nothing else than a type of perversity.
For love wounds those it delights

Et rursus ardebit iecur.
Simulare Reges sic sciunt
Vincuntur & vincunt tamen.
Paucis Bolena nutibus
815 Flammam excitabit maximam.
Haec est amoris magna vis
Nil ferre quod flammas premit.
Haec foeminae vis pervicax,
Voto potiri quod iuvat.
820 Victor resiste qui potes
Namque illa vincens opprimit
Bolena iam Regem tenet,
Flammam fovet, sed se negat,
Et dum negat flammam fovet.
825 Damnosa lateri fit comes,
Tractat dapes, tractat toros,
Tractando Regem decipit,
Tractando Regem lancinat. *
Perversitatis est genus
830 Miseros amore fallere.
Sic sauciat placens amor,

And slays the wounded even as they love.
But now, O King, you love in vain,
For Rome does not approve your lust.
835 We know that faith is always true
When it approves what God ordained.
Though Rome may be lenient often enough,
She is never inclined to betray the faith.
Judges shall importune the Rota,
840 But they in turn will uphold the marriage.
What the law upholds, no one disputes.
The law is a reliable rule of life.
Equity never approves a crime
When equity rules the tribunal.
845 Despite all this, that hard-hearted goddess
Will strive more fiercely than ever before.
Anne will ascend the royal throne,
Anne will grasp the royal scepter,
Anne will share the royal bed.
850 The throne, the scepter, the bed!
There ever remain the tears to be shed,
There ever remain the tears that are due.

Et amando saucios necat,
Frustra tamen, Rex hic amas.
Nam Roma non probat scelus,
835 Haec certa semper est fides,
Probare quod fecit Deus.
Favere Roma dum solet
Fallere fidem nunquam solet.
Prement Tribunal Iudices
840 Sed hi probabunt nuptias.
Quod lex probat; nemo improbat;
Lex certa vitae regula est.
Non aequitas probat nefas,
Cum fert tribunal aequitas.
845 Crudelis illa plus tamen
Saevire contendet Venus.
Thronum Bolena regium,
Sceptrum Bolena regium
Torum Bolena regium,
850 Ascendet, accipiet, premet.
Restare semper lachrymae,
Restare debent lachrymae.

Maidens, let us withdraw from hence
And let us weep fresh tears.
855 Tears can never move kings,
    Nor can destiny be altered by prayer.
    There remains but to bow down and accept
    The fate awaiting our native land.

    Nos hinc eamus Virgines
    Et lachrymas demus novas,
855 Nequeunt moveri lachrymis;
    Nec fata mutantur prece;
    Subire fortunam decet,
    Quam fata donant patria.

ACT III, scene i

Henry, Campeggio, Wolsey, Brian, Warham

Hen. Judges, let us return to the Council Chamber.* [860] A king should never be detained and the Queen seeks only delay. I cannot control the wayward impulses of my troubled heart. I lose courage; doubts about my salvation disturb and harass me and prove most troublesome. My judges, devote your full time to the case.

Cam. Such indeed is your wish. [865] But the Queen has been allowed a second trial. Furthermore, you have agreed that the Holy Father himself will be judge.

Hen. If she has appealed her cause, I take back the concessions I made. The case must proceed; I refuse to admit any further delay. Judges, come to a decision.

Wol. To forestall delay, [870] let us return to the Council Chamber;* we shall do here whatever we can and let the rest be settled elsewhere.

Bri. In accordance with the King's command, therefore, I shall proceed. I submit the written brief of Pope Julius,* lest there be any grounds for claiming deception. It is based on error.* The list of inaccuracies [875]

ACTUS TERTIUS, scena i

Henricus, Campegius, Volsaeus, Brianus, Varamus

    Hen. Rursum ad tribunal, Iudices;* Nunquam mora
860 Obesse Regi debet, & tantum moram
    Regina quaerit. Pectoris moti vagos
    Superare fluctus nequeo, succumbo mihi,
    Et dubia turbat, vexat, infestat salus.
    Vacate causae Iudices.
    Cam.   Equidem cupis,
865 Alia potestas facta Reginae fuit.
    Et ipse Iudex Pontifex Romae est datus.
    Hen. Si provocavit illa, concessa abnuo,
    Dicenda causa est, ferre iam nolo moras
    Pronuntiate Iudices.
    Vol.   Ne sit mora
870 Iterum ad Tribunal;* quicquid hinc, quicquid potest,
    Pars inde promat.
    Bri.   Regium nutum sequens
    Aggrediar ergo. Iulii scriptum Papae*
    Diploma promo, fraudibus ne sit locus,
    Errore constat:* ordo falsarum patet

is apparent to anyone. King Henry was very young, but this brief makes
no mention of this fact. He was only twelve years old.* The purpose of
the wedding was to insure the peace of the kingdom. But the boy was too
young [880] to think about peace; furthermore, when Catherine as wife
approached the royal bed, King Henry VII, the boy's father, had already
closed his last and fateful days.* Many petitions were addressed to
Rome, written entreaties were sent back and forth. But the youthful
[885] King knew nothing of these transactions;* not one of them bore
his mandate of approval. The Pope removed the impediment of affinity*
—we admit this—but a second impediment rendered the marriage invalid. No pope has the power to remove this latter impediment by his
own authority. [890] The fact is that the Queen was at that time contracted in marriage to Arthur her spouse; as his consort she submitted
to him and surrendered her virginity in wedlock. This basic impediment
of public honesty remains and no power in this world can remove it. No
decree ratified the concessions that followed. [895] Our decision is based
on civil and divine law.

Wol. Both sides of the case must be heard; let the party for the defendant
speak next. It is manifestly unlawful at this point to seek ways of evading
the issues a second time.

875 Cuicunque rerum. Regis Henrici fuit
      Aetas tenella, at istud hoc scriptum negat.
      Nam natus annos ipse bis senos fuit.*
      Hic nuptiarum finis, ut nostri foret
      Pax certa regni: poterat at nondum puer
880 Meminisse pacis; cumque regales toros
      Catharina consors adiit, Henricus Pater
      Tristi supremam clauserat fato diem.*
      Petita Romae multa, descriptae preces,
      Missae, remissae; quicquid est actum, puer
885 Nescivit hic Rex:* cuncta mandato carent.
      Affinitatis Pontifex obicem abstulit*
      Equidem fatemur; alius infirmas obex
      Semper reliquit nuptias, nec hunc suo
      Removere iure Pontifex unquam potest.
890 Coniuncta namque tunc suo Arthuro fuit
      Regina sponso, passa quae coniux virum est,
      Et dissoluto est vinculo exclusus pudor.
      Haeret potestas prima, nec quicquam hic potest.
      Et quod secutum est lege fit nulla ratum.
895 Coelestis haec, & Iuris humani est fides.
      Vol. Dicenda utrimque causa: nunc dicat rea;
      Diffugia rursum quaerere hic certum est nefas.

War. We fear no law,* either new or old, of a strict court of justice. Natural rights approve [900] the Queen's cause. No impediment invalidated the marriage. The King himself has conceded that the case should be appealed, with the Pope as final arbiter. Why is this tribunal reopened? In spite of this, I shall reply. The Queen's cause is entirely defensible from a legal standpoint. [905] You will admit, you say, that the Pope removed the impediment of affinity;* you claim there is a second impediment: namely, that since she was contracted in marriage to her spouse and submitted to him, it was forbidden for her to approach his brother's bed. This argument is fallacious. I shall not waste words but say truthfully [910] that no effect of affinity ever made the marriage invalid. In this case all human laws cease to apply. Nothing can interfere with the contract; no law has any force over it. You say the King was of tender age* at the time of the marriage. Believe me, age is no impediment [915] when the Holy Father proclaims his decision by an immutable decree. The royal alliance was an augury of peace;* the land of Britain has experienced the fruits of peace. I call to witness the territories of England that on all sides look down at the heaving sea. [920] Never could this kingdom enjoy greater prosperity. Our country is free

        Var. Nullam severi iuris aut legem novam,*
        Veterem aut veremur; iura Reginae probant
900 Humana causam, nuptias nullus ratas
        Obex resolvit. Provocatae cesserat
        Rex ipse causae, Summus est Iudex Papa.
        Cur hoc tribunal rursus? at dicam tamen,
        Carere iure causa Reginae nequit,
905 Affinitatis Pontifex obicem abstulit,*
        Fateris, inquis: alter est obex ais,
        Coniuncta sponso passa coniux est virum,
        Adire fratris potuit, haud unquam torum.
        Haec causa duplex. Verba non fallax feram,
910 Affinitatis ergo nulla vis ratas
        Dissolvit unquam nuptias: hic omnia
        Humana cessant iura, nil pactis obest,
        Vis nulla legum. Fuerit aetatis puer*
        Tum Rex tenellae; crede, non aetas obest,
915 Cum lege certa summus edicit ratum,
        Quod vult Sacerdos, Pacis augurium fuit*
        Regale foedus, pacis experta est bonum
        Brittana Tellus. Angliae testor plagas,
        Quacunque tumidum parte despiciunt mare,
920 Florere nunquam posset hoc regnum magis.

from war, all good things flow in desirable abundance. Your Sacred
Majesty, I here ask you to recall, as I swear by your scepter, that you
were often wont to say, [925] "This era of renewed prosperity is due to
my wife. It is the Queen and no other who blessed my kingdom with her
tears." But she submitted as wife to another man, the King's brother.*
O Monarch of Heaven, permit me to swear by your majesty and by the
sun's radiance: [930] Henry VII took precautions lest his son Arthur
be allowed to sleep with his spouse;* she was entrusted to a matron because the languishing prince was at the time afflicted with an infectious
disease. The Queen herself has testified that the marriage was not consummated.* Your Majesty, [935] I again call upon your memory,* I appeal to your word of honor: when she entered your royal bed she was
found to be a virgin. This is your own statement; I establish our case on
the honor of a king's word. Any objection you advance is inconsequential.
Furthermore the judges see the light of the truth. [940] It is improper to
engage in legal disputes over such petty subterfuges when the case of the
King is keeping the entire court on edge.
Cam. The case has been heard. Now what is the trouble? What do these
people want?

His arma cessant, omnium ubertas fluit
Optata rerum, Sacra Maiestas, tuam hic
Appello mentem, testor hoc sceptrum tuum,
Saepe, inquiebas, ista debentur novae
925 Felicitatis tempora uxori meae.
Una est beatum quae facit regnum suis
Regina lachrymis. Passa sed coniux virum est,*
Regisque fratrem. Si licet, testor tuum
Coeli Monarcha Numen, & Phoebi iubar.
930 Ne iungeretur coniugi Arthurus suae*
Pater ante cavit, cura matronae data est
Nam tabe Princeps corpus infirmum gravi
Languens trahebat; ipsa confessa est* probae
Regina vitae, rursus appello tuam
935 Rex magne mentem,* regiam appello fidem;
Inventa virgo est cum tuum intravit torum.
Tua ista vox est, regia nostram fide
Confirmo causam. Quicquid opponis, cadit;
Et veritatis Iudices lucem vident
940 Certare levibus non decet tantum dolis
Cum causa regis anxium exercet forum.
Cam. Audita causa est; quid tamen? quid hi volunt?*

ACT III, scene ii

Fisher, Campeggio, Wolsey, Ridley, King Henry

Fish. This is a new kind of tribunal,* a new type of trial. A court of law such as this is unusual for our kings. [945] The King himself pleads his case; the Queen in person is made the defendant. Majesty itself is on trial. Our morals have disintegrated; we no longer stand in awe of the eternal verities of Heaven. Behold, at this very moment the unimpeachable honor of the marriage tie is being threatened. Judges, it is not enough* [950] just to sit on those legal benches; here a great battle is being waged with trifling speeches. The case has been sufficiently probed and you have been assured without doubt of the King's spiritual wellbeing. That which is in jeopardy is the welfare of England our country.* Keep this thought uppermost. Stop these legal bickerings. [955] Look! The case has been settled in print.* Whoever challenges it is an enemy challenging the faith. God regards this heart, He sees the very marrow of my bones and the innermost recesses of my soul. If I have written lies,* let Him hurl on me flaming spheres that burst the clouds, [960] let Him plunge my head into the black Stygian waters. The divine prophecies of sacred scripture bear out everything this book contains. If the case so

ACTUS TERTIUS, scena ii

Roffensis, Campegius, Volsaeus, Rydlaus, Henricus Rex

    Roff. Novum hoc tribunal,* forma iudicii haec nova.
    Inusitatum Regibus nostris forum.
945 Rex ipse causam dicit, & causam simul
    Regina dicit; ipsa Maiestas rea est.
    Periere mores, Aetheris Magni polos
    Nondum veremur: certa connubii fides
    En hic laborat. Iudices, non est satis*
950 Solia ista premere; levibus hic ingens modo
    Fit pugna verbis, causa perspecta est satis
    Et nota vobis Regis in certo est salus,
    Periclitatur Angliae regni salus.*
    Hoc cogitate. Tollite ambages fori,
955 En scripta causa est,* quisquis oppugnat, fidem
    Oppugnat hostis. Cernit hoc pectus Tonans
    Istas medullas cernit, atque animi sinus,
    Si falsa scripsi* flammeos ruptis globos
    Iaculetur in me nubibus, caput hoc stygi
960 Immittat atrae. Sacra divini probant
    Oracla verbi quicquid hic claudit liber.

demands, I shall offer my life as testimony. Whatever blood remains in
this aged body of mine will bear witness to what I have said. Your
Majesty, [965] I testify by Heaven that there is no law on earth that has
the power to break the bond of your marriage. Study these books I have
here, and these.* Each and every rank of people devoted to spiritual
affairs within the realm is greatly disturbed.

Cam. Put down those books. And you, Ridley, what do you want to urge
in this matter?

Rid. I address the court* and this tribunal because I am roused [970] by
the injustice of this process. The legates are taking sides. The righteous
cause of the defendant is in jeopardy when a judge lacks courage. And
even though the case is clear, he cannot bring himself to pass judgment.
Where now is the strict sense of justice England once knew? Truth herself is feared, or else she is [975] hidden in the light she radiates. Look,
the radiance of this truth shines forth in these volumes. Ecclesiastical law
here confirms that the King's marriage is valid. This is the considered
opinion of righteous men. England is on the brink of ruin, victim to her
own injuries. Once the Queen [980] forsakes the royal chambers, dissensions, new sects, and doubts in the matters of faith will cleave the kingdom inwardly. The Emperor will foment wars and threaten our shores.
Then will citizens rush armed upon fellow-citizens; the price of madness

> Si causa poscit, morte testabor mea.
> Si quis senili est corpore in nostro cruor
> Vocem hanc probabit. Nuptias, O Rex, tuas,
> 965 Sit testis Aether, solvere in terris potest
> Vis nulla legum. Cernite hos, & hos libros;*
> Laborat ordo quisquis in regno est sacer.
> *Cam.* Depone libros; tu quid in causam hanc moves?
> *Ryd.* Iniquitate motus accedo forum;*
> 970 Et hoc tribunal. Arbitri in partes eunt,
> Iusta hic laborat causa dum Iudex timet;
> Et iudicare clara dum res est nequit.
> Ubi nunc severus Angliae quondam rigor?
> Etiam timetur Veritas; aut est sua
> 975 Invisa luce; lucis istius iubar
> En his refulget in libris; legum sacra
> Hic iura Regis nuptias firmas docent.
> Vox haec bonorum est. Anglia incumbit suis
> Iam prona damnis, deserat nam si suum
> 980 Regina thalamum schismata & sectae novae
> Dubiaque penitus dividet regnum fides.
> Hinc bella diris Caesar urgebit minis,
> Armatus inde Civis in Civem ruet,

will be that England shall fall to the sword.

Hen. [985] Judges, do you still remain undecided?* These men who pour out long speeches entertain fears that are groundless.

Cam. Let us not pass hasty judgment on a serious matter;* truth is favored by cautious deliberation. A man who judges hastily is usually unfair.

Hen. The problem is clear-cut and cries out for immediate decision. [990] You are not leaving the court yet?*

Cam. Yes, Your Highness, you will have to bear with these delays if the case proceeds slowly. A Roman legate does not make hasty decisions.

Wol. Nor have I the authority to settle the case* by my verdict alone. Your Majesty, be patient for a little while; [995] then summon this tribunal again when you so wish.

ACT III, scene iii

King Henry, Thomas More

Hen. What shall I do now? Look how my heart quakes with terror. Anger mounts up within me; love, like a serpent, glides through my veins. I am snatched up and swept along like the shifting sea. Why does my soul cower in hesitation? Could it be that I shall be forced to yield? [1000]

       Pretium furoris Anglia in ferrum cadet.
985 *Hen.* Haeretis iterum Iudices?* frustra timent
       Qui verba fundunt.
       Cam.   Subita ne properes rei*
       Iudicia magnae, veritas amat moram,
       Qui iudicando properat, iniustus fere est.
       Hen. Res ipsa poscit clara iudicium breve.
990 Etiam tribunal deseris?*
       Cam.   Sic est opus
       Si sera causa est Magne Rex patere has moras,
       Iudicia Romae subita Iudex non facit.
       Vol. Nec ipse nostro solus arbitrio* queo
       Finire causam; patere Rex tempus breve;
995 Et hoc tribunal coge cum rursus voles.

ACTUS TERTIUS, scena iii

Henricus Rex, Thomas Morus

       Hen. Quid igitur? Ecce pepulit hoc pectus tremor.
       Consurgit ira, serpit in fibras amor,
       Instabilis instar aequoris raptus feror.
       Quid, Anime, titubas? Vincar, & quod Rex volo
1000 Non obtinebo? Non decet Regem sequi

Shall I fail to achieve what I want? I, the King? It is not right for a king to submit to legal decisions; no king acknowledges a judge over him. I myself will be my own judge. Oh, Anne, how fiercely you smite my heart! Oh, Anne, with what terror you disturb my kingdom! Everyone detests you; I alone love you, the King alone. [1005] All England rises as your enemy. But come what may, I will bear it all for your sake. This love will turn to madness, or else they will approve this woman the King demands as his wife.

Thom. Your Majesty, if you have a moment,* I shall be brief.

Hen. [1010] Feel completely free to say what you will, Thomas.

Thom. I am here at the Queen's request.* It is her prayer that God may long preserve the King and his wife. Furthermore, Your Majesty must be informed that [1015] the Holy Father is recalling to Rome the judge he sent some time ago. He himself will act as judge; the case must be pleaded in Rome.

Hen. I am willing to have it so. I shall give special attention to the case so that the Holy Father may find the solution.

Thom. Your Majesty, you should have the papal commission announced publicly.

Hen. It suffices that I know of it; see that the legates are informed. [1020] Thomas, I know that you are courageous,* you have good judgment and

        Iudicia Legum; Iudicem nullus suum
        Rex confitetur; ipse mihi Iudex ero.
        Bolena, quanto pectus hoc motu quatis!
        Bolena, quanto concutis regnum metu!
1005 Te odere cuncti, solus ego te Rex amo.
        Consurgit hostis Anglia, et pro te feram,
        Quicquid ferendum est; hic amor fiet furor.
        Aut hanc probabunt coniugem, quam Rex volo.
        Thom. Rex magne, pauca proloquar, si das moram.*
1010 *Hen.* Eloquere More: plena libertas tibi est.
        Thom. Regina mittit,* quem vides; ut te Tonans
        Regem suumque Coniugem servet diu
        Eadem precatur. Scire Maiestas tua,
        Iam debet istud; Iudicem missum prius
1015 Revocat in urbem Pontifex; Iudex erit,
        Dicenda Romae est causa.
        Hen.   Dicatur, volo.
        Curabo causae ut Pontifex addat modum.
        Thom. Rex magne, publicare mandatum decet.
        Hen. Satis ipse novi; facite Legati ut sciant.
1020 Dic More, novi pectus* & mentem & fidem;

you are loyal. Tell me, will you approve of the King's new marriage?

Thom. I will never approve of it; you are looking upon a man whose mind is free. I will never approve.

Hen. And if I should want you to approve?

Thom. That which princes want is not always lawful. Your Majesty, let it be not your intention [1025] to reject your first wife. Such a decision will bring ruin on yourself and your kingdom.

Hen. Approve my course of action, Thomas. You shall rise to new offices in my service.

Thom. No man shall ever change my stand on this question, even though the highest-ranking [1030] position in your court might be mine. An upright man remains steadfast. One who is swayed by favors promised him cannot remain upright.

Hen. You will do nothing for me, Thomas?

Thom. Your Majesty, I will do anything for you. I will even submit to a violent death if it must be. But my conscience can make no concessions [1035] when you pursue something forbidden by law. I beseech Your Majesty to forsake your heart's desire.

Hen. You had better leave; you are asking for trouble in advance.

Thom. Behold, Your Majesty, the Queen approaches. Give your wife audience.

      Nunquid probabis nuptias Regis novas?
      Thom. Nunquam probabo: liberam mentem vides,
      Nunquam probabo.
      Hen.   Si velim?
      Thom.   Non hoc licet
      Quod semper optant Principes. Ne Rex velis,
1025 Eijcere primam coniugem si mens tibi est,
      Tibi tuaeque Patriae exitium paris.
      Hen. Mihi acquiesce, More, tu per me novo
      Honore surges.
      Thom.   Nullus hanc mentem mihi
      Mutabit unquam, sit licet primus tua
1030 Honos in Aula; vir bonus constans manet,
      Quem dona flectunt esse non potest bonus.
      Hen. Nil, More, pro me?
      Thom.   Crede Rex pro te omnia
      Et hoc acerbae corpus impendam neci
      Si sit necesse: ratio permittit nihil,
1035 Moliris istud quando quod leges vetant.
      Rex oro muta cordis hoc votum tui.
      Hen. Hinc tu recede, quod petis curae ocyus.
      Thom. Regina, Rex, en prodit, audi Coniugem.

ACT III, scene iv

Catherine, Henry, their daughter Mary

Cath. We are leaving, then, my dear husband. [1040] How the sound of that name afflicts my soul! To think that a husband should be free to cast out his own wife! To think that I, who once enjoyed your complete devotion, should now be banished from your heart. What a bitter fate! O Fortune, are you heaping these calamities upon me? Forcing me to leave you, O King? To be exiled from your palace? [1045] You will cause me less pain if you demand the last drop of my blood, cleave my heart with a sword, and pierce this bosom whose secrets you shared. There lies hidden in this heart more love than all the blood you will demand, my husband.

Hen. Husband? Why do you call me by this dubious title?

Cath. Do you think it dubious? [1050] It was no dubious wife that bore you this daughter. Will you, her father, insist on banishment?

Hen. Granted that this is our child, my mistake must be blamed on fate.

Cath. You, her father, want to blame fate for your daughter and your wife. Is it possible? [1055] O land of Spain, why did I forsake you? Why, O England, did I set foot on your shores? I could have lived in obscurity,

ACTUS TERTIUS, scena iv

Catharina, Henricus, Maria Filia

     Cath. Abimus ergo, chare Coniux, O nimis
1040 Mihi triste nomen! coniugem ut coniux suam
     Ultro repellat? iam tuo tota excidi
     Amata quondam pectore. O fatum grave!
     O sors! & istas ingeris clades mihi?
     Ut te relinquam? deseram hanc Aulam tuam?
1045 Potius per istud pectus, & notos tibi
     Sinus, cruoris ultimas guttas mei
     Ferro require; plus amoris hic latet,
     Quam tu cruoris exiges. Coniux.
     Hen.   Quid est?
     Dubium quid istud nomen?
     Cath.   Et dubium tibi?
1050 Hanc cerne prolem; Filiam hanc coniux tibi?
     Non dubia peperi. Nunquid eiiecies parens?
     Hen. Sit ista nata nostra, fortunae est meus
     Tribuendus error.
     Cath.   Nempe fortunae tuam
     Tribuere natam Genitor, & sponsam voles?
1055 Ibera Tellus cur reliqui te! tuos
     Britanna Tellus cur subivi limites!

but brightly have I shone on the Queen's throne. Would I had remained unknown—far better had I dwelt in the courts of my birth! But, oh, my husband! [1060] My dear husband!

Hen. Perhaps I was your husband when I considered this title a result of my marriage contract. But now the error has been exposed; I free myself from its restraint.

Cath. Will you deny your title of husband? Then recognize my other title, Your Majesty.

Hen. The problem at hand has no bearing on my kingship. [1065] The question concerns my spiritual welfare; I need the verdict of a judge.

Cath. Bear contentedly, then, with any delays the judge demands. Why do I, who have been your wife up to this time, displease you now? If I have been guilty of anything, tell me where I have failed. Whatever fault there may have been, on my knees I entreat you, my husband, to pardon it. You see me kneeling as your suppliant. [1070] Shall I say "your suppliant"? I am yours and, behold, this is your own daughter you gaze upon.

Hen. Rise, do not kneel.

Cath. By what title am I bidden to rise? As a poor, banished, unfaithful woman?*

Hen. I bid you rise as Queen.

Cath. If you address me by this title, I appeal as Queen to the sacred

---

        Latere potui; clara Reginae in throno
        Fulsi, ut laterem: melius ah! melius lares
        Potui paternos colere, Coniux O tamen!
1060 O chare Coniux!
        Hen.   Forsitan coniux fui,
        Hoc dum putabam foederis nomen mei,
        Nunc est apertus error, errorem exuo.
        Cath. Istud negabis nomen? admitte alterum.
        O Rex!
        Hen. In isto non ago Regem loco.
1065 Causa est salutis, iudicis vocem peto.
        Cath. Patere ergo quicquid postulat Iudex morae.
        Cur ante Coniux displiceo? Si quod meum est.
        Oppone crimen; si quod est, supplex precor
        Ignosce Coniux; supplicem cernis tuam
1070 Tuamne dicam? Sum tua, & natam tuam
        Hic ecce cernis.
        Hen.   Surge, ne terram premas;
        Cath. Quaenam ergo surgam? misera, deiecta, impia?*
        Hen. Regina surge.
        Cath.   Nomen hoc si das mihi,

honor of the King. [1075] No one can be Queen who is not at the same time your wife. Do you still not acknowledge me as wife? As your wife?
Hen. Rise, my wife.
Cath. My husband, I call upon your royal honor, upon the sacred rights of our marriage contract, and pray with suppliant hands and knees and in the name [1080] of this daughter of ours that you rid your heart of this shameful love. Lust alone, like an infamous monster, possesses you; look to your own reputation and mine. You will settle this case all by yourself—once this foul lust forsakes your heart.
Hen. [1085] This is not the reason. The stigma attached to the royal household forces me into this position. Will you take it upon yourself to rule my passionate soul?
Cath. Do not forget me.
Hen. I will not.
Cath. Remember your child. Look on this daughter, she is yours.
Hen. I acknowledge her as mine.
Mary. Father, have pity on my mother and [1090] have pity on your daughter.
Hen. Do not worry, Daughter, I will not forget you.
Mary. Have pity on my mother.

      Regina sacram Regis appello fidem
1075 Regina nulla est, aut simul coniux tua est.
      Nondumne nostri coniugem? nondum tuam?
      Hen. Assurge Coniux.
      Cath.   Per tuam Coniux fidem,
      Per sacra nostri iura coniugii precor,
      Per has manus, per hos pedes, per hanc meam
1080 Tuamque Natam, cordis excludas tui
      Turpes amores, una te infestat Venus
      Infame monstrum; consule & famae tuae
      Meaeque solus finies litem arbiter
      Libido pectus foeda si linquat tuum.
1085 *Hen.* Non ista causa est, Regiae opprobrium Domus
      Me cogit; ipsa fervidam hanc mentem regas?
      Cath. Mei memento.
      Hen.   Sum memor.
      Cath.   Prolis memor.
      En ista proles est tua.
      Hen.   Agnosco meam.
      Mar. Miserere Matris Genitor, & natae tuae
1090 Miserere.
      Hen.   Nata, sit satis, iam sum memor.
      Mar. Miserere Matris.

Hen. My daughter, your mother will experience no sorrow. What can I do to help you?
Cath. Let him do what a husband should do for his wife. Let him do what a king should do when [1095] his queen demands his loyalty.
Hen. Go now, you will lack nothing. I shall grant whatever royal majesty prescribes.

ACT III, scene v

Heresy, Lust, Impiety, Tyranny, King Henry

Her. See how he pines away, so helpless, so sad and listless. How he paces up and down. Look how his conscience grieves him. Take care that I do not lose him. [1100] The basic principles of our kingdom are strong concupiscence, rejected piety, and brute force. Stir up again the fires of his heart; let him burst into flames, let Anne torment his soul and arouse his passions.
Lust. Have you no blood in your veins? Your limbs are freezing with fear* [1105] and still you claim to love Anne? You do not love her, you have forgotten her completely. That very lady, yes, she who was the goddess of your heart! She, the radiance of your life, the lovely radiance of your life,* and now you no longer love her?

    Hen.   Nulla miseria est tuae
    O Nata Matris. Facere quid pro te queo?
    Cath. Faceret maritus quod sua pro coniuge;
    Faceretque quod Rex regiam quando fidem
1095 Regina poscit.
    Hen.   Vade nil deerit tibi
    Praestabo quicquid Regium debet decus.

ACTUS TERTIUS, scena v

Haeresis, Luxuria, Impietas, Tyrannis, Henricus Rex

    Haer. Ut ecce languet? impotens, tristis, vagus,
    Ut huc & illuc errat? ut sentit sui
    Animi labores? Agite ne pereat mihi,
1100 Initia nostri prima sunt regni, potens
    Libido, pietas pulsa, crudelis manus,
    Renovate flammas cordis, in flammas eat.
    Bolena mentem turbet, & motus ciet.
    Lux. Etiamne friges? membra torpescunt gelu*
1105 Et amas Bolenam? non amas, tota excidit;
    Illa, illa, sacrum cordis idolum tui.
    Lux illa vitae, grata lux vitae tuae;*
    Nec amas Bolenam?

Hen. I feel my whole being burning with desire. I love Anne, she is the beloved light of my life. [1110] But so many, alas, so very many people are anxious to prevent the fulfillment of my desires. The very heavens conspire against me. All of them are striving with every means in their power to destroy my love.

Imp. And meanwhile you are sick with fear, you worry about the marriage bond, you fear new legislation. [1115] When kings change the laws, they inevitably change them for their own advantage.*

Hen. England dreads the prospect of ruin, she fears war. Even at this moment she senses the invasion of countless terrors and disasters.

Tyr. Your Majesty's courage is already dwindling. A king who wants to rule by force despises all these threats. [1120] He strengthens his military forces, his hand consolidates royal authority by brandishing the sword. When a king fails to use force he is reduced to praying; but prayers do not befit a king. It is for kings to command; let him die who disobeys.

Hen. I love Anne; I swear by these flames in my heart [1125] that I love her. No one shall stand in my way. My mind is made up: either the judges will dissolve my marriage bonds at once or I will straightway put

      Hen.   Sentio ignescunt fibrae,
      Amo Bolenam; grata lux vitae est meae.
1110 Et impedire tot meos; heu tot meos
      Cupiunt amores? Ipse coniurat polus.
      Omnes laborant, ut meos, qua vi queunt
      Tollant amores.
      Imp.   Nempe dum langues pavens,
      Dum Ius vereris, dum novas leges times.
1115 Favere Iura Regibus semper solent
      Cum Iura mutant.*
      Hen.   Anglia exitium pavet,
      Veretur arma, tot minas, tot iam videt
      Instare clades.
      Tyr.   Cor tibi iam Rex labat:
      Regnare qui vult cuncta contemnit potens.
1120 Armatque dextram, stabilit Imperium manus
      Cum vibrat ensem. Quando Rex vim non facit
      Ultro precatur; non decent Regem preces.
      Iubere Regum est; occidat, qui non probat.
      Hen. Amo Bolenam; testor has cordis faces;
1125 Amo Bolenam; nullus obstabit mihi.
      Haec est voluntas, iura connubii mei,
      Vel mox resolvant Iudices; vel iam moras

a stop to all dawdling. Here and now I want to act as a king should act and arrogate whatever authority the good of my soul demands. [1130] Life and death lie side by side in a king's right hand.

Lust. Anne* is worth these burning desires of your soul.

Imp. Spurn your marriage bonds for the sake of Anne.

Tyr. Suppress by force whatever is unfavorable to Anne.

ACT III, scene vi

Longland, King Henry

Long. Your Majesty, the judge has departed.

Hen. My judge?

Long. [1135] He whom the Holy Father sent, Campeggio.

Hen. You say he has gone from here?*

Long. He has set foot outside the kingdom. The Holy Father recalled him; he was obliged to obey the sacred order at once.

Hen. He has left our kingdom? He has gone from here? Has my case been abandoned? [1140] Why does the Pope want him back? What does he want? What is the meaning of it? Does it mean the judges will not decide our case?

Long. The Holy Father himself will give the decision; it is he who wishes

> Abrumpo cunctas. Agere iam Regem volo,
> Et rapere nostra postulat quantum salus.
> 1130 In Regis una dextera est mors & salus.
> *Lux.* Istis Bolena* digna flammis est tuis.
> *Imp.* Tu pro Bolena iura contemnas tua.
> *Tyr.* Tu quod Bolenae non favet, ferro opprime.

ACTUS TERTIUS, scena vi

Longlandus, Henricus Rex

> *Long.* Iudex recessit, Magne Rex.
> *Hen.*   Iudex meus?
> 1135 *Long.* Quem misit ante Pontifex, Campegius.
> *Hen.* Et hinc recessit?*
> *Long.*   Extulit regno pedem;
> Revocavit illum Pontifex; mox mox sacris
> Parere iussis debuit.
> *Hen.*   Regno exiit?
> Et hinc recessit? causa deserta est mea?
> 1140 Quid iste rursum Pontifex? quid vult? quid est?
> Nec iura nostrae Iudices causae dabunt?
> *Long.* Dabit ipse iura Pontifex, Iudex tuae

to act as judge of your suit. It is only proper that you should submit to this great king and judge of the spiritual order. If it is your wish [1145] that a verdict be reached, he who exists as the official guardian of the spiritual order will give his decision.

Hen. Campeggio has gone, he has insulted the King by his stealthy withdrawal. Let there be no more delay. Anne is mine. She will enter the royal chamber as my wife. As Queen she will take her place [1150] with me on the royal throne. I will delay no longer; I will be my own judge.

Long. Let your reason control these passionate desires.

Hen. My reason commands me to carry out what I have in mind.

Long. At the present moment your heart is wrenched out of joint by blind passion. Do not act impetuously; take time to reconsider.

Hen. Look here, I am already making a mistake by pausing momentarily. [1155] Right now, time is standing in my way.

Long. It never takes long for sudden anger to rush headlong into a crime of lasting consequence.

Hen. Who would think it a heinous crime to marry Anne?

Long. Anyone who knows you already have a wife.

Hen. Anne will be my wife.

Long. But as long as your first wife is living, this is quite impossible.

      Vult esse causae; pareas tanto decet
      Regi sacrorum & Iudici: si ius sequi
1145 Tua est voluntas, ius dabit custos sacri
      Qui Iuris exstat.
      Hen.   Abiit, & Regem tacens
      Contempsit idem. Nulla ducatur mora;
      Mea est Bolena, Regium intrabit torum
      Mihi facta coniux; Regium ascendet thronum
1150 Regina mecum: nil moror, Iudex ero.
      Long. Ratione motus hos regas.
      Hen.   Ratio hoc iubet
      Quod mente verso.
      Long.   Coeca transversum rapit
      Iam pectus ira; siste, da tempus tibi.
      Hen. En ipse fallor dum breves patior moras;
1155 Iam tempus obstat.
      Long.   Tempus est semper breve
      Quando ira praeceps in nefas longum ruit.
      Hen. Ducere Bolenam, quis nefas dirum putet?
      Long. Qui scit te habere coniugem.
      Hen.   Coniux erit.
      Long. At esse Coniux prima cum vivit, nequit.

Hen. [1160] I will reject my first wife.

Long. That is forbidden. Let an impartial judge first render a decision. Your Highness, bear with these temporary postponements. One always lives to regret hasty decisions when there is no harm in temporary delay.

Hen. But right now there is harm in delaying.

Long. Still, this is not ordinarily the case when the act in question is morally good. [1165] The Holy Father himself will decide the case shortly.

Hen. Let him decide when he wants; right now I want Anne to be Queen, I want her to be my wife.

ACT III, scene vii

Heresy with her followers, Longland, Brian

Her. That was indeed a fitting conclusion. Shout with joy, O kingdom of Hell! O souls of the damned, rejoice! In another moment the kingdom of England [1170] will welcome me. This wedding is my work. The moment the King marries Anne, he embraces Heresy.

Long. Great God of Heaven, what disaster are you preparing for this wretched, terrified country! An icy numbness creeps through all my

---

1160 *Hen.* Istam repellam.
      Long.   Non licet, Iudex prius
      Decernat aequus; patere Rex parvas moras.
      Properasse semper poenitet, cum non potest
      Nocere tempus.
      Hen.   Iam mihi tempus nocet.
      Long. Operi nocere non solet tempus bono.
1165 Decidet ipse Pontifex causam brevi.
      Hen. Decidat ipse cum volet; nunc hoc volo,
      Bolena sit Regina, sit Coniux mea.

ACTUS TERTIUS, scena vii

Haeresis cum suis, Longlandus, Brianus

      Haer. Nempe hoc decebat; Tartari exulta Domus,
      Gaudete Manes, Angliae regnum mihi
1170 Iam iam patebit. Nuptiae sunt hae meae,
      Rex dum Bolenam ducit Haeresim accipit.
      Long. O magne Coelorum Tonans, ecquid paras
      Miserae & trementi Patriae! totos gelu
      Serpit per artus, corde confuso tremo,

body. I tremble, my heart is perplexed [1175] and the forebodings of this
day keep terrifying my soul.

Her. Today is the birthday of Heresy, this is your day, my sisters.

Lust. England will choose my wantonness. Whatever Lust does, England
will do.

Imp. She will cast off the yoke of righteousness, [1180] and whatever the
Christian Faith enjoins, the English will spurn.

Tyr. Their hands will redden with the blood of Christians; England will
sentence the wretched Christians to exile, to dark dungeons, to death by
fire, to slavery. It will overwhelm them with lashes and cruel torments.

Her. [1185] Such is the fruit of this wedding, the fruit of lawlessness. Oh,
how my soul is overjoyed by a wedding such as this! In a moment now it
will be official. The royal pair have joined hands and hearts and have
pledged their troth. The court is ringing with shouts of joy.

Long. Once more my heart trembles and cowers within me. [1190] O
God, let not the terrors I envision come to pass. Oh, what endless bloodshed and crime do I see in store for poor England! Brian is coming, my
heart beats with new terror. Brian, why this commotion?

Bri. The King's new marriage.* Anne is now the King's wife; she has
plighted her troth.

1175   Et ominosus territat mentem dies.
      Haer. Natalis ista est Haeresi natae dies
      Vestra est Sorores haec dies.
      Lux.   Luxum volet
      Meum Britannus; Luxuria quicquid facit
      Faciet Britannus.
      Imp.   Iuris excutiet iugum:
1180   Et Christiana quicquid iniungit fides,
      Nolet Britannus.
      Tyr.   Christiano sanguine
      Dextrae rubebunt; exilia, coecos specus,
      Ignes, catastas, verbera, & diras cruces
      Miseris Britannus Christianis adferet.
1185   *Haer.* Hic nuptiarum fructus est, hoc est nefas.
      Videre tales nuptias quantum iuvat?
      Iam iam licebit; dexteras, animos, fidem
      Iunxere Reges; Aula laetitiis sonat.
      Long. Iterum trementi pectore & fracto feror.
1190   Sim falsus augur O Tonans; O quot neces!
      O quot gementis Angliae intueor mala!
      Cerno Brianum, pectoris crescit tremor.
      Quid est Briane?
      Bri.   Nuptiae Regis novae.*
      Bolena coniux Regis est; fidem dedit.

Long. [1195] Who officiated at the ceremony,* I pray you?
Bri. I know not; the priest is quite unknown to me. But the deed is done. The King now wishes Anne to be graced with the royal crown. The entire court is ready to witness the coronation; they are all free to enjoy the ceremony. [1200] They are coming this way now—the King and his wife and all their attendants.

ACT III, scene viii

King Henry, Anne, Cranmer

Hen. May the benign and auspicious heavens be ever favorable to my England. My prayers have now been duly answered, yes, even generously answered. I have rid my mind of fear, I am supported by a decision freely made. [1205] No longer does my conscience torment me. This is our wife,* this is the pride of our England and a lady worthy of the King. There remains only to crown her with the sacred crown of the kingdom.
Anne. Your Majesty, command what you wish. It is your will that I become [1210] Queen Consort of your kingdom at the same time.
Hen. It was a proper decision and the heavens have favored it. Bishop Cranmer, place the royal crown on the head of my wife.

1195 *Long.* Quo teste tandem?*
     Bri.   Nescio, vix est satis
     Notus sacerdos; acta res est; hoc cupit
     Nunc Rex, Bolena regiam excelso ferat
     Vertice coronam; tota iam Regis Domus
     Parat triumphum, gaudiis vacat Domus.
1200 En Rex & ipsa, prodeunt cuncti simul.

ACTUS TERTIUS, scena viii

Henricus Rex, Bolena, Granmerus

     Hen. Quod Angliae foelix meae, & faustum diu
     Aspiret Aether, iam meis factum est satis
     Factum est abunde precibus; exsolvi meam
     Timore mentem, libero voto feror,
1205 Cessant tumultus conscii cordis male
     Haec nostra coniux,* Angliae nostrae decus,
     Et digna Rege: restat ut sacrum ferat
     Diadema regni.
     Bol.   Magne Rex quod vis, iube.
     Tua est voluntas, ut tui regni simul
1210 Sim facta consors.
     Hen.   Decuit, & favit polus:
     Granmere Praesul vertici imponas decus

Cran. This is as it should be. England wishes you joy, O King. May Your Highness rejoice to bear this scepter, now that your breast is freed from anxiety. [1215] England felicitates you, O Royal Lady, for the King in loving you has given his country a mistress.

Anne. My country will receive my love in return. I shall always love the English people and my mother country.

Cran. Let the Queen kneel. On your head I place [1220] the royal crown. Receive the scepter in your right hand. Long live the Queen!

Hen. I wish you joy. Now, my Queen, take your place at my side; be seated on the royal throne.

(*Acclamation*)

May she thrive! May she long endure!* Long may she live!
May she reign for aye!

Hen. May the skies be my witness, I swear by the heavens that look down: [1225] this new marriage was contracted to save my soul. I hereby renounce Catherine my previous wife. She is not Queen; I disclaim her. This lady is my wife; she is your Queen. Let there be holiday in the kingdom. Let the people celebrate the future prosperity of their royal mistress.

       Regale sponsae.
       Gran.   Sic decet, tibi Anglia
       Rex gratulatur, laeta Maiestas tua
       Quod liberato pectore hoc sceptrum gerat.
1215 Tibi gratulatur, regia O coniux, tuo
       Quod rex amore Patriae Dominam dedit.
       Bol. Etiam hunc amorem Patria accipiet meum,
       Anglos amabo semper, & Patriam meam.
       Gran. Regina flecte; regium impono decus
1220 Diadema capiti: dexteram sceptrum impleat
       Regina vive.
       Hen.   Gratulor, tu iam latus
       Regina claude; regium solium preme.

(*Acclamatio*)

Annet, perennet,* vivat, aeternum regat.

       Hen. Sit testis Aether, conscium testor polum
1225 Fuit salutis cura connubium hoc novum.
       Catharina coniux hactenus, nunc abdico.
       Regina non est, abnuo; haec coniux mea est,
       Regina vestra est. Festa sit regno dies;
       Auspicia Dominae plebis in ludos eant.

CHORUS

Of Vices and Virtues

Heresy and her companions on one side of the stage;
Reason with Piety and Clemency on the other.

Her. [1230] Let the souls of the damned ring out now with shrieks of joy. Let the turbulent Styx heave up her pitch-black waters, let Phlegethon and Acheron swell their waves. Lawful it is to laugh in Hell and enjoy fresh solace in the midst of torment. Lawful it is to satiate one's jealousy and fulfill one's rage. [1235] O damned spirits! O Hymen! Hymen! Sing out the wedding song in your throaty voices, for this is your daughter's wedding day. When the King lawlessly takes Anne to himself, then England takes me as her bride to destinies unknown.

Lust. I, Lust, shall preside over the wedding.
[1240] Leading the torch procession,
I shall proclaim your exploits.
Heresy never comes without my aid.
Lust is Heresy's mother,
Lust, or inordinate ambition.

Rea. [1245] The man who is an eager slave to his senses throws off the

CHORUS

Vitiorum & Virtutum

Ubi a parte una Haeresis cum suis, ab altera
Ratio cum Pietate & Clementia

1230 *Haer.* Nunc tandem laetis resonent ululatibus umbrae,
     Et piceos styx mota lacus Phlegetonque Acheronque
     Attollant undas; fas est ridere sub Orco,
     Et nova de mediis solatia sumere poenis,
     Invidiam satiare suam, rabiemque replere.
1235 O Manes, Hymenaee, Hymenaee instate sonoris
     Vocibus, haec vestrae nam sunt sponsalia Natae.
     Dum sibi Rex nulla coniungit lege Bolenam,
     Me sibi desponsat secretis Anglia fatis.
     Lux. Luxuria taedas praeferam,
1240 Et Nuptiarum pronuba,
     Tuos labores occinam.
     Per me Haeresis semper venit:
     Cui libido mater est,
     Vel ambitio sui impotens.
1245 *Rat.* Quisquis secutus sensuum celer impetum

yoke of reason, only to stumble and fall into ruin. England, this is the
fate that awaits you, for your King has rejected reason for the warm embrace of Venus.

Imp. Let this hand wave another torch.

[1250] Heresy, it is I who help your kingdom flourish,
For when Henry spurns Rome's sacred laws,
                    Heresy is born.

Pie. He who spurns God's masterdom
And inwardly rejects his laws,
[1255] Who forsakes religious worship
And recklessly violates sacred rights
Is rushing unwittingly to dark destruction.
From his lofty throne God looks down upon this sinner.

Tyr. At this juncture I, too, should bear a wedding torch of pitch,
[1260] And in my right hand bloody whips.
When Heresy, with armed right hand,
Strews the ground with victims,
When death follows death in dismal succession,
Then it is that the kingdom of Heresy is established
And its foundations made firm in blood,
While gentle rulers let their kingdoms languish.

Clem. [1265] The hard-hearted man

        Rationis excussit iugum, infirmo pede
        Cadit in ruinam. Hoc Anglia exitium est tuum.
        Ratione spreta dum fovet Regem Venus.
        Imp. Alteram taedam manus ista vibret
1250   Haeresis per me tua regna surgunt,
        Dumque Rex Romae pia iura temnit
                    Nasceris ipsa.
        Pie. Quisquis Domini temnit habenas,
        Quisquis sacras pectore leges
1255   Eiicit, & se substrahit aris,
        Nullo calcans iura timore,
        Hunc Deus alta despicit arce,
        Ruit exitii nescius atri.
        Tyr. Me quoque iam piceam decet hic protendere taedam;
1260   Et sanguinea verbera dextra,
        Haeresis armata dum spargit funera dextra,
        Cumulans mortes mortibus atris,
        Tum regnum stabilit, firmatque in sanguine sedem,
        Lenia languent regna regentum.
1265   *Clem.* Quisquis severo pectore

Whose mind and strength are diverted
By his thirst for innocent blood
Can give no thought to God.
Grown callous to every human value,
[1270] He is laid low by the first assault of Hell
And so loses his soul.
Her. Now the question is how to maintain our control over the kingdom.
A solution, my sisters! Find a solution, reach a decision.
Lust. As long as pleasure, debauchery, and venery are attractive, [1275]
you shall keep both England and the King completely in hand.
Rea. There is never any concern for God
In the midst of lust and sensual delights;
Debauchery always drags Heresy under her arm
And assists her as a bosom friend.
Imp. [1280] As long as England disdains the authority of Rome
You will reinforce your hegemony.
Pie. When a man belittles the rights of the sacred order
And the Fathers of the Church
And sets himself up as his own judge,
[1285] He can no longer remain a Catholic.
Tyr. As long as the Church continues to be dominated by the ready
sword of the State, you will flourish.

       Sitiens cruorem innoxium
       Oblectat animum & dexteram,
       Curare non potest Deum,
       Uno recedit impetu,
1270 Humanitatis & suae
       Expers salutem deserit.
       Haer. Querenda nunc est certa regnandi via.
       Modum, sorores, quaerite, & modum date.
       Lux. Donec voluptas, Luxus, & Venus placent,
1275 Tu possidebis Angliam, & Regem simul.
       Rat. Ubi voluptas & Venus
       Ubi nullus est usquam Deus.
       Secum trahit, secum fovet
       Libido semper haeresin.
1280 *Imp.* Donec Romanae contemnet iura Cathedrae
       Firmabis imperium tuum.
       Pie. Quicunque iura Ecclesiae,
       Sacrosque contemnit patres,
       Et arbiter sibi legis est
1285 Catholicus esse non potest.
       Tyr. Donec districto dominabitur ense, vigebis;

A fresh outburst of tyranny
Is always a boon to Heresy.
Clem. Heresy never fails to engender brutal natures.
[1290] It ravages by fire, rends asunder, destroys;
It cuts, kills, ruins, and demolishes.
Such calamities lie in wait for England.

        Crudelitatis est novae
        Firmare semper Haeresim.
        Clem. Animos severos Haeresis semper parit;
1290 Urit, revellit, destruit,
        Secat, necat, ruit, obruit.
        Misera haec videbit Anglia.

ACT IV, scene i

Longland, Catherine, her daughter Mary, Women-in-waiting

Cath. So we have failed. The King has issued his order and now Anne Boleyn, the King's mistress, occupies my chamber; the courtesan [1295] sits on my throne. I am evicted from the royal palace as an unworthy wife, the royal crown is swept off my anointed brow and the regal scepter slips from my hand. The King—how harshly that name sounds—the King in his folly has shut out of his heart [1300] all regard for me. I am rejected and must be banished—so he orders. I will make no objection. Let him disown me and drive me out, let him kill me.* Death will straightway put an end to the miseries I live to endure. Let execution come: it will claim an innocent victim. Oh, deceitful court!
Long. Control your anguish, [1305] my Queen.
Cath. Do not address me by that title—I am no longer Queen. Fortune begrudges me so great an honor.
Long. In any case, my noble Princess, let this bitter sorrow cease.
Cath. May the Eternal Father enable me to bear unflinchingly whatever punishment and terror [1310] the King or the Fates have in store

ACTUS QUARTUS, scena i

Catharina, Longlandus, Maria Filia, Pedisequae

Cath. Excidimus ergo; Regis Imperium datum est,
Torumque pellex iam meum, & meretrix thronum
1295 Tenet, Bolena; Regia expellor domo
Non digna Coniux, tollitur sacri decus
Regale capitis, & meae regni manus
Sceptrum relinquunt. Ipse Rex, heu dura vox!
Rex ipse nostros pectore exclusit suo
1300 Amens amores, exuli exilium imperat.
Nihil recuso; pellat, eiiciat, necet,*
Mors una nostrae finiet vitae mala.
Occidat, aberit a mea crimen nece.
O Aula fallax!
Long.   Pectoris luctum rege
1305 Regina.
Cath.   Nomen tolle, iam non sum amplius.
Fortuna tantum nomen invidit mihi.
Long. Tamen iste magnus pectoris cesset dolor
Generosa Princeps.
Cath.   Faxit aeternus Tonans,
Ut quicquid in me congeret seu sors mali,
1310 Seu Rex timoris, pectore invicto feram.

for me. I have known happiness, but willingly shall I embrace adversity.
Long. Good people are never corrupted by prosperity, nor do they succumb to adversity. Adversity tries the soul and makes it true; prosperity
drags the soul down to perdition.
Cath. [1315] If the King considers rejection of his wife too lenient a punishment, let him vent his royal anger by binding me in chains; let him
immure both mother and daughter in a gloomy dungeon. Yes, when he
so wills, my head will submit to the sword; my breast will wait in readiness. Let the sword be unsheathed [1320] and draw blood from this
heart in proof of my love. If this will not suffice, let him add the sacrifice
of a daughter to the slaughter of her mother. Oh, how bitter our lot!
Long. My Princess, you are succumbing again to grief. Your spirits are
sinking as quickly as they were rallying a few moments ago. [1325] Do
not yield to despair; for a lady so distressed God promises a better prospect.
Cath. Our sorrow has no counterpart in present history, nor does the
past provide a model.* My name is mentioned everywhere; I am the
laughingstock of the common people. Oh, how unbearable!
Long. On the contrary, the common people [1330] weep* over your
hardships; they recall your holiness, your devotedness, your chaste life.

      Tuli secundam, patiar adversam libens.
      Long. Nec insolescunt prosperis qui sunt boni,
      Nec rebus adversis cadunt: fortem probant
      Adversa mentem; prospera exitium trahunt.
1315 *Cath.* Eiicere Regi si parum est, oneret manus
      Regalis ira vinculis, claudat specu
      Tenebricoso filiam & matrem simul.
      Imo hoc patebit, cum volet, ferro caput.
      Patebit istud pectus; hinc stricta manu
1320 Pro amore ducat sanguinem: si non sat est,
      Addat Parentis funeri Natae necem.
      O sors acerba!
      Long.   Rursus incumbis tuo
      Princeps dolori, deficit quo mox suo
      Sese erigebat impetu sanguis tuus.
1325 Ne cede sorti, tempora afflictae Deus
      Meliora spondet.
      Cath.   Noster exemplum dolor
      Iam nescit ullum, prisca non aetas habet.*
      Ridenda vulgi fabula, O vulnus grave!
      Ubique dicor.
      Long.   Imo iam vulgus tuos*
1330 Deflet labores; sanctitas, pietas, pudor

In their eyes it is not adverse fortune but a vicious life that makes a
person disreputable. Your life proves you innocent. One who is overwhelmed by misfortune is guilty of no crime.

Cath. Come what may, I will embrace it joyfully. [1335] But my daughter's tears are eating into my heart. My poor child!

Mary. Mother, bid me go where you wish. I will obey you.

Cath. Daughter, your father disowns you and my husband disowns me;
as king he banishes us both. What a bitter cross! Will people say [1340]
that I bore my daughter in sin? Oh, I am drowned in grief!

Long. The world has always approved of your marriage. Believe me,
there is no question here of sin. Futhermore, everyone speaks of the
saintly life you have led.

Cath. Daughter, I will be both father and mother to you, [1345] I will
give you my name. Even though your father disowns you as his daughter, the land of Spain will give you the distinction of a famous title and
the prestige of lineage. Among your kin you will number grandfathers
and greatgrandfathers who were kings, and cousins who were emperors.

Long. Your ancestors are well known,* [1350] the whole world is aware
of the renown of your illustrious family.

      Animo recurrunt: crimen infamem facit,
      Adversa non sors; vita te excusat tua,
      Fortuna casu quem premit, non est nocens.
      Cath. Quaecunque veniet, grata sors veniet mihi.
1335 At Nata lachrymis perfodit pectus suis.
      O Nata!
      Mar.   Mater quo voles Natam voca,
      Sequar Parentem.
      Cath.   Nata, te Genitor negat,
      Et me, maritus; Rex, utramque exterminat.
      O dura fata! per scelus nunquid meam
1340 Genuisse dicar filiam? quo quo dolor
      Quo me resorbes?
      Long.   Nuptias Orbis tuas
      Semper probavit, crede nullum est hic scelus.
      Et sancta vitam fama collaudat tuam.
      Cath. Tibi, Nata, Genitor, & simul Genitrix ero,
1345 Habebis a me nomen; & quanquam parens
      Natam recuset, nominis magni notas
      Ibera Tellus, & decus stirpis dabit.
      Reges, avos, abavosque numerabis tuos;
      Et patrueles Caesares.
      Long.   Notum est genus,*
1350 Fortuna magnae cognita est mundo domus.

Cath. It is the King himself who grieves me. No matter how much he abuses me, he abuses one who loves him. He is always close to my heart. If only my tears might win salvation for my miserable King!

Long. My Queen, entrust his salvation [1355] to God's keeping. God will dispose of the future.

Cath. I do commend him to God. I submit willingly, I am ready to leave. Come with me, Daughter.

1 Woman. I will follow you, my Lady; your sorrows are mine, and your tears as well.

2 Woman. My lady, I join my lot to yours. [1360] Go where you will, I am at your side. Command your handmaid freely.

ACT IV, scene ii

King Henry, Brian, Wolsey, Warham

Hen. You say, Brian, that the Pope has issued his decree, that he has made an official pronouncement?*

Bri. Even so.

Hen. Could it be that he condemns my marriage?

Bri. He condemns your last marriage. It is his will that Anne Boleyn be

       Cath. Rex ipse nobis est dolor; quanquam opprimat,
       Opprimit amantem; corde sub nostro latet.
       O si redimere lachrymis possem meis
       Miseri salutem Regis!
       Long.   Hanc curam Deo
1355 Regina linque; fata disponet Deus.
       Cath. Commendo Regem; cedo, discedo, meae
       Venite mecum filiae.
       Ped. I   Dominam sequar.
       Tui dolores sunt mei, & lachrymae.
       Ped. II Fortuna, Domina, quae tua est, haec est mea;
1360 Quocunque pergis, pergo; tu famulam rege.

ACTUS QUARTUS, scena ii

Henricus Rex, Brianus, Volsaeus, Varamus

Hen. Quid ais, Briane? Pontifex legem dedit?
Pronuntiavit Pontifex?*
Bri.   Sic est.
Hen.   Meas
Num forte damnat nuptias?
Bri.   Damnat novas.
Domo Bolenam regia extrusam cupit.

thrust from the royal palace.

Hen. [1365] My Anne?

Bri. He approves your first marriage. He orders that Catherine be regarded as your lawful wife and that she bear the royal scepter as Queen of England. What is it, Your Majesty? Are your great hopes dashed?*

Hen. No matter, read the verdict; read it aloud.

(The decision of the Holy Father is read by Brian)

Bri. The pronouncement is so worded: your case has been decided.

Hen. [1370] My case has been decided.* Oh, Henry, what will you do? See how you tremble! I have no one to advise me. Shall I forsake Anne, my very life? Shall I pluck out my heart? The Supreme Pontiff so wills and ordains and threatens to hurl his sacred thunderbolt. I am a Christian: [1375] I must obey the Supreme Pontiff.

War. True, kings should obey the Supreme Pontiff.*

Hen. But my name will be degraded, the whole world will laugh over my amour.

War. The whole world will believe [1380] that the King fell into error and only later realized his mistake. One can hardly hold a person guilty

1365 *Hen.* Meam Bolenam?
     Bri.   Nuptias primas probat.
     Catharina Coniux sit tua, & regni decus
     Regina portet, imperat. Quid Rex? cadit
     Tuus ille fervor?*
     Hen.   Quicquid est, recita, lege.

     (Recitatur Sententia Pontificis per Brianum)

     Bri. Verba ista legis: causa decisa est tua.
1370 *Hen.* Decisa causa est.* Anime, quid restat tibi!
     Ut ecce trepidas? nulla consilii est via.
     Meam Bolenam deseram? vitam meam?
     Mihi revellam cor meum? summus cupit
     Mandatque Praesul, fulminis sacri minas
1375 Intentat idem. Christianus sum, meum est
     Parere tanto Praesuli.
     Var.   Regem decet
     Parere tanto Praesuli.*
     Hen.   At fiet meum
     Infame nomen, tota ridebit meos
     Tellus amores.
     Var.   Credet errorem prius,
1380 Sapuisse Regem postmodum. Vix est nocens

once he begins to repent.

Hen. But what is the way out of this difficulty?

War. Catherine must be restored to her former place of honor. Bid the Queen return—she is your lawful wife. Anne must leave. Believe me, now is the time [1385] to take your salvation in hand.

Hen. I will control my anger and force it to yield. Let Catherine return again to the King's chambers.* Let her return as Queen. Let Venus no longer delight me. Farewell, Anne, I fly your embraces. I forswear our marriage contract, I refuse to acknowledge it. [1390] Cardinal Wolsey, you have brought ruin on your King,* you are the author of my crime, you are the promoter of this most heinous offense. You it was who instigated my divorce.

Wol. I admit it, I alone was the instigator.* If I had not been, believe me, Your Majesty, I would be so at this moment. [1395] Your brother's wife can never be yours.

Hen. And because of this, behold the succession of tragedies* that has befallen the royal household! Because of this, witness all these afflictions!

War. You had no right* to upset the King's peace of mind; you had no right to undermine his firmly established marriage contract.

Wol. But the contract did not exist.

        Quem poenitere coepit.
        Hen.   At quisnam est modus?
        Var. Catharina rursus pristinum sumat decus.
        Regina redeat, vera quae coniux tua est,
        Abeat Bolena: Crede, cura nunc tuae
1385   Agitur salutis.
        Hen.   Ira decedas loco:
        Catharina rursus impleat Regis toros;*
        Regina redeat; nulla iam placeat Venus,
        Abi Bolena; desero amplexus tuos;
        Meum tuumque foedus eiuro, abnuo.
1390   Volsaee Regem perdidisti:* tu mihi
        Iniquitatis author, & magni nimis
        Sceleris minister; tu mihi divortii
        Causa extitisti.
        Vol.   Fateor, & solus fui.*
        Si non fuissem, crede Rex, iam iam forem.
1395   Tua esse Coniux fratris haud unquam potest.
        Hen. Et inde nostrae damna* tot passim Domus;
        Inde hi labores!
        Var.   Non tuum Regis fuit*
        Turbare pacem: nuptiarum non fuit
        Firmum movere foedus.
        Vol.   At nullum fuit.

War. [1400] Will you continue to doubt even after the Pope sanctions this contract by his decree? Do you see nothing wrong in this obstinacy? You are bloated with ambition, and since you cannot occupy the Holy Father's throne you change your tactics and betray your King. [1405] Anne Boleyn never fitted into your designs, but the sister of the King of France did. It was at your insistence that Catherine was banished so that your vindictive heart might harm the Holy Roman Emperor. You are guilty of high treason.

Hen. Withdraw from my presence. Your present title [1410] of Chancellor of England is hereby null and void.* The King so orders. Furthermore, I will your resignation.

Wol. I yield to you, I resign the chancellorship.

Hen. Let Thomas More receive this title; Thomas is my choice. Let him be Chancellor of England. This is my order. Cardinal Wolsey, withdraw; let Thomas More be informed of my decision.

Bri. [1415] I shall inform him. May he willingly accept this coveted office from the King's hands and promote the well-being of our kingdom.

War. And so let peace return to your troubled soul. The Roman Judge should be obeyed. Give orders that the Queen be restored immediately and banish the unworthy mistress [1420] from your palace and kingdom.

1400 *Var.* Dubitabis etiam Pontifex quando sua
Hoc lege sancit? Crimen hic nullum vides;
Ambitio tumidum reddit, & dum non potes
Primam occupare Praesulis sedem sacri,
Tua in ruinam consilia regis moves.

1405 Nunquam Bolena placuit, at Franci soror
Regis placebat; Caesari ut magno tuus
Ultor noceret animus eiecta est tuo
Catharina suasu. Regis es laesi reus.
Hen. Etiam hinc recede. Dignitas quae nunc tua est

1410 Et prima Regni cesset;* hoc Rex impero.
Imo abdicare te volo.
Vol.   Cedo, abdico.
Hen. Sit ista Mori dignitas; Morus placet,
Sit Angliae, nam mando, Cancellarius.
Volsaee, cede: quod volo, Morus sciat.

1415 *Bri.* Moro indicabo; Regis hoc munus sui
Ultro expetendum, capiat, & Regnum iuvet.
Var. Sic redde moto pectori pacem tuo:
Parere debes Iudici, actutum iube
Regina redeat, pellicem indignam eiice.

1420 Regno, domoque.

Hen. I shall ponder over these things, now that my heart has weathered its first outburst.

War. A righted wrong is the first step toward a better life; the second step is to continue no longer in that error.

ACT IV, scene iii

King Henry, Anne, Brian

Hen. What am I to do? A furious storm [1425] keeps pounding in my mind. My doubts dash me one way, then another. I pitch about like the boiling sea gathering and bursting in fury, and uncertainty clogs my heart as I toss. One moment my heart is swallowed up by love; the next it is wrenched with fear. What shall I do? Shall I drive Anne from the royal palace? [1430] The right thing to do is to obey the Pope: the other woman is my wife. The Pope has declared this officially and faith in his word leaves no room for doubt. I am not yet free of my passion for Anne; our love still burns feverishly deep within me. The right course to follow—I see this clearly—but my will hesitates; I am whirled about and swept along by my passions.

Bri. [1435] How utterly confused he appears! Grief has seized him on both sides and keeps spinning him round: his wavering mind seeks counsel. Once entrapped, it looks for a new way out.

Hen.   Consilia volvam mea;
Sedatus in me est pectoris moti furor.
Var. Correctus error primus est vitae gradus
Melioris; alter non sequi errorem amplius.

ACTUS QUARTUS, scena iii

Henricus Rex, Bolena, Brianus

     Hen. Quid fiet ergo? saeva tempestas meum
1425 Pertundit animum; dubius huc & huc feror:
     Et aestuantis seu Sali exundat furor,
     Sic erro, & errans pectus incertum traho.
     Amor hinc resorbet pectus, hinc turbat timor.
     Quid heu? Bolenam regia eiiciam domo?
1430 Parere iustum est; altera est coniux mea;
     Pronuntiavit Pontifex, certa est fides.
     Nondum hos amores exuo; nostras calor
     Agit in medullas, cerno quid fas sit sequi;
     Haeret voluntas; volvor, & sic effluo.
1435 *Bri.* Ut ecce totus haeret! abreptum dolor
     Utrimque versat; dubia consilium petit,
     Et implicata mens novam quaerit viam.

Anne. Are you still nursing those anxieties and terrible heartaches? Perhaps you have forgotten your Anne, [1440] perhaps I displease you already.

Hen. You are always pleasing to me.

Anne. Come, take this crown of glory from my head.

Hen. Whatever you possess is glorious. Hold fast to your crown.

Anne. My husband, you have pledged loyalty to me, your wife.

Hen. I maintain the loyalty I pledged.

Anne. [1445] But you are about to recall your other wife.

Hen. You are my wife.

Anne. Let the Queen return—this is what you want; you do not want me to be Queen. Is this indeed the meaning of a king's loyalty, of a king's love?

Hen. I shall never stain my love or my loyalty. Live, my Queen. All England [1450] now hails you as Queen.

Anne. But the Pope rejects me and fiercely hurls at me his savage thunderbolt. Will you tolerate this? And will you drive me from your royal palace?

Hen. Rest assured, you will always occupy the royal throne and bed. You are my dear wife. [1455] Why are your innocent cheeks defiled with

       Bol. Istos tumultus mentis, & cordis graves
       Pateris dolores? Excidi forsan tibi
1440 Et iam Bolena displicet.
       Hen.   Semper places.
       Bol. Age tolle, verticis nostri decus,
       Istam coronam.
       Hen.   Quodquod est tuum est decus.
       Retine coronam.
       Bol.   Coniugi Coniux mihi
       Fidem dedisti.
       Hen.   Quam dedi servo fidem.
1445 *Bol.* Revocanda Coniux altera est.
       Hen.   Coniux mea es.
       Bol. Regina redeat, hoc cupis: ne sim, cupis.
       Et ista Regis est fides? iste est amor?
       Hen. Nec amore quicquam, nec fide indignum gero;
       Regina vive, tota Reginam Anglia
1450 Iam te fatetur.
       Bol.   Pontifex sed me eiicit,
       Et fulmen in me barbarum intorquet ferus.
       Patieris? & me Regia expelles domo?
       Hen. Secura vive; regium solium & torum,
       Semper tenebis; dulcis es Coniux mea.
1455 Quid immerentes rore confundis genas?

tears? Come now, let the radiant sunlight of your soul gleam forth anew. Let the crimson lie unclouded on your lips. Be no longer sad.

Anne. The Pope brings on that sadness and I have good reason for fearing him.

Hen. You have no enemies in England.

Anne. [1460] Perhaps everyone is my enemy.

Hen. No one is your enemy.

Anne. As long as the King loves me, I shall fear no man.

Hen. The King will continue to love you. The Pope shall never remove this ardor from my heart. I will find a solution.

Anne. Your Majesty, I have sworn fidelity and so have you.

Hen. [1465] Yes, I have given my word of honor.

Anne. As King you esteemed me worthy of your embraces. My heart burns with love for you. If I am dear to you, hold fast to me as your own.

Hen. Anne, you are mine and I shall keep you mine. Brian, see that the Queen lacks nothing.

Bri. [1470] I shall do so. Is there anything further Your Majesty wills?

Hen. Let the Council be convened.

Bri. I shall see to it.

Age redde laetae mentis irradians iubar.
Iterum serenus ora perstringat rubor.
Compesce luctum.
Bol.   Pontifex luctum facit;
Nec vana metuo.
Hen.   Nullus est hostis tibi.
1460 *Bol.* Sunt forsan omnes.
Hen.   Nullus est hostis tibi.
Bol. Nullum timebo, Coniugem si Rex amet.
Hen. Te Rex amabo. Pontifex nunquam hunc meo
Ignem revellet pectore: inveniam modum.
Bol. Iurata mens est & mihi, & Regi tibi.
1465 *Hen.* Iurata mens est.
Bol.   Me tuo dignam toro
Rex iudicasti; pectus hoc nostrum tuo
Amore flagrat: si placeo, serva tuam.
Hen. Mea es Bolena, teque servabo meam.
Briane, cura deesse Reginae nihil.
1470 *Bri.* Curabo; num quid amplius forsan iubes?
Hen. Adsit Senatus.
Bri.   Aderit, hanc curam geram.

ACT IV, scene iv

King Henry, Heresy and her companions

Hen. The same turmoil all over again and the same anxieties tearing at my heart with scourges. I hesitate and I doubt; no one is at hand to advise me. The Pope drags my mind one way; [1475] Anne drags it back. I swing back and forth between certainty and doubt. I do not want something, and still I want it anyway. What I want I like; what I do not want is still the right thing to do. All England crouches over and hangs on my shoulders. The whole world keeps watching what my next move will be. On me will rest the name and the fame.

Her. [1480] And so you will obey? You will submit like a slave? You will bow your neck to the yoke, to the Pope's verdict? You, the King?

Hen. Why, yes, since the Pope has so decreed.

Her. You are going to submit when the Pope snatches away your wife? When he forbids you to love? Then surrender at once, pitiful, defeated King! [1485] The only kings who are awed by that church prince are those who inspire no fear. Rulers have great expansive natures. When a Pope curbs a ruler's pleasures, then it is degrading to obey. Sovereignty is yours; you alone tower above all others as head of the kingdom. No

ACTUS QUARTUS, scena iv

Henricus Rex, Haeresis Cum Suis

Hen. Rursum tumultus mentis, & rursum novi
Animum flagellant impetus; dubito, haereo,
Consilia desunt; Pontifex animum trahit,
1475 Retrahit Bolena; certus, incertus feror;
Nolo, voloque: quod volo gratum est mihi;
Quod nolo, iustum est. Anglia his humeris meis
Inclinat incubatque: quicquid hic agam
Spectabit Orbis, nomen atque omen feram.
1480 *Haer.* Parebis ergo? servies? legem & iugum
Patieris? & Rex?
Hen.   Nempe quando Pontifex
Pronuntiavit.
Haer.   Pontifex quando tuam
Tibi revellit Coniugem? quando tuos
Prohibet amores? Victe Rex, da da manus;
1485 Istum sacrorum Principem Reges timent
Qui non timentur. Indoles magnae regunt.
Parere turpe est, quando, quod prohibet, placet.
Tuum est supremum culmen, & regni caput

king can rule and still have room for fear.

Hen. [1490] But the Pope has control over kings. He is head of the world.

Her. He controls those kings whom he has made his pawns. Reassert yourself, vindicate your sovereignty, for powerful monarchs cannot possibly be underlings to anyone. Only the God of kings enacts the law for kings.

Hen. [1495] He is the prince of the spiritual order. As Vicar of Christ he has care of all men's souls and keeps the sacred traditions of our ancient faith inviolate.

Her. Let the Tarpeian Ruler rule over his Roman rocks. It is your responsibility to rule over your subjects in the kingdom of England and to establish the religion of your people. [1500] Every kingdom must have a head of its own and only one head; you alone can and should be both king and pope. Let your subjects embrace whatever religion the king favors, make them submit to any law the king demands. Your Majesty, make the law fit your needs.

Hen. [1505] Then he will not be able to take away my wife.

Her. Not your present wife, or any other you might wish. Go through with this, Your Majesty. Be pope of the English church. Make everyone proclaim you pope. If anyone resists, let him die. He is truly a king who

       Tu solus exstas, qui timet Rex, non regit,
1490 *Hen.* At ille Reges dirigit; Mundi caput.
       Haer. Mancipia quos fecit sibi Reges, regit.
       Tibi redde temet, vendica culmen tuum:
       Namque esse Reges nil supra magnos potest.
       Dat iura solus Regibus Regum Deus.
1495 *Hen.* Princeps sacrorum est, & vices Christi gerens
       Hominum salutem curat, & fidei sacra
       Antiquae servat.
       Haer.   Saxa Tarpeius regat
       Romana Rector: Angliae in regno tuum est
       Et regere populos, & dare populis fidem.
1500 Opus est ut unum regno in uno sit caput.
       Et Rex & esse Pontifex solus potes,
       Et esse debes, subditi accipiant fidem,
       Quam Rex amabit: subditi legem ferant,
       Quam Rex iubebit. Pone tu legem tibi.
1505 *Hen.* Non ergo nostram coniugem avellet mihi.
       Haer. Nec hanc, nec illam quam voles: hoc Rex agas
       Ecclesiae sis Anglicanae Pontifex.
       Fateantur omnes: si quis obsistat, cadat.
       Rex ille verus, qui sibi indulgens, nihil

looks out for himself [1510] and fears absolutely nothing. A king should be allowed to do whatever he wants.

Imp. Royal scepters and pious practices make poor bedfellows.* Sovereignty alone ought to be worshiped. The man who must worship others is a wretched hireling. Powerful! Ruthless! Warlike! Omnipotent! [1515] These are the great names given to kings—never are they heralded as "pious." That epithet is reserved for private individuals.

Hen. My mind is made up at this instant. I will be king from now on. O unjust Pontiff, so you will threaten me with your thunderbolt! I will be pontiff and king.

Tyr. Keep this firmly in mind: there is only one way to rule: [1520] by wielding the sword. You will have to be powerful and secure England by an iron rule. The blood of Christians shed in England will prepare your advance to a peerless throne.

Hen. I see my Council approaching. I shall complete what remains to be done.

Her. Our work is done, the land of the Britons will change her faith.

1510 Usquam veretur: quod volunt Reges, simul
      Hoc posse debent.
      Imp.   Sceptra conveniunt male
      Pietasque:* debet sola maiestas coli,
      Alios colere qui debet, est servus miser.
      Fortes, Severi, Bellicosi, Maximi
1515 Sunt magna regum nomina, haud unquam Pii,
      Privata sors est.
      Hen.   Iam ratum est, iam Rex ero.
      Iniuriose Pontifex, ergo mihi
      Fulmen minaris? Pontifex & Rex ero.
      Tyr. Haec firma mens sit, una regnandi est via
1520 Districtus ensis, Angliam ferro potens
      Teneas oportet: Christianus hic cruor
      Fusus parabit sortis excelsae thronum.
      Hen. Sed en Senatum cerno, quod superest, agam.
      Haer. Satis est, Britanna Terra mutabit fidem.

ACT IV, scene v

King Henry, Cranmer, Fisher, Thomas More, other Councilors

Hen. [1525] My lords, in the past I have taken counsel with you, as I should have, about matters concerning my reputation and my spiritual welfare. Our mutual deliberations in this hall have weathered violent storms. You have borne my burdens. England herself has bewailed our misfortunes, while my reputation is being injured by a world uninjured by me. [1530] But vicious rumors have been repudiated; the sincerity of my love for Anne has overcome popular prejudice. I bask in my happiness and rejoice, for my prayers have been answered. But, my lords, give heed to the next proposal I am about to make. A short time ago the Pope threatened me with his thunderbolt* [1535] and doomed me to Hell at a time when I was grieviously concerned about the state of my soul. First of all I took a wife and thereupon endowed my country with this new mistress. The Pope condemned my action—he was forced by the Emperor to assume this position. So much for that. My present wish is this:* [1540] that the King be made Pontiff and Head of the Church of England. That the name "Pope" nevermore be mentioned. That whoever mentions his name, takes cognizance of him, acknowledges him or

ACTUS QUARTUS, scena v

Henricus Rex, Granmerus, Roffensis, Thomas Morus, Senatores Alii

1525 *Hen.* Consulere me decebat & famae & meae,
Proceres, saluti. Vester hic mecum labor
Subiit tumultus; onera portastis mea,
Et ipsa nostris Anglia ingemuit malis,
Dum laedit Orbis laesus haud famam meam.
1530 Sed victa fama est, vicit invidiam meus
Sincerus ardor; gaudio incumbo meo
Votique compos laetor: at quod nunc volo,
Percipite, Proceres, Pontifex nuper suum
Vibravit in me fulmen,* & nostrum caput
1535 Devovit Orco dum meae incumbo anxius
Multum saluti. Coniugem primo mihi,
Dominam deinde patriae novam dedi.
Ipse improbavit, Caesar in partes Papam
Pertraxit istas. Sit satis, nunc hoc volo*
1540 Ut Anglicanae Pontifex Ecclesiae
Caputque sit Rex, nominet nemo Papam.
Qui nominabit, noscet, agnoscet, colet,

honors him, be guilty of treason and be liable to death. That the offspring of Anne be legally mine [1545] and that my subjects likewise
acknowledge this child as heir to the throne. That anyone denying this
be guilty of treason and subject to death. My lords, this is my will. It is
for you to obey it.

Cran. Your wish is lawful* and so we owe you our obedience. Your
Majesty, I reverence you as supreme head of the English Church; [1550]
I hereby renounce the Pope of Rome. I acknowledge the daughter of
Anne Boleyn as your heir and successor to the throne. The actions of your
Sacred Majesty, even to the present moment, win my complete approba-
tion. Your conscience has constrained you to act thus.

Thom. [1555] This sudden proposal* is a very grave matter. His Majesty's personal desires enjoin on us all a decision that is serious indeed.

Cran. Thomas, do you not recognize and acknowledge your King?

Thom. I do recognize and acknowledge my King and I reverence him.

Cran. Do you not pay homage to him as Head of England?

Thom. The King is head of England, but not head of the English Church.

Hen. [1560] Is this the recompense I receive for your recent promotion?
Is this the way you show gratitude to your King, Thomas?

Thom. I am profoundly grateful to honor Your Highness; however, if

         Sit perduellis, debeat morti caput.
         Proles Bolenae sit mea & regni simul
1545   Haeres, fateri subditi debent mei:
         Sit perduellis, qui negat, mortis reus.
         Haec est voluntas, hanc sequi Proceres, decet.
         Gran. Iusta est voluntas,* nos sequi iustam decet.
         Ego te Anglicanae Rex, supremum Ecclesiae,
1550   Veneror caput, Quiritium eiuro Papam.
         Ego Bolenae filiam haeredem tuam
         Regnique fateor. Sacra Maiestas tua
         Quicquid peregit hactenus, totum probo.
         Necessitatem dubia permovit salus.
1555   *Thom.* Haec causa praeceps,* una rem tantam iubet
         Regis voluntas.
         Gran.   More non regem tuum
         Noscis, fateris?
         Thom.   Fateor & nosco meum,
         Venerorque Regem.
         Gran.   Non caput Regni colis?
         Thom. Regni est caput non Anglicanae Ecclesiae.
1560   *Hen.* Et dignitatis iste fructus est novae?
         Sic More Regi gratus es?
         Thom.   Grata colo

I am obliged to approve your every inclination, I must resign.* I forfeit the highest position of the realm.

Hen. Thomas, you never do come round [1565] to my way of thinking.

Fish. Your Majesty, if your desire were law, I should perhaps obey you. But you are commanding something unlawful. At no time whatever has anyone acknowledged a king to be prince or supreme head of the Church.

Cran. Not even of the English Church?

Fish. No, never; [1570] the Pope is supreme head of all churches.

Cran. His Highness personally has never ceased distinguishing you with new titles, and now you disdain His Majesty's command. Acknowledge your King and his daughter. You can be forced to do so. His Majesty will exercise his authority and make you obey.

Fish. [1575] Let him use the weight of his authority or the threat of death. My death will bring him no victory. Besides, an old man like myself scorns the thought of being intimidated, or of dying.

Hen. This ingrate rebels against his King late in life. Perhaps a dungeon will make him less bold. They will both be crushed. [1580] Let rebels who refuse to support their King instead support fetters in foul dungeons.

         Te mente Regem; Dignitatis si meae est
         Probare quod vis; abdico: * primum decus
         Resigno regni.
         Hen.   More, tu nunquam mea
1565 Ad vota transis.
         Roff.   Magne Rex, si lex tua
         Esset voluntas, forte parerem tibi.
         Iubes iniquum: nemo Regem Ecclesiae
         Agnovit unquam principem, aut summum caput.
         Gran. Non Anglicanae?
         Roff.   Nemo, namque est omnium
1570 Ecclesiarum Pontifex summum caput.
         Gran. Te dignitate semper ornavit nova
         Rex ipse; Regis iussa nunc temnis tui.
         Agnosce Regem, & filiam: cogi potes,
         Authoritate coget ipse Rex sua.
1575 *Roff.* Authoritate cogat, aut certa nece;
         Non morte vincet, & metum, & mortem mea
         Temnit senectus.
         Hen.   Impium in Regem caput
         Sero rebellat: augeat carcer metum,
         Vincentur ambo; vincula & tetros specus
1580 Ferant rebelles, ferre qui Regem negant.

Thom. Then let us go. Happy am I to acknowledge God's benevolence. Our prison shall become a home of cherished quietude and a haven of rest.

Fish. Yes, let us go. I am ready. [1585] I hereby inaugurate a new life. My death shall unlock a new era. Oh, happy old age that sinks to its close in death and wins a crown! Lead this old man where you will.

Cran. Guard, take them away. Their defiance must be paid for. You who remain must bind yourself by oath. Do you favor His Majesty's edict?

1 Coun. [1590] I acknowledge the King as head of our church. I consider the daughter of Anne Boleyn to be rightful heir to the throne.

2 Coun. I acknowledge and venerate the King as supreme head of the sacred order. I abjure the sacred order of the Pope and his detestable name.

3 Coun. I likewise approve and swear that whatever his Majesty commands [1595] must be obeyed. King Henry, be both king and pontiff. I detest him whom Rome reverences as its Father.

Hen. All is as it should be. Now, Archbishop Cranmer, let it be your responsibility* to proclaim my wishes to the very ends of England moated by seas. [1600] Every subject must acknowledge my edict and solemnly swear to abide by it. Kings have the authority to establish the creed and

        Thom. Eamus ergo, laetus agnosco Dei
        Benignitatem; carcer optatae Domus
        Tranquillitatis fiet, & portus simul.
        Roff. Eamus, ecce nil moror, vitam novam
1585 Hinc inchoabo, mors diem pandet novum
        Foelix senectus, morte quae sera cadens
        Reperit coronam: quo voles, abduc senem.
        Gran. Abduc Satelles, ista libertas rea est.
        Iurate reliqui. Regis edictum placet?
1590 *Sen.1* Agnosco Regem Ecclesiae nostrae caput.
        Regni Bolenae filiam haeredem probo.
        Sen.2 Sacri supremum culminis Regem caput
        Fateor coloque, sacra Pontificis nego,
        Dirumque nomen.
        Sen.3   Et probo, & quae Rex iubes
1595 Servanda iuro, Pontifex & Rex simul
        Henricus esto, Roma quem patrem colit
        Detestor illum.
        Hen.   Sic decet, nunc sit tuae
        Granmere curae,* nostra qua late Anglia
        Vallatur undis publicare quod volo,
1600 Fateantur omnes, & data iurent fide.
        Regum est fidem legemque subiectis dare.

law for their subjects. When the sun drives his flaming steeds back into the western sea, summon the guilty recusants before the tribunal.

ACT IV, scene vi

Cranmer and Councilors

Cran. Proceed, Crier, proclaim His Majesty's new decree. [1605] People are prone to disregard orders they do not understand.

(*The royal proclamation is read aloud.*)*

All England must be traversed and the King's decrees made clear to everyone—to bishops, religious communities, and townspeople. Whoever refuses to acknowledge the new dispensation must be put to the sword. The law [1610] is to be sanctioned by bloodshed.

1 Coun. Perhaps we should make an example of someone for all to see. The commoners understand such a lesson well, and others are horrified. Everybody is horrified by the sight of flowing blood, by a corpse paraded through the towns, or by someone's head on a pike. Soon they will all be wary and use discretion.*

2 Coun. [1615] Then let us first summon Bishop Fisher* and bring him here to the tribunal. If he falls under the sword, nobody will want to

> Cum sol reducet flammeos undis equos
> Voca ad tribunal conscios rursum reos.

ACTUS QUARTUS, scena vi

Granmerus, Senatores

> *Gran.* Age, Praeco, Regis publica edictum novum;
> 1605 Cum nesciuntur iussa contemni solent.

(*Recitatur edictum Regis.*)*

> Lustranda tota est Anglia, & cuncti sciant
> Decreta Regis, Praesules, Sacrae Domus,
> Urbes; probare qui novam non vult fidem,
> Feriatur ense. Fusus hanc legem cruor
> 1610 Sancire debet.
>   *Sen.1*   Forsan exemplum volent
> Videre cuncti, vulgus exemplo sapit,
> Terrentur alii. Si quis exundet cruor,
> Si quod per urbes funus, atque haustum caput
> Percellat omnes, sapere* mox cuncti volent.
> 1615 *Sen.2* Huc ad Tribunal ergo Roffensem prius
> Revocemus:* illum, si cadat, nemo sequi,

follow his example. Even Thomas More might have a change of mind.
Cran. Guard, bring the prisoner forward. If he decides to act discreetly,
many others will follow his lead. The commoners have a great esteem for
this man [1620] and regard him as a saint.
3 Coun. He will not change his mind. He is a wise old man and his
mind is unconquerable. Death in no form will ever daunt him in the
least. Do you not mark how the old fellow hurries this way with his face
all beaming?* For all his physical weakness he spurns the thought of
death like a proud warrior; believe me, this man is too wise to be discreet.

ACT IV, scene vii

Cranmer, Fisher, Councilors

Cran. [1625] Once more you face the tribunal,* Your Grace. Have you
not yet made up your mind to exercise discretion? Life or death now
hangs in the balance. Do not wait until it is too late to make a prudent
decision. Accept the King as your pope and Anne Boleyn's daughter as
heir to the throne. Your Sovereign has enacted this law—he whom you
should hold in awe.
1 Coun. [1630] Such stubborn adherence to a foolish idea is never com-
mendable. Or do you insist on being the only man of discretion here?
Fish. My advanced years help me remain steadfast to the truth. Life

       Nec ipse Morus mente mutata volet.
       Gran. Reduc Satelles; sapere si forsan volet
       Multi sequentur, suspicit vulgus virum
1620 Colitque sanctum.
       Sen.3   Non volet, mens est seni
       Invicta docto, nulla mors ipsi metum
       Iniciet unquam. Cernite, ut laeto senex
       Vultu propinquat?* Pectore infracto necem
       Contemnit audax; credite, hic nimium sapit.

ACTUS QUARTUS, scena vii

Granmerus, Roffensis, Senatores

1625 *Gran.* Iterum ad Tribunal,* Praesul, an nondum sapis?
       Necessitas suprema nunc fati tui est.
       Ne sero sapias. Pontifex sit Rex tibi,
       Haeres Bolenae filia. Hanc legem tulit,
       Quem tu vereri Principem debes tuum.
1630 *Sen.1* Laudandus iste pertinax mentis furor
       Nunquam est; an ipse sapere solus hic cupis?
       Roff. Rectae tenacem mentis haec aetas facit.

holds no appeal to a man who welcomes its close. The present opportunity is an occasion of joy, for it will exchange a new life [1635] for the
one I forsake.

2 Coun. Why do you rejoice at the prospect of death? Your death is im-
minent if you refuse to comply. Swear and return to the King's graces.
He is your pope: acknowledge him under oath.

Fish. He is not my pope.

3 Coun. Do you acknowledge him as head of the English Church?
[1640] As head of the realm?

Fish. No one who does so can be called a man of discretion. He is not
head of the English Church,* nor can any king be head. There is only
one head, the Roman Pontiff himself. It is he who is Lord of the world.
The King ought not to feel betrayed because we cling fast to our religion.
Nor should these white hairs deceive him.* All through history [1645]
our people have clung to the ancient faith; the Bishop of Rome has defined our obligations in spiritual matters. I refuse absolutely to comply
with these innovations. The King has no power to suppress the traditional religion of this country.

Cran. He is guilty of treason; he thinks he alone is wise. Pronounce
sentence.

Fish. I am ready for the verdict.

        Speranda non est vita cum finem cupit.
        Occasione laetor, haec vitam dabit
1635 Hinc cum relinquam.
        Sen.2   Morte quid gaudes tua?
        Vicina mors est si negas: iura & tuo
        Te redde Regi, Pontifex ipse est tuus;
        Fateare, iura.
        Roff.   Pontifex non est meus.
        Sen.3 Nec Anglicanae noscis hunc Ecclesiae
1640 Caputque Regni?
        Roff.   Nullus agnoscens sapit.
        Non est,* nec esse Rex potest. Unum est caput,
        Romanus ille Praesul, & mundi est caput.
        Decipere Regem nostra non debet fides,
        Non haec senectus:* hactenus nostri fidem
1645 Tenuere primam, iura Romanus dedit
        Sacrata Praesul. Quod novum est constans nego:
        Rex hic receptam tollere haud potest fidem.
        Gran. Est perduellis, sapere sic solus cupit.
        Pronuntietur.
        Roff.   Nil moror, pronuntia.

1 Coun. [1650] Because you deny the King to be head of the church, because you refuse to acknowledge the daughter of Anne Boleyn as rightful heir, I hereby pronounce you guilty of treason and sentence you to death. Executioner, go and cut off the old man's head.

ACT IV, scene viii

Fisher, Executioner

Fish. The King's sentence is a harsh one, but I am grateful for it. [1655] Death is the greatest moment of life, and certainly not the greatest evil. A wise man is not wont to shudder at death, especially after he has welcomed it. Everyone must face it eventually. I suddenly feel a strange energy coursing through my body.* I am an old man—yet I am being transformed. I feel myself growing stronger and stronger. [1660] O God! This grace is a proof of your bountiful kindness. I have not deserved it. You call one even so undeserving as I to untold bliss. It is a glorious thing to die for You.

Exec. Come, Your Grace, do not tarry along the way.*

Fish. Old age is sluggish; yet there is only a short way to go. [1665] But this old man has no need of support; my staff, I leave you here, farewell.* My feet must hurry me along to glory. I am reborn and my youth is fresh upon me.

1650 *Sen.1* Ecclesiae quod deneges Regem caput,
     Et quod Bolenae filiam haeredem haud probes,
     Te perduellem dico, & addico neci,
     I lictor, istud amputa seni caput.

ACTUS QUARTUS, scena viii

Roffensis, Lictor

    Roff. Vox ista Regis dura, sed grata est mihi.
1655 Mors summa vitae est, nec tamen summum est malum.
     Horrere sapiens non solet, certam omnibus.
     Ipsi invocatam. Nescio quis se meos,
     Agit per artus ardor,* immutor senex,
     Novumque crescit robur, & vires novae.
1660 Benignitatis hic tuae est, Tonans, favor,
     Non hunc merebar. Gloriam ad tantam vocas
     Etiam immerentem; gloria est pro te mori.
    Lic. Hinc est eundum; ne trahas, Praesul, moras.*
    Roff. Tarda est senectus, parva sed restat via.
1665 Fulcro senectus non eget; bacule hic vale.*
     Properare nostri ad gloriam debent pedes,
     Iterum renascor, & Iuventus est nova.

Te Deum laudamus,* Te Dominum confitemur
Te aeternum Patrem, omnis terra veneratur

[1670] O Supreme King of kings, O Christ, abide with me. Deign to accept kindly the sufferings of your Bishop. Farewell, my countrymen; O wretched England, fare you well. Carry on your work, Executioner. See, I shall offer my neck for the blow.

CHORUS
Of English Exiles or Refugees

Our cities of England must now be forsaken,
1675 We have decided to leave our motherland homes.
Farewell, our English mountains,
Farewell, our English fountains.
O land of England, receive and hold dear
The new-minted coins of our deep-seated groans.
1680 Banished from England, we give you these tears,
We miserable English now pledge you these tears.
We are falsely accused, falsely, alas!
We who know and acknowledge
Our Pontiff in Rome.

Te Deum laudamus,* Te Dominum confitemur
Te aeternum Patrem, omnis terra veneratur

1670 Rex summe Regum, Christe tu praesens ades,
Tui labores praesulis gratos habe.
Valete cives, Anglia O misera, O vale.
Tu perage, Lictor, ecce cervicem dabo.

CHORUS
Anglorum Exulum, seu Profugorum

Ergo Patriae linquendae Urbes
1675 Linquere patrias certum est sedes.
Valete Montes Angliae,
Valete Fontes Angliae.
Anglica Tellus ultima nostri
Munera luctus impressa tene,
1680 Has tibi lachrymas, has tibi lachrymas,
Profugi & miseri solvimus Angli.
Poscimur, heu, heu, poscimur heu heu!
Quicunque Romam noscimus
Et qui fatemur hic Papam.

1685 And so poor England is lost,
       The devoted daughter of Rome;
       The Christian folk are surrendered to slaughter.*
       Our holy priests are drenched in their blood
       And pour out their lives in torture and pain.
1690 Our churches lie gutted and burned to the ground,
       Blessed ashes are whirled on high by the winds,
       Ungodly flames our altars destroy,
       While Christ is driven from his sacred shrines.
       Gold in the churches is greatly desired,*
1695 So shrines are plundered for the riches they yield.
       The plunderer revels in riches around him,
       The poor are found guilty and inherit the cross.
       Screams rise and fall with the crack of the scourge,
       Groans are heard everywhere, tears are shed everywhere.
1700 When the oath is administered, he who refuses
       Is driven at once from his fields and his home,
       And ruthlessly dragged to a horrible death.
       And so as exiles we take our departure;
       We are leaving our fields and our homes.
1705 No longer can England sustain her own sons

1685 Sic misera perditur Anglia
       Devota Romae filia.
       Gens Christiadum devota neci est.*
       Sacri multo sanguine patres,
       Laceram fundunt sub nece vitam,
1690 Delubra iacent obruta flammis,
       Sacros rapiunt cineres venti,
       Destruit aras impius ignis,
       Christusque suis pellitur aris,
       Multum in templis perplacet aurum,*
1695 Aurumque reas efficit aras.
       Populator amat quicquid ditat.
       Pauper reus est & crucis haeres.
       Verbera mixto resonant planctu,
       Undique luctus, undique lachrymae,
1700 Quisquis renuit iurare prius,
       Pellitur agris, patriaque Domo.
       Trahitur durae victima morti.
       Sic nos abimus exules;
       Agros domosque linquimus.
1705 Heu Christianos Anglia heu non fert suos!

For Christians are fleeing the land of their birth.
We ask you, O King now grown tyrant,* why
Are you driving your subjects to faraway lands?
But now we sail to harbors unknown
1710 And leave behind our native seas.
One would think you would deem it drastic enough
To have stripped us bare of our ancestral goods.
We English subjects are pressed into exile;
We must remain true to our ancient faith
1715 While we dwell in the lands of foreigners.
O Shades of our Fathers! Shades of our Fathers!
In your graves you will weep for your children
Who must quit their ancestral homes,
Who must leave England because of their faith.
1720 Yea, the tombs are pried open* by force
And the dead are exposed in their tombs.
We will go, alas, we folk
Who were wont to live in fair meadows.
Some will dwell on Belgian soil,*
1725 Some inhabit fields of Italy
And others will touch on western Spain.

Heu Christiani patriam fugiunt suam!
O Rex Tyranne* quo tuos,
Procul repellis subditos!
Externa regna quaerimus
1710 Aequorque nostrum linquimus,
Dum non tibi bonis sat est
Nos exuisse patriis,
Angli exulare cogimur
Et exterorum per plagas,
1715 Servare debemus fidem.
Manes Patrum! Manes Patrum!
Etiam sepulti flebitis,
Hinc dum Nepotes ob fidem
Sedas relinquunt patrias;
1720 Et mortuorum iam iacent,
Sepulchra* ferro diruta.
Ibimus eheu, assueta prius
Placidis heu Gens vivere campis.
Pars Belgiacas incolet oras,*
1725 Pars Italicos incolet agros,
Pars Occiduos viset Iberos.

Nameless, wretched exiles we will be,
Scattered in a trice all over the world.
England lies here, Ireland beyond.
1730 O dearly beloved mother country,
O land of England, O land of our fathers,
We now bid farewell, we bid thee farewell.
But hear yet our sad lamentations
And treasure our tears, for without tears
1735 We never could leave our dear land.
How often our eyes will long to look back;
How often our souls will desire to speak.
Our England forever is lost,
She will never possess us in death,
1740 But our tears she will ever possess.
Once more, farewell, a final farewell,
O land of England, our native land,
We bestow our last tears,
Our last kisses are yours.
1745 Never will these tender farewells
Let us forget our country beloved.
Again farewell, forever farewell.

Sparsi toto protinus Orbe
Miseri latebimus exules.
Alibi Anglia, alibi Hybernia.
1730 O dulcis & chara patria!
Anglia Tellus, Patria Tellus,
Nunc ergo Vale, nunc ergo Vale,
Sed adhuc nostros imbibe questus
Imbibe lachrymas; non sine lachrymis,
1735 Linquenda nobis patria est:
Cernere retro quoties oculi;
Dicere quoties cupient animi;
Perdita nostra est Anglia nobis
Non nos habebit mortuos;
1740 Nostras habebit lachrymas.
Rursum ergo vale, rursum ergo vale,
Anglica Tellus, patria Tellus
Has ultimas tibi lachrymas
Haec ultima ferimus oscula!
1745 Meminisse semper Patriae
Haec sera facient oscula.
Rursus Vale, aeternum Vale.

ACT V, scene i

The Catholic Religion, Reason, Piety, Clemency

Rel. O earth, sky, sea, and whatever else is embraced by this vast fabric of being! [1750] O great begetter of time, you who evolve all ages in your course; O moon, queen of the night! You stars gleaming with your wandering fires! O air, O billowing clouds, and all else nature controls aloft; O rivers and mountains, O endless waters [1755] of swift-flowing fountains, O crags and caverns! All of you, join me in my grief. England has lost me and I, alas, have lost England—England who has been my own. I am Religion, Heaven's daughter and mother of Rome. See how I am plunged into grief and detested. My virgin bosom [1760] is lacerated, I am bruised and drenched with blood. On one side I am tortured with fire, on the other I am abused; I am driven out and crushed. To think that he—so recently my defender—oh, the shame of it! That illustrious king who guarded our sacred doctrines with his pen! That disgraceful Henry —tears choke my voice—now [1765] rushes on me as I stagger, bares his hand to uproot me and scatter me, banish me and kill me. O my Christians, your only alternatives are cruel banishment or bitter death. Perse-

ACTUS QUINTUS, scena i

Religio Catholica, Ratio, Pietas, Clementia

Rel. Coelum, solumque, & Aequor, & quicquid suo
　　　　Immensa rerum machina amplexu capit,
1750　Tu magne Genitor temporum volvis tuo
　　　　Qui saecla cursu; Luna tu noctis regens;
　　　　Vos spendicantes ignibus stellae vagis,
　　　　Aer, globique nubium, & quicquid supra
　　　　Natura versat; Flumina, & Montes, Aquae
1755　Levium perennes fontium, Rupes, specus,
　　　　Iuvate nostras lachrymas. Perii Angliae,
　　　　Mihique periit Anglia, heu quondam mea!
　　　　Religio Coeli filia, & Romae parens,
　　　　Demersa luctu, foeda, virgineos sinus
1760　Lacerata, fracta, sanguine effuso madens,
　　　　Hinc uror, inde vexor, expellor, premor,
　　　　Defensor ille, pro pudor! nuper meus,
　　　　Rex ille, calamo nostra qui asseruit sacra;
　　　　Henricus ille, (lachrymae vocem obruunt)
1765　In me ruentem pellit ac stringit manum;
　　　　Ut me revellat, dissipet, tollat, necet.
　　　　O Christiani, restat exilium grave,
　　　　Aut mors acerba: lenta succedent mala,

cutions will continue relentlessly, will keep raging even after you die. Our enemies [1770] will cruelly drag the spirits of the dead to a second death. On all sides I am afflicted, my victims lie everywhere. Torture racks groan with countless burdens of saintly heroes, and ransacked churches greedily devour the flames from hurled firebrands. Monastery cloisters stream with blood. [1775] Death is heaped on death, the burial records are crowded with the slain.* Nor are these calamities reserved for England alone; Ireland, too, is oppressed. There, anyone who clings to Roman Catholicism is condemned to ignominious death. How long will this go on? To whom can I look for help? [1780] Is there no hope left?

Rea. No hope at all, for once the King dismissed from his mind all dictates of right reason, he rushed fiercely and boldly to the attack. He still acts in a blind rage.

Rel. Are you sure there is no hope?

Pie. None whatsoever, for he has only contempt for the wrath of Heaven; he suppresses human rights and laws. [1785] The King is mad—he no longer believes in God.

Rel. But is there no hope at all?

Clem. None. When a man with a raging soul feeds on blood, he is com-

```
        Ultraque mortem saevient; Manes sua
   1770 Crudelitate rursus in mortem trahent.
        Ubique luctus est meus, funus meum:
        Gemunt onustae tot viris sacris cruces,
        Et fracta iactas templa corripiunt faces.
        Coenobiorum claustra confudit cruor.
        Et fracta iactas templa corripiunt faces.
        Coenobiorum claustra confudit cruor.
   1775 Mors morte premitur, funeri est funus grave.*
        Nec una tantis Anglia est satis malis;
        Hyberna Tellus premitur, hic quisquid fidem
        Servat Quiritum mortis infandae est reus.
        Quousque tandem? cuius implorem manum?
   1780 Nec ulla spes est?
        Rat.            Nulla spes, quando suo
        Exclusit animo recta quod ratio iubet,
        Ruit, impetuque surgit, & coecus furit.
        Rel. Nec ulla spes est?
        Pie.            Nulla spes, quando poli
        Contemnit iras, iuraque & leges premit.
   1785 Rex esse nullum cogitat demens Deum.
        Rel. Nec ulla spes est?
        Clem.            Nulla spes quando furens
```

pletely distraught. He has outlawed human kindness from his heart.
Rel. O Great Heavenly Ruler, O Father of the world! [1790] If all is
hopeless, breathe strength into my children. Help them triumph over
whippings and buffetings, over flames and torture racks. Let them be
exalted in death. But look! The King approaches in person. What does he
want? I am completely unnerved with fear. He is planning fresh disasters
because I am so grieved.

ACT V, scene ii

King Henry, The Catholic Religion, Reason, Piety, Clemency

Hen. [1795] How dreadfully this furious disturbance shatters my peace
of mind! On either side of me anxieties are drawn up like soldiers; they
hem me in. Only a few of my subjects cower in the face of royal threats.*
They refuse to comply with the enactment I have drawn up. They refuse
to take the oath; [1800] they refuse to acknowledge me as head of the
English Church. They prefer to die, even to die in flames and torture.
Shall I allow my own subjects to deny me, their King? Shall my own subjects offer resistance to me, to their King? Never! If I cannot have my
way by persuasion, I will have it [1805] by force, by blood. It is this

Animus cruore pascitur; totus furit;
Benignitatem pectore exclusit suo.
Rel. O Magne Coeli Rector, O Mundi parens!
1790 Si nulla spes est, robur aspira meis.
Vincant flagella, verbera, ignes & cruces,
Et augeantur mortibus. Sed en venit
Rex ipse: quid vult! tota concutior metu.
Meditatur iterum misera quod nimium gemam.

ACTUS QUINTUS, scena ii

Henricus Rex, Religio Catholica, Ratio, Pietas, Clementia

1795 *Hen.* Immane quantum pectoris saevo quies
Turbata motu est! longa curarum cohors
Utrimque cingit; subditi Regis minas
Pauci verentur,* quam dedi legem, negant;
Iurare nolunt, Anglicanae me caput
1800 Ecclesiae non confitentur, & mori,
Etiam per ignes & cruces malunt mori.
Et me negabunt subditi Regem mei?
Et mihi resistent subditi Regi mei?
Non ita, cruenta quod volo fiet manu.

phalanx of Christian subjects that provokes me to such wrath. They face
slaughter fearlessly, and stubbornly persist in clinging to their Roman
faith. This insidious religion is causing great damage. Either I will be
their King or it will be wiped out of England.

Rel. Behold, Your Majesty, I am here. [1810] I, Religion, stand before
you. Why will you overthrow me by force? Will you banish me? Will
you drive me from your English shores? There was a time when you
raised your sword in my defense. Do you now intend to turn barbarian
and suck my blood to the last drop? Will you drain my lifeblood and
pour it out like a savage?

Hen. [1815] I have made up my mind to be head of the English Church.
Unless you submit to this, you will have to leave.

Rel. Your Majesty, by demanding this you force me to leave England.
But still you cannot be head of the church. There is only one head, and
that head is the Roman Pontiff.

Hen. Let him remain Pontiff of Rome, but let my subjects acknowledge
me as head.

Rel. [1820] But there must be only one head since there is only one
church.

Hen. Is it right for the Pope to make laws for me? Should he exercise any
control over my kingdom, over my subjects?

1805 Si non quieta. Christianorum Phalanx
      Istas in iras me vocat; temnit necem,
      Suamque tantum pertinax Romam colit.
      Ista, ista Religio nocet. Vel Rex ero,
      Vel hinc recedet.
      Rel.   Ecce Rex adsum tibi
1810 Religio, nunquid me tua evertes manu?
      Me exterminabis? Anglia expelles tua?
      Tu me solebas ense tutari tuo,
      Et nunc cruoris ultimas guttas mei
      Sorbebis atrox, hauries, fundes ferox?
1815 *Hen.* Ecclesiae caput Anglicanae sim, volo.
      Vel hinc recedes.
      Rel.   Quando Rex istud petis,
      Hinc me repellis, esse non potes caput.
      Unum est, & istud Pontifex Romae est caput.
      Hen. Sit ipse Romae, me mei agnoscant caput.
1820 *Rel.* Unum esse debet, una tantum Ecclesia est.
      Hen. Et iura mihi det Pontifex? regnum meum
      Meosque fraenet subditos?

Rel. He rules over the moral and spiritual needs of your kingdom, and by establishing your subjects in their faith he looks after their spiritual welfare.

Hen. It is I who establish faith and law for my people.

Rel. [1825] But this is not your prerogative; you should do only what is befitting a king.

Hen. I shall force the rebels to submit.

Rel. A Christian cannot be forced, even by death.

Hen. I shall strew the ground with a thousand victims.

Rel. While you are doing so, a thousand new Christians will be born.

Hen. The violence of my attack will prevent this.

Rel. When such cruel violence cuts us down, it serves only [1830] to increase our fruitfulness.

Hen. I shall use fire and water to punish them.

Rel. My children always emerge more beautiful from such treatment. I grow fruitful with buffeting; I wax strong under affliction.

Rea. Be reasonable. A king should not pursue something prohibited by law.

Pie. It is still not too late [1835] to appease Heaven, provided you act reasonably. The Holy Father is benevolent, he will pardon your waywardness.

      Rel.   Mores regit
Et sacra regni, & subditis donans fidem
Curat salutem.
      Hen.   Do fidem & legem meis.
1825 *Rel.* Hoc non tuum est, tu quod decet Reges, ages.
      Hen. Cogam rebelles.
      Rel.   Christianus non potest
Vel morte cogi.
      Hen.   Mille diffundam neces.
      Rel. Dum mille tolles, mille nascentur novi.
      Hen. Furor cavebit.
      Rel.   Ille qui resecat furor,
1830 Crudelis auget.
      Hen.   Igne & undis opprimam.
      Rel. Hinc pulchriores semper emergunt mei.
Foecunda fio cladibus, cresco malis.
      Rat. Compone mentem; non decet Regem sequi
Quod iura nolunt.
      Pie.   Sero, si tamen sapis,
1835 Placatus Aether fiet, errorem auferet
Tibi benignus Pontifex.

Hen. Alas, O Sovereign Pontiff! How you throw me and my kingdom into confusion!

Rel. Acknowledge him as your Father—the Pope is the Father of kings.

Hen. Never! Begone. I am head of our England. [1840] Let him oppose me. Come what may, I will still triumph.

Clem. You will never triumph. When power heaps crime upon crime, it grows callous and inflexible. Kingdoms are governed better by more humane rule. Cruelty begets cruelty.

Hen. One thing alone is necessary: they must obey my will. [1845] When kings command, they have a right to be obeyed. I am king and I will likewise be pope for my people.

ACT V, scene iii

Cranmer, King Henry, Councilors, Alice (wife of More),
and their daughter Margaret

Cran. All this raging violence is futile, Your Majesty. Few subjects heed your enactments. Every sacred order is actually growing rebellious. They pay no attention to your threats. [1850] They do not worry in the least about what the outcome will be. And this will astonish you still more: they actually desire to endure a cruel death by the sword.

Hen. In spite of this I am determined to use violence. I shall make the

      Hen.   Heu Pontifex!
      Heu me meumque Pontifex regnum moves!
      Rel. Agnosce Patrem, Pontifex Regum est pater.
      Hen. Nunquam; recede: sum Angliae nostrae caput.
1840 Obsistat ille, quicquid est vincam tamen.
      Clem. Nunquam; potestas scelere diffundens scelus
      Violenta durat; mitior melius manus
      Regnum gubernat: efferat, quicquid ferum est.
      Hen. Unum est necessum: pareant, sit quod volo.
1845 Parere iustum est Regibus quando iubent.
      Sum Rex, & idem Pontifex ero meis.

ACTUS QUINTUS, scena iii

Granmerus, Henricus Rex, Senatores, Aloysia Mori Uxor, Margareta Filia

      Gran. Saevire frustra est Magne Rex, pauci tua
      Edicta curant, ordo quicunque est sacer
      Ultro rebellat: nil minas curant tuas,
1850 Nil fata curant; quodque mireris magis,
      Etiam cruento confici ferro petunt.
      Hen. Saevire certum est attamen: flectam impios

rebels submit or do away with them completely.

1 Coun. Popular opinion is swayed by the example of Thomas More. Every educated man takes him for his ideal.

Hen. [1855] This one man can have more influence than the King.* Let him be summoned again. If he remains obstinate, let him die. The death of one such famous figure might terrify the people.

2 Coun. His wife is here. She will sway her husband with her tears. And here is his daughter. Her tears will be added to her mother's.

Hen. [1860] Let us use them. My Lady, why do you prostrate yourself and grieve so bitterly?* What is your petition? My young maiden, what do you implore on your knees?

Alice. Restore my husband. In my grief I beg you to restore him.

Marg. Give me back my father. By these tears I beg you to release him.

Hen. I shall restore husband to wife and father to daughter. [1865] Let him yield, let him obey his king. Go and persuade him.

Alice. But first let him be released from his chains.

Hen. This I cannot allow. However, you shall be allowed to visit him in prison.

Cran. My daughter, throw your arms around your father's neck and plead with him. [1870] He will never be able to resist your tears.

Aut morte tollam.
Sen.1   Morus exemplo movet.
Illum imitari quisquis est doctus cupit.
1855 *Hen.* Vir unus ipse plus potest,* quam Rex potest.
Iterum vocetur, pertinax si sit, cadat.
Mors una tanti forte terrebit viri.
Sen.2 En uxor, ipsa lachrymis flectet virum.
En Nata, matris lachrymis iunget suas.
1860 *Hen.* Utamur illis. Prona quid tanto petis
Matrona luctu?* Virgo, quid supplex cupis?
Aloy. Reddas maritum, repetit hic luctus virum.
Marg. Reddas parentem, lachrymae hae repetunt patrem.
Hen. Reddam maritum coniugi, & natae patrem.
1865 Flectatur ipse, pareat regi suo
Ite & movete.
Aloy.   Vinculis sed sit prius
Suis solutus.
Hen.   Non licet, carcer tamen
Vobis patebit.
Cran.   Nata tu patrem move
Affusa collo, lachrymas nunquam tuas
1870 Feret obstinatus.

Marg. I shall clasp him in my arms and the sight of my anguish will break down his resistance.

Cran. He will refuse his wife nothing.

Alice. May God so ordain. Since the head of the family has been taken from us, the entire household has been thrown into confusion.

3 Coun. And so he alone can preserve the entire household. [1875] Go and change his mind. Make him obey and his deliverance is assured.

Hen. As to the next move, go once more and publicly proclaim the death penalty for recusancy.

Cran. It is useless to do this a second time. The entire Order of Friars of the Observance,* immune as they are to whatever cruel destiny awaits them, [1880] are growing insolent. The followers of Francis accuse the King of crime and defend the Papacy before the excited crowds.

Hen. They accuse the King of crime?

Cran. Precisely! Of crime. They condemn Anne Boleyn's marriage, they deny that the King is the supreme head of the English Church. [1885] Their following is so strong that the people are taking sides. And so all England is lost.

Hen. O accursed sect! No establishment of the Friars must remain standing. Go and burn them, drive out this foul pestilence. Make them leave

    Marg.   Vinciam amplexu meo,
    Constansque pectus luctibus vincam meis.
    Gran. Nihil negabit Coniugi.
    Aloy.   Faxit Tonans;
    Confusa patre est tota sublato Domus.
    Sen.3 Servare totam sic potest solus Domum.
1875   Ite & movete; pareat, parta est salus.
    Hen. Quod restat, ite rursus & poenam ultimam
    Denunciate.
    Gran.   Vanus hic rursum labor.
    Ordo Minorum totus Observantium*
    Qui dura supra fata, Francisci genus,
1880   Ultro insolescit, arguit Regis nefas,
    Et concitata plebe defendit Papam.
    Hen. Nefasne Regis arguit?
    Gran.   Sic est, nefas.
    Damnat Bolena nuptias, Ecclesiae
    Negat Anglicanae maximum Regem caput.
1885   Istos secutus populus in partes abit.
    Sic tota perditur Anglia.
    Hen.   O sacrum Genus!
    Coenobiorum nulla perduret Domus;
    Injicite flammas, pellite infandam luem,

and quit this country; banish them or let them die.

1 Coun. [1890] The Carthusian monks are also taking sides.* They refuse
to admit the King as head of the church.

Hen. Let them also incur death by being burned alive. Wipe them out;
make them pay the death penalty for their crime.

2 Coun. Even this will be of no avail. There is only one thing [1895] that
will terrify the entire populace: the death of Thomas More.

Hen. Let More die, let him perish. Let him fall unless he acknowledges
me as sovereign of our land.

ACT V, scene iv

Thomas More, Alice, Margaret

Thom. Dear Wife, what are you doing here? This prison is no place for
you. And there is no need for you to cry over my present misfortune.

Alice. Thomas, do not allow your wife to weep.* [1900] You know my
sorrow is great beyond measure. Come back to me as a husband should.
It is in your power. You would not leave me, would you? You would not
forsake your country and your daughter! Oh, dear Husband, I call upon
your love for me; dear Husband, I beseech you by the power of these

    Abeant, recedant, exulent, fato occidant.
1890 *Sen.1* Carthusiana Gens quoque in partes abit.*
    Regem fateri Ecclesiae non vult caput.
    Hen. Etiam hi per ignes ultimum fatum ferant;
    Exterminate, morte delictum luent.
    Sen.2 Nec hoc iuvabit; una mors Mori omnium
1895 Terrebit animos.
    Hen.   Occidat, pereat, cadat.
    Vel me supremum patriae dicat caput.

ACTUS QUINTUS, scena iv

Thomas Morus, Aloysia, Margareta

    Thom. Quid cara Coniux? Carcer hic non te decet.
    Nec iste noster lachrymas poscit labor.
    Aloy. Ne patere, More, coniugis lachrymas tuae.*
1900 Cernis dolorem, magnus excedit modum,
    Tu redde te mihi coniugem; Coniux potes.
    Num me relinques? Patriam Natam tuam?
    O chare Coniux, si quid est in te mei
    O chare Coniux, si quid hae lachrymae queunt,
1905 Per te, per istud pectoris Numen tui,

tears, [1905] for your own sake and in the name of God within you; for my sake, Husband, for the sake of these tears, my Husband, do have pity on your wife and children.

Thom. My wife and children are always in my thoughts.

Alice. Let the thought of life affect you.

Thom. Of my life?*

Alice. Yes, Husband, yours. [1910] You may well live another twenty years on this earth.

Thom. Twenty years! Yet even that is a short time. No person in his right mind would exchange eternity for twenty years. You are worried, dry your tears. It is all for my good.

Alice. But believe me, Thomas, it is not so good for your wife. [1915] For my part, if you die, everything dies. The day that robs me of my husband will rob me of my life as well. You are our life. Alas the day! Alas, alas the day! Am I to hold your lifeless body to my bosom, am I to behold your face bereft of its radiance? [1920] What empty hopes! O Fortune, how deeply you wound my heart. Husband, you stood forth as the light of your country; now you are an object of shame. Not long ago you were gleaming, you were England's foremost jewel. Now you are stripped of honor and a prison holds you fast. [1925] Now, Thomas, you are tasting the cruel reversal of Fortune.

      Per me, per istas lachrymas, Coniux, meas
      Miserere, Coniux, liberorum & coniugis.
      Thom. Et liberorum, & coniugis vivo memor.
      Aloy. Miserere vitae.
      Thom.   Num meae?*
      Aloy.   Coniux tuae.
1910 Bis forte denos vivere annos hic potes.
      Thom. Bis forte denos? Numerus annorum est brevis,
      Aeternitate nemo mutet qui sapit,
      Sollicita tolle lachrymas, Moro est bene.
      Aloy. Bene, crede Coniux, coniugi non est tuae.
1915 Mihi cuncta pereunt, si peris: quae te dies
      Mihi maritum tollet, haec vitam auferet.
      Tu vita nostra est. Heu dies! Heu heu dies!
      Ego te peremptum claudere hoc possim sinu?
      Et istud oris cernere extinctum iubar?
1920 O spes inanes! vulnere O quanto meum
      Fortuna pectus laedis! O Coniux! tuae,
      Lux extitisti patriae, nunc es probrum;
      Nuper nitebas Angliae primum decus,
      Nunc dignitate carcer exutum tenet.
1925 Vires vicesque More fortunae subis.

Thom. I am master of my fate. No man should fear destiny. Furthermore, through hope a wise man triumphs over every adversity of fate.
Alice. But if you face certain death, what is there to hope for?
Thom. [1930] For something beyond death.
Alice. That is a good thing, certainly. It is always right to go on hoping, but it is not always right to die. You can still say one thing and mean another.
Thom. An upright man can never dissemble simply to win his own freedom. [1935] God detests equivocation in this matter.
Alice. Oh, Thomas, your uprightness will destroy you.
Thom. Uprightness can never destroy anyone. God always extols an upright heart.
Alice. But our family's good name now perishes with you.
Thom. An honest man's reputation is immortal: [1940] our good name will be enhanced by my death. My Lady, cry no longer. Come, dear Daughter, compose yourself.
Marg. If only I could! I would gladly do anything at all that would help. Why are you the only one who cannot comply with the King?
Thom. Such complicity is forbidden [1945] when it offends God.

          Thom. Sors omnis in me est, quae mea est: non est viri
          Timere sortem: quisquis est sapiens sua
          Spe vincit omne sortis adversae malum.
          Aloy. Sperare quid vis certa si mors sit tibi?
     1930 *Thom.* Mortem quod ultra est.
          Aloy.   Istud est quodquod bonum.
          Sperare fas est semper, haud semper mori,
          Simulare mentem iam potes.
          Thom.   Nunquam bonus
          Simulare mentem vir potest quando suae
          Causam salutis sustinet: fictas Deus,
     1935 Odit loquelas.
          Aloy.   Ista te perdet tua
          O More probitas.
          Thom.   Perdere haud probitas potest.
          Sincera semper pectora extollit Deus.
          Aloy. Sed fama nostrae perditur tecum domus.
          Thom. Perire iusti fama non potest viri;
     1940 Augebo famam mortuus. Coniux tuas
          Compesce lachrymas: Nata tu luctus tene.
          Marg. Utinam liceret; si quid est ultra, dabo.
          Obtemperare solus an Regi nequis?
          Thom. Obtemperare non licet Regi suo,
     1945 Obtemperando laeditur quando Deus.

Marg. But the case is doubtful, and in such a case you can take the benefit of the doubt.

Thom. There can be no doubt about something which faith makes absolutely certain. The Pope is the head of all Christendom and as such he possesses complete ecclesiastical jurisdiction; the old faith so teaches.

Marg. [1950] The Bishop of Rochester made you think this way.

Thom. I admit that I esteem and venerate the Bishop as a holy man, but I have thought this way for a long time.

Marg. Still, so many bishops throughout England are taking the oath;* so are learned men, both young and old, as well as noblemen and holy people.

Thom. [1955] But more of them are recusant. The rest of the world does not agree with those Englishmen who approve the royal edict. The Fathers of the Church also think otherwise, and they are the authorities on Christian orthodoxy.

Marg. Your King drew up the enactment and the English Parliament approves it. Father, will you still be the only one who refuses to acknowledge it?

Thom. Daughter, I have no choice. My reason [1960] and my loyalty to the faith demand it. No edict of kings can abrogate something which our faith makes certain.

Marg. Still, Father, I am afraid.

       Marg. At dubia res est, flectere hic mentem potes.
       Thom. Res dubia non est, quam facit certam fides.
       Ecclesiarum Pontifex quod sit caput
       Ius omne dicit, prisca decernit fides.
1950 *Marg.* Roffensis ille Praesul hanc mentem facit.
       Thom. Veneror coloque Praesulem, sanctum virum,
       Fuit ista pridem nostra mens.
       Marg.   At tot tamen
       Iurant ubique praesules,* iurant senes,
       Iuvenesque docti, Nobiles, sancti viri.
1955 *Thom.* Plures recusant. Reliquus hoc Orbis negat,
       Quod hi fatentur. Sentiunt aliter Patres
       Fidei Magistri.
       Marg.   Regis edictum est tui,
       Probat Senatus Angliae, tune hoc parens
       Solus negabis?
       Thom.   Ipsa sic ratio iubet
1960 Pietasque, Nata; quod facit certum fides
       Lex nulla Regum tollit.
       Marg.   At vereor parens.

Thom. My dear, why are you afraid?

Marg. Because I will be overwhelmed with grief.

Thom. Over my death? No fear, no power on earth shall conquer my soul. It is not through any merit of my own that I feel such confidence: [1965] this is God's doing. The loving Father who endowed me with reason will also grant me strength of soul. Daughter, why are you beginning to cry again?

Marg. Our whole family is weeping for you, for their father and lord. And look how wretched Mother is—all but dead with grief.

Thom. If only there were some way I might relieve you of this anguish! [1970] But God who eases every burden will lighten your cross. Fare thee well, dear Wife.

Alice. I cannot fare well without you.

Thom. And goodbye, Daughter. All will go well with you.

Marg. Not without my father. How cruel life would be without a father like you.

ACT V, scene v

Cranmer, Thomas More, Councilors

Cran. Let More be summoned,* the King's edict so enjoins, [1975] for those guilty of crime should not be allowed to go on living indefinitely.

> *Thom.* Quid tu vereris Nata?
> *Marg.*   Quod nimium gemam.
> *Thom.* Meamne mortem? nullus hoc pectus timor,
> Vis nulla vincet; spem facit tantam Tonans,
> 1965 Non merita vitae. Qui dedit mentem, dabit
> Vires benignus. Nata quid rursus gemis?
> *Marg.* At tota Dominum nostra te Domus gemit.
> Et ecce misera se enecat lucta parens.
> *Thom.* Utinam dolorem tollere hunc vestrum queam.
> 1970 Sedabit illum cuncta qui sedat Deus.
> Coniux vale.
> *Aloy.*   Valere sine te non queo.
> *Thom.* Et tu valebis Nata;
> *Marg.*   Nempe sine patre.
> O dura vita Patre quae tanto caret.

ACTUS QUINTUS, scena v

Granmerus, Thomas Morus, Senatores

> *Gran.* Hic Morus adsit;* Regis edictum iubet;
> 1975 Vivere nocentes namque non debent diu.

This is the ultimate guarantee of the public good: namely, obedience to royal injunction. More, now that you are in the presence of this just tribunal, speak what befits a loyal and upright subject of the King. This is the place where a man should exercise good judgment.

Thom. [1980] I have always been a loyal subject of the King;* I am so right now and will continue so as long as I live. I have no wish to offend anyone here. I have never intended to offend anyone. I wish well to all mankind and I pray for every man.

Cran. One thing remains to be done: acknowledge the King as head of the church.

Thom. He is not the head. [1985] I find it impossible to admit this statement.

Cran. You insist on holding stubbornly to this view. You can be forced to yield.

Thom. Notwithstanding, such action would be unjust. Let him use force and put me to death. As long as my body has life in it I will be of this mind.

Cran. You are an ingrate, More. Will you concede your King nothing?

Thom. [1990] I will concede my body and this life that he demands of me. The King knows my devotion and loyalty. I am a loyal subject and I love my King, but I can never approve of his enactment, even though the

      Hoc est salutis publicae pignus novum
      Servare Regum iussa. More, dum vides
      Iustum hoc tribunal, loquere, quod verum decet
      Probumque Regis subditum, sapere hic licet.
1980 *Thom.* Regi fidelis subditus semper fui;*
      Sum, vivo talis. Laedere hic nullum volo;
      Laesisse nunquam mens fuit; bene omnibus
      Volo, precorque.
      Gran.   Restat hoc tantum, caput
      Agnosce Regem Ecclesiae.
      Thom.   Non est caput.
1985 Istud fateri non queo.
      Gran.   Semper tua
      Haeret voluntas pertinax: cogi potes.
      Thom. Certe est iniquum: cogat & mortem inferat:
      Dum vita corpus hoc reget, mens haec erit.
      Gran. Ingrate More, nil tuo Regi dabis?
1990 *Thom.* Hoc corpus, atque hanc, quam petit vitam dabo.
      Rex pectus istud novit, & nostram fidem;
      Amo fidelis subditus Regem meum.
      Probare legem quam tulit nunquam queo.

King has so decreed.

1 Coun. This fellow is the only wise man alive.* [1995] Just think how many bishops are mentally inferior to this great More! Even the lords and the members of Parliament are stupid. The King is wrong, all the people who approve this law are wrong.

Thom. I am not impressed by what a few English lords believe. The whole world feels the way I do and the Fathers of the church in the past [2000] have had the same opinion.

1 Coun. More is a public enemy, a traitor, and an enemy of the Crown.*

Thom. I have never been so. I have been a loyal subject of the King every moment of my life and I shall die a loyal subject. I swear by the high heaven and by God who knows my every thought [2005] that my heart is upright and my tongue is true. I pray for the King's happiness and health and for the kingdom's weal.

2 Coun. There is no point in going on talking. An end to quibbling! More, do you or do you not approve of His Majesty's law?

Thom. My word is final: I do not approve.

3 Coun. Then why should we delay? He is guilty of high treason.

Cran. [2010] Pronounce sentence, or else let him change his mind before the verdict.

1 Coun. We pronounce you a traitor and guilty of high treason. Execu-

---

          Lex ista regis sit tamen.
          Sen.1   Solus sapit;*
1995 Antistites tot inter hic Morus sapit;
          Et optimates, & Senatus desipit.
          Rex errat, errant quotquot hanc legem probant.
          Thom. Nil optimates Angliae paucos moror;
          Mecum ipse sentit orbis, & patrum vetus
2000 Ita sensit aetas.
          Sen.1   Perduellis, proditor
          Et Regis hostis Morus est.*
          Thom.   Nunquam fui:
          Regi fidelis hactenus servus fui;
          Moriar fidelis; testor aethereas plagas,
          Nostraeque testor conscium mentis Deum,
2005 Nec fictus animus, ficta nec lingua est mihi.
          Felix, valensque Rex sit, & Regnum, precor.
          Sen.2 Tot verba frustra; tollat ambages; probas
          Regisne legem More.
          Thom.   Dixi, non probo.
          Sen.3 Haeremus igitur? Regis est laesi reus.
2010 *Gran.* Pronuntietur; mutet aut mentem prius.
          Sen.1 Te perduellem & Regis offensi reum

tioner, go cut off More's head with a sword. He has seen his day.

Thom. Eternal Father, I thank You freely and joyfully. [2015] I shall be privileged to die for You, since my death on this day will be in your honor.

1 Coun. Enough of this, no more delays. Executioner, lead him away; I shall accompany you.

ACT V, scene vi

Thomas More, Councilor 1, Executioner, The Catholic Religion

Thom. Do not weary yourself by helping me; I shall go ahead of you un-assisted to the very last step. The skies have never seemed [2020] brighter than now. I am about to give my body back to England and my soul back to God.

Exec. But that cloak of yours must come off, More.*

Thom. My cloak is yours, Executioner. Here, take it.

Rel. And shall England strip off her foremost glory, [2025] her model of prudence, of loyalty, and of public service? And shall that body stretch out its bared limbs? That body that houses a brilliant mind, that citadel of integrity, that throne of unswerving fidelity?

<blockquote>

Pronunciamus. Lictor I Moro caput
Rescinde ferro, vixerit.
Thom.   Grates tibi,
Aeterne Genitor, liber & gaudens ago.
2015 Haec grata mortis causa, cum pro te mori
Hodie licebit.
Sen.1   Sit satis, tolle hinc moras.
Comitabor, illum Lictor abductum trahe.

</blockquote>

ACTUS QUINTUS, scena vi

Thomas Morus, Senator 1, Lictor, Religio Catholica

Thom. Ne te fatiga, libero en promptus pede
Ultro praeibo; gratior nunquam mihi
2020 Illuxit Aether; Angliae reddam meae
Mortale corpus, spiritum reddam Deo.
Lic. At exuenda More, vestis est tua.*
Thom. Tua ista, Lictor, vestis est, vestem cape.
Rel. Et exuetur Angliae primum decus?
2025 Prudentiae, Virtutis, officii decus?
Et corpus istud, inclytae Mentis Domus,
Arx illa Honoris, & thronus Constantiae,
Nudata pandet membra?

1 Coun. Now that the time has come, More, I forbid you to address the crowd.*

Thom. [2030] This also is unjust.* A loyal subject of the King and servant of God should be allowed at least to say this: I ascribe to the faith of Rome by dying for it.* My beloved England, I call you to witness that I die a true Englishman. And as a Christian do I pour out my blood. [2035] Christ, make me strong. I am ready to die.

Exec. Pardon me, More,* for dealing the death-blow but I must do it.

Thom. I am grateful for dying this way, Executioner, and I thank you. I am your friend. Here, let me embrace you,* and kindly accept this kiss of peace and my coat [2040] as a pledge of our friendship.

Rel. Almighty God!* Behold this head! Will an unrighteous sword strike it off? And that neck! Will this neck of England be smitten?

Exec. Allow me to blindfold you, More.*

Thom. I will blindfold myself, I will use this handkerchief I have.

Rel. [2045] Withdraw your face, O sun, for behold England's sun declines. Clothe yourselves in black, you heavens, for behold Thomas More is about to die. That illustrious head of radiance is veiled.

Thom. Jesus, have mercy. Executioner, I await your blow.

        Sen.1   Nunc dum tempus est,
        Te verba More proloqui ad plebem, veto.*
2030 *Thom.* Etiam hoc iniquum est;* liceat hoc saltem loqui.
        Regis fidelis servus, & servus Dei
        Fidem Quiritum morte consigno mea.*
        Te chara testor Anglia, occumbo tuus.
        Et Christianus sanguinem effundo meum.
2035 Tu Christe robur adde, nil mortem moror.
        Lic. Ignosce, More* cogor, ut mortem inferam.
        Thom. Mors ista grata est Lictor, & grates ago.
        Habes amicum, pectus amplectar tuum,*
        Et pacis istud osculum accipies meae.
2040 Et pignus istud.
        Rel.   O Tonans?* Et hoc caput
        Caput hoc secabit impiae ferrum manus?
        Et illa cervix, Angliae haec cervix cadet?
        Lic. Permitte vultum, More, velabo tuum.*
        Thom. Velabo memet, linteo hoc utar meo.
2045 *Rel.* O sol recede, en Angliae Phoebus perit.
        Coelum tenebras indue, en Morus perit;
        Velatur illud Luminis clari caput.
        Thom. Miserere Jesu. Lictor, en cervix patet.

ACT V, scene vii

Religion, Margaret, an Angel

Rel. It is done; the head of all England has been severed.* [2050] O land of Britain, behold how your glory has faded! O land of Britain, see your pillar of state lie in ruins! O land of Britain, it is you that lie here in death, for behold, you lie here slaughtered with More. All Englishmen perish with this man. [2055] Oh, Thomas, what grief lies in store for your England!

Marg. Is it all over now? There is nothing to do, then, but mourn.

Rel. This death should put all England in mourning.

Marg. Nothing remains? Nothing at all? No sign of life? Alas! Where now is that face that shone as the glory of England? [2060] And is that voice stilled? The voice that rang out for justice! And does that body that was the mainstay of England now lie pale, silent, lifeless, desolate? King Henry, you are the one who perpetrated this outrage; you who ordered his execution. And now he is slain, [2065] he who could never be won over by your schemes and your bribes. Oh, my poor father! Your daughter now realizes how saintly you were: I venerate you. I venerate your

ACTUS QUINTUS, scena vii

Religio, Margareta, Angelus

    Rel. Actum est, recisum est Angliae toti caput.*
2050 Britanna Tellus, en tuum cecidit decus.
        Britanna Tellus, en tuum columen iacet.
        Britanna Tellus, en iaces, ipsa hic iaces
        Hoc ecce Mori funus est funus tuum.
        Moriuntur omnes unus hic quando perit.
2055 Heu More quantus Angliae est luctus tuae!
        Marg. Ergo peractum est? sufficit nunc ut gemam.
        Rel. Lachrymetur ut tota Anglia, hoc funus sat est.
        Marg. Et nil relictum est? & nihil? vitae nihil?
        Ubi vultus ille, heu, Angliae quandam iubar!
2060 Et reticet os, os aequitatis organum?
        Et corpus illud Angliae fulcrum suae;
        Exanime, mutum, mortuum, abiectum iacet?
        Henrice facinus hoc tuum est; iussu tuo
        Iacet peremptus, qui tuis flecti dolis
2065 Donisque nunquam potuit. Ah, ah, ah Parens!
        Ego Nata certum iam colo Numen tuum;
        Ego Nata Manes veneror, & colo tuos.

departed spirit and cherish your memory. As I lay you to rest in this grave,* receive my offering of tears, the last gift a daughter can give.

Rel. [2070] Alas, what shall I do? Whose aid shall I beg? Shall I forsake this land? Will he live on? How long will this treacherous king go on living? May lightning strike him down! O Mighty Warden of the skies, when will your voice begin thundering? Will not the earth soon split wide open [2075] and all Hell gape beneath?

Angel. Religion, be of good hope. Revenge is already storming Heaven and sin will incur unprecedented punishment. Still it will be a long time before you return to England, a long time. Meanwhile may your children bear up with slaughter and banishment, with prisons and torture racks. [2080] They must go underground. Heresy will employ her wiles to hold the kingdom in her clutches and there is no escaping the woman's iron rule.* Fate will decide the issue. A country that rejects Christianity scarcely ever recovers, and then only at the price of bitter retribution. [2085] The pains of expiation are long in arrears.

Rel. But will our children endure persecution?

Angel. Yes, many of them. Generous natures will lay down their lives. Yes, martyrs will mount to Olympus from English soil, martyrs radiant in their garments of blood. No torture whatsoever will daunt the up-

       At dum sepulchro corpus hoc condo tuum*
       Lachrymas, supremum filiae munus, cape.
2070 *Rel.* Quid agam? quid eheu? cuius implorem manum?
       Et hinc abibo? vivet? & vivet diu
       Hoc fulminandum perfidi Regis caput?
       Et non tonabis magne Coelituum Parens?
2075 Patebit Orcus?
       Ang.   Religio, spera bene,
       Vindicta Coelos pulsat, & poenas scelus
       Inusitatus sentiet. Sero tamen,
       Sero redibis; interim clades tui
       Ferant Alumni, exilia, carceres, cruces.
2080 Latere debent, Haeresis regnum sua
       Tenebit arte, & foeminae Imperium grave*
       Pati est necessum. Fata decernent viam.
       Quae Christianam regio contemnit fidem,
       Vix recipit unquam, vel graves poenas luit.
2085 Sunt debitarum longa poenarum mala.
       Rel. Etiamne nostri perferent?
       Ang.   Multi ferent.
       Generosa vitam pectora effundent suam.
       Etiam hinc cruore Martyres pulchri suo
       Scandent Olympum. Nulla mors vincet bonos;

right. [2090] The fields of England and Ireland will run deep with blood and furious persecution will rage, but to no avail.

Rel. Then let us prepare to suffer whatever the fates decree. But in the end, may God still have mercy on England.

ACT V, scene viii

King Henry, Brian, Councilor 1, Anne Boleyn, Warham

Hen. Oh, how I am dogged by this endless retinue of anxieties that keep haunting me! [2095] A king can have no peace whatsoever. My body is more bloated* each day and the swellings grow worse. And then this fear never gives me a free moment. Tell me, has Thomas More met his doom yet?*

1 Coun. His life is ended. "I die a loyal subject of my country and my King," he said, "and I keep the faith of my fathers [2100] by dying for it."

Hen. Oh, Thomas, Thomas, how you prolong my torture!

1 Coun. He died a Christian and swore his allegiance to the Pope of Rome.

Hen. He was always steadfast.

War. Your Majesty, the former Queen Catherine your wife has likewise passed away.*

2090 Hyberniaeque & Angliae campos cruor
   Replebit altos, sed fremet frustra furor.
   Rel. Patiemur ergo, fata decernent modum.
   Misere tamen O Angliae tandem Deus.

ACTUS QUINTUS, scena viii

Henricus Rex, Brianus, Senator 1, Bolena, Varamus

   Hen. Heu pallidarum longa curarum cohors!
2095 Pax nulla Regi est; intumescit hoc meum*
   Crescitque pondus corporis, nec me metus
   Unquam relinquit. Morus an fato occidit?*
   Sen.1 Vixit: fidelis Patriae & Regi meo
   Occumbo servus, inquit, & patrum fidem
2100 Moriendo servo.
   Hen.   More, More quo meos
   Trahis dolores?
   Sen.1   Christianus & Papam,
   Confessus obiit.
   Hen.   Semper hic constans fuit.
   Var. Catharina vixit, illa Rex Coniux tua.*
   Regina quondam, vixit.

Hen. She also? Now a fresh wound [2105] strikes my heart.

War. As she lay dying, she sent you these papers. Here they all are for you to read. Wounded by her love for the King, she sank to death, grieving over you to the very end. I know not how many times she began to cry all over again, how frequently she repeated [2110] while dying: "O Christ, grant pardon to my husband."

Hen. Read through the papers; I am overwhelmed with grief!

*(The letters of Queen Catherine are read to the King)**

War. These are the papers she sent.

Hen. No tears I shed can satisfy this.* The grief this sorrow deserves is greater than grief itself. About Anne—is it really true that she ridicules my love?* [2115] No! It cannot be that Anne scorns me.

Bri. She is already a disgrace to your court; she defiles the royal bed shamelessly. She is a common harlot. With her very own brother has she sinned and is happy about it.* The Queen's gross appetite makes her an easy conquest for all suitors.*

Hen. By this head, I swear! [2120] I swear by this scepter in my hand, now you will pay the penalty.

          Hen.   Hoc nostro est novum
     2105 Sub corde vulnus: vixit?
          Var.   Has ad te dedit
          Moriens tabellas; inspice & totas lege;
          Amore regis saucia occubuit sui;
          Sollicita pro te semper, O quoties novas
          Quaesivit ipsa lachrymas, quoties ait
     2110 Moriens, marito Christe condona meo.
          Hen. Perlege tabellas; turbat hunc animum dolor!

          *(Leguntur Reginae Catharinae ad Regem Litterae)**

          Var. Hae sunt tabellae.
          Hen.   Fletus haud noster sat est.*
          Lugendus ipso maior est luctu dolor.
          Et heu amores illa contemnit meos?*
     2115 Illa, heu, Bolena?
          Bri.   Iam tuae est Aulae probrum;
          Et impudica Regium spurcat torum;
          Vulgare scortum est; fratris amplexu sui
          Potita gaudet;* una Reginam omnibus
          Libido facilem subiicit.*
          Hen.   Iuro caput,
     2120 Istudque Sceptrum iuro, iam poenas dabis.

Bri. Here she comes now.

Anne. What is this silly talk about me?* About casting blame on your wife? What does all this mean, Your Majesty?

Hen. Put down that scepter.

Anne. What! I the Queen should put down my scepter?

Hen. Take that crown off your head. I command you, [2125] take off that crown. If she refuses to obey, carry the lewd woman off by force. You vile slut, so you are polluting my court and my bed?

Anne. Husband!

Hen. Hold your tongue, you are not—leave this place—you are not my wife. Be still!

Anne. You will throw me out? Me, your heart's desire?

Hen. [2130] I will throw out a slut; cut off this accursed head. I myself have witnessed the fact, yes, I myself. You are the royal palace prostitute. Leave this place, get out.

Anne. I beseech you in your kindness . . .

Hen. Away with you, begone!

Anne. By your royal scepter, I pray you . . .

Hen. Away with you, begone!

Anne. Husband, if you refuse [2135] to love me, at least let me live.

       Bri. En ipsa prodit.
       Bol.   Nempe me rumor tuam*
       Accusat ergo Coniugem? Quid Rex? quid est?
       Hen. Depone sceptrum.
       Bol.   Nempe deponam meum
       Regina sceptrum?
       Hen.   Verticis ponas decus,
2125 Ponas coronam; iubeo, si non est satis,
       Trahite impudicam: vile scortum, tu meam
       Aulam, torumque polluis?
       Bol.   Coniux.
       Hen.   Tace,
       Non es, recede, non mea es Coniux, tace.
       Bol. Et me repelles cordis idolum tui?
2130 *Hen.* Scortum repellam; tollite hoc sacrum caput;
       Vidi ipse, vidi; Regiae es scortum Domus.
       Abi hinc, recede.
       Bol.   Per tuum pectus precor.
       Hen. Abi hinc, recede.
       Bol.   Per tuum sceptrum precor.
       Hen. Abi hinc, recede.
       Bol.   Si mihi Coniux negas
2135 Tuos amores, da meam hanc vitam mihi.

Hen. She must die.* Go, take her away, let her be straightway executed. Let the sword cut off her shameless head.

Anne. O mighty King!

Hen. Now shall you realize I am King! Let her die!

Anne. My dear husband!

Hen. I was never dear to you. [2140] Let her lewd neck fall under an iron hand. Away with you, get out of my sight.

Bri. You must submit, Anne. The case is settled: you must die. The King so wills. Executioner, go and behead her.

Anne. O King, have mercy! Have mercy, Husband! O God!

ACT V, scene ix

Religion, an Angel, Brian

Rel. [2145] This punishment is a just one; no one can sin with impunity. A haughty sinner's heyday is always short-lived; slowly the gradually accumulated guilt draws vengeance down with itself. The arm of that loving Ruler of the celestial order is slow in threatening, but finally the time comes [2150] when the just God hurls flaming thunderbolts from the sounding sky and avenges crime with bitter retribution. Witness how Anne Boleyn now lies slain—she who was the source of evil and the

> *Hen.* Moriatur;* ite, abstrahite, moriatur cito;
> Et impudicum concidat ferro caput.
> *Bol.* O magne Rex!
> *Hen.*   Jam senties Regem! peri.
> *Bol.* O chare Coniux.
> *Hen.*   Non tibi charus fui.
> 2140 Cadat impudica ferrea cervix manu.
> Abi hinc, & oculos libera aspectu meos.
> *Bri.* Bolena cede, iam ratum est, debes mori.
> Ista est voluntas Regis, I Lictor, feri.
> *Bol.* Miserere Rex! miserere Coniux! O Tonans!

ACTUS QUINTUS, scena ix

Religio, Angelus, Brianus

> 2145 *Rel.* Haec iusta poena est, nullus impune est nocens;
> Animi insolentis semper est regnum breve.
> Et sera secum culpa vindictam trahit.
> Benignus ille Machinae aethereae Tonans
> Lento minatur brachio, tandem tamen
> 2150 Tonante vibrat flammeos coelo globos.
> Iustusque dura vindicat poena nefas.
> Iacet en Bolena, nempe principium mali

cause of grief. O Almighty, will You bring an end to my sufferings only when it is too late?

Angel. [2155] The King who rages against you will also meet his doom and his conscience will turn him into a maniac. At this very moment he is convulsed and his feverish condition is sapping his strength. His pain is slow and relentless and his death will be long drawn out.

Rel. This is a just retribution!* Let him perish and then [2160] I can finally return to my duties; let him perish and I can again resume my spiritual functions; let him perish so my children may live once more.

Angel. There is no question about it, he will die. He is already dying as he witnesses his slow disintegration; he is dying at this moment as the storms rage within his brain. He is dying at this instant [2165] as his stricken soul shudders at death's approach. Let him endure what fate has ordained. An entire lifetime of painful expiation is not enough to pay for his crime.

Bri. The crisis has come,* the King's final relapse will be fatal, the swellings in his body keep growing worse. Furthermore, he is mentally unable to endure his sufferings and protracted misery. [2170] His face is bloated and his chest and feet are swollen, while his heaving torso is shaken with horrible spasms. Right now as I speak the entire court is stricken with grief and continues to lament. Even the princes are fearful.

       Et causa luctus. O Tonans nunquid meo
       Finem labori sero, sed sero, dabis?
2155 *Ang.* Etiam iacebit ipse Rex, qui in te furit.
       Stimulosque Mentis consciae demens feret.
       Iam iam laborat intus, & seipsum suo
       Fatigat aestu; longa mors lentus dolor.
       Rel. O iuste vindex!* pereat, & tandem meo
2160 Reddar labori; pereat, & rursum meos
       Cultus resumam; pereat & vivant mei.
       Ang. Certum est, peribit; iam perit dum se videt
       Perire lente; iam perit dum sustinet
       Mentis tumultus; iam perit dum iam mori
2165 Perculsus horret. Patere quod fatis ratum est.
       Unum severae saeculum haud poenae sat est.
       Bri. Actum est,* supremus tendit in mortem labor,
       Regisque corpus intumescit amplius;
       Nec mens dolores ferre, nec moram potest?
2170 Tumet ipse vultus, pectus, & pedes tument.
       Et horror intus turbidum pectus quatit.
       Iam tota tristes Aula singultus trahit.
       Tremunt & ipsi Principes.

Rel. God's vengeance is at work and God is just. The King cannot possibly escape.

Bri. [2175] Look at him! So burdensome is the weight of a throne; he gasps for each breath, his face fills with fear as he looks on death.

ACT V, scene x

Cranmer, King Henry, Brian, Religion

Cran. Your Sovereign Highness, the final hour has come, you are losing blood. Arouse your mind and collect your senses. Not even the greatest monarchs are exempt [2180] from death's single stroke. Such is Nature's inexorable law. Down into shadows will fall the holy splendor of your royal head.

Hen. I feel both death and darkness creeping toward me.* Only at great hazard can I move my swollen limbs, while fears keep swirling in my brain. I have become bloated with disease, [2185] and my mind is more deteriorated than my body, swollen and corpulent though it is.

Cran. Rally your spirits and take courage.

Hen. Worries crowd in on me; like angry mobs they press me in on all sides. Is there anything for me to look forward to?

     Rel.   Haec est Dei
     Vindicta iusti: effugere Rex nunquam potest.
2175 *Bri.* En ille, tantum pondus est sedis grave,
     Et mortem anhelans turbido aspectu tremit.

ACTUS QUINTUS, scena x

Granmerus, Henricus Rex, Brianus, Religio

     Gran. Fatalis hora est, Magne Rex, Corpus tuum
     Sanguis reliquit; concita mentem & tuos
     Attolle sensus; maximos Reges quoque
2180 Mors una tollit, certa Naturae est via;
     Et istud alti verticis sacrum iubar
     Cadet in tenebras.
     Hen.   Sentio & mortem, & meam
     Instare noctem:* turbido afflatos metu
     Vix tutus artus urgeo: intumui miser,
2185 Et ipsa tumidum pondere evincit suo
     Mens lapsa corpus.
     Gran.   Erige & mentem & tuos
     Compone sensus.
     Hen.   Turba curarum ingerit
     Se parte ab omni. Restat an aliquid mihi?

Bri. Your life is still yours.

Hen. Yes, life which is a living death. [2190] What a cruel existence! Alas, with every breath I inhale death. Can it be that my reign is over? Death, come! Come and blast my life asunder.

Rel. Your sins torment you; your soul overflows with grief, for now the righteous arm of Almighty God is smiting you fiercely.

Hen. O God! Alas! O my God! [2195] Are even monarchs prey to such devouring pain? Where am I? What kind of man am I? And what have I been? What will happen to me now?

Cran. He is out of his mind; his fear is overwhelming him.

Bri. Does this horror oppress his body as it does his soul?

Rel. He is being punished by his guilty conscience! His crimes haunt him. [2200] Sinners always cringe like this in the face of death.

Hen. How wretched is the life of kings! Alas, must even they perish? And yet does Nature keep running its course?

Cran. Strengthen your heart in the hope that never fails.

Hen. In hope! In what can I place any hope of mine?

Cran. In God.

Hen. In God! Hah! [2205] After so many bloody slaughters of innocent

       Bri. En vita restat.
       Hen.   Vita quae mors est mihi.
2190 O dura vita! vivus heu mortem traho.
       Etiamne rexi? Mors veni, mors hanc meam
       Abrumpe vitam.
       Rel.   Te tuum torquet scelus:
       Intus redundas, iusta iam saevit Dei
       Manus Tonantis.
       Hen.   Heu Tonans! heu heu Tonans!
2195 Etiam Monarchas tantus infestat dolor?
       Ubi sum? quid ego sum? quid fui? quid nunc ero?
       Cran. Emota mens est; vincitur pectus metu.
       Bri. Ut terror intus, terror exterius premit?
       Rel. Haec poena mentis consciae est! hoc est scelus;
2200 Scelesta semper vita sic mortem timet.
       Hen. O misera Regum vita! vah etiam mori?
       Et effluentis spatia Naturae ruunt?
       Cran. Spes certa firmet pectus.
       Hen.   O spes! O mea
       Ubi spes relicta est?
       Cran.   In Deo.
       Hen.   Nempe in Deo,
2205 Post tot cruentas capitis innocui neces;

victims, after destroying so many churches and confiscating so many possessions?

Bri. It was through you that the faith of England was firmly established.

Hen. It was through me that the faith of England was destroyed.* It was I who destroyed it.

Cran. Many subjects accept your faith.

Hen. [2210] But many more refuse to accept it. The ones who approve are afraid of the King. How I wish no one had accepted my faith!

Cran. His mind is in turmoil. Life has been gradually slipping away and he is no longer completely conscious.

Rel. His crimes frighten his soul and the life he has led floods his heart with anxiety.

Bri. [2215] He is stirring again.

Hen. No longer can I look for any peace of soul. It is over, it is all over. Oh, to save my soul!

Cran. You have always been solicitous about your spiritual welfare.

Hen. Hah! In the very act of seeking to save my soul I have lost it. I will not be saved. Oh, Henry, what will you do? Alas! Oh, alas! What will you do?

Cran. [2220] You are king and head of the Church of England. Why are you afraid? You still live.

       Eversa post tot templa, tot raptas opes.
       Bri. Firmata per te est Angliae fides tuae.
       Hen. Eversa per me est Angliae fides meae.*
       Eversa per me est.
       Gran.   Tot tuam probant fidem.
2210 *Hen.* Plures recusant; qui timet Regem, probat;
       Utinam probare nemo potuisset fidem.
       Gran. Turbata mens est; vita paulatim effluit,
       Seseque nescit.
       Rel.   Territat mentem scelus,
       Et acta pectus vita confundit metu.
2215 *Bri.* Turbatur iterum.
       Hen.   Nulla iam restat quies.
       Actum est, peractum est. O salus!
       Gran.   Semper tibi
       Fuit salutis cura.
       Hen.   Nempe dum meam
       Quaero salutem, perdidi; non est salus.
       O Anime quid ages? heu, quid heu? quid ages? quid heu?
2220 *Gran.* Ecclesiae caput Anglicanae Rex times?
       Tibi vita restat.

Hen. I have destroyed—but it is too late—I have destroyed the English Church! How wretched I am! O Christ, do you now summon me the king to your final judgment? Come, destroy me, destroy me, let lightning strike me down, let me live no longer. [2225] Must I face the great tribunal? Let me be annihilated, let me live no longer.

Rel. Look at the pope of the English Church. Behold him who in his rage spilled forth the blood of bishops. Behold him who denies the Sovereign Pontiff's decrees. Behold him at the tribunal of the Final Judge—he quakes—a maniac.

Bri. [2230] It is almost all over.

Hen. How evil it is, alas, to die as I do! Now I see how evil it is to have lived as I have lived. I cannot be saved. There is no hope for me. Oh, my nobles! How my chest fills with scalding pain. Give me wine, hurry!*

Rel. There is no drink that will allay this burning fever.

Cran. [2235] Come, Your Majesty, you must spend your final moments with discretion.

Hen. It is over, it is all over. We have lost everything.*

Bri. He sinks in death, his life is fled.

Rel. Nothing remains of such a king—only this corpse and lasting woe.

Cran. Come, let him be borne away. O England, this is your demise.

      Hen.   Anglicanam Ecclesiam
      Heu sera fata! perdidi. O miserum caput!
      Tuum ad tribunal, Christe, me Regem vocas?
      Imo imo tolle, effulmina, non sim amplius.
2225 Heu ad tribunal? Sim nihil non sim amplius.
      Rel. En Anglicanae Pontifex Ecclesiae;
      En qui cruorem Praesulum effudit furens;
      En qui supremi iura Pontificis negat,
      Summi tribunal Iudicis demens pavet.
2230 *Bri.* Vix restat aliquid.
      Hen.   Quam malum est heu sic mori!
      Vixisse sic quam nunc malum est! quantus meum
      Spes nulla, Proceres o mei! quantus meum
      Infestat ardor pectus? Huc vinum date.*
      Rel. Extinguet istum nullus ardorem liquor.
2235 *Gran.* Hic sapere Rex in morte iam debes tua.
      Hen. Actum est, peractum est, cuncta perdidimus.*
      Bri.   Iacet,
      Extincta vita est.
      Rel.   Rege de tanto nihil,
      Nisi hoc cadaver restat, & longus dolor.
      Gran. Agedum efferatur; Anglia hoc funus tuum est.

ACT V, scene xi

The Catholic Religion

[2240] O Just Ruler of Heaven! O avenging God! The enemy is laid low, both your foe and mine. Will You not look favorably on England your country? Will that day never come? If a century must first pass—even for a century, let us wait hopefully. Let our faith live on in secret, [2245] let the faithful remain in hiding. They in no way refuse to endure the rule of the woman Heresy; they will go down dying for You with undaunted courage. Readily will they endure banishment and foul prisons, and any other torments a savage tyrant will ordain. Yet grant someday* [2250] the faith return to England, that someday You bless her kings with true hearts. Grant someday they may acknowledge your church, that Rome again number the English as hers, and that I may boast again of my Catholic Irish. Someday, O Christ! by your death* I implore You. [2255] By your cross, O Christ! I beg You, someday.

THE END

ACTUS QUINTUS, scena xi

Religio Catholica

2240   O iuste Coeli Rector! O vindex Tonans!
      Occumbit igitur hostis, atque hostis tuus
      Meusque, nunquid Angliam aspicies tuam?
      Aliquando nunquid? saeculum si sit satis,
      Etiam moremur saeculum; lateat fides,
2245   Lateant fideles; foeminae Imperium pati,
      Nihil recusant; pectore infracto necem
      Pro te subibunt; exilia, tetros specus,
      Et quod iubebit efferae mentis furor,
      Ferent parati; sed tamen, tandem tamen*
2250   Redire dona, Regibus veram novis
      Infunde mentem, fac tuam noscant fidem;
      Et rursus Anglos Roma connumeret suos,
      Rursusque Hibernos Religio iactem meos.
      Aliquando Christe! per tuam mortem* peto.
2255   Aliquando Christe! per tuam crucem peto.

FINIS TRAGOEDIAE

EXPLANATORY NOTES

Foreword

The notes that follow are meant to serve a fourfold purpose: (1) to summarize the issues involved in individual scenes and furnish a brief critical assessment of their artistry as revealed in structure, characterization, imagery, and theme; (2) to point the rhetorical and metrical graces; (3) to document the playwright's use of sources by indicating his adherence to them, his deviation, compression, elaboration, or omission; included at this point is the attempt to evaluate the historical accuracy of the facts that appear in the play and its sources in the light of present-day knowledge and scholarly opinion; and (4) to indicate such features of staging and performance as are suggested by the text of the play.

Because of the frequency of their occurrence, the following documentary sources are indicated by the abbreviations here designated:

S-L: Sander-Lewis, Rise and Growth of the Anglican Schism. As stated in Chapter IV, note 1, this is David Lewis' excellent translation of the first edition of Nicholas Sander's *De schismate anglicano* (Cologne, 1585). Lewis' translation is cited whenever the English version is considered adequate for the documentation required.

L&P: Letters and Papers, foreign and domestic of the reign of Henry VIII. Ed. J. S. Brewer, J. Gairdner, and R. H. Brodie.

Span. Cal.: Calendar of Letters, Despatches, and State Papers relating to the Negotiations between England and Spain. Ed. G. A. Bergenroth, Pascual de Gayangos, M. A. S. Hume, and R. Tyler.

Ven. Cal.: Calendar of State Papers and Manuscripts relating to English affairs, existing in the Archives and Collections of Venice. Ed. Rawdon Brown.

Notes to the Title Page

NOTE: *As stated on page 76, asterisks are used within the English and Latin texts to direct the reader to the Explanatory Notes. In the poetry, line numbering is marginal; in the Latin prose and in the translation (choruses excepted) it is internal. Line references in the Explanatory Notes are to the Latin text. In both the Latin prose and in the translation, a bracketed small Roman numeral precedes the line it indicates.*

Schisma Anglicanum. The alternate title of the play was very probably suggested by Sander's *De origine ac progressu schismatis anglicani.*

Exhibita Ludis Encenialibus: the New Year holidays, lasting throughout the first week of the new year. *Henricus Octavus* was performed during the opening week of 1624. The other favorite time for school plays was during the *Ludis Remigialibus,* the week beginning October 1 (feast of St. Remy or Remigius), which marked the opening of the scholastic year. A large number of the Louvain students enjoyed scholarships which required attendance in college for their duration. The staging of school plays was one of the methods used by masters to keep their charges alert and occupied during the vacation season.

In Collegio Porcensi. Henricus Octavus was first performed at Porc College, probably in the refectory of the main hall. It is clear from the Dedicatory Letter (ll. v-vi) that the play was likewise presented in the University theater. It was this second public performance that the Reverend Desbois attended (Dedicatory Letter, ll. xxiv-xxv). (See also below, n. to ll. v-vi of the same letter.)

Philippi Dormalii. Louvain printer Philip Dormalius (Van Dormael) printed many of Vernulaeus' books. Of the various vignettes he used to ornament the title pages of the works issuing from his press, the best known is the engraving of Pegasus in flight. It may be seen on the title page of Vernulaeus' *Academia Lovaniensis* (1627). See Nève, *Renaissance des lettres . . . en Belgique,* p. 382, n. 1.

Notes to the Dedicatory Letter

Vernulaeus dedicated *Henricus Octavus* to the Very Reverend Engelbert Desbois (1578–1651), who was currently Provost of St. Pierre de Lille and later Bishop of Namur.

iii. *A Iosepho ab Arimathia primum acceperat* (. . . initially received
. . . from Joseph of Arimathea). "The Britons are said to have been first
converted to the faith of Christ by Joseph of Arimathia" (*S-L*, Preface,
p. cxlv). The second edition of Sander's *De schismate anglicano* (Rome,
1586) supplies the marginal gloss: "Polydorus probat ex antiquissimo
Gilda lib. 2 & 4." Glastonbury, perhaps the oldest Christian sanctuary in
England, still nurtures its earliest legend of the Arimathean hero who,
after burying the body of Christ, journeyed to Somersetshire with the
Holy Grail and built a church of wattles in Avalon. The story is known to
every student of English literature through the *Idylls of the King*. Under
a "world-old yew tree," Tennyson has Sir Percivale relate the story to his
fellow-monk Ambrosius:

> The cup, the cup itself, from which our Lord
> Drank at the last sad supper with his own.
> This, from the blessed land of Aromat—
> After the day of darkness, when the dead
> Went wandering o'er Moriah—the good saint
> Arimathean Joseph, journeying brought
> To Glastonbury, where the winter thorn
> Blossoms at Christmas, mindful of our Lord.
> "The Holy Grail," II. 46–53.

For further details, see Abbot Gasquet, *The Great Abbeys of England*
(London: Chatto & Windus, 1908), pp. 99–101; Thomas Dugdale, *Cu-
riosities of Great Britain: England and Wales Delineated* (3 vols.; London: L. Tallis, n.d.), III, 834–38; M. R. James, *Abbeys* (London:
Spottiswoode, Ballantyne and Co., 1926), p. 20.

v–vi. *Publico Lovanii theatro* (Louvain public theater). Vernulaeus
reminds his patron that *Henricus* was performed in the public Arts Auditorium. This auditorium, formerly situated on Vanderkelenstraat, is
commemorated by a plaque at the entrance of the present branch library.
The inscription reads: Van 1444 tot 1797 "Gemeene Schole Vicus"/Der
Fac. Artium/dei Universiteit.

vii–viii. *Gladio styloque asseruerat* (he had hitherto championed
with sword and pen). In answer to Martin Luther's *De captivitate baby-
lonica ecclesiae praeludium* (October, 1520), Henry VIII wrote *Assertio
septem sacramentorum*, which was solemnly presented to Leo X in full
consistory on September 15, 1521. The full title of Henry's work is *Assertio septem sacramentorum aduersus Martinum Lutherum, aedita ab
inuictissimo Angliae & Franciae rege, Do. Hyberniae Henrico, eius
nominis octauo* (Antwerp: Michael Hillen, MDXXII Kalend. Aprilis).

xxviii. *Oculi maduerunt* (tears came to your eyes). The impact of Vernulaeus' play on his patron, together with Desbois' appraisal after the performance, remains one of the few extant references to audience reaction in the Vernulaeus theater.

xxxi. *Legant alii quae vidisti* (May others read what you have witnessed). The great majority of academic plays remain unprinted. Vernulaeus clearly intended to reach a larger audience, as he indicates at this point. All his plays were printed, nine of them under separate title. Bernard Heymbach, Louvain professor and contemporary of Vernulaeus, attested to the latter's popularity as a playwright and to the labors of the Louvain press in printing his tragedies. See *Otium itinerarium,* printed as an appendix in *Tragoediae, in duos tomos distributae* (2d ed.; Louvain: P. Sassenus & H. Nempaeus, 1656), unnumbered page 15, counting from the beginning of the essay.

xxxv. *In sacris Academiae Spatiis* (the sacred halls of the University). Desbois obtained his licentiate in both canon and civil law at Louvain (Paquot, *Mémoires,* XII, 399).

xxxvi–xxxviii. *Hinc Romam . . . abivisti* (From here you went to Rome . . .). Upon completion of his studies in jurisprudence, Desbois was ordained priest and received a canonship of the metropolitan See of Cambrai. Vernulaeus' allusion to Desbois' studies in Rome seems to be our unique authority for this fact.

xxxix. *Nicolaus Michaut* (Nicolas Michaut). Michaut was Knight, Lord of Indevelde, Orp, and Huyssinghen, prefect hereditary of Binche, counselor to the Conseil privé, Knight and Treasurer of the Golden Fleece. Born in Brussels September 17, 1518, Nicolas Michaut (Micault, Miscault) served Charles V, Philip II, and Mary of Hungary. He was appointed counselor in 1554; he likewise served as ambassador for Queen Eleanor of France, sister of Mary of Hungary. He died September 15, 1589. The inscription of his tomb (as well as that of his wife, Mary Boisot, 1529–79) may be found in J. B. Christyn, *Basilica Bruxellensis, sive monumenta antiqua, inscriptiones, et coenotaphia* (2 vols.; Mechlin: Laurence Van der Elst, 1743), I, 76–77. The Michaut family were related to the Desbois: Engelbert's mother was Françoise Verreycken; her brother Louis married Louise Miscault. See Andreas Walther. *Die burgundischen Zentralbehörden* (Leipzig: Duncker & Humblot, 1909), pp. 54, 62, 79; C. P. Hoynck van Papendrecht, *Analecta belgica* (3 vols. in 6 parts; The Hague: Gerard Block, 1743), I, ii, 592; Alexandre Henne, *Histoire du règne de Charles-Quint en Belgique* (10 vols.; Brussels: Émile Flatau, 1858–59), VII, 302; de Vocht, *Monumenta,* p. 640.

xli–xlii. *Ut cum virtute prudentiam comparares* (so that you might develop a sense of prudence to match your native gifts of character). The
distinction between personal morality (*virtus*) and morality in social
conduct or politics (*prudentia*) is clearly implied. The relation between
ethics and politics, deriving from Aristotle's *Nicomachean Ethics*, was in-
corporated into the Renaissance concept of history via the Tacitean tradition.

xlvi. *Columnae, Farnesii, Madrutii* (Colonna, Farnese, and Madruzzo
families). These were noble and powerful Renaissance families that furnished generals, prelates, and statesmen in the service of the Church and
other powers.

The Colonna, a noble Roman family, is represented by Pope Martin V
(1417–31) and by poetess Vittoria Colonna, friend of Reginald Pole.
Her husband, Ferrante de Avalos, was a noted captain of Charles V. Another Colonna, Carlo Gaudenzio, was created cardinal (Ingolstadt) in
1604 (*Enciclopedia italiana . . .*, XXI, 854–55).

From 1545 to 1731, the Farnese were rulers of the Duchy of Parma and
Piacenza (since 1512 part of the papal states). Alessandro Farnese, who
succeeded Clement VII as Pope Paul III (1534–49), summoned the
Council of Trent; he likewise created Pole cardinal. Alessandro Farnese
(1545–92), Duke of Parma and famous general of Philip II of Spain,
spent the whole of his rule in the Flemish wars. His son Odoardo was
created cardinal in 1591 by Gregory XIV (*ibid.*, XIV, 825–28).

The Madruzzo (Madruzzi) family of Trent served the Church chiefly
in the person of Christopher Madruzzo, who was created cardinal by
Paul III in 1543. Esteemed by both Charles V and his brother King
Ferdinand I, afterward Emperor (1556–64), Cardinal Madruzzo was
employed by Ferdinand in many important and delicate missions. As
Cardinal-Bishop of Trent and temporal ruler of that principality, he
naturally played a prominent part in the Council. Upon his resignation of
the bishopric of Trent in 1567, he was succeeded in that office by his
nephew Ludovico (*ibid.*, XXI, 854–55).

xlix–l. *Nimirum . . . conformare* (. . . patterning . . . on the example of
industrious men). Vernulaeus' conviction that political prudence could
be learned from examples of illustrious men has already been stressed.

li–lii. *Metropolitana Cameracensis Ecclesia* (the metropolitan See of
Cambrai). Presumably after his Roman studies, Desbois returned to
Cambrai as archdeacon. As mentioned earlier, he had been awarded a
canonship there upon ordination (Paquot, *Mémoires*, XII, 399; Andreas,
Bibliotheca belgica, p. 204).

lvi–lvii. *Insulensis Ecclesiae Praeposituram* (Provost of the Church of Lille). In 1619 (Desbois was then forty-one), Philip II appointed Vernulaeus' patron Provost of St. Pierre de Lille (Paquot, *Mémoires*, XII, 399).

lviii–lvix. *Tibi maius debeatur* (merit a still higher post). Vernulaeus' estimate of Desbois' ability and worthiness for advancement was corroborated officially five years later (October 31, 1629) when his patron was appointed seventh bishop of Namur (J. B. L. de Castillion, *Sacra Belgii chronologia* [Ghent: Petrus De Goesin, 1719], II, 453–54; Paquot, *Mémoires*, XII, 399).

lxii. *Tuus ... Avunculus Ludovicus Verreickius* (... your uncle Louis Verreycken). Françoise, sister of Louis Verreycken, was Engelbert's mother. Louis Verreycken, secretary of state of Philip II and councilor of Archduke Albert and Isabella, derived from a famous royal family of Flanders. In the employ of the King from 1583–1619, he died October 23, 1621; his wife, Louise Micault, followed him July 8, 1622 (see Cornelius Van Gestel, *Historia sacra et profana archiepiscopatus Mechliniensis* [2 vols.; The Hague: Christian Van Lom, 1725], II, 97–98, cited hereafter as *Historia sacra;* J. van der Leene, *Le théâtre de la noblesse du Brabant* [Liege: J. F. Broncaert, 1705], pp. 239, 280–82, cited hereafter as *Le théâtre;* Em. Dony, "Verreycken Louis," *Biographie nationale de Belgique,* Vol. XXVI, col. 682).

lxv. *Commissum ... Audientiarii (Audientiarius)*. The position of secrétaire audiencier involved, among other duties, the clearance of legal suits before arraignment.

lxix. *Eius in Filio Cognato tuo* (his son and your cousin). Louis-François Verreycken, son of Louis Verreycken, succeeded his father in the office of "premier secrétaire audiencier" on November 19, 1621, three years before Vernulaeus wrote this dedicatory letter. Louis-François was a cousin of the Reverend Desbois. His wife, Anne Marie de Busleyden, was the daughter of Gilles de Busleyden and Catherine van der Dilft. Louis-François Verreycken died on May 6, 1654. His son Charles succeeded him as secretary of state by appointment of Philip IV on March 4, 1650. Thus three generations of Verreyckens served the kings of Spain as secretaries of state in the Netherlands (Van Gestel, *Historia sacra,* II, 97–98; van den Leene, *Le théâtre,* pp. 239, 280–82; Em. Dony, *Biographie nationale de Belgique,* Vol. XXVI, col. 682; de Vocht, *Jerome de Busleyden,* p. 24, n. 1).

To the Reader: The Subject Matter of the Tragedy

The purpose of this letter is to indicate briefly the contents of the tragedy, the attitude of the author toward his subject matter, and the source to which he was indebted. Both in content and conduct, Vernulaeus' introductory remarks adhere closely to the Preface of S-L. To avoid the tedium of a line-by-line juxtaposition of the two texts, the relevant passages from S-L (Preface, pp. cxlv–cxlvii) are here gathered:

The Britons are said to have been first converted to the faith of Christ by Joseph of Arimathia. . . . From that day almost to the twenty-fifth year of the reign of Henry VIII., for about a thousand years, none other than the Roman Catholic faith prevailed in England. . . . But Henry VIII., solely for the reasons I am about to set forth, changed the faith of Christ, and severed the realm of England from the communion of the Roman Pontiff.

Arthur, the elder brother of Henry, married to Catherine, the daughter of the Catholic sovereigns of Spain, not only died without issue, but more than that, on account of his sickly youth, and because of his death, which soon ensued, never lived with his wife. Thereupon Henry, by Papal dispensation, for the preservation of peace between the Spaniards and the English, took Catherine for his wife, and having lived with her for some twenty years, put her away, seemingly, because she had been married to his brother, but in truth that he might put Anne Boleyn in her place. . . . Henry then, in order to marry this woman, put away Catherine, and apostatised from the Roman Church. . . . He set up a new Church, of which he called himself the supreme head on earth.

Vernulaeus' reference to the offspring of Henry and Catherine is likewise based on Sander: "Henry and Catherine had five children, three sons and two daughters of whom . . . Mary alone . . . was alive when Henry and Catherine were dead" (S-L, pp. 5–6). A. F. Pollard corroborates Sander on this fact and supplies the documentation (*Henry VIII*, pp. 175–77). Nicholas Pocock, in the Preface to his *Records* (I, xlii), attests that Sander alone, of all historians, gives the correct number of Catherine's children. "These little particulars," he goes on to say, "afford the strongest guarantee for his accuracy in other matters."

i. *Nulla fabula aut figmentum* (no fairy tales or flights of fancy). *Figmentum* is postclassical. Vernulaeus takes pains at the very outset to insist on the historical truth on which his tragedy is based. It is curious to note that Burnet, in his attack on Sander's book, echoes Vernulaeus' expression at this point. Burnet says: "Those who intend to write romances, or plays, do commonly take their plot from some true piece of history. . . . Some such design Sander seems to have had in his book" (Burnet-Pocock, *History*, IV, 543).

xxi. *Vide praeter alios* (In addition to other sources). Vernulaeus invites the reader to consult other sources in addition to Sander's volume. For details of More's execution, Vernulaeus drew on Stapleton's biography in *Tres Thomae*; see especially below, notes to verses 2022, 2030, 2038, 2043. It is likewise possible that he reinforced Sander's account with that of Polydore Vergil (nn. to vv. 226, 2111*a*), the *Paris News Letter* (n. to v. 1994), the anonymous *Vita Henrici VIII* (nn. to vv. 123, 168, 173, 191, 1195) and Cardinal Pole (n. to v. 226). Apart from Stapleton, however, there seems to be no convincing evidence that Vernulaeus departed from Sander in any way that cannot be explained by dramatic expedience. On the other hand, Vernulaeus helped Valerius Andreas classify the holdings of the University of Louvain library, and could easily have acquainted himself with the published works and manuscripts of Sander's fellow-polemicists (see Nève, *Renaissance des lettres ... en Belgique*, p. 414). Unfortunately, the 1914 and 1940 destructions of the Louvain library leave room only for speculation.

Cast of Characters

It should be observed that the *Personae Tragoediae* fails to list Dr. Ridley, who defends the Queen's cause in a spirited speech (III, ii, 969–84). The text of the play likewise contains lines (II, vi, 746–48) attributed to the Queen's procurator (*Procur.*), namely, William Warham, as well as to two of Catherine's waiting-women (*pedisequae*) who console their mistress (II, i, 497–99, 501–02) and accompany her in banishment (IV, i, 1356–60). Neither the designation of Warham as procurator, nor the *pedisequae* are listed in the cast of characters.

ACT I, scene i (1–71)

The opening scene serves a threefold function: expository, thematic, and atmospheric. With remarkable economy Vernulaeus employs four allegorical figures to outline the critical situation facing England in the person of its infatuated king. The main theme is announced: England will expose her body to disaster. As instigator and chargé d'affaires, Heresy plans her campaign, which she delegates to her allegorical companions.

Vernulaeus clearly indicates that the ensuing struggle will be psychological and moral: the battleground of the forces of good and evil will be the King's conscience. No less clear is the identification of the national crisis with the moral decision of the protagonist.

The atmosphere of gloating horror, reminiscent of Seneca, is largely created by the use of black-white contrasts and by recurring images of shipwreck, pestilence, devouring flames, imprisonment, streaming blood, and wounds. In addition, the marked antipapal attitude of Heresy adds spice and puts an edge on the issues involved. Finally, the announcement of Henry's approach at the close of the scene leads naturally to the second scene, mortising it with the first.

Although Vernulaeus is ultimately indebted to the medieval morality and mystery plays for the precedent of allegorical figures, their function in this scene was anticipated in his *Gorcomienses* (1609), where Lutheranus, Calvinia, and Memnonistica rise to the proscenium from Hell to join Inquisitio, who plots a similar disaster for Holland (I, ii, iii).

1–2. *Orbem sepultum, lucis immunes domos/Tetrumque ... infernae chaos* (The buried world, the dwellings bereft of light, and the lower regions ...). Vernulaeus uses three periphrastic expressions of the classic underworld to describe the Christian Hell from which the allegorical figures have just emerged.

4. *Titan.* Latin personification of the sun, from Helios, the sun-god.

12. *Fiat hoc, fiat scelus* (May any wickedness I conceive come to pass). Use of anaphora (repetition of initial word in successive clauses) with *fiat* to secure sudden climax. Vernulaeus uses anaphora frequently.

13–14. *Dirum, novum,/Inusitatum, triste, terribile, efferum* (cruel, novel, strange, sorrowful, frightful, savage). The use of asyndeton (omission of conjunctions ordinarily joining co-ordinate words or clauses) to pile up a series of adjectives for an effect of horror is characteristic of Seneca.

15. *Anguineum hoc caput* (by this snaky head). In swearing by her snaky head, Heresy informs us further of her forbidding appearance on stage. For her black garments, see v. 9. Evidently the audience was familiar with the myth of Medusa slain by Perseus.

16. *Stygis Arbitrum* (the lord of hell): either Minos or Rhadamanthus, the two rulers of the lower regions, according to classical legend. In the present context, the *"Arbitrum"* also suggests Satan.

18. *Phlegeton* (Phlegethon): a river of Hades flowing with fire.

22. *Fidei Quiritum* (Roman Catholic faith). Literally, the faith of the Roman citizens, the Roman Catholic faith.

23–24. *Ille Tarpeia tonans/E rupe Rector* (Let him who thunders from the Tarpeian Rock): Tarpeian Rock of the Capitoline hill (a periphrasis of *Jupiter Capitolinus*), here used in a transferred sense to indicate the Pope's Roman headquarters. The thundergod Jupiter (*Tonans*), by similar transfer, refers to the Pope. *Tonans* (Jupiter) is frequently used by Ovid.

25. *Funera & diras neces* (deaths and cruel executions). An example of Vernulaeus' use of the rhetorical figure hysteron-proteron (reversal of chronological sequence of events).

35. *Et quam nefando genuit incestu Pater* (whom he sired in wicked incest). Although Sander did not invent the slander that Anne Boleyn was the daughter of Henry VIII and Lady Boleyn, he gave it wide currency by his statement (*S-L*, pp. 23–24):

Anne Boleyn was the daughter of Sir Thomas Boleyn's wife; I say of his wife, because she could not have been the daughter of Sir Thomas, for she was born during his absence of two years in France on the king's affairs. Henry VIII sent him apparently on an honourable mission in order to conceal his own criminal conduct.

Finding a child born on his return, Sander continues, Sir Thomas Boleyn refrained from prosecuting his wife on learning from her "that the child Anne was the daughter of no other than Henry VIII" (*ibid.*). In a marginal gloss to the above passage, Sander noted the source of this story: "This is recounted by Judge William Rastell in his life of Thomas More." Sander was accused of having invented Rastell's book as a basis for his slander. Yet the fact that Rastell had written a life of his uncle is undeniable: the surviving fragments (MS. Arundel 152) were published in *Analecta Bollandia*, XII, 248–70, by Franciscus Van Ortroy in 1891, and again by Elsie Vaughan Hitchcock for the Early English Text Society in 1932 (see Harpsfield's *The Life and Death of Sir Thomas More*, App. I, cited hereafter as *Life of More*).

Sander was by no means the only historian to adopt this gross story of Henry's incestuous union with Anne Boleyn (see Harpsfield, *Pretended Divorce*, pp. 236–37). The King's licentious life, particularly his relations with Mary Boleyn, exposed him to such rumors. For other rumors in regard to this question, see Pocock, *Records*, II, 468, 566–68; for the currency of this malicious gossip on the Continent since about 1536, see Van Ortroy, *Analecta Bollandia*, X, 159–60. By propagating the lurid slander, both Sander and Vernulaeus leave a stigma on their work that is not easily erased, even by their otherwise proven respect for historical fact.

36–38. *Frustra tuum/Ab Urbe lenta fulmen excuties manu/Pater Quiritum* (In vain, O Father of Roman Catholics, . . . the thunderbolt of excommunication . . .). The classical allusion to Jupiter's thunderbolts is here transferred, in typical Humanist manner, to the pope's powers of excommunication. The reference to Clement VII's "dawdling hand" is historically accurate. See n. to v. 1362*a*.

42. *Torreas Regis iecur* (parch his liver). The liver as the seat of the passions is frequently referred to by Roman poets.

44. *Nostris perustus ignibus totus furit* (Our flames already burn through his body . . .). There seems to be no documentation extant for establishing the date of Henry's first attraction to Anne Boleyn. Authorities now incline to believe that Anne was born in 1507. About 1519 she was sent as maid of honor to the French queen, Claude (Pollard, *Henry VIII*, p. 188). In 1522, Anne was recalled to the English court (*L&P*, III, 1994), at which time, March 4, 1522, she took part in an entertainment at Wolsey's house (*Revels Accounts, L&P*, III, 1559). Although it is quite possible that the fifteen-year-old Anne caught Henry's eye, it would seem that the King was currently more interested in Anne's sister, Mary. "About 1527," says Gustave Constant (*La réforme en Angleterre*, p. 23), "Anne Boleyn had captured the king's eye and heart." Substantiation for this date (1527) is suggested by the King's famous love letters to Anne— the earliest conjecturally assigned by Brewer to July, 1527. *L&P*, IV, 3218–21, 3325–26, 3990, 4383, 4403, 4410, 4477, 4537, 4539, 4597, 4648, 4742, 4894.

The statement made by Lust (I, i, 46) that Henry had already determined to marry Anne suggests the date for the opening action of *Henricus Octavus* to be late in 1526 or early in 1527. Pollard believes (*Henry VIII*, p. 189) that the divorce proceedings began at least as early as March, 1527. The subject of the divorce seems to have been mooted as far back as 1525, and the first mention of the divorce, of which we have any record, is contained in a letter from Warham to Wolsey. Referring to some other business, Warham says, "It will be better not to proceed further, till this great matter of the King's grace be ended" (*L&P*, IV, 1263, quoted in J. M. Stone, *The History of Mary I. Queen of England*, p. 36, cited hereafter as *Mary I*).

Actually, the divorce proceedings began with the hearings of the secret legatine court before Wolsey at his house at Westminster on May 17, 1527, and again on May 20 and May 31. Considerable secrecy was at first observed, as may be seen by Sampson's letter to Wolsey (*L&P*, IV, 3302) written July 25, 1527; but Don Inigo de Mendoza had informed the Emperor early in July of the King's intention (*ibid.*, p. 3312). It was not until the next year that application was made for a legate to be sent to act with Wolsey. The attempt to get the judgment of the universities belongs to the following year, October, 1529 (see Harpsfield, *Pretended Divorce*, p. 322, note to p. 177, l. 20; see also Stone, *Mary I*, pp. 37–38).

71. *Amans amensque* (madly in love). The play on words juxtaposes effectively the characteristics of the lunatic and the lover.

Nec sit suus (no longer his own master). The classical expression is ordinarily "Nec sit sui compos."

ACT I, scene ii (72–142)

The opening soliloquy of Henry, an example of Vernulaeus' considerable poetic ability, is a series of variations on the theme of outward splendor and inward anguish. Moving from a general statement of this theme (embodied in contrasts of gleaming, sparkling, blazing ornaments that entangle, corrupt, and vanquish the spirit), Henry particularizes the object of his torment in the person of Anne Boleyn. Like the deceptive splendor of the royal accouterments, her peculiar attractiveness fires, burns, and enslaves his soul.

The soliloquy yields to a debate between Henry and the allegorical figures. Their persuasions and temptations to tyranny are countered by Henry; he rejects his evil impulses personified in Lust, Impiety, and Tyranny, but the seeds of lawlessness are planted. The announcement of Anne's entry at the close of the scene keeps the action flowing effortlessly.

Vernulaeus' portrayal of Henry in his first appearance is sympathetic and dramatic in its objective handling. The audience witnesses the inner tension of a monarch who is sensitive to moral issues and candid in his analysis of their urgency. This scene, like the previous one, is studded with classical allusions to Seneca, Vergil, Horace, and Ovid. Its ultimate basis on Sander is disguised by the playwright's poetic transmutation and dramatic vividness.

72. *Iubar* (gleams and glistens). A nimbus-like light emanating from a heavenly body, sometimes used to suggest the majesty radiating from man's soul. In the present context, the source of the majestic brilliance is the King's scepter.

73. *Purpura* (this purple): purple color; metonymy for royal purple robes.

73–74. *Sacrae micat/Diadema frontis* (on my anointed brow the royal diadem sparkles). *Sacrae* is taken to modify *frontis* literally, although there is a possibility of its reference to the crown (*diadema*) by means of hypallage, or an interchange of two elements for aesthetic reasons—a rhetorical figure occasionally found in Vernulaeus.

78–79. *Pectus dolor/Intus flagellat* (anguish whips the heart within me). *Dolor* is personified to secure a vivid action image.

83–84. *Fascino nam me suo/Occidit illa* ... (She slays me with her enchantment...). Vernulaeus' portrait of Anne, as seen through the eyes of Henry, is the playwright's first radical departure from Sander, who describes her thus (*S-L*, p. 25):

> Anne Boleyn was rather tall of stature, with black hair, and an oval face of a sallow complexion [*colore subflavo*], as if troubled with jaundice. She had a projecting tooth under the upper lip, on her right hand six fingers. There was a large wen under her chin, and therefore to hide its ugliness she wore a high dress covering her throat. ... She was handsome to look at, with a pretty mouth, amusing in her ways, playing well on the lute, and was a good dancer.

For verification of the sixth finger, see *L&P*, IV, Introduction, p. ccxxxvii; for the wen, *ibid.*, VI, 585. John D. Mackie (*The Earlier Tudors, 1485–1558* [ed. G. N. Clark], p. 323) ridicules Sander's portrait of Anne as a physical and moral monstrosity:

> No one can believe that the heart of the English king, already well experimented according to the theory, was carried away by a fairy with an oblong face of jaundiced hue, a projecting tooth, an extra finger on her right hand, and a large wen under her chin.

The secret of Anne's fascination, Pollard notes (*Henry VIII*, p. 191), was a puzzle to observers. A Venetian ambassador wrote on October 31, 1532 (*Ven. Cal.*, IV, 824):

> Madam Anne is not one of the handsomest women in the world; she is of middling stature, swarthy complexion, long neck, wide mouth, bosom not much raised, and in fact has nothing but the King's great appetite, and her eyes, which are black and beautiful.

Vernulaeus' flattering description of Anne was undoubtedly prompted by dramatic exigence: his refusal to follow Sander at this point indicates his intention of making Henry's infatuation and consequent struggle as intensive as possible. On the other hand, it is clear that the imagery he selected to portray Anne's attraction for Henry (grief, murder, burning, slaying, imprisoning in fetters, slavery) left the Louvain schoolboys controlled by their professor's moral attitude to the infatuation. One may also observe that Vernulaeus makes the most of the attractive features of Anne which Sander somewhat grudgingly admits: her "pretty mouth," "black hair," and general handsome appearance.

85. *Vernus decor* (springtime beauty). The play of words involving *"vernus"* and "Vernulaeus" occurs more than once in the eulogistic verses of the playwright's admirers, but seems to have no connection here.

87–88. *Comae/Animum hunc amoris vinculo blando ligant* (her hair imprisons my soul . . .). Anne capitalized on her long black hair by wearing it loose. On her way to the coronation, Cranmer describes her as "sytting in her heere" (see Henry Ellis, *Original Letters Illustrative of English History*, First Ser., II, 37, cited hereafter as *Original Letters*; see also *Ven. Cal.*, IV, 802, 912).

91*b*–92. . . . *hoc scilicet/Regnare tandem est, velle quod mentem iuvet* (. . . this is what it means to be a ruler . . . to will whatever you please). The specious arguments advanced by Lust would be recognized as such by Vernulaeus' students. In 1623, one year prior to the appearance of *Henricus Octavus*, the playwright had published his *Institutionum politicarum libri* wherein he clearly distinguishes between the nature of a king and a tyrant. A tyrant, explains Vernulaeus, is a sovereign who sacrifices the common weal for personal advantage (see *Institutionum politicarum*, p. 26). The 1647 edition of the same work, expanded with sources and examples, adds this apt phrase (p. 9): "That well-known maxim, 'My wish is my command, let will substitute for reason' holds good for the reign of a tyrant."

95–97. *Regii vultus decor,/Virilis aetas* . . . (The splendor of the royal countenance, the virile manhood . . .). Sander does not fail to point out the young Henry's physical endowments (*S-L*, p. 5): "Henry VIII., in the eighteenth year of his age [was] handsome and majestic in person." And again, (p. 164): "The king . . . ruined a most admirable constitution by unsatiable gluttony." Eyewitness reports are unexceptionally favorable:

The King is the handsomest potentate I ever set eyes on; above the usual height, with an extremely fine calf to his leg, his complexion very fair and bright, with auburn hair combed straight and short . . . and a round face so very beautiful that it would become a pretty woman.

L&P, II, 395; III, 402; *Ven. Cal.*, II, 1287.

98–99. *Cura* . . . *flagellat* (. . . no trifling urgency that flogs my sad spirit). Vernulaeus is fond of using personification to secure concrete vividness. See n. to vv. 78–79.

102*a*. *Regina placuit* (Yet till now I have been content with the Queen). The first years of Henry's marriage seem to have been happy enough. They were spent in a series of celebrations in which Henry took great pleasure (see *L&P*, I, 224, 338; Constant, *La réforme*, pp. 21, 339–40; Stone, *Mary I*, pp. 5–6). The probability of miscarriages, in addition to Catherine's five children, affords certain evidence that Henry lived with Catherine as wife until 1518 (see Pocock, *Records,* I, xlii; for further details of Henry's early life with Catherine, see Pollard, *Henry VIII,* pp. 174–78).

103–04. *Veneris haud miles novus . . .* (You are by no means a new soldier of Venus marching forth to battle). Using a common Ovidian figure, Lust taunts Henry. Vernulaeus here follows Sander (*S-L,* p. 8): "Meanwhile Henry was giving the reins to his evil desires, and living in sin, sometimes with two, sometimes with three of the queen's maids of honour, one of whom, Elizabeth Blount, gave birth to a son, whom Henry made duke of Richmond." Sander's reference to Henry's illegitimate son by Elizabeth Blount, sister of Lord Mountjoy, is a matter of historical record. "Possibly, even probably," Pollard says, "there were other lapses from conjugal fidelity, for in 1533, the Duke of Norfolk told Chapuys that Henry was always inclined to amours" (*Henry VIII,* p. 185). The statement concerning the King's "ten mistresses" in 1528 (*L&P,* IV, 3748) is shorn by Pollard of its modern signification and interpreted merely as an allusion to gentlewomen (*Henry VIII,* pp. 185–86).

106. *Implevit illum mater* (Her mother did). There is no evidence extant to corroborate Sander's statement that Lady Boleyn bedded with Henry, here followed by Vernulaeus (see n. to v. 35). It is generally admitted that Henry was not a father at sixteen.

Implevit soror (and so did her sister [Mary Boleyn]). Vernulaeus follows Sander (*S-L,* p. 24), "The king, who had sinned before with the . . . elder daughter, turned his thoughts now to the other daughter, Anne." Pollard (*Thomas Cranmer and the English Reformation,* p. 35, n. 1) corroborates Sander's statement about Mary and Anne:

These relations of Henry with Mary Boleyn were long believed in England (cf. Le Bas, *Life of Cranmer,* i., 18) to be a Roman Catholic libel similar to the assertion that Henry VIII. was father of Anne Boleyn. The latter, indeed, is fiction, but there is no doubt about the relations between Henry VIII. and Mary Boleyn.

See also Harpsfield (*Pretended Divorce,* p. 236), who likewise reports this as fact, and Ehses (*Römische Dokumente,* p. xxxiii) for the documentary evidence.

109. *Amare pellex non volo, coniux volo* ("I do not wish to love you as your mistress . . ."). Vernulaeus includes this bit of expository material by having Henry quote Anne. Sander (*S-L,* p. 26) gives the background of Anne's resistance:

On her return to England she was taken into the royal household, and there easily saw that the king was tired of his wife. She also detected the aims

of Wolsey, how much the king was in love with herself, and how quickly
he changed in his lawless affections. Not to speak of strangers to her family,
she saw how her mother first, and then her sister, had been discarded by the
king. What was she, then, to hope for in the end if she did not take care of
herself at first?

111. *Lenimen . . . nullum facit* (. . . she allows me no means of alleviating my lovesick heart). Vernulaeus follows Sander's view that Anne had
no sexual relations with the King during the early period of the infatuation. "The more the king sought her, the more she avoided him, sancti-
moniously saying that no one but her husband should find her alone"
(*S-L*, p. 26). Protestant Simon Grynaeus writes to Bucer in another
strain:

> Whether she has had children by the king I do not know. She has not any
> acknowledged as such: they may probably be brought up in private, which,
> if I am not mistaken, I have heard more than once, though there are those
> who positively deny that the king has any intercourse with her, which in my
> opinion is not at all likely.

(Ellis, *Original Letters*, No. cclvi, quoted in *S-L*, p. 26, n. 2). It should
be noted that the judgment of Grynaeus, a stranger and only occasional
visitor at court, has dubious value, if any.

123. *Caesar & Reges* (The Emperor and other sovereigns). The reference is to Emperor Charles V and especially Francis I. Henry's fear derives from Sander (*S-L*, p. 33):

> But Henry was held back not so much by his respect for the laws of the
> Church as by his fear of the Emperor Charles V.; for he knew too well that
> the emperor would not patiently endure the divorce of his aunt, and that his
> own subjects would be angry if he entered into new and questionable rela-
> tions with the French, and deserted the ancient alliance of the house of Bur-
> gundy, with which they were bound by the gainful bonds of trade.

The anonymous Latin Chronicle, written in the summer of 1557 and
formerly attributed to Nicholas Harpsfield, is remarkably close to the
succinct expression put in Henry's mouth: "That which checked him
was, on the one hand, the fear of the Emperor, who would have liked to
avenge the insult to his aunt, and on the other, the uncertainty of peace
with France, and finally the opinion of his people" (Charles Bémont
[ed.], *Le premier divorce de Henri VIII, et le schisme d'Angleterre.
Chronique latine . . .*, p. 100, cited hereafter as *Vita Henrici VIII*). Pollard points out (*Wolsey*, p. 231) that it was Wolsey, not Henry, who
feared the imperial reprisal. Charles V had seen one sister, Mary, driven
from her throne in Hungary, and another, Isabella, from her throne in

Denmark without lifting a finger to restore them. Why should Henry anticipate greater concern for an aunt? Charles V would not, and did not, make war on Henry for the sake of Catherine (*L&P*, VIII, 182: Charles V to Chapuys, February 6, 1535; No. 189: Chapuys to Charles V, February 9, 1535); on the other hand, he did make war in Italy to retain his dominions and his influence over the papacy. After all, Rome was essential to papal-delegate Wolsey, but not to the English king.

131. *Privata languent tecta, non Aulae gemunt* (the homes ... grieve but palaces ... do not lament). *Languent* and *gemunt* personify their subjects.

137. *Herois in me est sanguis, & Divus vigor* (I have the blood of heroes ... and my strength is that of a god). The words *herois* (demigod, hence superman) and *Divus* (god-like) suggest the divinity hedging in a king. The divine right of kings, a frequent theme in Vernulaeus, is invariably advanced by secular rulers as a pretext for encroaching on sacral authority.

138. *Manet hoc repostum corde* (There lies hidden in my heart). The syncopated form for *repositum* is used by Vergil (*Aeneid*, i. 26): "Manet alta mente repostum," as well as by Lucretius and Horace.

139. *Est turpe Regem pectoris flammam pati* (It is scandalous for a king to burn with unholy passion). Vernulaeus depicts Henry at this early stage of his infatuation still imbued with piety, an attitude that Impiety will gradually alter. Sander (*S-L*, p. 33) supplies the King's attitude:

He remembered the account he had one day to give before the judgment-seat of God. The thought of this pursued him night and day; he could come to no decision, and was unable to sleep. Whether he had friends he knew not, but he was certain he had enemies; and besides this, his own conscience condemned him, and he regarded his life as joyless.

142. *Mihi me abstrahit* (she unnerves me completely). Parataxis, or juxtaposition of related pronouns, is a cherished device of Vernulaeus.

ACT I, scene iii (143–208)

Vernulaeus introduces Anne as a carefree, engaging creature who immediately senses Henry's despondency and seeks to alleviate it. Henry ignores her attempts and importunes her for the personal solace he longs for. Anne remains evasive. Upon further solicitation, she refuses firmly, unequivocally. The structural key to the lovers' interchange consists in their seizing of the last reference of the other contender and volleying it back with a qualifying rejoinder. The method is highly effective in producing a kind of dialogue that reflects two minds in unrehearsed repartee—an effect of immediacy not regularly found in Neo-Latin drama.

At the departure of Henry and Anne, Brian moves upstage and soliloquizes on the love affair. His choric commentary is urbanely amoral and dispassionate. Allusions to shipwreck, crippling, slaying, and wounding, in his characterization of Anne's attraction for Henry, aid considerably in prolonging the theme of disastrous love established earlier. They serve likewise in controlling the point of view intended by the playwright.

143–52. *Quid Rex* ... (What is wrong, Your Majesty ...). The opening exchange between Anne and Henry revolves on the central image of light-darkness. This contrast of open-minded carefreeness in the person of Anne and the secretive gloomy introspectiveness of Henry serves as a mutual foil in characterizing the lovers. It also recalls the light-darkness imagery of the opening scene, in which Vernulaeus juxtaposed the underworld gloom with the radiance of the earth. The playwright thus establishes a parallel between the underworld "bereft of light" and Henry's darkened, tortured soul. Anne's allusion to the sun's radiance would not be lost on late-Renaissance students, for whom the correspondence between Phoebus and kingship would be an automatic association.

161–62. *Cum voles, iungo manum;/Animumque iungas* (When you will, I will offer you my hand ...). Anne offers Henry her hand, presumably as an invitation to dance. Henry accepts the gambit and ripostes on another level.

168. *Hanc castitatis nemo decerpet rosam* ... (no one shall pluck my rose of virginity unless he first marry me). Vernulaeus retains Sander's key words: "Sancte dictitans *nemini* se *virginitatis florem,* praeterquam viro suo dedicaturam." (*De schismate anglicano,* p. 17 [italics mine]). The anonymous *Vita Henrici VIII,* written at least two decades before Sander's book on the schism, may have been Sander's source. It has Anne say similarly (p. 47), "Vitae ego hujus potius quam pudicitiae despondium faciam, o rex! Virginitatis meae florem marito (quicumque is futurus est) semel consecravi."

173–76. *Tu iuncta Regi* . . . (Once you surrender yourself to the King . . .). Sander makes no overt statement of Henry's advances to Anne, although he implies them. Again the *Vita Henrici VIII* is explicit on this point: "Brought before the king without witnesses, she [Anne] interpreted his indecent proposition as probably made in jest and done simply to try her."

180. *Pax parta regno est* . . . (Peace has come to your kingdom . . .). For the fundamentally peaceful character of Henry's reign, see Pollard, *Henry VIII*, pp. 66–68.

191–95. *Levare moestam iam decet mentem* . . . (It is now you should lighten your melancholy spirit with jests . . .). In having Anne encourage Henry to forget his anxieties by substituting a life of merriment, song, dances, and tender displays of affection toward her, Vernulaeus adheres to the spirit of Sander's remarks at this point (*S-L*, p. 26):

> The more the king sought her, the more she avoided him. . . . Nevertheless she did not think there was any want of modesty in talking, playing, and even in dancing with the king. In this way she so fed the fire of the king's passion that he became more and more determined to put away Catherine his wife, and to put a woman of such admirable modesty in her place.

The *Vita Henrici VIII* (p. 100) gives a similar account:

> "I cannot marry you and am unworthy to do so, but I do not wish to be a royal mistress." These words served merely to fan the flame in the heart of the king and, not being able to expect anything from a clandestine affair, he resolved to repudiate Catherine and marry Anne; moreover, he had already begun to grow tired of Catherine.

ACT I, scene iv (209–252)

Two colorfully robed figures bustle onstage as Brian recedes. Cardinal Wolsey monopolizes the conversation as Bishop Longland, the King's confessor, attends him. Circuitously, Wolsey lays the groundwork of his purpose with Longland, then suddenly discloses his thoughts of the illegality of Henry's marriage with Catherine. He urges Longland to inform the King and thereby serve the royal conscience and passion simultaneously. Longland is passively submissive and promises cooperation.

Scene iv contrasts sharply with preceding scenes by its straightforward exposition and absence of imagery. Its purpose is to advance the action and prepare for the following encounter with Henry. This it does economically. In addition, two important personages are introduced in characteristic attitudes: Wolsey, puffing, worried, conniving; Longland, obsequious and circumspect. Brian's contribution to the discussion helps contrast his man-of-the-world view of the situation with Wolsey's sanctimonious display. Vernulaeus adheres closely, both in spirit and content, to the account given by Sander.

226–35. *Nuptias Regis ratas/Nemo probabit doctus* . . . (No learned person . . . will consider it valid . . .). For Wolsey's disclosure to Longland that Henry's marriage to Catherine was invalid, Vernulaeus again relies on Sander (S-L, p. 15):

> Burning with wrath at the emperor's conduct, and seeing that the king was becoming more and more estranged from Catherine, and that his own ambitious temper was extremely offensive to the latter, he [Wolsey] resolved to bring about the divorce of the king and queen. . . . He sends for John Longland, the confessor of Henry VIII., and tells him how very much he thought of the king's salvation. He could not be silent any longer about a matter of such grave importance, nor did he think it right to speak of it to anyone before he spoke to the king's confessor, who knew well all the secrets of the king. At last he spoke out, saying that he did not think the king's marriage was valid, and gave many reasons for his opinion. Longland thought the man was sincere in what he said and did not venture to contradict him on account of his rank.

Polydore Vergil's account (*The Anglica Historia* [ed. and trans. Denys Hay], p. 325) agrees substantially with Sander's:

> It came into Wolsey's head to change his queen and find a new one. . . . Certain of achieving his plan as soon as it had occurred to him, he had a friendly discussion with John Longland bishop of Lincoln, because the latter was the person who heard the king's confession. . . . Taking upon themselves more than was proper, as if they had been most learned theologians but with more presumption, they looked for difficulties where there were none (as the saying is) and readily decided that the marriage was neither valid nor sound.

The question of Wolsey's role in the instigation of the divorce has continued to challenge historians. In general it can be said that contemporary opinion believed Wolsey to have been the author of the idea. In his *Life of More* (pp. 40–43) and *Pretended Divorce* (pp. 175–76), Harpsfield depicts Wolsey as the originator of the divorce. The part Longland is supposed to have played at Wolsey's instigation is qualified by the record of Longland's denial: "Thus say some of the Bishop of Lincolne; though himself (as we have shewed) denied that he was one of the first movers of this matter" (*Pretended Divorce*, p. 176). Tyndale, in the "Practice of Prelates" (1530) asserted that Wolsey "imagined the diuorcement betwene the king and the Queene" (quoted in S-L, p. 15). On the other hand, Reginald Pole (. . . *pro ecclesiasticae unitatis defensione*, Bk. III, p. lxxvi), writing to Henry in 1536, goes back ten years and recalls that Anne first put into Henry's mind that the marriage with Catherine ought to be voided. Finally Mackie (*The Earlier Tudors*, p. 322) cites a list of contemporary statements concerning Wolsey as instigator and concludes that "contemporary opinion must have believed that Wolsey was the author of the divorce."

Modern historians, like their predecessors, have disagreed both on the facts and interpretation of the divorce instigation. Pollard (*Wolsey*, p. 340) and H. A. L. Fisher (*The History of England from the Accession of Henry VII. to the Death of Henry VIII.*, p. 275, cited hereafter as *The History of England*), while admitting Wolsey's partial responsibility for the divorce, claim that he was not the instigator. Gairdner ("New Lights on the Divorce of Henry VIII.," *English Historical Review*, XI, 674) shares their view. Busch, on the contrary (*Historisches Taschenbuch*, 6te Folge, VIII., 273–88), argues that Wolsey prompted Henry to divorce Catherine in order to strengthen the French connection, and then found to his dismay that the Boleyns were plotting to raise Anne to the throne. Philip Hughes (*The Reformation in England*, I, 157–59) places the responsibility squarely on Henry's shoulders; Mackie (*The Earlier Tudors*, pp. 322 ff.) also is inclined to impute the germinal idea to Henry. One may conclude that Sander's view of Wolsey as instigator of the divorce, while reflecting the general contemporary opinion, has been considerably qualified by modern scholarship. Wolsey adopted but did not originate the divorce (Fisher, *The History of England*, p. 275).

252. *En concitato properat ipse Rex gradu* (Look, the King himself is walking this way excitedly). Brian's sight of the King approaching from offstage allows this scene to flow unbroken into the next.

ACT I, scene v (253–303)

Wolsey's proposal of having the royal marriage annulled is expedited by the entrance of Henry. In plain language, contrasting noticeably with Henry's colored rhetoric, Wolsey repeats the strategy used earlier on Longland. Alleging the purity of his motives and his devotion to the common weal, he states bluntly what is on his mind and adduces arguments. The scene ends with Henry's decision to pursue Wolsey's course of action.

Henry's initial objection, followed closely by approval, is sadly lacking in motivation. The playwright is obviously in a hurry to get on with the meatier scenes. Thus the plot is furthered at the expense of psychological credibility on the part of Henry. The scene is streamlined to the point of bareness; its lack of complication and its unwarranted reversals reveal Vernulaeus at one of his uninspired moments.

256–57. *Ponti . . ./Incerta . . . unda* (the inconstant current of the

Pontic Sea). The Pontus Euxinus, or Black Sea. Compare Shakespeare's
Othello, III, iii, 454–58:

> ... Like to the Pontic sea,
> Whose icy current and compulsive course
> Ne'er feels retiring ebb, but keeps due on
> To the Propontic and the Hellespont,
> Even so my bloody thoughts ...

275. *Sacrae loquuntur paginae* (the sacred scriptures speak out). Periphrastic expression for the Bible, together with personification of the
"pages" as speaking.

278–80. *At iudicata res fuit* ... (But the case was judged ...). Henry's
cautionary interruption of Wolsey's statement concerning the invalidity
of Henry's marriage is based on Sander: "The King, as soon as he saw
what he [Wolsey] had come to speak about, interrupted him and said,
'Beware of disturbing settled questions'" (*S-L,* p. 16). Harpsfield (*Pretended Divorce,* pp. 175–76) gives a similar account of Henry's reaction:

> At the first hearing whereof, the king, somewhat astonished, held his peace
> awhile, not a little marvelling at this matter so moved unto him. At length
> he answered thus: "Take heed, I beseech you, reverend father, and well
> consider what a great and weighty enterprise you now take in hand"; and
> speaking much in the commendation of his wife, said that his marriage was
> allowed by the most learned and virtuous bishops of the realms of England
> and Spaine, and confirmed also by the Pope's authority.

292–94. *Longlande, ... actutum expedi* (Longland, take action immediately). Henry's instructions to Longland to inform Rome of the King's
doubts concerning his marriage with Catherine are not found in Sander.
It seems likely that Vernulaeus, in the interest of dramatic economy, had
Henry entrust Longland with handling the Roman correspondence, an
eventuality historically inaccurate, but dramatically plausible.

300–01. *Sit alia magni Galliae Regis soror* ... (That someone else
might be the sister of the powerful King of France ...). Wolsey's suggestion of a specific lady to replace Catherine is taken from Sander:
"Wolsey broke in and said that there was a woman of great beauty and
nobleness in France, Margaret, sister of the most Christian king, formerly married to the duke of Alençon, and a fitting bride for the king"
(*S-L,* p. 16). In his *Life of More* (p. 43), Harpsfield likewise mentions
Wolsey's suggestion of "one of the french kinges sisters, the Dutchesse of
Alanson." See also his *Pretended Divorce* (p. 176). This common error,
which ultimately found its way into the Shakespearean *Henry VIII* (III,
ii, 85), comes originally from Polydore Vergil and was repeated by later

writers. The Duchess of Alençon (generally known as Margaret of
Navarre) had already been married to Henry, king of Navarre, in the
preceding January. Wolsey wanted Henry to marry Renée, daughter of
Louis XII. A year later (June 28, 1528) Renée was married to Hercule
d'Este, afterward Duke of Ferrara. See Gairdner, "New Lights on the
Divorce of Henry VIII.," p. 681; for details on the proposed marriage
between Henry VIII and Renée, see Pollard (*Henry VIII*, p. 222) and
Mackie (*The Earlier Tudors*, p. 223).

302. *Sile* (let no word of this be mentioned). Sander supplies the
King's admonition (*S-L*, p. 16):

> "We will speak of this hereafter," said Henry; "now silence is necessary
> above all things, lest the matter be bruited abroad before everything is ready,
> and leave a stain on our honour," for he knew well whom he should marry
> if he could once put queen Catherine out of the way.

Modern historians corroborate Sander at this point. Hughes (*The Reformation in England*, I, 177) claims that "Henry, from the beginning,
had done his best to prevent any knowledge of the suit coming to the
queen until it would be too late for her to oppose it effectively." Garrett
Mattingly (*Catherine of Aragon*, p. 182) is more vehement in his de-
nunciation of Henry's connivance:

> A surreptitious, conspiratorial attempt to declare her [Catherine's] marriage
> null from the beginning, herself, consequently, no wife, and her daughter a
> bastard, an attempt he launched without a word of prior warning or the
> slightest opportunity for her to enter her defence. The whole nature of the
> proceedings marked the case as prejudged and the court as hostile.

On the other hand, it is a matter of record that Henry did eventually
allow Catherine means of defense. Two Belgian lawyers were appointed:
Giles de la Blocquerie, provost of Our Lady of Tongres, and Louis de
Schore, member of the Mechlin Parliament. The appointment of Luis
Vives was also granted. Vives advised the Queen to desist from every
defense and rely merely on her right and guiltlessness. The resultant displeasure of the Queen compelled Vives to leave England in disgrace;
the Queen, nevertheless, did follow his advice (see de Vocht, *Monumenta*, pp. 34–43).

ACT I, scene vi (304–350)

In Act I, scene ii, the evil allegories were seen surrounding the protagonist and pommeling his mind with arguments for fulfilling his desires. The present scene presents the good allegories invading Henry's

conscience in similar fashion. The two scenes offset each other as contrasting panels: Lust is here opposed by Reason; Impiety by Piety; and
Tyranny by Clemency. In the earlier scene the good impulses of the
King engaged in debate with his evil propensities, personified allegor-
ically; here the King's virtues are externalized and storm the evil side
of his nature. The argument proceeds logically by thrust and counter-
thrust, each parry prompting a shift in the attack.

The end of the scene marks an advance in the interior struggle (morally, a retrogression) by the fully advertent decision of the King to sup-
plant Catherine by Anne. The moral issues are clearly delineated; their
importance is made paramount. Henry faces the tragic choice between
good and evil: he chooses what is objectively evil—yet the audience
realizes, sympathetically, that his evil desires masquerade as an apparent
good.

304–09. *Iam certa sors est* . . . (Now my future is certain . . .). The
opening soliloquy indicates Vernulaeus' decision to omit the period of
Henry's studious procrastination as related by Sander (*S–L*, p. 17):

The king having obtained a promise of secrecy, gave his whole mind to
the divorce. He read and re-read, and compared together, with certain
theologians, those passages of Scripture . . . which he thought most to the
purpose. . . . But after spending nearly a year in this secret examination of
the question, he could find nothing for his purpose in the sacred writings, not
a flaw in the Pontifical Brief, . . . and so he and those whom he consulted
came to the conclusion that the matter could be carried no further.

Sander adds (*ibid.*) that it was in part Wolsey's insistence and in part
the King's eagerness for a divorce that kept the question from being
abandoned.

308. *Abdico, eiuro, abnuo* (I disown . . . abjure . . . refuse to recognize . . .). Vernulaeus uses the Senecan device of securing a sudden
climax (see n. to vv. 13–14).

317b–18. *Sponsam mei/Retinebo fratris? Non licet* (Shall I hold fast
to the wife of my brother? It is unlawful). The passage from Leviticus
xx: 21 was crucial in the divorce trial: "He that marrieth his brother's
wife, doth an unlawful thing; he hath uncovered his brother's naked-
ness: they shall be without children."

322b–26. *Tibi non placet/Tam sancta coniux* . . . (. . . you are dissatisfied with such a virtuous wife . . .). The religious qualities of Queen
Catherine are frequently referred to by Sander: The King "saw also that
men loved and admired the queen for her goodness" (*S–L*, p. 33). "Catherine's life was one of soberness and modesty" (*ibid.*, p. 11). After listing

the Queen's daily practices of devotion, Sander (*ibid.*, pp. 7–8) concludes: "Can anyone be astonished that so saintly a woman was to be tried in a greater fire of tribulation, so that the fragrance of her goodness might be the more scattered over the Christian world?"

Historians, without exception, pay tribute to Catherine's uprightness. Pollard, for example (*Henry VIII*, p. 192), writes:

> If Henry's motives were not so entirely bad as they have often been represented, neither they nor Anne Boleyn's can stand a moment's comparison with the unsullied purity of Catherine's life or the lofty courage with which she defended the cause she believed to be right. There is no more pathetic figure in English history, not one condemned to a crueller fate. No breath of scandal touched her fair name, or impugned her devotion to Henry.

327b–28. *Scilicet curam tuae/Geris salutis* (You have good reason to be worried). The word "*scilicet*" in Vernulaeus is usually indicative of irony, but the tone in this instance is rather one of scornful reproach.

331b. *Nempe te pietas movet* (Piety is your motive, indeed). Vernulaeus intends an ironical implication here.

337b–38. *Scilicet Veneri tuae/Tonans favebit* . . . (Oh, yes! The Almighty will favor your lust . . .). The rebuke of Piety is again meant to be ironical.

341. *Saecli* (of our age). The syncopated form of *saeculi* to satisfy metrical demands is common in classical poets.

ACT I, Chorus (351–415)

At this point one must imagine five students, dressed as English maidens, filing onstage or rising in the orchestra. The signal given, they recite ensemble the sixty-five verses constituting the first chorus. The audience is immediately aware of the change in metrical pattern, the iambic senarius of the preceding scenes now giving way to the flowing anapaestic rhythm.

The chorus has four natural divisions. The first section (351–76) is an apostrophe to cruel Love: the symptoms of the malady are catalogued; the imagery involves shipwrecks, shackles, enslavement, and devouring flames. The second part (377–87) is a direct address to Henry, bemoaning the loss of his schoolboy ideals and early education. The third part (388–99) shifts to an impersonal recitation of appropriate *sententiae*. The final section, in turn, looks forward prophetically and dismally.

Verses 372–73, 392–93, and 414–15 are written in iambic dimeters which relieve the anapaestic pattern at well-timed intervals. The chorus, furthermore, is clustered with classical allusions and displays many rhetorical artifices. Its main artistic purpose is to digest the preceding action and afford a religious commentary, thus helping the audience to dwell on the essential moral problem and its significance in a thoroughly orthodox and pious context. This it succeeds in doing effectively. As a pedagogic instrument, it summarizes the issues and anticipates those that are to follow.

353. *Gargara*: the town of Gargara and its plain (at the foot of Mt. Gargara), famous for fertility.

354. *Euripus:* the channel between Boeotia and Euboea, noted for its driving current.

366. *Ostro* (Tyrian purple): a red dye, metonymy for purple garments; properly, the "oyster" or shell fish from which the dye was derived. Tyre was the center for production of this dye—hence, "Tyrian purple."

375. *Quidvis sperat, metuit quidvis* (He hopes for everything, everything he fears): an effective use of chiasmus combined with epanadiplosis—a figure in which a verse begins and ends with the same word.

376. *Aestuat horrens, torpet anhelans* (While shivering he burns, while panting, is benumbed). The juxtaposition of the sensations of burning and numb listlessness presents a vivid image of the sensual lover.

380. *Miserum misere* (torments . . . miserably). The parataxis, or juxtaposition of cognate forms (difficult to render in English), re-enforces the theme of wretchedness by repetition and titillates the ear by the variation of the endings.

391. *Inter Scyllas atque Charybdes* (through Scylla and Charybdis). Vernulaeus freshens the well-worn image, familiar to every Renaissance schoolboy, by use of the plural form. The translation into English might be rendered freely: As the lover sails heedlessly between treacherous whirlpools (*Charybdes*) and rocks (*Scyllas*).

393. *Non est suus* (He is not his own master): used in place of the classical expression, "non est sui compos" (see n. to v. 71).

ACT II, scene i (416–503)

The opening scene of the second act introduces two major characters who will oppose the protagonist steadily and be eventually victimized: Queen Catherine and Thomas More. The longest scene of the play (87 verses) is taken up with Catherine's soliloquy, followed by an interchange between her and More.

Catherine's set speech begins with an apostrophe to the Ruler of the universe, followed by a typical transfer to the sun and the moon. Revolving on the question of a providentially ordered cosmology as opposed to one ruled by mere hazard, the lamentation rehearses Catherine's avowed neglect by the Deity in the face of persecution from Henry. Catherine, in spite of her prayerful life and record of integrity, foresees only the ignominy of royal repudiation and banishment. The prospect is climaxed by her bursting into tears.

More enters to counsel and console. He meets each of the Queen's perturbations with common sense and worldly wisdom; even the Senecan-like dreams that rack her nightly are discredited by More's objective point of view. He assures her that the English people, the Emperor, the Pope, and Spain will make her rights prevail. Even he will pledge his life in her cause. Catherine, fortified by trust in Providence, leaves with her maidservants.

The scene represents a dramatic expansion of a few hints afforded by Sander, but is largely the playwright's invention. There is no account in Sander, for example, of More's private meeting with Catherine; nor is there any evidence extant to support this particular episode. On the other hand, there is no evidence to contradict its possibility. More was on friendly terms with both Henry and Catherine, and was commonly summoned by them because of his pleasant disposition (see William Roper's *Life of Sir Thomas More* [ed. E. V. Hitchcock], p. 11). The main purpose of the scene is to introduce Catherine and More in characteristic attitudes, to dramatize the issues involved in the Queen's cause, and to advance the action by the pledge of More's support.

416–53. *Beate rerum Rector* ... (O Blessed Ruler of the universe ...). Catherine's opening soliloquy is a rhetorical expansion of Sander's sentence: To Catherine above all, the arrival of Campeggio was "painful, and her nights and days were spent in mourning and in weeping" (*S-L*, p. 43).

421–23. *Ergone incerto fluunt/Humana casu* ... (Can it be that human affairs flow in aimless succession ...). In his political writings Vernulaeus treats Catherine's question of whether the universe is ruled fortuitously or providentially and concludes that changes in nature and government are presided over by a beneficent Creator, not dictated by hazard. The origin of political disaster is due to human vices (*Institutionum politicarum*, [1623], p. 43).

424–25. *Magne saeclorum Parens/Lucisque Rector* (father of the ages and lord of light): periphrastic expressions for Phoebus or the sun.

425–26. *Tuque quae noctu vagas/Regis* (O Moon, you who nightly rule): periphrasis for Diana, moon goddess.

445–47. *Et nunc . . . Et nunc . . . Et nunc* (and now . . . and now . . . and now). This triple repetition of initial phrases serves as a rhetorical and emotional climax to Catherine's soliloquy, an effect that must have been noted by an audience trained in rhetorical niceties.

448. *Expulsa, & abdicata & eiecta, & vaga* (driven out as a vagrant, and repudiated, and banished). Vernulaeus' use of polysyndeton (repetition of conjunctions in close succession) prolongs the plangency of the verse and emphasizes the key words in the lament.

449. *Videre cogar exul, atque exul pati* (Shall I be forced to see myself . . . driven into exile). The chiasmic construction throws the emphasis effectively on *exul*.

450–51. *O immerentes! immerentes sed tamen/O ite lachrymae* (The tears . . . innocent tears, undeserved tears . . .). The repetition of *immerentes* drives home the radical injustice of the divorce proceedings as seen from Catherine's point of view.

463–64. *Impetu sese . . . franget* (This infatuation will dash itself to pieces . . .). More's statement that Henry's devotion to Anne was merely a temporary infatuation that would soon run its course is attributed by Sander to Wolsey, not to More: "Wolsey, indeed, was not ignorant of the king's passion for Anne Boleyn, but he never imagined that the king meant to marry her; he persuaded himself that Henry would treat her as he had treated her sister . . . before, who never had any expectations of being raised to the throne" (*S-L*, p. 22). It seems likely that Vernulaeus gave these lines to More, rather than to Wolsey, simply because Wolsey was not on speaking terms with Catherine, whereas More was her confidant.

468. *Scelus istud Anglus non feret* (The English people will not tolerate this crime). Again Sander (*S-L*, p. 31) forms the basis for Vernulaeus' statement:

Everybody was at this time talking of the divorce. All those urged it on in every way who thought that their advancement could be secured only by disturbances, for they saw a road open to the highest honours through the divorce. On the other hand, those who confessed the faith, loving only the truth, defended the cause of the queen, abandoned openly by men, as the most just.

Sander adds later, "The king, seeing the indignation of the people at his attempt to put away so noble a woman as his wife for the sake of a woman unclean of life . . ." (*ibid.*, p. 44). And again Sander emphasizes the opposition of the people: "Throughout England, every man of sense, modesty, and honour—every man who feared God, hated exceedingly the divorce of the queen and the marriage of Anne" (*ibid.*, p. 28).

Sander's account is historically accurate. The murmuring in the lobbies of the Commons came to a boil in Temse's famous speech in 1532 (quoted in Hughes, *The Reformation in England*, I, 236), a speech that expressed the majority opinion of the lower house:

> The best fortification was to maintain justice in the kingdom and friendship with the emperor; and to this end the house should petition the king to take back his wife and treat her well, otherwise the kingdom should be ruined. . . . The discord which the marriage suit was provoking would ruin the kingdom.

Fisher (*The History of England*, pp. 280–81) likewise corroborates Sander's view of popular opposition to the divorce:

> In London popular sympathy ran strong and warm for Catherine, and Henry, always sensitive to the eddies of public opinion, judged that the moment had come for frank explanation. Summoning the notable persons of the court and the city to Bridewell on 8 November [1528] he made a speech admirably calculated to quiet disturbed consciences and to silence the tongue of slander. His sense of dignity would not permit him to answer the common talk of the town, which attributed his action to a vulgar amour.

Ambassador Falier, writing in 1531, stated his opinion (quoted with source in Constant, *La réforme*, I, 366–67):

> The Queen is so beloved, so respected, that the people are already beginning to murmur, and there is no doubt that if some leader of a faction appeared, the English nation, which leans toward novelty and change, would take up arms for her, especially if he had in mind to marry the princess Marie.

The fact is that continual watch was kept across England to prevent an uprising. Henry was aroused not merely by the gossip of the people but by the threat that the Imperialists might stir his subjects against him in Catherine's behalf (see DuBellay to Montmorency, *L&P*, IV, 5016).

469. *Et prava Regem Consilia secum auferent* (and wicked counselors will win the King . . .). Catherine foresees the decisive influence of wicked counselors. Thomas More, writing from the Tower to his daughter Margaret, looked back with the wisdom of personal experience as he wrote: "And surely, daughter, it is a great pity that any Christian prince should by a flexible Council ready to follow his affections, and by a weak clergy lacking grace constantly to stand to their learning, with flattery be so shamefully abused" (Roper's *Life of Sir Thomas More*, p. 78).

476b–78. *Brevis est furor/Ab amore semper; illa quae Regi placet,/ Mox displicebit* (Passionate love is always short-lived . . .). Vernulaeus gives another example of More's common-sense, objective attitude toward Henry's amour. Actually Anne's marriage lasted three years and several months: married to Henry January 25 (?), 1533, she was executed May 19, 1536.

478b–84. ... *Et dubia noctis pectus excruciat fides*...(... the dubious evidence of nightly dreams ...). Catherine's report to More of her nightmares and ill-boding dreams, not mentioned by Sander, is Vernulaeus' application of a Senecan technique to instill horror and foreshadow subsequent events.

ACT II, scene ii (504–547)

The stage is momentarily deserted for the first time with the exit of Catherine, her maidservants, and Thomas More. In their wake enter Henry and Brian, and later Anne. By abandoning his usual practice of announcing the entrance of new characters, the playwright succeeds at this point in distinguishing between the action of the King's cause and that of the Queen.

The King's cause advances logically from its previous position in Act I, scene vi, where Henry had privately resolved to have his marriage dissolved. The obstacles he will meet as a public figure are now investigated by his interview with Brian, a flattering counselor. Brian assures Henry that the commoners, Parliament, and clergy, with proper persuasion and bribery, can be manipulated to the royal will. Henry accepts Brian's counsel and turns his attentions to Anne.

Again Henry besieges the fortress of Anne's virtue and is again repulsed by the lady's ultimatum: only by marrying her will the King enjoy her person. Archly, Anne maintains her stance till the scene closes with the announcement of Longland's approach.

Vernulaeus clearly emphasizes in the latter half of the scene that Anne's insistence on marriage directs the subsequent action the protagonist will take. Her resistance proves an obstacle the King can overcome by circumvention only.

504. *Briane* (Tell me, Brian). Vernulaeus modifies the historical portrait of Sir Francis Brian to typify the "evil counselors" suspected by Catherine in verse 469. He takes his lead, undoubtedly, from this passage in Sander (*S-L*, p. 24):

The royal household consisted of men utterly abandoned—gamblers, adulterers, panders, swindlers, false swearers, blasphemers, extortioners, and even heretics; among these was one distinguished profligate, Sir Francis

Bryan, of the blood and race of the Boleyn. This man was once asked by the king to tell him what sort of sin it was to ruin the mother and then the child. Bryan replied that it was a sin like that of eating a hen first and its chicken afterwards. The king burst forth into loud laughter, and said to Bryan, "Well, you certainly are my vicar of hell." The man had been long ago called the vicar of hell on account of his notorious impiety, henceforth he was called also the king's vicar of hell.

The historical Brian shared almost all of Henry's amusements and therefore acquired an unrivaled reputation for dissoluteness. In a letter to Gardiner, Cromwell calls Brian "the vicar of hell"—a popular nickname which his cruel indifference to the fate of his cousin Anne Boleyn proves that he well deserved (see "Sir Francis Bryan," *DNB*).

517. *Ast* (But). Poetical variation of *at*, prompted by metrical necessity.

521*b*–25. *Regibus quicquid lubet/Istud licet* . . . (Whatever kings find agreeable is lawful . . .). Brian's equation of tyranny with kingship would not deceive Vernulaeus' students. A tyrant, wrote Vernulaeus in 1623, is one who disregards law and seeks his personal advantage (*Institutionum politicarum*, p. 196).

527. *Pallidum* . . . *metum* (pale-faced fear): an example of the figure of hypallage, or transferred epithet, since the pallor in question is proper to the person made pallid by fear.

533. *Medullas* (innermost being). Meaning literally "the innermost parts" and extended to signify "marrow of the bones" or "innermost feelings," the expression is a classical commonplace.

534. *Vultu vulneror* (sight of your face wounds). The paronomasia, or play on words, is striking in economy and suggestiveness, juxtaposing as it does the face of Anne and its destructive power with the vulnerability of Henry's heart. The image crystallizes in two words the tragic theme as envisioned by the protagonist, the playwright, and his source.

ACT II, scene iii (548–607)

Awaiting the arrival of Longland, Henry confides to the audience the evils attendant on men who rule. The verses given him by the playwright are sympathetically conceived and heightened by imagery befitting a magnanimous sovereign. His very determination to emerge undaunted in the face of universal antagonism bears a natural nobility of purpose discernible even in tyrants. Vernulaeus clearly takes pains to maintain sympathy with the protagonist throughout the scene by making his desolation credible on the psychological level.

Longland's report on the divorce situation serves as a point-by-point contradiction of Brian's previous diagnosis. Henry's spirits plunge progressively lower as Longland enumerates the opposition of theologians and scholars, the attachment of the English people to saintly Catherine, the threats of the Emperor. At the climax of despair, Henry is informed of the Pope's decision to send Campeggio to try his case, an eventuality that fires his soul with new hope.

The action of the scene is ordered to secure the maximum of dramatic impact. Longland's report, manifestly sincere and respectful, is counterpoised tellingly with the sycophantic counsel of Brian. Furthermore the arguments of Longland are arranged to lead progressively to Rome, the ultimate seat of authority. It is from this unexpected quarter that a reversal of the King's fortune seems forthcoming.

549. *Fluctibus fractis* (as the waves buckle). The alliterating fricatives suggest the buckling of waves and flying spume. Cf. Coleridge, "The Rime of the Ancient Mariner," Part the Second: "The fair breeze blew, the white foam flew/The furrow followed free."

556–57. *Nullus in Regem est satis/Iustus tumultus* (No rebellion . . . is justified). But Vernulaeus' students had been taught that there were times when rebellion against a *tyrant* was justified. See the section entitled, "Is it lawful to kill a tyrant who has a legal right to rule?" (*Institutionum politicarum*, p. 200). On the whole, however, Vernulaeus cautions against tyrannicide, suggesting patience, endurance, even death in preference to violent remedies (see also nn. to vv. 91–92, 521–25).

557. *Arguant, damnent, fremant* (Let them accuse . . . condemn . . . rage). The playwright's use of asyndeton secures the desired climax of Henry's tirade, an effect extremely difficult to convey adequately in English.

558. *Sceptrum Bolena capiet, & Regis thronum* (Anne shall assume . . .). The key words gain emphasis from their position at the extremities of the verse.

566. *Praesulum . . . Pater* (the Father of bishops): periphrasis for the Pope.

578b–84. *Forsitan Caesar tibi/Rex, est timendus* . . . (Perhaps Your Highness should fear the Emperor . . .). Longland cautions Henry to abandon the divorce venture for fear of inciting the armed vengeance of Charles V. See also n. to v. 123.

591–94. . . . *Debet hic multum* . . .(. . . He is greatly indebted to me . . .). Henry's allusion to the Pope's indebtedness to him is mentioned by Sander (*S-L*, pp. 33–34):

Knowing also that he had rendered such services to Pope Clement, in return for which he might confidently expect that the Pope would do for him all that he was asking him to do, and that both the neighbouring princes and his own subjects would yield before the authority of the Pope, he [Henry] doggedly made up his mind . . . to put Catherine away.

Sander's account at this point is historically accurate. In a letter to Campeggio written in January, 1528 (Burnet-Pocock, *History*, IV, 59), Wolsey stated that the King

has conceived such a confidence, both from the justice of his case and from his own filial devotion to the pope, that he can by no means whatever persuade himself that his confidence can ever be frustrated ["Ex rei justitia, tum ex sua in sanctissimum dominum nostrum filiali devotione, spem concepit, ut illo pacto sibi persuadeat umquam fieri posse ut sua expectatione frustretur. . ."].

For further documentation on Henry's insistence on securing the divorce from the Pope as a favor for continued support of papal policies and as a service due to him in consideration of his merits, see Hughes, *The Reformation in England*, I, 160–62.

594b–96. *Novit tuam/Iam Roma causam* . . . (Rome is already aware of your problem . . .). Longland assures Henry of Clement's sympathy for the King's predicament. Sander explains that Clement VII wished to have the question of the divorce discussed by various theologians (*S-L*, p. 37):

If it could be shown that the king's petition could be lawfully granted, he [Clement] would not only grant it, but would congratulate himself that he had an opportunity of showing how thankful he was to so great a prince, who, by the most learned work he had written in defence of the seven sacraments of the Church, had rendered such great services to the Church at large, and who also had lately come to the assistance of the Apostolic See, and, above all, had placed the Pope under infinite obligations by delivering him out of the hands of his enemies.

A study of the Rome correspondence shows clearly that if Clement VII showed any inclination toward partiality, it was not in favor of Catherine or Charles V, but rather of Henry VIII and the English. The above statement of Sander is taken almost literally from Clement's letter to the bishops and lords of England, September 27, 1530 (Ehses, *Römische Dokumente*, p. 163):

Nos enim amamus regem ipsum ut filium carissimum, et cum eius praeclaras virtutes et tam multa et maxima *in nos atque in Sedem Apostolicam merita* . . . nihil est, quod non illius causa cupiamus, nihil, quo eius Maiestatem dignissimam non iudicemus. . . . Itaque *a principio,* cum regii oratores ad nos huiusmodi causam detulerunt, *animi nostri propensionem magis quam viris vigorem secuti comisimus* (italics mine).

See also Salviati to Campeggio, from Rome, April 13, 1532, *ibid.,* p. 198; for a full documentation of Clement VII's sympathy for Henry, see Constant, "Clément VII et le divorce d'Henri VIII, 1527–1533," pp. 151–61.

599–600. *E purpuratis Patribus Campegium./Volsaeus alter iunctus est Iudex simul* (Campeggio, one of the Cardinals . . . Wolsey has been added as a second judge). Campeggio, Longland reveals to Henry, is being sent as judge by Clement to join Wolsey. "Lorenzo Campeggio and Thomas Wolsey, Cardinals, priests, and bishops, were appointed judges in the cause" (*S-L,* p. 40). It was Wolsey who directed his agents to Rome to press for the appointment of a legate. Clement VII finally granted the commission on June 8, 1528 (*L&P,* IV, 4345). Wolsey had been made *legatus de latere* on May 17, 1518, to "watch and control Campeggio" (Pollard, *Wolsey,* p. 170), who was en route to England to encourage interest in a crusade. In 1519, Leo X prolonged Wolsey's legacy for two years and, under Adrian VI, two further extensions were granted. Wolsey finally managed to secure his commission for life from Clement VII.

604*b*–05. *Subitque regnum* ([Campeggio is] entering the kingdom). Sander mentions that Campeggio arrived in London October 7, 1528 (*S-L,* p. 42). Vernulaeus disregards the unhurried journey of Campeggio to England—Rome to London was less than a six-week journey even in winter. The Cardinal embarked for France July 25, 1528, arrived at Dover September 28, and entered London more than a week later, as Sander records. For Campeggio's own account of his journey, see *L&P,* IV, 4857.

ACT II, scene iv (608–677)

The Queen's cause is eloquently promoted by speeches of Bishop John Fisher and Thomas More in a scene of the playwright's own invention. Both speeches are admirably fitted out in their own right: Fisher's, grandiloquent and forceful in its rhetorical indignation; More's, lower-keyed and almost casual in its marshaling of biting evidence. Fisher's speech is meant to warn the King against inviting God's destruction on the English nation by sacrificing Catherine for lust; More's speech, on the other hand, expresses the commoners' low regard for Anne Boleyn and the ignominy that would result in her marriage with the Defender of the Faith.

Henry parries both thrusts in a marvelous display of self-control. It is not a question of lust, he assures Fisher, but a matter of conscience. The opinion of the people, he reminds More, is manifestly untrue to the facts, since Anne's integrity is beyond reproach.

The scene is a remarkable example of the art of eloquence as a handmaid to academic drama. No longer could any schoolboy in the audience doubt the power of spoken Latin, either in its Ciceronian fullness or in its Senecan succinctness. Within a dramatic context, Louvain's *rhetor publicus* displays his masterly power of communicating ideas that were vital in the age of religious wars.

611. *Anglia expandit manus* (England extends her hands). The personification of the mother country is apt in the rhetorical context of Fisher's address.

621–23. . . . *horrescunt* (quake) . . . *pavescant* (cower). These inchoative forms may suggest the early stages of trembling and cowering.

629. *Non feret, nunquam feret* (He will not tolerate, He will never tolerate). The repetition of *feret* at the end of successive clauses acts as a fist hammering emphatically.

654–68. *Quid Fama dicet* . . . (What will the people say . . .). In More's assessment of Anne Boleyn, Vernulaeus avails himself of the lurid remarks of Sander concerning Anne's youthful delinquency.

654–55. *Vulgus* [Bolenam] *infamem putat/Et impudicam* (The commoners think her . . . shameless). As Speaker of the Commons, More is in character here, an innovation made by Vernulaeus.

657. *Vicina testis Gallia est, scortum hic fuit* (. . . she was a harlot there). Sander's frankly vulgar comments about the mother of Queen Elizabeth (*S-L*, pp. 25–26) are bowdlerized by Vernulaeus to some extent. Sander says that Anne Boleyn "appeared at the French court, where she was called the English mare, because of her shameless behaviour; and then the royal mule, when she became acquainted with the king of France." Henry's plans to marry Anne reached France, Sander adds (*ibid.*), "and there it became a common report that the king of England was going to marry the mule of the king of France."

658–59. *Et nostra testis Anglia est; virgo hic prius/Fregit pudorem* (And our own England is a witness . . .). Sander is more explicit: "At fifteen she sinned first with her father's butler, and then with his chaplain, and forthwith was sent to France" (*S-L*, p. 25).

664. *Sectam Lutheri sequitur* (She follows the sect of Luther). Following Sleidan (trans. Bohun, IX, 170), Sander writes (*S-L*, p. 26): "She embraced the heresy of Luther to make her life and opinions consistent,

but nevertheless did not cease to hear mass with the Catholics, for that was wrung from her by the custom of the king and the necessities of her own ambition." Sleidan (and Sander) are supported by Chapuys, who reported that Anne Boleyn and her father were more Lutheran than Luther himself, that they were the true apostles of the new sect in England (*L&P*, V, 148, 850, quoted in Pollard, *Henry VIII*, p. 274).

666–67. *Ecclesiae/Defensor* (Defender of the Church): Henry's title of *Defensor Fidei*. Presented by Leo X on September 15, 1521. See above, *Dedicatory Letter*, n. to ll. vii-viii.

ACT II, scene v (678–702)

In one of the shortest scenes of the play, Cardinal Campeggio is ushered into the royal presence. After extending the Pope's blessing and good wishes to Henry, the legatine Cardinal states his business clearly and unequivocally. If Catherine can be persuaded to join a nunnery, the inconvenience of a formal trial will have been obviated. Henry welcomes the suggestion and the private audience with Catherine is prepared.

The advent of Campeggio from Rome marks a turning point in the play's progress. Up to this point, the dramatist has been concerned with delineating the opposing issues of the King and the Queen. Supporting Henry's cause are Wolsey, Anne, Brian, and, ostensibly, Longland. Catherine, in turn, has the support of Fisher and More. Beyond this human situation are the forces of Good and Evil incarnated in the allegorical figures but temporarily withheld from the conflict. Campeggio's entry heralds the beginning of the divorce proceedings, the expected terminus of which will be the decision of Rome in the persons of Campeggio and Wolsey. It is at this point that the beginning of the action yields logically to the middle; the direction of the middle action, in turn, will be determined by Catherine's decision in the forthcoming scene. The present scene, however telescoped for dramatic economy, adheres to Sander's account and is historically accurate.

678–80. *Urbemque & Orbem . . . Arbiter felix tibi/Iubet esse Regnum* (He who rules the city and the world . . . bids your kingdom bring you joy). Sander (*S-L*, pp. 42–43) says of Campeggio's first appearance: "Campeggio arrived in London October 7, 1528, and on being introduced to the king by Wolsey, on behalf of the Pope, the Cardinals, the clergy, and people of Rome, he offered their services to Henry as the one whom they regarded as their deliverer." Pocock, in his edition of Harpsfield's *Pretended Divorce* (p. 323) establishes the precise dates: Campeggio crossed from Calais September 29, 1528. He was at Canterbury October 1, but did not arrive in London until October 8. The meeting of the King at Bridewell occurred on Thursday, October 22.

690–91. *Si causa nostro caperet arbitrio modum,/Gauderet Orbis* (If the case could be settled by our own arbitration [outside of court], the whole world would rejoice). Sander mentions (*S-L*, p. 42) that the Pope instructed Campeggio "to make every effort to reconcile the king and the queen, and if he should fail, then to persuade the latter to become a religious." Again Sander is accurate in his account. In the letter of John Casali, December 17, 1528 (Burnet-Pocock, *History*, IV, 67; Le Grand, *Histoire du divorce*, III, 117), in which the writer gives an account of an audience with the Pope, the fact is thus stated: "Ego, (inquit) [Pontifex] illi [Campeggio] imposui, ut divortium regi dissuaderet, persuaderet reginae." Writing to Salviati from London, October 17, 1528, Campeggio had said previously (Ehses, *Römische Dokumente*, p. 49) that his first business as legate was to persuade Catherine, in the Pope's name, not to stand on her rights, but to become a nun and let her case go by default, undefended.

ACT II, scene vi (703–748)

On her first appearance in Act II, scene i, Queen Catherine impressed the audience as a pathetic figure overwhelmed by adversity and powerless to resist it. The present scene evokes a new aspect of her character. Faced by Wolsey, she bristles, countering his advances with controlled disdain. Wolsey's commission as investigator of her marriage provokes her to a spirited defense of her cause. Like William Morris' Guenevere, she stands defiantly before the officious prelate and defends her marriage. At the climax of her speech she launches into a personal attack on Wolsey, accusing him of instigating the divorce proceedings. It is this same righteous indignation that fires her resolution to face the legatine court.

The scene likewise introduces Warham, Archbishop of Canterbury and chief counsel of the Queen in the divorce trial. The Queen's decision to face the legatine court carries the action forward: action results from character. The material of the scene is based on Sander; its historical accuracy, except for the absence of Campeggio, is noteworthy.

703–04. *Quis iste rumor . . .* (What is this I hear . . .). The news of Clement's appointment of the legatine judges comes to Catherine as a painful surprise. See n. to v. 302.

715. *Volsaeus eccum* (Wolsey is approaching). Vernulaeus departs from Sander and from historical fact in having Wolsey alone conduct the legatine interview with Catherine prior to the trial. Sander (*S-L*, p. 45) gives the following account:

Campeggio persuaded the king to allow the matter to be settled in a friendly way, and not by means of an unfriendly lawsuit. The king was pleased with the advice he gave, and the Cardinals with his consent went to the queen to induce her to enter some religious order.

Vernulaeus heightens the Wolsey-Catherine conflict by the exclusion of Campeggio in this scene; he likewise succeeds in motivating Catherine's spirited rebuttal more convincingly, fired as she is by Wolsey's personal animosity to her and the Emperor. For the preliminary visit of Campeggio and Wolsey to the Queen, see Campeggio to Sanga, October 17, 1528, in *L&P*, IV, 4858.

716–20. *Regina vive; Nempe, Reginam vocas . . .* (Long live the Queen. That title sounds strange on your lips . . .). The stychomythic fencing of Wolsey and Catherine is highly effective dialogue, and original with the playwright. Catherine betters the Cardinal in the exchange of thrusts, a nicety that probably delighted the audience of students and clerics.

723–32. *Nempe connubium ut meum . . .* ("to investigate" my marriage . . .). Catherine's reply to Wolsey's proposal is based on Sander (*S-L*, p. 45):

But when they had said, by way of preface, that they had received a commission from the Pope to try the question of the validity of her marriage, she interrupted them at once, and told them that they were opening a question settled for ever—settled not only in the councils of two of the most prudent monarchs, but in the consistory of the Pope, Pope Julius.

Sander's account of Catherine's reply seems to be modeled on that of Hall (*The Vnion of the Two Noble and Illustre Famelies of Lancastre & York*, p. 55, cited hereafter as *Chronicle*), for it is substantially the same. Cavendish likewise echoes Hall's recorded speech of Catherine before the legates, but incorporates it in Catherine's speech at the session at Blackfriars on June 18, 1529 (Cavendish, *Life of Wolsey*, pp. 80–81). The accuracy of Sander and of the sources he relied on is proved by the account of Campeggio to Salviati October 26, 1528, and again two days later (see Ehses, *Römische Dokumente*, pp. 53–59, 59–60; *L&P*, IV, 4875).

729–30. *Ecce bis denos simul/Habitamus annos* (. . . We have lived together these twenty years). Catherine and Henry were married on June 11, 1509; the two Cardinals approached the Queen on October 27, 1528. See Campeggio to Salviati, October 28, 1528: "Hieri . . . Eboracense et io . . . andammo . . . alla regina" (Ehses, *Römische Dokumente*, p. 59).

732. *Quid nunc? & actam rursus agere rem cupis* (Will you now stir up . . .). Catherine's reproach to Wolsey recalls Henry's similar admonition when the Cardinal broached the subject of the divorce (see I, v, 278–80).

733–37. *Volsaee . . . causa tu solus* . . . (Wolsey, you alone are the one . . .). In having Catherine accuse Wolsey of being the instigator of the divorce, Vernulaeus takes his cue from Sander (*S-L*, p. 45):

Then, looking to Wolsey, she added, "I am indebted for this sorrow to you alone, who persecute me with so much hatred, either because I have not been able to endure your ambition and your immoral life, or because my nephew the emperor took no pains to obtain for you the Papacy."

Hall (*Chronicle*, p. 755) or Harpsfield (*Pretended Divorce*, p. 180) may have been Sander's source for Catherine's attack of Wolsey as instigator of the divorce as a means of revenging himself on Charles V. Campeggio does not mention Catherine's outburst against Wolsey, but he does record the extremities to which Wolsey went, breaking out into English and falling on his knees before the Queen, pleading with her to change her mind for the good of all:

And I spoke at length, and having finished, the Cardinal of York replied (but in English) and finally he fell on his knees before the Queen and for a long time begged and pleaded with her to follow this good advice, and profit by the good will of the king for her own honor, convenience, and profit—all this, moreover, in English.

(Ehses, *Römische Dokumente*, p. 60; see also *L&P*, IV, 4880.) There seems to be no doubt that Sander and contemporary historians of the divorce inclined to make Wolsey more criminal a scapegoat than is borne out by modern historical evidence. Furthermore, Catherine seems to have modified her view of Wolsey's role in the divorce instigation after the Cardinal's fall from power. By September, 1529, she had come to believe that the case "originated entirely" in her husband's "iniquity and malice," and by December she had "shown some pity for the Cardinal's fall" (*Span. Cal.*, pp. 236, 368, quoted in Pollard, *Wolsey*, p. 283; for related matters concerning Wolsey as divorce instigator, see n. to vv. 226–35).

744–47. . . . *cernis hos fletus meos* . . . (. . . You see these tears . . .).
Sander writes (*S-L*, p. 46): "Then, when they saw her great distress, and
the tears which she could not control, they thought it better to refrain
from further discussion and to do the rest of their work by the mouth of
others."

746. *Proc[ur]* (Proc.). This speaker's tag does not appear in the *Personae Tragoedia* or in the list of characters prefixed to the scene in question. Vernulaeus undoubtedly meant *"procurator"* to designate Warham,
who appears in this scene as chief counsel for Catherine during the divorce proceedings.

ACT II, scene vii (749–799)

Vernulaeus' dramatization of the first session of the divorce trial adheres closely to the account given by Sander. Sander leaves the impression that the formal opening of the court, the beginnings of the trial
itself, the objection of Catherine to the judges, their refusal to honor her
objection, the Queen's personal appeal to Henry together with his acquiescence to her wishes—that this entire catalogue of incidents took
place at the opening session of May 31, 1529. In point of fact, however,
the above business extended over the period of one month, reaching successive climaxes in three sessions of the legatine court. These sessions, together with the events relevant to each, may be recalled at this point.

First Session: May 31, 1529, Blackfriars. The opening session was taken
up with the nomination of different officers and the serving of the ci-
tations on the King and on the Queen (*L&P*, IV, 5613, 5636). The court
then appointed the following session (*ibid.*, No. 5613) and adjourned.
For further details, see Campeggio to Salviati, June 4, 1529 (Ehses,
Römische Dokumente, p. 99). On June 15, 1529, Catherine paid a visit
to Campeggio, who was in bed with the gout (*L&P*, IV, 5681), but left
him in doubt as to what course she would pursue. The following day she
drew up her appeal to the Pope and her protestation against the jurisdiction of the legates (Pocock, *Records*, II, 609).

Second Session: June 18, 1529. The Queen, to the astonishment of all,
appeared in person and read a carefully drawn protestation against the
fitness of the court to try the case, the judges being suspect as subjects of
Henry. Henry was not present, being represented by Sampson and Bell.
The legates fixed the following Monday for their answer (*L&P*, IV, 5685,
5694, 5695, 5702). For the appeal of the Queen, see Pocock, *Records*, II,
609; for Campeggio's report to Salviati, see Ehses, *Römische Dokumente*,
pp. 103–04.

Third Session: June 21, 1529 (Monday). Both the King and the Queen were present. The following events, correctly described by Harpsfield (*Pretended Divorce*, p. 181), Cavendish, and Sander, occurred in this sequence:

1) Henry made a long speech, arguing violently that his cause was just, recalling his devotion to the Pope as he did so; that all he sought was the truth and the relief of his conscience, that he had confidence in the legates (see Campeggio to Salviati, June 21, 1529, Ehses, *Römische Dokumente*, p. 106; Harpsfield, *Pretended Divorce*, p. 181).

2) The legates rejected Catherine's objections, declaring themselves a competent court (Ehses, *Römische Dokumente*, p. 109).

3) The Queen appealed to the Pope (*ibid.*).

4) The Queen threw herself before Henry, calling upon him to bear her out that she had come to him a virgin, that she had ever been to him a loyal and obedient wife. She then begged him for the honor of her family to allow her the means of presenting her case (Burnet-Pocock, *History*, IV, 118).

5) Henry remained silent until the Queen left the court.

6) Henry then delivered a panegyric on Catherine's virtues (*L&P*, IV, Introduction, p. cccclxxv).

Vernulaeus eliminates certain features of these three historical sessions but merges all three into this scene. The structural advantage of tele-scoping the events consists in having the temporary victory of the Queen's cause serve as the climax of Act II. The scene itself shows effective use of surprise and reversal, of momentary deadlock, and resolution. On the other hand, it suffers from lack of elaboration (fifty verses), from failure to exploit adequately the predicament of Catherine and the possibilities of impassioned oratory, and from the strain it puts upon the reader's credibility in accepting Henry's sudden acquiescence.

749–50. *Optanda fuerat optimae pacis quies* . . . (A peaceful settle-ment . . .). Sander does not refer to Campeggio's disappointment that a peaceful settlement had not been arranged outside of court, but Vernu-laeus' reference is, nonetheless, accurate. See Campeggio to Salviati, October 26, 1528: "Her [Catherine's] obstinacy in not accepting this reasonable advice is not greatly to my satisfaction" (Ehses, *Römische Dokumente*, p. 59).

753–54 [Stage direction between lines]. *The papal commission is read aloud.* Vernulaeus does not include the text of the commission, thus leav-ing the reader in doubt about the precise wording that was used. The Bull of Clement authorizing Campeggio and Wolsey to pronounce judgment on the divorce case was granted April 13, 1528, and renewed in June, 1528. (It is printed in Ehses, *Römische Dokumente*, pp. 28–30.) It seems likely that Vernulaeus composed a papal commission of his own at this point, for even had he recourse to a copy of the original, the text of the bull is rather too lengthy for inclusion.

759–60. *Pro Rege causam . . ./Aggrediar* (. . . I shall commence the case for the King). Brian is entrusted by Vernulaeus with representing the King's cause. Sander does not mention Brian at this point; nor does he refer to the King's proctors by name: "Then Henry is first summoned by name, and two proctors appeared on his behalf" (*S–L*, p. 52). Vernulaeus' choice of Brian as chief counsel for the King is dramatically convenient but historically inaccurate: both Brian and Gardiner left England for Rome late in 1528 and did not return to England until after the third session was completed. See *L&P*, IV, 4976 [November 27, 1528, Brian and Vannes sent to Rome]; 4977 [their instructions]; 5650, 5715 [their return, June 25, 1529].

760*b*–62; 764*b*–66. *Agedum postulat nondum hoc locus . . .* (Wait! It is not yet time . . .). Vernulaeus departs from Sander in having Warham, chief counsel for the Queen, enter his objection in the Queen's name. The playwright's innovation is effective, however, in bringing about a head-on clash between the opposing proctors.

771*b*–73. *. . . Mandata promas . . .* (. . . Produce your rescript . . .). "The Legates would not allow the appeal unless the queen could show by a rescript from the Pope [*nisi Regina scripto quodam Apostolico doceret*] that their powers had been withdrawn" (*S–L*, p. 52). At this juncture, Sander indicates a lapse of time between court sessions (*ibid.*): "The queen presents herself again on the next sitting of the court [June 18, 1529] and gave in her objections in due form of law, as well as her reasons for appealing to the Pope." As explained in the introduction to this scene, Vernulaeus dovetails the two sessions for the sake of continuity and preparation for the climax.

774–81. *Nec iste Iudicii locus; nec Iudices/Favent querelae . . .* (Neither the location of the trial nor the judges are favorable to my complaint . . .). The objections of the Queen in Vernulaeus are simply summary statements of those recorded by Sander (*S–L*, pp. 52–53):

> The first, that the trial was held in a place where she could not hope for justice, she being a Spaniard by birth and a foreigner; and that Henry, who began the lawsuit, was the king of all England.
> The second, that the judges were in their own persons not only under obligations to the king, but also in his power: Wolsey holding the bishopric

of Winchester, the archbishopric of York, and many abbeys; Campeggio holding the see of Salisbury, given him by the king.

Finally, she declared solemnly on her oath that nothing but fear, most justly grounded, moved her to decline in that place, and in that cause, the sentence of the judges.

780. *Nullus pectus infestat timor* (no fear about this . . . besets my heart). Vernulaeus reverses the role of fear in the final statement of the Queen, as set down by Sander. Vernulaeus' Catherine is unperturbed about the outcome of the trial; Sander's Catherine confesses her fear. The about-face on Vernulaeus' part is consistent with his practice of allowing heroes (but not villains) to confront affliction with undivided souls.

782*b*–87. *Quid tuas tanto genas/Regina fletu spargis* . . . (Why do you drench your cheeks . . . O Queen . . .). Vernulaeus heightens the dramatic intensity at this point by having Henry address the Queen directly, rather than the assembly, as in Sander (S–L, p. 53): "Standing before the court himself, he made a public declaration that in these proceedings he was not urged on by any dislike of the queen, but by scruples of conscience and the judgment of most learned men." The moral significance of Henry's case of scrupulosity still troubles historians, notably the foremost Roman Catholic priest-scholar of England today. "Was Henry really telling the truth?" he asks (Hughes, *The Reformation in England*, I, 159–60).

Had he really been in good faith, worried in conscience, when he began his long siege of the Roman Curia and Pope Clement VII? Or was he—as some coolly unsympathetic observers, then and since, have thought—merely determined to have Anne Boleyn for his wife, and, to that end, ready to tell any lie he thought sufficient to win a judgment in his favour? The point is of very great importance, even for the political and social historian; what is in question is the spirit in which this quasi-absolute prince began the business which was to change the Englishman's idea of the kind of being God is and of the way God works with mankind—to change greatly, therefore in the course of centuries, the national character and destiny.

788–89. *Nil provocatae Iudices* . . . (Will the judges pay no heed . . .). Catherine's appeal to the judges and their refusal follow immediately in Sander (S–L, p. 53): "When the king had spoken, the queen insisted on the allowance of her appeal. The judges refused."

790–99. *O Rex, per istas lachrymas* . . . (O My King, by these tears . . .). The final dramatic appeal of the Queen and the King's temporary acquiescence versifies Sander's version (S–L, pp. 53–54):

Thereupon the queen, who was sitting on the left side of the court, rose from her place and went up to the king, who was sitting under a canopy on the other side. Falling upon her knees before him, she most humbly prayed him, who was at home in his own kingdom, to allow her, a foreigner, to prosecute her appeal in Rome, before the common father of all Christians, and also the judge whom the king himself acknowledged. The king rose from his seat, and looking at the queen with the utmost affection, declared that he gave her leave.

The rhetorical plea of Catherine, as phrased by Vernulaeus, seems influenced by the famous appeal of Dido to Aeneas (cf. Vergil, *Aeneid*, iv., especially 314–19).

ACT II, Chorus (800–858)

Written in faultless iambic dimeters, the second chorus reveals five divisions, three of them foreshadowing the action of the coming act, which will terminate in the triumph of the King's cause. Henry's submission to Catherine will be forsaken for Venus (800–19); already Anne is besieging Henry daily with a barrage of enticements (820–32). But Anne's maneuvers will be checked by the decision of the Roman Rota in favor of Catherine (834–44). Eventually, however, Venus will conquer: Anne will usurp the royal throne, scepter, and bed (845–50). The destiny awaiting England cannot be forestalled by prayer; it must be met with stoic resignation (851–58).

The second chorus is largely expository in function. Its second section discloses the strategy carried out by Anne behind the trial scenes and indicates the lapse of time between sessions.

826–28. *Tractat . . . Tractando . . . Tractando . . .*: the variations of *tractare* are subtle and effective in Latin, but difficult to render in English without resorting to slang.

ACT III, scene i (859–942)

The third act begins with a long formal disputation in court, where the Queen's cause is prosecuted by Brian and defended by Warham. The scene enables Vernulaeus to display two lengthy, closely reasoned models of deliberative oratory that advance both sides of the dramatic conflict without providing a resolution. The rather amazing historical accuracy of the formal debates is explainable only by the playwright's adherence to Sander, whose access to the Rome sources may explain his knowledge of the facts of the divorce proceedings, long thought a fictitious invention.

859–69a. *Rursum ad tribunal, Iudices* . . . (Judges, let us return . . .). Henry countermands his concession to the Queen and resummons the session, as described by Sander (*S-L*, p. 56): "Henry indeed for the moment granted the request of the queen, but it was done in order that he might not seem uncourteous; for he urged the Legates in every way to pronounce sentence at once." Henry did indeed extol the Queen's virtues, Pollard reminds us (*Henry VIII*, p. 222), adding, "But these qualities had nothing to do with the pitiless forms of law. The legates overruled her protest, refused her appeal, and summoned her back. She took no notice and was declared contumacious. The proceedings then went on without her."

869b–71a. *Ne sit mora* . . . (To forestall delay . . .). The stage direction implied in Wolsey's order to return to the council chamber involves a rapid change of scene that must be explained. Our lack of information about the physical arrangement of the stage in the Louvain public theater or in the Porc College, prompts the conjecture that at this point the main curtain was withdrawn, thus exposing the council chamber. The actors took their positions as before (II, vii) and the next session began. This explanation, however, cannot be advanced with any certainty.

872–75. . . . *Iulii scriptum Papae* . . . (I submit the written brief of Pope Julius . . .). Brian begins the King's case by a general indictment of the brief. Sander (*S-L*, p. 56) writes that Henry

urged the Legates to . . . pronounce the Brief of Pope Julius null and void. His proctors therefore, when the Papal dispensation was produced in court, maintained that on many grounds it was not a sufficient justification of the marriage of Henry and Catherine.

The question of the brief of Pope Julius (sent to the dying Isabella in November, 1504) is not to be confused with the bull authorizing Henry's marriage with Catherine, sent to Henry VII early in 1505. The two documents were antedated December 26, 1503 (the brief is reprinted in Burnet-Pocock, *History*, IV, 61–62; the bull, *ibid.*, pp. 15–16). The protracted discussion about the validity of the brief is not sufficiently relevant in Vernulaeus to deserve lengthy notation. For a treatment of the question, see Hughes, *The Reformation in England*, I, 180–86; Pollard, *Henry VIII*, pp. 218–19. For the discussion concerning the validity of the brief, see Wilhelm Busch, *England Under the Tudors*, I, 376–78; Paul Friedmann, *Anne Boleyn*, II, 329.

874–95. *Errore constat* . . . (It is based on error . . .). Sander enumerates six objections presented by Henry's lawyers—the second, fourth, fifth, and sixth of which Vernulaeus simplifies and puts into the mouth of Brian.

875–77. First Objection: *Regis Henrici fuit/Aetas tenella* . . . (King Henry was very young, but this brief makes no mention of this fact. He was only twelve years old). Sander is followed literally (*S–L*, p. 56): "Nothing is said in the Brief of the age of Henry, who was then only twelve years old, and therefore not marriageable." It seems very likely that Sander is relying on the official documents he had access to in Rome (now available in Ehses, *Römische Dokumente*). For evidence of this, see entry No. 19 in Ehses, entitled "Consilium super causa Anglicana" and identified as "Kurzes Protokoll einer Beratung vor dem Papste über die von englischer Seite vorgebrachten Ehescheidungsgrunde." The third objection submitted to the Roman canonists reads: "Tertio quia nunc temporis impetratae dispensationis erat XII annorum, et sic non legitimae aetatis."

878–82. Second Objection: *Hic nuptiarum finis* . . . (The purpose of the wedding was to insure the peace of the kingdom. But the boy was too young to think about peace; furthermore, when Catherine as wife approached the royal bed, King Henry VII, the boy's father, had already closed his last and fateful days). Compare Sander (*S–L*, pp. 56–67):

Besides, that this marriage was allowed for the purpose of preserving peace— the final cause of the dispensation—between Ferdinand and Isabella of Spain on the one hand, and Henry VII., king of England, on the other hand; but Henry VIII., not then of age, never thought of peace, and Henry VII. and Isabella were dead when the marriage was solemnised.

Sander here may well have drawn upon the second and fourth objections outlined in the "Consilium" (Ehses, *Römische Dokumente*, p. 21):

In the second place, they say that the purpose for contracting the marriage— namely, for maintaining union and peace—is not a sufficient cause for granting a dispensation, since no war had preceded; nor do they admit that the purpose of maintaining peace was a sufficient cause in this case.

   Fourthly, since some of the persons named in the letters of dispensation were already dead at the time, the letters themselves are surreptitious because of this untrue statement.

883–85. Third Objection: *Petita Romae multa* . . . (Many petitions were addressed to Rome, written entreaties were sent back and forth. But the youthful King knew nothing of these transactions). Vernulaeus follows Sander (*S–L*, p. 57):

That the petition presented to the Pope was the petition of Catherine and Henry by name, and yet they had given no instructions on the subject, in virtue of which their parents could lawfully act on their behalf. A false recital vitiated the whole grant.

Again the Rome documents relating to the divorce (Ehses, p. 21) corroborate Sander:

First of all, because it is set down in these petitions that the king himself wanted to marry—and this statement is false, since he did not make any petition; nor did he know about letters granting a dispensation of this kind.

886–95. Fourth Objection: *Affinitatis Pontifex obicem abstulit* . . . (The Pope removed the impediment of affinity . . .). The brief of Pope Julius removed the impediment of *affinity*, but did not remove the impediment of *public honesty*; hence the invalidity of the marriage. Sander explains this clearly (S–L, p. 57):

Lastly, that there were two impediments to the marriage—one of affinity, arising out of the former marriage [*ex carnali copula*] of Catherine and Arthur; the other resting on what is due to public decency [*iustitiae publicae honestatis*], the consequence of the contract of marriage, though the marriage may never have really taken place. Pope Julius by this Brief removed the impediment of affinity, but he said nothing about removing the other impediment of public decency. That being so, they asserted that because this second impediment had not been removed, the marriage of Henry and Catherine was not lawful and not valid.

Sander's account is borne out by Wolsey's contention that Catherine and Arthur, being married "*in facie Ecclesiae* and contracted *per verba de praesenti*, there did arise *impedimentum publicae honestatis*, which is no less *impedimentum ad dirimendum matrimonium* than affinity, whereof the bull maketh no express mention" (Wolsey to Henry VIII, July 1, 1527, L&P, IV, 3217). According to canon law, there are two kinds of impediments to the marriage contract: (1) *impedimentum dirimens*, which makes it impossible to enter upon a valid contract; (2) *impedimentum impediens*, which renders the marriage illegal but does not annul the contract. Now among the diriment impediments listed are those of affinity and public honesty. The latter is the relation arising from a contract not yet consummated. Wolsey held that the bull of Julius, while dispensing from the impediment of affinity, left that of public honesty untouched (see E. L. Taunton, *Thomas Wolsey, Legate and Reformer*, pp. 180–82). For the Roman Catholic law on impediments to marriage, explained above, see H. Noldin and A. Schmitt, *Summa theologiae moralis* (Vol. 3, "De sacramentis"; 30th ed. by Godefridus Heinzel; Westminster, Maryland: Newman Press, 1954), pp. 469–71.

898–941. Warham's rebuttal: *Nullam severi iuris aut legem novam* ... (We fear no law ...). Sander explains (*S–L*, p. 57) that "though the queen would have nothing more to do with the two judges, her lawyers, nevertheless, lest they should be considered as having no legal defence, either in law or equity, replied immediately to all the arguments of their adversary." Ignoring the third objection of the King's lawyers, Warham answers the remaining objections in the order indicated below.

905–13. General Answer to the Fourth Objection: *Affinitatis Pontifex obicem abstulit* ... (You will admit ... that the Pope removed ...). Warham gives a straightforward statement of its irrelevance. He shelves his other arguments temporarily but returns to them later. However, he insists that "no effect of affinity ever made the marriage invalid" because Catherine did not consummate her marriage with Arthur.

913–16. Reply to the First Objection: *Fuerit aetatis puer* ... (You say the King was of tender age ...). Warham insists that a papal decision nullified the alleged impediment of Henry's youthfulness. Sander's account reads (*S–L*, pp. 58–59):

There was no reason for referring to the want of age on the part of the king, for that alone, touching the person or the matter, is necessarily to be spoken of which is against the law. ... The matter in this case was not the want of age on the part of the king, for that was a natural defect which the Pontiff could not remedy. ... Besides, as to marriage nothing is necessary but the capacity of the persons, and certainly he is not unfit who is only twelve years of age.

Sander does not state explicitly that the Queen's lawyers used the above arguments in their rebuttal. Sander received his degree in canon law at Oxford and was undoubtedly interested in expressing his own closely reasoned verdicts on the case.

916–27. Reply to the Second Objection: *Pacis augurium fuit* ... (The royal alliance was an augury of peace ...). Warham meets this objection by adducing the a posteriori argument of England's current prosperity, together with Henry's avowal that Catherine's piety was the cause of the national weal. Vernulaeus' version at this point is independent of Sander.

927–38. Reply to the Fourth Objection: *Passa sed coniux virum est* ... (But she submitted as wife to ... the King's brother ...). Vernulaeus has Warham disregard the alleged impediment of public honesty (see n. to vv. 886–95); instead Warham marshals a threefold argument to prove that the marriage of Arthur and Catherine was never consummated.

930–33. *Ne iungeretur coniugi Arthurus suae* . . . (Henry VII took precautions lest his son Arthur be allowed to sleep with his spouse . . .). Sander (*S–L*, p. 63) supplies this account: "Henry VII., on account of the illness of the prince at that time, had placed him and Catherine under the charge of a discrete [*sic*] matron."

933–34. *Ipsa confessa est* . . . (The Queen herself has testified that the marriage was not consummated). Sander (*S–L*, p. 63) notes: "Secondly, her most serene highness the queen herself had deponed upon oath, in the presence of John Talcarne, public notary, before many bishops and other witnesses, that the marriage had never been completed." (The record of Catherine's oath, attested by John Talcarne, may be found in Pocock, *Records*, II, 431.) Catherine gave Campeggio leave to communicate to the Pope that she told him under seal of confession that her marriage with Arthur was not consummated: "And first of all, she affirmed in conscience that from the fourteenth of November (when she married Arthur) to the second of April of the following year (when he died) she did not sleep with him except seven nights, and that she came away from him as intact and virginal as she was from her mother's womb." (Written October 26, 1528, Ehses, *Römische Dokumente*, p. 59; see also *L&P*, IV, 5681. For the depositions against Catherine's virginity made during the trial, see *L&P*, IV, 5774).

934–37. *Rursus appello tuam/Rex magne mentem* . . . (Your Majesty, I again call upon your memory . . .). Sander (*S–L*, p. 63) relates: "And again, when the queen had repeated her declaration in court publicly, in the presence of the king himself, Henry did not contradict her, and in so grave a matter it must be taken for granted that the king assented to the statement which he did not deny." Pole (. . . *pro ecclesiasticae unitatis defensione*, Bk. III, p. lxxviii) had information of a letter to Charles V in which Henry admitted Catherine's virginity:

Well, Your Highness, do you believe your own words? And if you do, you did assert yourself that you married a virgin; and you asserted this to the Emperor, to whom it was least expedient to admit such a thing if you were thinking at that time of a divorce. But there is no doubt whatsoever that you did say it at that time.

(See the letter of Ferdinand of Spain in confirmation of the above statement in Pocock, *Records*, II, 426.) Thus Warham concludes his reply by establishing his case "on the honor of a King's word" (937*b*–38).

942. *Quid hi volunt* (What do these people want). The final verse of

this scene indicates a commotion in court and thus prepares for the unexpected rise of Fisher in the Queen's defense.

ACT III, scene ii (943–995)

The preceding court scene overflows into the present one, which is implemented by two eloquent pleas, both in support of the Queen's cause. Fisher summarizes the case, presents his own writings on the divorce question as evidence, castigates the legatine judges for their hesitation in pronouncing sentence, and warns them against the internal dissension and imperial aggression that will result from an unjust verdict. The King's impetuosity is offset by Campeggio's calculated stalling. However, the unexpected proroguing of the court that concludes the scene is anticlimactic: Vernulaeus fails to exploit the dramatic possibilities of Campeggio's brilliant evasion and of Wolsey's heroic decision—a deficiency that prevents this scene from attaining excellence.

The account of this scene follows immediately in Sander (S–L, p. 66): "Then, when all the arrangements had been made which are necessary for the discussion of questions of the ecclesiastical law, John Fisher, bishop of Rochester, stood forth."

943–46. Novum hoc tribunal . . . (This is a new kind of tribunal . . .). Fisher's introductory words, not found in Sander, are strangely similar to those of Cavendish, Life of Wolsey, p. 78, ll. 8–13.

949–52. Iudices, non est satis . . . (Judges, it is not enough . . .). Fisher inveighs against legal bickering and the judges' indecisiveness in the face of incontrovertible evidence. He warned them (S–L, p. 66) "against searching for difficulties where none existed, or allowing either the plain truths of Scripture, or the laws of the Church, which in this matter were abundantly clear, to be set aside."

953–54. Periclitatur Angliae regni salus . . . (That which is in jeopardy is the welfare of England our country. . . .). Sander (S–L, p. 66) enumerates the hazards that place the welfare of England in jeopardy:

Still further, he begged them to consider carefully the great mischief likely to follow upon the divorce; the enmity between Henry and the emperor Charles and the princes who took their part; wars, not foreign only but civil; and, worse than all, dissensions in matters of belief, schism, heresies, and sects innumerable.

955. En scripta causa est (Look! The case has been settled in print). Fisher holds out the book he wrote. "He presented to the Legates a book he had written—and a most learned book it is—in defence of the marriage" (S–L, p. 66). Since Henry forbade under pain of death to sell

or exchange any of the works of Fisher or More (Bémont, *Vita Henrici VIII*, p. 113), Sander must have read Fisher's book in manuscript, perhaps in Harpsfield's *Pretended Divorce*, of which it forms the opening book. Fisher's treatise was entitled *Matrimonii cujusdam . . . brevis apologia;* it circulated, says Bémont (*ibid.*), in many copies.

958–66. *Si falsa scripsi* . . . (If I have written lies . . .). Vernulaeus models Fisher's conclusion on Sander (*S-L*, pp. 66–67):

'As for myself,' said the bishop, 'as I have taken great pains in the matter, I am bold enough to say, and I have not only proved it clearly in my book, on the authority of the Scriptures and of the holy Fathers, but I am also ready to seal my testimony with my life's blood, that there is no power on earth that can break the bond of this marriage, which God Himself has made.'

For the evidence supporting Sander's account of Fisher, see the letter of Floriano, Campeggio's secretary, written from London, June 29, 1529, the day following the speech of Fisher (see Ehses, *Römische Dokumente*, pp. 116–18; *L&P*, IV, 5732, Introduction, p. cc-cclxxix).

966. *Cernite hos, & hos libros* (Study these books I have here, and these). The other books that Fisher produces are presumably those written by Clerk, Tunstall, West, Abel, Powell, Fetherston, and Ridley (see *S-L*, p. 67).

969–84. *Iniquitate motus accedo forum* . . . (I address the Court . . .). Ridley's address to the court follows only loosely the speech assigned him by Sander. Ridley's preoccupation with the evils of religious dissension, for example, is attributed by Sander to Fisher. The account of Ridley reads (*S-L*, p. 68):

But Ridley, a sound and devout Catholic, to whom all flattery was hateful, complained in open court of the injustice of the Legates, who had exacted an oath of the queen's lawyers, and of the queen's lawyers only, that they could neither say, nor write, nor do anything in the cause otherwise than in strict accordance with the ecclesiastical laws. 'For,' said he, 'if the like oath had been exacted of the king's lawyers, the process would have been already ended, and our opponents would not have denied that the truth is on our side. He would suffer any punishment they pleased if the king's lawyers, on being compelled to take such an oath, did not range themselves on the side of the queen.' All the king's lawyers held their peace.

Cavendish (*Life of Wolsey*, p. 86) records Ridley's heated tussle with Wolsey over the evidence adduced for Catherine's relations with Arthur, but does not follow Sander's account above. Floriano, Campeggio's secretary, writes (Ehses, *Römische Dokumente*, p. 117) that Fisher was followed by Standish, Bishop of St. Asaph, who, in turn, was succeeded

by "un doctore ductus decanus de Arcubus [Dr. Ligham, then Dean of
the Arches] praefectus curiae Cantuariensis." No mention is made of
Ridley.

985–86. *Haeretis iterum Iudices* . . . (Judges, do you still remain
undecided . . .). Neither Wolsey nor Cardinal Campeggio, says Sander
(*S-L*, p. 68), "saw his way to go on with the cause, for the proofs of the
validity of the marriage were all so clear and beyond doubt. Nevertheless, the king, as usual, was pressing them to pronounce sentence at
once in his favour." There is abundant evidence to prove that Henry,
from his first summoning of the court (*L&P*, IV, 5611) to its adjourn-
ment was increasingly impatient and restless. "The King and the
Cardinal of York," Campeggio wrote to Sanga, "not only solicit my
compliance with them, but the expediting of this business with all
possible despatch. . . . They will endure no procrastination" (*L&P*, IV,
4881). The King's insistence on speed in pressing the Pope may be
seen in his letter of June 23, 1529, to his ambassadors Dr. Bennett,
Sir Gregory de Casalis, and Peter Vanne, analyzed in *L&P*, IV, 5707,
and printed at length in Burnet-Pocock, *History*, I, ii, No. xxviii.

986*b*–88. *Subita ne properes rei* . . . (Let us not pass hasty judgment . . .). In having Campeggio warn Henry of being overhasty,
Vernulaeus follows Sander (*S–L*, pp. 68–69):

> Cardinal Campeggio then seeing that anything he could say would have no
> weight with the king . . . at last spoke out with courage and freedom, and
> said that he had been a lawyer for many years . . . but had never known such
> hurry before, not even in matters of little moment, still less in a cause so
> weighty and important as this.

990–92. *Etiam tribunal deseris* . . . (You are not leaving the court yet).
Campeggio prorogues the court. Sander (*S–L*, p. 69) reports the final
events of the royal trial accurately:

> Campeggio would not pronounce any sentence, and suggested daily new
> reasons for delay; he also lengthened the process, contrary to all expectation,
> so that when the end of the month had come he announced that it was the
> custom in Rome for the courts there to be closed till the month of October.

On July 23, 1529, Campeggio prorogued the court until the first of
October (*L&P*, IV, 5791). Hughes says (*The Reformation in England*,
I, 189), with all fairness to Henry, that "in the legal game the king had
been out-tricked. Campeggio had, unashamedly, and in desperation
(as his letters show), pulled the winning trump out of his sleeve before
the very eyes of his opponents." It may be noted here that Catherine's

appeal to the Pope had already been granted by Clement VII, who avocated the cause before himself by a brief signed July 15, 1529. The decision reached England August 4, 1529, a fortnight after Campeggio's prorogation (see J. H. Blunt, *The Reformation of the Church of England: its History, Principles, and Results*, I, 152, cited hereafter as *The Reformation of the Church of England*).

993–94. *Nec ipse nostro solus arbitrio* ... (Nor have I the authority to settle the case ...). In having Wolsey announce his inability to pronounce a decision independent of Campeggio, Vernulaeus was undoubtedly misled by Sander's comment: "Wolsey, however, though he was the first in the commission, held his tongue, for he was very much alarmed" (*S–L*, p. 70). The fact of the matter is that Wolsey, as well as Campeggio and Henry, knew that *either* of the legates was empowered by Clement VII to pass *independently* on the validity of the marriage. The Bull for the commission (Ehses, *Römische Dokumente*, p. 29) makes this clear: "We confer our complete authority on you two to act in our stead, either jointly, or independently of each other in case one of you is unwilling or incapacitated, and this without any consideration of your personal or jurisdictional differences, and without any right of refusal or appeal" (see also *L&P*, IV, 5789). Neither Sander nor Vernulaeus seems to have been able to rise sufficiently above the contemporary opinion that regarded Wolsey as the villain of the divorce to perceive that Wolsey's final decision was undoubtedly the most heroic act of his career.

ACT III, scene iii (996–1038)

The series of public hearings is succeeded by several private scenes, the first of which dramatizes Henry's reaction of angry frustration at the failure of the legatine court, together with his interview with Thomas More. Drawing upon imagery of tempestuous seas and serpents, Henry projects his inner perturbation convincingly in a sequence of questions. The dialogue with More stands in sharp contrast to Henry's soliloquy by its informal conversational style. More's refusal to support Henry's cause, following hard upon Rome's revocation of the case, eliminates another alternative course of action for the protagonist and thus confines him in an ever tightening noose of necessity.

1009. *Si das moram* (if you have a moment). Vernulaeus' fondness for word play allows More to make a pun on his name: *si das moram* [*Morum*].

1011–16. *Regina mittit* . . . (I am here at the Queen's request . . .).
Sander (*S–L*, p. 72) provides Vernulaeus' material for having More convey Catherine's message to Henry: "The queen sent to the king Sir
Thomas More . . . to say that the Pope had withdrawn from the Legates
their commission, and had summoned him and the queen to plead by
their attorneys in the court of the Rota." On July 15, 1529, Clement VII
revoked the case to Rome but the news did not reach England until after
Campeggio's postponement of the marriage hearings (see *L&P*, IV, 5777,
5780, and 5791; see also n. to v. 990).

1020–37. *Dic More, novi pectus* . . . (Thomas, I know that you are
courageous . . .). Henry questions More privately, offering bribes for
his support of the marriage annulment. Vernulaeus builds this interview
on an earlier account of Sander, inserting it at this point as an effective
contrast to the previous public hearings. Sander's account (*S–L*, pp.
31–32) reads:

> He sends for Thomas More, whom he knew to be a man of the highest
> ability, exceedingly learned and perfectly honest, and asks him of his opinion
> about the marriage. More at that time was a member of the council, but he
> was not yet chancellor. He answered candidly that he did not at all approve
> of the divorce. Henry did not like the answer, but he would leave no stone
> unturned to serve his purpose, so he promised the highest rewards to Sir
> Thomas if he would conform his view to that of the king.

Roper (*Life of More*) mentions three occasions on which the King
attempted to gain More's consent to the divorce (pp. 31–33; 37–38;
49–50), these three occasions being repeated by Harpsfield in his *Life
of More* (pp. 44–46; 48–49; 56–57), with a fourth (pp. 47–48) not
cited by Roper. For this latter meeting, see More's letter to Cromwell
(*English Works*, p. 1425), quoted in the notes to Roper's *Life of More*,
p. 115, n. 31/16–18; see also *L&P*, VII, 289.

ACT III, scene iv (1039–1096)

For the first and last time the stage is occupied by the unattended
royal couple and their daughter Mary. Resuming the pathetic role
assigned to her in private scenes, Catherine climaxes her farewell by
falling on her knees before Henry and refusing to rise until addressed
by her lawful title. The prostration of wife and daughter, together with
their irrefutable feminine logic, softens the King's harshness. He bids
them remain at court and enjoy their royal prerogatives.

This second temporary victory of Catherine over her wayward husband is entirely Vernulaeus' invention and without historical foundation. Thematically, the scene is successful in objectifying the playwright's depiction of a monarch torn between the demands of wedded love and of illicit passion. At this midpoint of the play's action the King is still unconfirmed in his evil intent; his attraction to the good is credibly demonstrated in his restoration of Catherine and Mary. The reversal of action following upon Henry's decision is thus an effective instrument in emphasizing the humaneness of the protagonist and in maintaining sympathy with him as a tragic figure.

1072. *Misera, deiecta, impia* (poor, banished, unfaithful woman): Vernulaeus' use of asyndeton enhances the pathos of Catherine's plea.

ACT III, scene v (1097–1133)

After dismissing Catherine and Mary, Henry paces the stage restlessly. Left alone, he is again besieged by selfish emotions that haunt him in the persons of the evil allegories. Clustering round the King as they had done in Act I, scene ii, Heresy, Lust, Impiety, and Tyranny harass him for his cowardly desertion of Anne Boleyn. Henry resists their taunts with arguments of expedience, but is gradually vanquished. In a burst of passion he resolves to have his marriage annulled, either by the judges or, if necessary, by his own authority.

The scene locates the battle between good and evil within the soul of the protagonist. The crisis of this inner action of the play is reached in verses 1126–29 with Henry's deliberative choice of forsaking Catherine for Anne. From this decisive turn in the middle of the third act, the Queen's cause begins to decline as the King's cause prospers.

1104. *Membra torpescunt gelu* (Your limbs are freezing with fear). The inchoative form of the verb emphasizes the opening stages of Henry's loss of passion for Anne, according to Lust.

1107. *Lux illa vitae, grata lux vitae tuae* (She, the radiance of your life . . .). The effectiveness of this verse is rhetorically oriented by the use of epanalepsis (repetition of *lux* and *vitae* in successive phrases) and chiasmus of *lux*, thereby emphasizing *grata*.

1115–16a. *Favere Iura Regibus semper solent/Cum Iura mutant* (When kings change the laws, they inevitably change them for their own advantage). This easily recognized fallacy ignores the distinction between *rex* and *tyrannus* (see nn. to vv. 91–92, 521–25, 556–57).

1131–33. The repetition of *"Bolena"* (Anne) in three successive verses, and in the same position in each verse, serves as a triple seal on Henry's critical decision at this point.

ACT III, scene vi (1134–1167)

Henry seizes upon the departure of Campeggio (announced previously in III, iii, 1014–15) as the pretext for marrying Anne before a
decision has been announced. Bishop Longland counsels him against
the rash move, but the King, now thoroughly disgusted with delays, has
resolved on his course of action. Let Rome decide later, Henry insists.
At this moment he will be his own judge.

The dialogue between the King and his confessor is dramatically
conceived: its direction represents "*la peinture de la pensée*" in the act
of its emergence. Structurally, the scene makes public the private decision of the protagonist in the foregoing scene and leads causally to
the wedding ceremony that will follow.

1136–37. *Et hinc recessit* . . . (You say he has gone from here . . .).
"Campeggio received letters from the Pope ordering him to return to
Rome immediately" (*S–L*, p. 73). The Cardinal left London October 5,
1529 (*L&P*, IV, 5995), was held up at Dover where his baggage was
searched (*ibid.*, No. 6003), and finally sailed October 26 (*ibid.*, No.
6050).

ACT III, scene vii (1168–1200)

While the secret marriage of Henry and Anne Boleyn is fittingly performed offstage, the larger implications of the event are revealed to the
audience. No scene in the Vernulaeus canon is more indicative of the
playwright's preoccupation with forging the academic theater into an
instrument for expressing the moral significance of history and the
responsibility of princes who determine its course. This dramatization
of the inner meaning of the ceremony is synchronized with its progress
offstage. Just as Anne is welcomed to Henry's arms, so is Heresy embraced by the English nation. The other allegorical figures join with
Heresy in predicting the disasters that will succeed the birthday of
Heresy in England.

1193b–94. *Nuptiae Regis novae* . . . (The King's new marriage . . .).
Sander (*S–L*, pp. 92–93) refers to Henry's sudden decision: "The king,
now impatient of further delay, though everything had not yet been
duly prepared, determined to marry Anne Boleyn secretly on the 14th of
the following November." Hall (*Chronicle*, p. 794) gives a similar account: "The King . . . married privily the lady Anne Bulleyn on St.
Erkonwald's Day [November 14], which marriage was kept so secret
that very few persons knew it till she was great with child at Easter
after." Sander relates in detail the dramatic secret wedding of Henry

and Anne, emphasizing the deception used by Henry to calm the scruples of the officiating clergyman (*S–L*, p. 93). For the evidence supporting January 25, 1533, as the date of the marriage (so recorded by Cranmer and Stow), see Pollard, *Thomas Cranmer and the English Reformation*, p. 60, n. 1. Sander's date (November 14, 1532) is that given also by Hall and Holinshed. Pollard supposes that the antedating of the marriage to November was intended to shield Anne's character—a gesture scarcely to be expected from Sander.

1195–96. *Quo teste tandem* ... (Who officiated at the ceremony ...). According to Sander, the celebrant of the wedding ceremony, unknown to Brian, was Rowland Lee, later Bishop of Lichfield. The anonymous *Vita Henrici VIII* (Bémont, p. 109) says, "L'officiant fut Rowland Lee, plus tard évêque de Lichfield." Blunt (*The Reformation of the Church of England*, p. 182) and J. M. Stone (*Mary I*, p. 53) likewise mention Lee as the celebrant. On the other hand, Chapuys, the imperial ambassador, reported as early as February 23 (*L&P*, VI, 180) that Cranmer was the priest, but the Archbishop himself denied this (Cranmer, *Works* [ed. Parker Society], II, 246).

ACT III, scene viii (1201–1229)

The coronation of Anne Boleyn is re-enacted with simple dignity. From his first appearance in this scene, Bishop Cranmer becomes the clerical mouthpiece of the King's cause. He places the crown on the kneeling Queen, places the scepter in her right hand, after which Queen Anne takes her seat next to Henry on the royal throne. The tableau is concluded amid the shouts of the courtiers.

The King's cause reaches its zenith in this final scene of Act III. The King has fulfilled his ambition by repudiating Catherine and marrying Anne. Vernulaeus preserves dramatic objectivity by allowing the principals to speak for themselves without interruption of choric commentary. The scene is an excellent example of Vernulaeus' command of eloquence fitted out in simple language that is both chaste and economical.

1206–08. *Haec nostra coniux* ... (This is our wife ...). Of the coronation of Anne, Sander (*S–L*, p. 110) says simply: "Anne therefore was on that day, the day kept in honor of our Lord's burial, the 12th of April [1533], brought forth before the world as the king's wife, and on the 2d of June next following was crowned." See also C. Wriothesley, *Chronicle of England*, p. 17: "The 12th day of April, Anno Domini 1533, beinge Easter Eeaven, Anne Bulleine ... was proclaymed queene at Greenwych." It is accepted today that Anne Boleyn was crowned on Whitsunday, 1533 [June 1]; Sander, therefore, was in error on this date (see *L&P*, VI, 583, 584, 585, 601).

1223. *Annet, perennet* . . . (May she thrive! May she long endure . . .). Vernulaeus delights in ringing off modulations of *"Anna" Bolena: annet, perennet*. Actually, the coronation of Anne in Westminster Abbey was marked by an absence of popular enthusiasm approaching general stupefaction. Henry had caused his own and Anne's initials—H. and A.— to be interwoven in every imaginable device, but the people interpreted them derisively—Ha! Ha! (*L&P*, VI, 263, 266, 295; see also Stone, *Mary I*, p. 56).

ACT III, Chorus (1230–1292)

The third chorus draws on pageantry, stage grouping, action, and a variety of meters to convey the significance of the wedding of Henry with Anne Boleyn. Modeled loosely on the Roman marriage procession and ode, it allows each of the evil allegorical figures to explain her peculiar contribution to the victory of Heresy. The second half of the chorus follows a similar pattern in outlining the strategy by which Heresy will maintain her hegemony. Interwoven with these speeches of the vices are comments by the corresponding virtuous allegories. Thus from either side of the stage where the opposing allegories are placed there issues an alternating stream of impassioned verses that modify and re-enforce each other.

There is also a suggestion of the diabolical wedding procession getting under way. Lust leads with a flaming torch; she is followed by Impiety and Tyranny, who likewise brandish flambeaus, the latter swinging a bloody whip in tempo.

Vernulaeus lets the Chorus pour out its song in a profusion of meters that suggests reckless abandon. Twenty-eight verses are iambic dimeters (1239–44, 1265–71, 1276–79, 1280–85, 1287–88, 1290–93); fourteen are dactylic hexameters (1230–38, 1259, 1261, 1263, 1280, 1286). Nine verses of anapaestic dimeter are included (1253–58, 1260, 1262, 1264); eight verses of iambic trimeter (1246–48, 1272–75, 1289); the final variation is a sapphic strophe (1249–52).

ACT IV, scene i (1293–1360)

The coronation of Anne Boleyn involves the repudiation of Catherine and Mary and their forced withdrawal from the royal palace. Vernulaeus now devotes a lengthy scene to the banishment. Catherine's inner struggle results from the sudden adjustment demanded as the wheel of Fortune dips from prosperity to adversity. The immediacy of the affliction meted out to her by the King she loves and the usurpation of her dignities and rights by Anne put an edge to her grief that is not easily assuaged by Longland's review of eternal verities. The scene comes to an end after Catherine has emptied her soul of bitterness; she then accepts the cross as a token of the inscrutable will of Providence and leaves for exile with all the joy that accrues to the courageously submissive. This final appearance of Catherine and Mary is entirely Vernulaeus' invention.

1301. *Pellat, eiiciat, necet* (. . . disown . . . drive out . . . kill . . .): climactic function of asyndeton. See nn. to vv. 13, 308, 557, 1072.

1326b–27. *Noster exemplum dolor/Iam nescit ullum, prisca non aetas habet* . . . (Our sorrow has no counterpart in present history . . .). The Renaissance practice of viewing history as a catalogue of exemplary precepts and patterns is mirrored in these verses of the playwright.

1329b–33. *Imo iam vulgus tuos* . . . (. . . the common people weep . . .). On July 14, 1531, Henry took leave of Catherine at Windsor, never again to see her (Blunt, *The Reformation of the Church of England*, I, 180; Hall, *Chronicle*, p. 871). From this time onward, Catherine was separated permanently from her daughter Mary. The humiliation of the Queen and her daughter was deeply resented by the people, who, says Chapuys (*L&P*, VI, 918), though forbidden on pain of their lives to call Catherine "Queen," shouted it at the top of their voices.

1349b. *Notum est genus* (Your ancestors are well known). Catherine of Aragon was the daughter of Ferdinand and Isabella of Spain. Her father was the son of John II of Aragon; her mother, the daughter of John II of Castile by his second wife, Isabella, the daughter of John I of Aragon. Through both parents, Isabella was thus a descendant of John of Gaunt.

ACT IV, scene ii (1361–1423)

With the banishment of Catherine and Mary, the King's cause is subjected to a series of threats that force the protagonist to decision. With each decision, Henry is driven into positions he cannot defend without resorting to tyrannical measures. The first disturbance of the *status quo* is the official pronouncement of Clement VII ratifying the marriage of Catherine and Henry and demanding the repudiation of Anne. As a loyal Christian, the King sees no alternative but submission to Rome.

Postponing this distasteful decision, Henry turns on Wolsey as the cause of his plight, deprives him of the chancellorship, and appoints More to succeed him. The scene closes with the King still faced with the choice of Anne or Rome.

1362. *Pronuntiavit Pontifex* (he has made an official pronouncement). Of the official pronouncement of Clement VII, Sander says: "The Roman Pontiff, after the most rigid examination of the question between Henry and Catherine, declared them bound together in the bonds of lawful wedlock beyond the power of man to sunder" (S–L, pp. 101–02). For evidence of the above statement, Sander quotes the sentence of Clement VII, dated July 11, 1533, and beginning "Cum pendente lite," in which the Pope declared Henry's marriage with Anne null and void and Henry excommunicated, the effects of the sentence to be suspended until the end of the following September. This bull was printed, seemingly for the first time, in Sander's *De schismate anglicano* (1585), pp. 102–03, and is reprinted in Ehses, *Römische Dokumente*, pp. 212–13.

Actually there were three admonitory bulls prior to "Cum pendente lite." The first, March 7, 1530, forbade Henry under pain of excommunication from contracting a new marriage, the trial having not yet been terminated. For the copy of this bull, see Le Grand, *Histoire du divorce*, III, 446–53; also *L&P*, IV, 6256. The second admonition, January 5, 1531, may be seen in Le Grand, *ibid.*, III, 531–40; Pocock, *Records*, II, 109; see also *L&P*, V, 27. The third admonition, November 15, 1532, is given also in Le Grand, *ibid.*, III, 588, and Pocock, *ibid.*, II, 378. The bull quoted by Sander is next, chronologically. The final and definitive statement of the validity of the marriage of Henry and Catherine was pronounced in Clement's bull of March 23, 1534 (see *L&P*, VII, 362).

1367–68a. *Cadit/Tuus ille fervor* (Are your great hopes dashed). It is likely that Vernulaeus supplied student Johannes de Traux, who played Brian's role, with the Latin text of the bull of July 11, 1533, which may be found in Sander (S–L, pp. 102–03). To aid in understanding the impact of the bull upon Henry, and upon the audience, the English translation is here given:

'Clement Pope VII.—Whereas the validity of the marriage contracted by Our most dearly beloved children in Christ, Catherine and Henry VIII., king and queen of England, has been disputed, and the cause brought before Us, and by Us, in a consistory of the most reverend Cardinals, committed to Our beloved son, Paul Capisucchi, auditor of causes in the Sacred Apostolic Palace, and dean; and whereas the aforesaid Henry, while the cause was still pending, has put away the said Catherine, and *de facto* married one Anne,

contrary to Our commandments, and in contempt of Our prohibitions contained in Our letter *in forma Brevis* [first admonition, March 7, 1530], and
sent forth after counsel had with Our brethren the Cardinals of the Holy Roman Church, thereby temerariously disturbing the due course of law;—

'We, therefore, in the fulness of that power given Us, unworthy as We are,
in the person of the blessed Peter, by Christ the King of kings, sitting on the
throne of justice, and looking unto God alone, do, by this Our sentence, which
We pronounce, by Our duty constrained, and with the advice of Our venerable brethren, the Cardinals of the Holy Roman Church, in consistory
assembled, declare that the casting out of the said Catherine the queen, and
the withholding of her wifely rights and royal dignity, whereof she stood
possessed when the suit was begun, and also the marriage contracted by the
aforesaid Henry and Anne—all manifest and notorious deeds—to be what
they are and were, null and unjust and contrary to law, to have been and
to be tainted with the defects of nullity, injustice, and contempt of law; and
We further declare by the same sentence that the children, born or to be born
of that marriage, are and have always been bastards: We also declare that the
said Catherine the queen is to be restored to, and reinstated in, her former
rank, and quasi-possession of her wifely rights and royal dignity, and that the
king aforesaid must put away and remove the aforesaid Anne from his house
and quasi-possession of wifely and royal rights, and by this sentence in writing
We restore and reinstate, put away and remove, the aforesaid persons respectively.

'Moreover, by this same sentence, after due deliberation had, in virtue of
Our office, We pronounce the aforesaid Henry to have fallen, to his own
damnation, under the censure of the greater excommunication, and to have
brought upon himself the other censures and penalties in the aforesaid Brief
expressed, because of his disobedience thereto, and contempt thereof, and
We command all the faithful to avoid him.

'Nevertheless, as a father tender of heart, We wish to deal gently and
mercifully with the said Henry, and so We suspend the effects of this sentence from this day to the end of September next, that he may the more
easily obey Our sentence and decrees aforementioned.

'And if within that time he shall not have submitted himself, and shall not
have reinstated the said Catherine in her former rank, in which she was when
the lawsuit began, and if he shall not have put the aforesaid Anne from his
house and her quasi-possession of the rights of wife and queen, and if he
shall not have effectually purged this contempt, then We will and decree
that this present sentence shall take effect now as then.—So We say.'

1370–76. *Decisa causa est* . . . (My case has been decided . . .). As set
down by Vernulaeus, Henry's qualms of conscience after receiving the
news represent a radical departure from Sander and from historical
fact. Sander gives the true account of Henry's reaction (S–L, p. 104):
"Henry regarded the sentence as a wrong done to himself, and then,
to be avenged of the Pope for his vexation, took measures for the aboli-

tion by Parliament of the oath which the English clergy took to the Pope." Upon receiving the second admonition (January 8, 1531), Henry told the nuncio that he did not care three straws for excommunication and that if the Pope designed to wrong him, he would proceed in arms to Rome and take vengeance (*L&P,* V, 287). As to the final sentence (March 23, 1534), Chapuys wrote that Henry took no account of it and was making as good cheer as ever (Chapuys to Charles V, April 12, 1534, *L&P,* VII, 469). "Yet inwardly," adds Chapuys, "his spirit is not at rest" (*ibid.*).

1376b–77. *Regem decet/Parere tanto Praesuli* (True, kings should obey the Supreme Pontiff). Since Warham died August 23, 1532, his appearance at this point and in later scenes is historically inaccurate. Dramatically, however, the anachronism enables Vernulaeus to prolong the theme of official opposition to the repudiation of Catherine, embodied in Warham, without the disadvantage of so late an introduction of a substitute. Vernulaeus' anachronism of character has no foundation in Sander, it should be noted.

1386. *Catharina rursus impleat* . . . (Let Catherine return again . . .). Vernulaeus again dramatizes the sudden reversals of Henry's conscience, an invention without basis in Sander or in historical fact. Henry and Catherine never met after July 14, 1531 (Constant, I, 41; for the evidence, *ibid.*, p. 384, n. 186. See also n. to vv. 1329–33).

1390–93a. *Volsae Regem perdidisti* . . . (Cardinal Wolsey, you have brought ruin on your King . . .). Vernulaeus increases the tension by having Henry confront Wolsey in person—a departure from Sander. Sander, earlier in the story, wrote (*S–L,* p. 74):

But Wolsey, knowing nothing of that which had been contrived against him, had gone to the king, then staying in a place near St. Alban's, where, with him and his council, he discussed many things that would have to be done in the trial to be held in Rome. Stephen Gardiner was also there, one of the king's secretaries, who knowing himself to be suspected of having been the cause of the divorce, asked Wolsey openly to declare in the interests of truth, publicly before the king and the council, who they were who had been the first movers in the matter.

1393b–95. *Fateor, & solus fui* . . . (I admit it, I alone was the instigator . . .). "I will never deny," Sander has Wolsey say (*S–L,* p. 74), "that I alone have done it; and I am so far from regretting it, that if it had not been begun, I would have it begun now." There seems to be no documentary evidence to corroborate Wolsey's admission of being sole instigator of the divorce.

1396–97a. *Et inde nostrae damna* . . . (. . . behold the succession of tragedies . . .). Vernulaeus here disregards Sander, who adds merely (*S–L*, p. 74), "At that time, however, the king remained silent."

1397b–1408. *Non tuum Regis fuit* . . . (You had no right . . .). Warham's vicious appraisal of Wolsey is Vernulaeus' invention. For the similarity of motives attributed to Wolsey by Warham and by Catherine, see n. to v. 733.

1409–14. . . . *Dignitas quae nunc tua est/Et . . . cesset* . . . (. . . Your present title of Chancellor of England is hereby null and void . . .). Sander (*S–L*, p. 75) gives the true account of Henry's tendering Wolsey's resignation of the chancellorship and appointing Thomas More in his stead: "Not long after that [the departure of Campeggio] he [Wolsey] was arrested at the king's command . . . and compelled to resign . . . the chancellorship, which was given without delay to the illustrious Sir Thomas More."

A bill of indictment for *praemunire* had been presented against Wolsey in the Court of King's Bench, and on October 22, 1529, the Cardinal acknowledged his liability to the penalties (*L&P*, IV, 6017). Three days later, October 25, More succeeded Wolsey as chancellor (*ibid.*, No. 6026). Wolsey died on November 29, 1530.

ACT IV, scene iii (1424–1471)

The next two scenes dramatize Henry's torture on the horns of a dilemma. The opening soliloquy discloses his unshaken faith in Rome as head of the spiritual order and his full awareness of his duties as a Christian king. The issues are crystal clear. The universality of the tragic choice between reason and passion is sympathetically projected. The entrance of Anne, her taunts and tears, her delicate badgering of Henry and appeals for protection against the Pope tip the scales of judgment in her favor. Henry vows that he will never desert her. The scene is written with considerable sympathy; its evocation of the psychological torment involved in moral decision is both sensitive and powerful. No less remarkable are the playwright's insight into the feminine mind and his ability to re-create a woman's strategy when faced with a threat to her security.

ACT IV, scene iv (1472–1524)

The previous scene depicted Henry's temporary decision, not altogether ignoble, of shielding Anne from anxiety. Vernulaeus now narrows the battleground to Henry's conscience. The tug of war between Anne and Clement VII for the King's allegiance is intensified by the entrance of the evil allegories. In a display of logic that would do credit to a master theologian, Henry meets the taunts of his evil nature blow for blow: church and state are discrete orders involving distinct sovereignties. At this point Heresy plants the seed that will take root in the King's decision and bear fruit in the act of royal ecclesiastical supremacy: namely, that England requires a union of church and state under one head, the king. The decision to be both pope and king of England is eagerly embraced by the protagonist as a solution to his dilemma. Henry's choice marks a crisis in the internal action that will issue in tyranny. The chain reaction of evil is now fully evolved: lust has led to heresy and impiety (cleavage from Rome) and will enforce its position by tyranny.

1511b–16. *Sceptra conveniunt male/Pietasque* . . . (Royal scepters and pious practices make poor bedfellows . . .). The fallacious reasoning of Impiety is best understood in the context provided by Vernulaeus' books on political theory and practice. Both piety and religion are necessary virtues for sovereignty, he insists. As a result, the Machiavellian dictum that these two virtues are proper to private persons, not to princes and kings, is erroneous and detestable (*Institutionum politicarum*, p. 63).

ACT IV, scene v (1525–1603)

Henry's decision in the previous scene leads logically to its public enactment in the present Parliamentary session. The King confronts his council and enjoins on them the Act of Supremacy and the Act of Succession. Bishop Cranmer and the three councilors serve as foils, in their obsequiousness, to Fisher and More, who balk at the issue of ecclesiastical supremacy, refuse to take the oath, and are sentenced to the Tower. Cranmer is then commissioned to serve the oath on all English subjects.

Structurally, the scene is dovetailed with the preceding scenes and leads in turn to the dramatization of the resistance to Henry's reformation. This latter aspect in the career of the protagonist will occupy Vernulaeus' principal attention.

1533–36. *Pontifex nuper suum/Vibravit in me fulmen* . . . (A short time ago the Pope threatened me with his thunderbolt . . .). See n. to v. 1362.

1539–47. . . . *nunc hoc volo* . . .(My present wish is this . . .). Vernulaeus here telescopes the various enactments of the Reformation Parliament from its first session on November 3, 1529, to its climax in November, 1534. To simplify the processes involved in the legislative, financial, and judicial breach of the *Ecclesia anglicana* with Rome, he singles out three enactments which he has Henry propose to Parliament for their approval: (1) the spiritual supremacy of the king in England, (2) the repudiation of the pope, and (3) the right of succession of Anne Boleyn's issue. Vernulaeus' choice of these key proposals was undoubtedly dictated by the nature of his audience—students who could readily grasp their import and significance. The more elaborate account of this Parliamentary process is given by Sander (*S–L*, pp. 114–16). For the best discussion of the new ecclesiastical autonomy called into being by Parliament, see Hughes, *The Reformation in England*, I, 207–81.

1548–54. *Iusta est voluntas* . . . (Your wish is lawful . . .). Vernulaeus' use of Cranmer as a foil to Fisher and More has its precedent in Sander (*S–L*, p. 88) only by implication: "Cranmer is therefore nominated, on the condition that, being archbishop, he will, though the Roman Pontiff should give sentence in favour of the marriage, give sentence against the sentence, and that Catherine must be put away."

1555–87. *Haec causa praeceps* . . . (This sudden proposal . . .). Fisher and More refuse the oath. The playwright dramatizes the account offered by Sander (*S–L*, pp. 110–11): "That oath was tendered to John Fisher, the bishop of Rochester, and to Thomas More. . . . They refused to take the oath, and were thrown into prison." For the documentation of Fisher's and More's refusal to take the oath tendered them at Lambeth April 15, 1534, see Cranmer's letter to Cromwell from Croydon, April 17, 1534, *L&P*, VII, 499. Actually, Fisher was sent to the Tower directly upon his refusal of the oath at Lambeth. Four days later More followed him (see Blunt, *The Reformation of the Church of England*, I, 419). John Fisher was imprisoned in the Bell Tower and Sir Thomas More in Beauchamp Tower (Ernst E. Reynolds, *Saint John Fisher*, p. 226).

1563–64a. . . . *abdico* . . . (. . . I must resign . . .). The suicide of ecclesiastical authority in England was accomplished by the Submission of the Clergy Act, May 15, 1532; the act was delivered to the King on May 16. The following day, May 17, 1532, More resigned his high office (see Hughes, *The Reformation in England*, I, 239; Pollard, *Henry VIII*, p. 294).

1597b–1601. . . . *nunc sit tuae/Granmere curae* . . . (. . . let it be your responsibility . . .). Vernulaeus invents this deputation of authority and, for purposes of economy in characterization, ascribes to Cranmer the task that was actually ordained by Parliament to commissioners (see "The Royal Supremacy," May 14, 1534, *L&P*, VII, 665).

ACT IV, scene vi (1604–1624)

In a short transitional scene, Vernulaeus shows the royal proclamation being announced publicly by a crier and the decision of the King's commissioners to make use of Bishop Fisher as a warning to the common people, who regarded him as a saint. Fisher is summoned and is seen approaching his trial with joyous eagerness at the prospect of martyrdom.

1605–06 (between). *Recitatur edictum Regis (The Royal Proclamation is read aloud.)* Vernulaeus gives no indication of the actual wording of the "stage" proclamation. One form of the oath, entered in the Journals of the House of Lords, is reproduced by Blunt (*The Reformation of the Church of England*, pp. 417–18). It begins in this way:

> Ye shall swear to bear your faith, truth, and obedience only to the King's Majesty, and to the heirs of his body, according to the limitation and rehearsal within this Statute of succession above specified; and not to any other within this realm, nor foreign authority, prince or potentate.

It seems likely that Vernulaeus wrote a stage version of the proclamation for the crier at this point.

1614. This first ambiguous use of *sapere* (to be discreet, to be sensible, to capitulate, to compromise, to fall in line) begins a series of variations on the theme of worldly wisdom versus integrity.

1615–17. *. . . ergo Roffensem prius/Revocemus . . .* (Then let us first summon Bishop Fisher . . .). Vernulaeus attributes to the Second Councilor the motive for killing Fisher that Sander (*S–L*, p. 121) attributed to Henry, who "resolved at last to put to death the bishop of Rochester first, to see whether More afterwards could be made to change his opinion."

1622–24. *Cernite, ut laeto senex/Vultu propinquat . . .* (Do you not mark how the old fellow hurries this way with his face all beaming . . .). Fisher's advanced years and physical weakness are contrasted with his moral fortitude, as anticipated by Sander (*S–L*, p. 121): "There was not in England a more holy and learned man than John Fisher, bishop of Rochester. He was now worn out by age, and though he had been offered more than once a better endowed see, he could never be persuaded to leave the poor church to which God had first called him."

ACT IV, scene vii (1625–1653)

This scene and the following are devoted to the trial and execution of Bishop Fisher. Faced by Cranmer and the King's councilors, the venerable Bishop is unequivocal in his adherence to Rome and refuses to take the oath. His sentiments at the prospect of death reveal stoic resignation blended with Christian joy at the prospect of paradise. The conflict between the royal commissioners and the accused is quickly resolved by the sentence of execution.

1625. *Iterum ad Tribunal* (Once more you face the tribunal). The first interrogation of Fisher in the Tower by the commissioners involved the Bishop's papers. These questions and answers (undated MSS.) may be seen in *L&P*, VIII, 856 (June 11, 1535), 858 (June 12, 1535), and 859; they are tentatively dated by Reynolds (*Saint John Fisher*, p. 228, n. 2) around April 27. On June 14, 1535, Fisher was again questioned by Thomas Bedyll and three others (*L&P*, VIII, 867). Three days later, June 17, 1535, Fisher was finally tried and condemned (*ibid.*, No. 886).

1639–41. . . . *Non est* (. . . He is not head of the English Church). Sander (*S–L*, p. 121) records simply that Fisher "would not acknowledge the ecclesiastical supremacy of the king." The exact words of Fisher (*L&P*, VIII, 886, iii) were: "The king our sovereign lord is not Supreme Head in Earth of the Church of England."

1644. *Non haec senectus* (Nor should these white hairs deceive him). Born in 1469, Fisher was sixty-six years old at the time of the trial.

ACT IV, scene viii (1654–1673)

Before bending his neck to the sword, Bishop Fisher pauses to repeat his Stoic-Christian acceptance of the death penalty. Suddenly, at the urging of the executioner, the gaunt old man straightens up, throws away his cane, and strides youthfully to the execution block. With a voice miraculously reinvigorated, he intones the *Te Deum* and sings it through to the end. Then he willingly bows his neck and awaits the blow.

1657–59. . . . *Agit per artus ardor* . . . (I suddenly feel a strange energy coursing through my body . . .). There seems to be no explicit reference to Fisher's miraculous renewal of strength in the extant sources, although such an eventuality is implied in the account of his final actions immediately prior to the beheading.

1663. . . . *ne trahas, Praesul, moras* (. . . do not tarry along the way). William Rastell, who witnessed the execution of Fisher, records that the

Bishop was carried in a chair by four of the sheriff's officers from the Tower gate to East Smithfield and set down near the scaffold (see *The Rastell Fragments* in Harpsfield's *Life of More*, App. I).

1664–65. . . . *bacule hic vale* (. . . my staff, I leave you here, farewell). Of this episode Sander says: "As soon as he came in sight of the place where he was to be conqueror in the glorious contest, he threw his staff away, saying, 'Now my feet must do their duty, for I have but a little way to go'" (S–L, p. 122). Sander probably drew on Rastell (*Fragments*, pp. 243–44) for this incident:

And when he cam to the foott of the scaffold, they that caryed hyme wold haue helped hyme vp the stayres of the scaffold. But then sayed he unto them: 'Nay, Maisters, now lett me alone, ye shall see me goo vp to my death well ynough myself, wythout help.' And so went he vpp the scaffold stayres without help, to no lytle marveill of them that knewe his weekness and debylitie, by reason of his age and infirmytie.

The staff that Fisher cast aside is still preserved as an heirloom in the family of Mr. Eyston of East Hendred (see Pollen, "Dr. Nicholas Sander," p. 45).

1668–69. *Te Deum laudamus* . . . Sander (S–L, p. 122) says of this moment: "Having reached the place of his martyrdom, he lifted up his eyes to heaven and said, 'Te Deum laudamus, Te Dominum confitemur.' When he had finished the hymn he bowed his head beneath the sword of the executioner." Again Sander's account agrees with Rastell's eye-witness report (*Fragments*, p. 245), though Rastell is more detailed and graphic:

He knyled downe on both his knees, and sayed certene prayers; and, as some reported, he sayed than the psalme or canticle "Te deum laudamus," etc. to the end, and "In te domine speraui, non confundar in eternum." Then was he blyndfolded with an handekerchiefe abowt his eyes. And than, liftyng vp his handes and hart devoutlie towardes heaven, he sayed a few prayers, whiche were not long, but feruentlie devout. Which done, he layd downe on his bely, flat on the floore of the scaffold, and layd his lene necke vpon a little blocke, so that his body was on the one syde of the blocke, and his head on the other syde, so that his necke was iust vpon the middes of the blocke. And than came quickely the executioner, and wyth a sharpe and hevy axe cut asunder his nekke, and so seuered the head frome the bodie.

ACT IV, *Chorus (1674–1749)*

The refugee theme, charged with plangency and studded with concrete pictures of England's desolation, unravels mournfully. Pictures of burning churches, gutted shrines, exposed tombs, shrieking victims on torture racks, and widespread slaughter are soon following in the wake of the royal injunction. Interspersed with these harrowing experiences are the exiles' reiterated farewells to their native land. There is no attempt at securing effects by understatement: the theme of banishment is given full vent.

The metrical scheme presents a shuttling from anapaestic dimeter to iambic dimeter. Verses 1674–75, 1678–82, 1687–1702, 1723–27, 1731–34, 1736–38, 1741–42 are anapaestic; the remaining verses, with the exception of 1705–06 (iambic trimeters), are iambic dimeters. Verse 1707 is thematically noteworthy in its reference to Henry as a tyrant: a king who, according to Vernulaeus' definition, sacrifices the common good to private advantage.

1687–89. *Gens Christiadum* . . . (The Christian folk . . .). Vernulaeus' reference to the slaughter of clerics and laymen could have been suggested by accounts of Sander, *passim*, and particularly S–L, pp. 117–20.

1694–96. *Multum in templis perplacet aurum* . . . (Gold in the churches is greatly desired . . .). Concerning the plundering of shrines, Sander (S–L, p. 140) records the destruction of Walsingham, Ipswich, Worcester, Willesden, Canterbury, and others.

1707. *O Rex Tyranne* (O King now grown tyrant). Henry's degeneration, seen on the political level, represents the greatest threat to monarchy: the possibility of a king becoming a tyrant. This theme is developed at regular intervals throughout the play (see nn. to vv. 91, 521, 556, 1511).

1720–21. *Et mortuorum iam iacent,/Sepulchra* . . . (Yea, the tombs are pried open . . .). It is possible that Vernulaeus drew on the anonymous *Vita Henrici VIII* (pp. 128–29), which lists twenty-two of the more important tombs in England that were pried open and their contents burned.

1724. *Pars Belgiacas incolet oras* (Some will dwell on Belgian soil). The reference to Belgium as an asylum for the English refugees undoubtedly impressed the Louvain audience with the reality of the dramatic situation.

ACT V, scene i (1748–1794)

The first three scenes of the final act are concerned with the resistance to royal innovations, the sufferings of the old religion, and the gradual callousing of Henry to beneficent influence. Resuming the theme introduced by the preceding chorus, a character personifying Mother Church exhibits her lacerated, bruised, and bleeding figure and recounts her vilification at the hands of Henry, her erstwhile defender. She seeks consolation from Reason, Piety, and Clemency, but they foresee no alternative but death or exile for Mother Church and her loyal servants.

1775. *Mors morte premitur, funeri est funus grave* (Death is heaped on death, the burial records are crowded with the slain): a striking example of Vernulaeus' juxtaposition of cognate forms.

ACT V, scene ii (1795–1846)

Henry enters in a state of anguish over the widespread resistance to his decrees, an invention of the playwright unwarranted by historical fact. As he resolves to establish his will by force, he confronts Mother Church and her allegorical sisters, who appeal to his dwindling sense of justice. Henry lingers over the suggestion of submitting to the Pope and restoring England to her traditional faith, but finally remains unshaken in his resolution to remain king and spiritual head of England. The scene enables the playwright to dramatize Henry's spiritual degeneration. His decision, at this point, is unaffected by the urgency of lust; it is rather a deliberate act of the will to persevere in a course from which he can no longer swerve with impunity.

1797–1809. *Subditi Regis minas/ Pauci verentur* (Only a few of my subjects cower in the face of royal threats). Both Sander and Vernulaeus seem to exaggerate the extent of the Catholic opposition to the King's oath. Modern historians, both Catholic and Protestant, refer to the widespread lack of resistance. Fisher (*The History of England*, pp. 341–42) concludes:

When all allowance has been made for the terror, it still remains a surprising fact that the abrogation of the papal authority was accepted with so little demur in the country. The pope was on the popular side in the divorce question, and derived an adventitious advantage from this circumstance. Yet, with few exceptions, the whole body of the English clergy, regular and secular, abjured his authority.

Catholic historian Philip Hughes, whose extensive research on this phase of the Reformation is unparalleled, bows to the facts (*The Reformation in England*, I, 271):

All the evidence goes to show that the act was very thoroughly administered. The clergy made almost no resistance at all. We have the signatures of more than 6,500 of the secular clergy in the dioceses of Lincoln, London, Canterbury, Rochester, Worcester, Bath, and Wells and Exeter, and long lists of the signatories in the chapters of 1,470 canons and monks in 106 monasteries great and small. . . . The clerical abjurers . . . are unmistakably conscious that they are renouncing a specific religious belief . . . and not merely assenting to an administrative or juridical change.

On the other hand, it should be kept in mind that Henry, except for his refusal to submit to Rome, kept to the Catholic faith. Notwithstanding the reign of Edward VI, it was only toward the end of the sixteenth century under Cecil that England was protestantized. Nor should it be forgotten that Henry's demand for supremacy was approved by such intelligent Englishmen as Gardiner, Tunstall, and even Warham. The ordinary Englishman seems not to have been greatly perturbed. For example, the Thomas More household conformed outwardly to the Henrican supremacy, whatever their inward reservations. Even Thomas More's final stand on the supremacy of the pope was arrived at, as he admitted under oath, only after seven years of study. For an illuminating discussion of the traditionally precarious position of papal prerogatives in England and the perspective it provides for understanding England's seeming lack of resistance, see Henri de Vocht, *Acta Thomae Mori*, pp. 9–14.

Sander, living abroad among a band of enthusiastic Catholics, seems to have adhered to his ultramontane position, partly by failing to appreciate the growth of nationalism in England during his absence. Vernulaeus, by overemphasizing the theme of Catholic resistance, succeeded in maintaining the exterior conflict between good and evil (as he saw it) and thus sustained the interior conflict of the protagonist. He likewise accentuated the values of heroic Catholic resistance as embodied in the English martyrs—values that were still viable to his Catholic students currently involved in similar issues of the Thirty Years' War.

ACT V, scene iii (1847–1896)

Vernulaeus continues to dramatize Henry's progress in tyranny. Disregarding Cranmer's admonition of the ineffectuality of violence, the King insists on pursuing his strong-arm policy. When the wife and daughter of Thomas More request permission to visit the prisoner, Henry seizes the occasion to turn them to his advantage. Meanwhile the infuriated monarch orders the recalcitrant Franciscans and Carthusians to be executed and their establishments demolished.

1855–57. *Vir unus ipse plus potest* . . . (This one man can have more influence than the King . . .). Henry's decision to liquidate the upright and influential Thomas More would be recognized by Vernulaeus' students as the prime indication of tyranny. Their master's book on political science (*Institutionum politicarum*, p. 198), published contemporaneously, placed this crime first on the list of "Tyrannorum Arcana."

1860–66. *Prona quid tanto petis/Matrona luctu* . . . (My Lady, why do you prostrate yourself and grieve so bitterly . . .). Henry's personal interview with More's wife and daughter is Vernulaeus' invention. It has, of course, no basis historically; nor is it provided by Sander. On the other hand, it is dramatically effective in personalizing the relations of Henry with the More household and in emphasizing Henry's eagerness for More's support. Sander does refer, however (*S–L,* p. 123), to the role which the nobles urged Alice to play in winning her husband to the King's side: "Many of the chief nobles went to see him, for the purpose of winning him over; but when they could not succeed in the slightest degree, they intrusted the matter at last to Alice, his wife."

1878–89. *Ordo Minorum totus Observantium* . . . (The entire Order of Friars of the Observance . . .). Sander (*S–L,* pp. 112–13) furnishes Vernulaeus the material for having Henry, on hearing of the aggressive opposition of the Franciscans, order their execution and the burning of their houses:

Out of all the clergy, none withstood the divorce with greater freedom than the Friars minor, commonly called the Observants. They, indeed, both in public disputations and in their sermons, most earnestly maintained that the marriage of Catherine was lawful. . . . For this the king so hated all the friars of the Observance, that on the 11th of August he drove them out of every monastery of their order.

Fisher (*The History of England,* p. 343), following *L&P* (VII, 1095 [Chapuys to Charles V, August 29, 1534]), corroborates Sander:

On June 17 [1534] two carts full of friars drove through London to the Tower. The victims were drawn from the friaries of Richmond and Greenwich, which two days earlier had confronted Bishop Rowland Lee and Thomas Bedyll with their firm intention to live and die in the observance of St. Francis' religion. An excuse was thus afforded to obliterate the whole order of Observants. Their seven houses were cleared, and those friars who were not sent to the Tower were dispersed among other monasteries, where, according to Chapuys, they were bound in chains and treated worse than common prisoners. . . . It was Henry's first experiment in the suppression of a religious order.

The fact that the friars were trained by non-English superiors may account for their stand on the royal supremacy.

1890–93. *Carthusiana Gens quoque in partes abit* . . . (The Carthusian monks are also taking sides . . .). For the account of the martyrdoms of the Carthusians, together with elaborate documentation, see S–L, pp. 117–20; Fisher, *ibid.*, pp. 343–44.

ACT V, scene iv (1897–1973)

The four scenes that follow are devoted to the final days and martyrdom of Thomas More. Sharply contrasting with the previous scene of the tyrannical Henry, the present depiction of the More circle is deeply affecting in its portrayal of the domestic tragedy that lies ahead. Both Alice and Margaret search vainly for arguments to forestall the catastrophe. Thomas meets their pleadings tenderly but firmly. He is fully aware of the pain he will cause others by his decision; nevertheless, he is constrained by allegiances that cannot be forsworn. For all its poignancy, the scene is not without its lighter moments: Alice maintains her traditional role of awkward outspokenness and guilessness; breaking forth in homely comments that amuse her husband and add freshness to the somber prison atmosphere.

1899–1907. *Ne patere, More, coniugis lachrymas tuae* . . . (Thomas, do not allow your wife to weep . . .). Alice's supplication is an amplification of Sander (S–L, p. 123): "Alice, his wife . . . was to persuade her husband not to give up herself, his children, his country, and his life."

1909b–12. *Num meae* . . . (Of my life . . .). Vernulaeus preserves More's quip about time and eternity as related by Sander (S–L, p. 123):

> As she harped on this [the many years to come], More said to her, 'And how long, my dear Alice, do you think I shall live?' 'If God will,' she answered, 'you may live for twenty years.' 'Then,' said Sir Thomas, 'you would have me barter eternity for twenty years; you are not skilful at a bargain, my wife. If you had said twenty thousand years, you might have said something to the purpose; but even then, what is that to eternity?'

The similarity of Alice's plea to that of Catherine (782b–87) and the echoes in both of Dido's speech is noteworthy. See n. to vv. 790–99.

1952b–54; 1957b–59. *At tot tamen/Iurant ubique praesules* . . . (Still, so many bishops throughout England are taking the oath . . .). Margaret's reference to the precedent set by holy and learned men who submitted to Henry is not found in Sander. Vernulaeus may be relying on the account in the *Paris News Letter* (Harpsfield, *Life of More*, App. II, 263; Harpsfield likewise mentions the precedent [*ibid.*, p. 195]).

ACT V, scene v (1974–2017)

More's trial before Cranmer and the King's councilors proceeds with a minimum of irrelevance and elaboration. The former Chancellor of England twice refuses to acknowledge under oath that Henry is the head of the English church. At the same time he ignores the precedent of other English clerics and laymen who chose to subscribe to the royal decrees. Basing his decision on his own convictions and the consensus throughout Western Christendom, he takes his stand firmly, insisting all the while that he has never been disloyal to his sovereign. His sentence of execution he receives joyfully, without trace of rancor or regret.

1974–77. *Hic Morus adsit* . . . (Let More be summoned . . .). More was summoned to trial on July 1, 1535. At this point the first edition of Sander's *De schismate anglicano* (Cologne, 1585) plunges *in medias res,* whereas the second edition (Rome, 1586) prepares the scene (p. 139), as does Vernulaeus: "After spending approximately fourteen months in prison, he [More] was summoned to court from the Tower of London . . . and questioned." On the other hand, Vernulaeus may have relied on Stapleton's *Tres Thomae* (Douay, 1588, p. 318), which gives the same account.

1980–83. *Regi fidelis subditus semper fui* . . . (I have always been a loyal subject of the King . . .). More's reply is paralleled in Sander, *De schismate anglicano* (1586), p. 141.

1994*b*–2000. *Solus sapit* . . . (This fellow is the only wise man alive . . .). The jibes of the First Councilor and More's rejoinder are found in Sander (Rome, 1586), pp. 143–44. See also the *Paris News Letter* for a similar account (pp. 263–64).

2000*b*–01. *Perduellis, proditor/Et Regis hostis Morus est.* (More is a public enemy, a traitor, and an enemy of the Crown). Sander says (S–L, p. 125): "He had hardly ended his answer when they all cried out that More was a traitor and a rebel."

Act V, scene vi (2018–2048)

As More advances unaided to the scaffold, doffs his robe, embraces the executioner, and blindfolds himself, Religion looks on and comments on the significance of the events. The great esteem in which Thomas More was held by continental Europe and by the Louvain playwright reveals itself clearly in the scene of his execution. There is no doubt that Vernulaeus' emphasis on More's role in the drama of the English schism was intended to serve as a model for most of the Louvain students who would serve church and state as laymen. There is no conflict within the soul of the victim. His beautiful death as a Catholic martyr is made to contrast strongly with the agonizing last moments of King Henry that are soon to follow.

2022–23. *At exuenda More, vestis est tua* . . . (But that cloak of yours must come off, More . . .). The incident of More giving his cloak to the executioner, not found in Sander, was very likely prompted by Stapleton's remark that the jailer had furtively substituted a robe of drugget for More's rich robe, a present from Bonvisi (see *Tres Thomae*, p. 340).

2029. *Te verba More proloqui ad plebem, veto* (I forbid you to address the crowd). None of the editions of Sander that I consulted alludes to this restriction. Harpsfield (*Life of More*, p. 202) mentions it, as does Stapleton (*Tres Thomae*, p. 341): "Ubi conscendisset, verba ad populum facturus a praetore prohibetur."

2030–34. *Etiam hoc iniquum est* . . . (This also is unjust . . .). More's brief statement before dying is provided by Stapleton (*ibid.*, p. 341): "Unde breuissime dixit. *Ego fratres contestor me & fidelem Regi, & seruum Dei, & in fide Catholica moriturum.*"

2032. *Fidem Quiritum morte consigno mea* (I ascribe to the faith of Rome by dying for it). Sander (*S–L*, p. 126) writes of More's final prayer and words to the spectators: "When he had ended his prayer, had called the people to witness that he was going to die in the Catholic faith, and had said the psalm *Miserere* . . ." See also Stapleton, *Tres Thomae*, p. 342.

2036. *Ignosce, More* . . . (Pardon me, More . . .). "The executioner came forward, and, according to the custom, asked him to forgive him" (*S–L*, p. 126).

2038–39. . . . *pectus amplectar tuum* . . . (. . . let me embrace you . . .). More's embrace of the executioner and kiss of peace, not recorded by Sander, is mentioned by Stapleton (*Tres Thomae*, p. 342), "Having finished his prayer and rising quickly he first granted pardon to the executioner, who asked for it as is customary, and then kissed him sweetly."

2040–42. *O Tonans* . . . (Almighty God . . .). Through the eyes of Religion, Vernulaeus sees More's execution symbolically as the execution of England. This pattern was supplied by Sander (*S–L*, p. 126): "That done, he struck off the head of justice, of truth, and of goodness. All England mourned the dead, regarding the blow as having fallen not so much upon the martyr of Christ as upon itself."

2043–44. *Permitte vultum, More, velabo tuum* . . . (Allow me to blindfold you, More . . .). More blindfolds himself with his own handkerchief. Stapleton (*Tres Thomae*, p. 342), not Sander, supplies Vernulaeus with this incident: "Finally, when the executioner wished to blindfold him, he [More] said, 'I will do it myself.' Thereupon he took the handkerchief he had brought along with him and wrapped it around his face."

ACT V, scene vii (2049–2093)

Religion, Margaret, and an Angel mourn the passing of Thomas More, the unexcelled ornament of England. Through her grief Margaret grasps the secret of her father's heroism and venerates him as a saint as she lays his body in the grave. Religion meanwhile receives little comfort from the Angel, who prophesies long years of persecution and illustrious deaths of English and Irish recusants. A country that embraces heresy and rejects Christianity, the Angel explains, scarcely ever recovers. The scene brings the More episode to an end and prepares the stage for the catastrophe of the protagonist.

2049–54. . . . *recisum est Angliae toti caput* . . . (. . . the head of all England has been severed . . .). For the identification of More with England, see n. to v. 2040.

2068. *At dum sepulchro corpus hoc condo tuum* (As I lay you to rest in this grave). Sander treats at some length the actions of Margaret during and immediately after the death of her father, including the legend of her miraculous financing of the burial shroud: "Comforted by the miracle, she took up the linen, wrapt her father's body therein, and honourably buried the martyr of Christ. No one disturbed her in her pious duty, for they respected the woman, especially the child [*filiam*]" (*S–L*, pp. 127–28). Vernulaeus chooses to concentrate on Margaret's anguish and its expression (2058–67), but mentions the burial.

2081–82. *Foeminae Imperium grave* (the woman's iron rule). The woman is, of course, Heresy.

ACT V, scene viii (2094–2144)

The King's mental convulsions are now accompanied by advanced stages of the illness that will soon cause his death. The report of the death of Thomas More unnerves him; a moment later a messenger announces the death of Catherine. As her last letter is read to him, Henry breaks down in genuine grief. Remorse immediately gives way to fury at the news of Anne Boleyn's multiple infidelities. When she enters, Henry abuses her vehemently, orders her stripped of her dignities, and sentences her to prompt execution.

The scene is intensely dramatic and filled with surprises. The repudiation of Anne is accomplished with terrible violence. The juxtaposition of the deaths of three major characters is dramatically effective, though somewhat forced. On the other hand, their triple impact on the mind of the protagonist prepares the way for his eventual despair.

2095–96. . . . *intumescit hoc meum* . . . (. . . my body is more bloated . . .). This is the first allusion to Henry's physical ailments. Sander (*S–L*, p. 164) says: "The king having ruined a most admirable constitution by unsatiable gluttony, was now grown so unwieldy that he could hardly enter by the doors, and was wholly unable to mount up the stairs." On Christmas Eve, 1546, Van der Delft wrote the Queen-Regent at Brussels (*Span. Cal.*, VIII, n. 371, quoted in Hughes, *The Reformation in England*, II, 71–72): "The king is so unwell that, considering his age and corpulence, fears are entertained that he will be unable to survive further attacks, such as he recently suffered at Windsor." Pollard (*Henry VIII*, p. 240) likewise refers to Henry's ailments but does not document his statement: "Henry's physique was no longer proof against every ailment; frequent mention is made about this time of headaches [*L&P*, IV, 4546] which incapacitated him from business, and it was not long before there appeared on his leg the fistula which racked him with pain till the end of his life, and eventually caused his death."

2097–2102. . . . *Morus an fato occidit* . . . (. . . has Thomas More met his doom yet . . .). Henry's inquiry about More's execution and the King's anguish, unrecorded by Sander, is found in Stapleton (*Tres Thomae*, p. 344):

When news of Thomas More's execution was brought to King Henry (it so happened that he was playing at dice), he was stricken with horror and said, 'Is it all over with him now?' When they who brought the news said that it was so, he turned his gaze on his own Anne Boleyn who was sitting next to him and said, 'You are the cause of this man's death.' And immediately rising from his seat he rushed to his room and wept bitterly.

Vernulaeus makes no reference to the dice game, nor to Anne.

2103. *Catharina vixit, illa Rex Coniux tua* (Your Majesty, the former Queen Catherine your wife has likewise passed away). Vernulaeus has Warham announce Catherine's death to Henry. For the historical impossibility of Warham's role at this point, see n. to v. 1376*b*. Catherine died on Friday, the day after Epiphany, 1536, about two o'clock in the afternoon. See *Span. Cal.*, V, Pt. II, 3 (Chapuys to Emperor, January 9, 1536).

2111 (between 2111–12). *Leguntur Reginae Catharinae ad Regem*

Litterae (The letters of Queen Catherine are read to the King). At this point Vernulaeus probably furnished student-actor Nicolaus Bottinus, who played the role of Warham, the Latin text of the letter cited by Sander (S–L, p. 131). The English version reads:

My lord, king Henry, the love which I bear you makes me now, when the hour of my death is drawing nigh, put you in mind of your soul's salvation, which you should prefer to all things in the world. I forgive you myself, and I pray God to forgive you. I recommend to you our child, my three maids, and all my servants. Let the former be well provided in marriage; and let the latter have a year's wages in addition to what is due to them now.

On the other hand, Vernulaeus may have used the longer letter recorded by Polydore Vergil (*The Anglica Historia,* pp. 334, 336), or again that cited by Harpsfield (*Pretended Divorce,* pp. 199–200).

2112*b*–13. *Fletus haud noster sat est . . .* (No tears I shed can satisfy this . . .). Henry's reaction to Catherine's letter follows Sander (S–L, p. 131): "The king could not refrain from tears when he read the letter." Harpsfield (*Pretended Divorce,* p. 200) gives the same report. In point of fact, however, Henry seems to have been relieved at Catherine's death. "You could not conceive the joy of Henry," Chapuys wrote to Charles V, reporting the King as saying, "God be praised that we are free from all suspicion of war" (*L&P,* X, 141).

2114–15. *Et heu amores illa contemnit meos . . .* (About Anne—is it really true that she ridicules my love . . .). Vernulaeus, at the risk of introducing the motive for Anne's waywardness that would involve the introduction of Jane Seymour, chose to leave Anne's supposed infidelity to Henry unmotivated. But he adapted the account given by Sander (S–L, p. 132), who says that after Catherine's death "Anne Boleyn seemed now to be delivered from all fear of any rival. But God is just; He raised up another rival to her forthwith, and a more dangerous rival than Catherine had ever been; for the king began to grow weary of Anne, and to give his affections to another woman." Sander proceeds to tell of Anne's miscarriage ["the 29th of January, queen Anne was delivered of a man-child before her time, which was born dead."] and of Henry's forsaking her.

2117–18. *Fratris amplexu sui/Potita gaudet* (With her very own brother has she sinned and is happy about it). In the accusations of incest, Vernulaeus again follows Sander (S–L, pp. 132–33), but disregards Anne's motives:

But when Anne saw that she had hitherto not been the mother of a boy to Henry, and that now there was no hope of her ever being so, she resolved to try whether, in some way or other, she, who was the wife of a king, might not become the mother of a king also. She considered that her sin would be more secret if she sinned with her own brother, George Boleyn, rather than with any other.

George Boleyn, Viscount Rochford, was arrested May 2, 1536, after the famous May Day Tournament; he was executed on a charge of "incest and treason" on May 17, two days before Anne met the same fate.

2118–19. *Una Reginam omnibus/Libido facilem subiicit* (The Queen's gross appetite makes her an easy conquest for all suitors). Of the charges of Anne's later infidelities, Sander (*S–L*, p. 133) remarks: "But as her incest prospered not, she gave herself up to a lewd life, having not only Norris, Weston, and Brereton, who were gentlemen, but also Mark her musician, as her companions in sin." On May 2, 1536, Anne was examined at Greenwich, charged with adultery, and sent to the Tower. Musician Mark Smeaton and Henry Norris had preceded her through the Traitor's Gate and six hours later she was followed by her brother Rochford. Sir Francis Weston, William Brereton, Thomas Wyatt, and Sir Richard Page were added to the list of prisoners. On May 12, Smeaton, Norris, Weston, and Brereton were tried, found guilty of treason as paramours of the Queen, and condemned to die the traitor's death. Smeaton, racked by torture and in hope of pardon, had confessed to guilt, but the other three protested their innocence to the end. On May 15, 1536, Anne and Rochford were tried in the Tower before the peers and Anne was declared guilty by unanimous verdict. On May 17 the sentence was carried out upon the Queen's brother and the four other condemned men (see *Span. Cal.*, V, 55 [Chapuys to the Emperor, May 19, 1536]; Fisher, *The History of England*, pp. 386–87; Pollard, *Henry VIII*, pp. 345–46).

2121*b*–44. *Nempe me rumor tuam . . .* (What is this silly talk about me . . .). The confrontation of Henry and Anne seems to be Vernulaeus' invention.

2136–37. *Moriatur . . .* (She must die . . .). Concerning the sentencing of Anne, Sander (*S–L*, pp. 133–34) writes: "Anne was led into prison, and by Sir Thomas Boleyn himself, sitting among the judges at the commandment of the king, was found guilty of adultery and incest, and was beheaded May 19 [1536], having borne the title of queen not quite five months after the death of Catherine." To the end, Anne confessed her innocence. "The lady who had charge of her," writes Chapuys (*L&P*, X, 908), "had sent to tell me in great secrecy that the concubine, before and after receiving the sacrament, affirmed to her on the damnation of her soul that she had never been unfaithful to the king."

ACT V, scene ix (2145–2176)

The purpose of this scene is to prepare the audience for the death of the protagonist. Both Religion and the Angel entertain righteous satisfaction at the prospect of his passing and the punishment awaiting the tyrant who has persecuted the Church. Brian's detailed report of Henry's illness, more graphic than that of the Angel, is nevertheless instinct with human sympathy. The tones generated by the supernatural creatures and by Brian's reactions to the King's sufferings fall strangely and somewhat ambiguously on the modern reader, who finds it difficult to re-create the violent animosities characteristic of the era of religious wars. Yet it is evident that Vernulaeus meant the audience to share the viewpoint of Religion and the Angel, rather than Brian's.

2159–66. *O iuste vindex* . . . (This is a just retribution . . .). The prospect of Henry's death incites Religion and the Angel to sentiments of "righteous vengeance" that strike one as radically unchristian and reminiscent of the gloating associated with Seneca. On the other hand, the passage is dramatically effective.

2167–73. *Actum est* . . . (The crisis has come . . .). Brian's description of Henry's physical and mental anguish prepares the audience for the coming death-scene of Henry onstage. For the documentation of Henry's disease, see n. to v. 2095.

ACT V, scene x (2177–2239)

Like the many deaths the protagonist has endured in the course of the play, this final dissolution, though terrifying and cautionary, is not unsympathetically treated. In spite of the sententious commentary of Religion, the final impression left by Henry's death is a tragic one: both pity for the tyrant and fear of the inescapable retribution of vice dominate the scene. The King's clear-eyed retrospect of the havoc he has wrought and his impulse to rectify the situation are given voice; nevertheless, he is rendered powerless and dies in despair. The catharsis exercised by this deathbed scene was not lost on the future Bishop of Namur, who approached the playwright tearfully after the performance and confessed how deeply he had been stirred.

2183*b*–86. *Sentio & mortem, & meam/Instare noctem* . . . (I feel both death and darkness creeping toward me . . .). Henry describes his physical and mental torment. Dr. Walter Cromer (d. 1547) became King's physician in Ordinary to Henry in 1539–40. A list of his medicines for the King is contained in Sloane MS. 1047, from which it was reprinted by Furnivall for the Early English Text Society (E. S. 53, 1888). See Sylvester's note in Cavendish's *Life of Wolsey*, p. 241, n. 121/11.

2208–11. *Eversa per me est Angliae fides meaa* . . . (It was through me that the faith of England was destroyed . . .). Henry's momentary regret of having caused the schism with Rome is related by Sander (*S–L*, p. 160):

> When the king saw, as the hour of death was approaching, that in his greed, or rather in his rage, he had broken away from the unity of the Church, he consulted secretly with some of the bishops how he might be reconciled to the Apostolic See, and the rest of Christendom.

The only documentation extant that partially supports Sander's statement are the words of Henry to the papal nuncio in London, reported by Chapuys to Charles V on March 31, 1533 (*Span. Cal.*, IV, 1057):

> It was very true that he had, in other days, composed books in favour of the pope, but since then he had studied better and found the contrary to what he had written, and it could be that he might be given occasion to study more deeply still and to confirm anew what he had once written— wishing to hint that it depends only on the pope being willing to fall in with his wishes.

2230–33. *Huc vinum date* (Give me wine, hurry). "When he was told that he was at the point of death," Sander writes (*S–L*, p. 164), "he called for a goblet of white wine." There seems to be no documentation for this statement of Sander.

2236. . . . *cuncta perdidimus* (. . . We have lost everything). Sander (*S–L*, p. 164) supplies Henry's last words for Vernulaeus: "Turning to one of his attendants, he [Henry] said, 'All is lost.'" David Lewis, quoting from *Prevarication of the Holy Church's Liberties* (iv. 31, Eyston MS), furnishes the following report to document Sander (*S–L*, p. 164, n. 2): "In his last sickness always muttering out, 'Monks and friars,' and desperately concluding his life with these his last words, 'Bryan, we have lost all!'" Pollard (*Henry VIII*, pp. 424–25) gives the following account of Henry's last moments:

When the king woke he felt his feebleness growing upon him, and told Denny to send for Cranmer. The Archbishop came about midnight: Henry was speechless, and almost unconscious. He stretched out his hand to Cranmer, and held him fast, while the Archbishop exhorted him to give some token that he put his trust in Christ. The King wrung Cranmer's hand with his fast-ebbing strength, and so passed away about two in the morning, on Friday, the 28th of January, 1547.

Hughes (*The Reformation in England*, II, 73) gives a similar account:

And then . . . the king collapsed. This time it was the end, and none dared say the word until a matter of hours before the end came. Cranmer, summoned in haste from Croydon, reached St. James's to find the king all but unconscious, and, to a question whether he placed all his trust in the merits of Christ, able to do no more than press the archbishop's hand.

ACT V, scene xi (2240–2255)

The final scene of the tragedy is a prayer for the return of England and Ireland to the ancient fold. Artistically, the final words of Religion soften the grimness of the protagonist's death by disclosing a new horizon of spiritual courage that lies ahead and by lifting the play into a spiritual dimension that balances the bitterness and rancor of religious strife. The historical tragedy, essentially a religious drama, is fittingly concluded by a prayer.

2249. *Tamen, tandem tamen.* (someday . . . someday . . . someday . . .). The use of repetition secures the effect of elegiac supplication.

2254–55. *Mortem . . . crucem* (death . . . cross). The repetition of elements with a minimum of variation emphasizes these key words.

APPENDICES

A. List of Textual Emendations and Preferred Readings

B. List of Student Actors

C. Chronological List of the Works of Vernulaeus

APPENDIX A

List of Textual Emendations and Preferred Readings

During the course of the seventeenth century, *Henricus Octavus* was printed three times. The first edition (Louvain: Philip Dormalius) appeared in 1624. The drama was reprinted seven years later in a collected edition of ten Vernulaean plays, *Tragoediae decem* (Cologne: J. Oliverius & C. Coenestenius, 1631); later it appeared in a posthumous publication of Vernulaeus' fourteen dramas entitled *Tragoediae, in duos tomos distributae* (Louvain: P. Sassenus & H. Nempaeus, 1656).

The present edition of *Henricus Octavus* is based on the Folger Shakespeare Library copy of the first edition. Since no manuscript copies of any of Vernulaeus' plays have survived, one must presume that the second edition of the play was set up by the Cologne printers from the original printed copy. This second publication corrects a number of typographical errors present in the first edition; at the same time, however, it introduces new ones. The third edition, similarly, exhibits further corrections and errors not found in the preceding editions. Thus by collating these three printed editions of the play and bearing in mind that the first edition was set from the author's manuscript copy, one can determine a text that is more faithful to the playwright's original intention than any single edition hitherto published. This I have done in the present edition of *Henricus Octavus*. In general, the first edition is remarkably free from error and affords a reliable basis with only occasional exceptions. I designate this first edition by "*A*"; the second and third printings of the play are referred to as "*B*" and "*C*," respectively. The following entries, by verse number, comprise the complete list of emendations and preferred readings.

17. Et qui tremendam flebili tundit *domum*. *A* and *B* read *donum*. *C* gives the correct reading, *domum*, evidenced by the context and the meter, as well as by the syntactical demands of the feminine form of the adjective, *tremendam*.

32. Amens rebellat, sceleris *infandi* est reus. *A* has *nifandi*; *B* reads *nefandi*; *C* corrects the transposed letter of *A* and *B* and restores *infandi*, undoubtedly the author's intention, since it alone satisfies the metrical demands of an iambic foot in the fourth position—Vernulaeus' habitual practice.

40. Tandem Sorores pergite. Hic partes tuae. *A* neglects the pointing after *pergite*, supplied by *B* and *C*.

100. Impletque celsa regios Coniux *toros*. *A* and *B* read *thoros*. *C* prefers the classical spelling. For the sake of uniformity the classical spelling has been maintained throughout the present text.

208 (between 208 and 209). Scena IV. *A* misprints this caption as "Scena II," an error rectified by *B* and *C*.

280b. *Fatear*, erravit tamen. *A* reads *fateor*; *B* and *C* read *fatear*. The subjunctive form is taken as the preferred reading, the context of Wolsey remonstrating politely with King Henry VIII seeming sufficient justification.

304. Iam certa sors est, sortis inveni modum. The sense demands a full stop after *modum,* although none of the texts supplies it.

350 (between 350 and 351). Chorus Virginum *Anglicanarum.* A has *Anglicarum; B* substitutes *Angelicarum,* an improbable alternative which *C* repeats. Vernulaeus evidently intended *Anglicanarum* (*Anglicanus-a-um*), as evidenced by his use of this adjectival form elsewhere. Cf. Title Page: Schisma *Anglicanum,* and Letter to the Reader, Ecclesia *Anglicana.*

415*a. Pedisequae.* All three editions have *Pedisseque.* The classical spelling of "waiting women" and the correct plural ending was undoubtedly intended by the author.

524–25. Amare primum quod volunt, dein frui,/Regum est voluptas. *A, B,* and *C* show a full stop after *frui.* Substitution of a comma at this point seems to be demanded by the sense.

898. Nullam severi iuris aut legem *novam. B* and *C* correct the typographical error (*vovam*) of *A.*

1038 (between 1038 and 1039). Scena IV. *A* designates this scene as Scena III, an error righted by *B* and *C.*

1046–47. Sinus, cruoris ultimas guttas mei/Ferro require. All three texts have a full stop after *mei,* an impossible reading.

1086. Me cogit; ipsa fervidam hanc mentem regas? The interrogation point, present in *B* and *C,* compensates adequately for the absence of terminal punctuation in *A.*

1110–11. Et impedire tot meos; heu tot meos/Cupiunt amores? *A* and *B* insert a comma after the second *tot,* a needless pointing ignored by *C.*

1121. Cum vibrat *ensem.* The typographical error of *A* (*cnsem*) is corrected in *B* and *C.*

1128. Abrumpo cunctas. Agere iam Regem volo. Although all three editions register a comma after *cunctas,* together with initial capitalization of *Agere,* the full stop after *cunctas* is dictated by the sense.

1136*a.* Et *hinc* recessit? *B* and *C* substitute *hic* for *hinc,* an undesirable emendation.

1190. Sim falsus augur O *Tonans. B* and *C* correct the typographical error (*conans*) of *A.*

1200 (between 1200 and 1201). *Granmerus.* Although all three texts have *Grammerus* at this point, the preferred Latinized spelling of Cranmer is indicated in the *Personae Tragoediae* and elsewhere.

1207. Et digna Rege: *restat* ut sacrum ferat. *A* reads *eestat,* corrected by *B* and *C.*

1220. Diadema *capiti. A* has *cap.ti,* which *B* and *C* correct.

1241. Tuos labores *occinam. B* substitutes *occinans* ungrammatically; *C* corrects *B* with *occinens.* The *occinam* of *A* is quite satisfactory and hence retained.

1266. Sitiens cruorem *innoxium. A* and *B* have *in noxium; C* restores the correct adjectival form, *innoxium.*

1272. Quaerenda nunc est certa regnandi via. The terminal punctuation is blurred in *A; B* and *C* supply an interrogation point. The context requires a period after *via.*

1435. Ut ecce totus *haeret*! *B* and *C* emend to *haeres*, but there is no need for Brian's observation to be interpreted as direct address. Brian here serves a choric function, a convention often used by Vernulaeus.

1481*b*–82. Nempe quando Pontifex/*Pronuntiavit*. *A* reads *pronunciavit*; *B* and *C* print the classical spelling.

1496–97. . . . fidei sacra/*Antiquae* servat. The *antiqua* of *A* would have to modify *sacra*; Vernulaeus evidently intended the idiomatic expression *Fides antiqua*, supported by *B* and *C*.

1545. Haeres, fateri subditi debent mei: The terminal colon supplied by *B* and *C* is preferred to the lack of end punctuation in *A*.

1549–50. Ego te *Anglicanae* Rex, supremum Ecclesiae/Veneror caput. The terminal ligature of *Anglicanae* in *A* is indistinct, hence the incorrect form *Anglicana* in *B* and *C*. The genitive case, *Anglicanae*, is controlled by *Ecclesiae*.

1628. Haeres *Bolenae* filia. *B* and *C* correct the illogical form, *Bolena*, printed in *A*.

1634–35*a*. . . . haec vitam dabit/*Hinc* cum relinquam. All three texts furnish *hunc*, thus entailing the simplest emendation possible.

2062. *Exanime*, mutum, mortuum, abiectum iacet? Although all three texts have *examine*, the context demands a word designating "lifelessness."

Appendix B. List of Student Actors: *Margareta* Mori filia, & Ratio. *A* reads *Maria*, instead of *Margareta*; in *B* and *C* no list appears. Both daughters (More's and Catherine's) are entered correctly in the *Personae Tragoediae*: Maria Filia Catharinae, Margareta Mori filia.

APPENDIX B

List of Student Actors*

Haec Tragoedia Exhibita Lovanii in Publico Theatro
Ludis Encenialibus Egerunt in ea Ingenii Iuvenes
Collegii Porcensis Alumni & Studiosi.

Henricus Rex
  Antonius de Monin Namurc. [Namur, Belgium]
Catharina Regina
  Georgius de Humyn Luxemb. [Luxembourg, Belgium]
Thomas Morus
  Georgius Bottinus Marchiensis [Marchienne-au-Pont, Belgium]
Brianus
  Ioannes de Traux Castellanus [Casteau? Castillon?, Belgium
                                Castellane?, France]
Longlandus
  Gaspar van der Hofstat Malinas [Mechlin or Malines, Belgium]
Volsaeus
  Petrus Mulderus Sylvaeducensis [Hertogenbosch or Bois-le-Duc, Holland]
Campegius
  Petrus Scellenius Boxtellanus [Boxtel, Holland]
Varramus
  Nicolaus Bottinus Marchiensis [Marchienne-au-Pont, Belgium]
Religio
  Robertus Schutteput Lovanien. [Louvain, Belgium]
Granmerus
  Adamus Prudentius Fleuricens [Fleurus?, Belgium; Fleury?, France]
Senatores
  Georgius Pisroux Marchiensis [Marchienne-au-Pont, Belgium]
  Joannes de Saincte Wauriensis [Ware, Belgium]
  David Clancius Nobilis Hiber [of Irish nobility]
Roffensis Episcopus
  Antonius Matthei Blaruesiensis [Blaricum?, Holland]
Bolena
  Philippus Godefridi Belloramus [Beauraing?, Belgium]
Haeresis
  Franciscus Staes Lovaniensis [Louvain]
Impietas
  Ioannes du Molin Orchiacensis [Orchies, France]
Tyrannis
  Ioannes Genin Lovaniensis [Louvain]
Luxuria & Aloysia
  Antonius la Riviere Iprensis [Ypres, Belgium]

* The list of student actors for *Henricus Octavus* is appended to the first edition
of the play.

Margareta Mori filia, & Ratio
  Cornelius Vranx Lovaniensis [Louvain]
Angelus
  Ioannes Gogels Lovaniensis [Louvain]
Exules
  Ludovicus Vranx Lovaniensis [Louvain]
  Carolus Schutteput Lovaniensis [Louvain]
  Cornel. de Vleeschouvver Lovaniensis [Louvain]
Virgo & Clementia
  Eurardus de Bacher Lovaniensis [Louvain]
Virgo & Pietas
  Ioannes Impens Lovaniensis [Louvain]
Virgo
  Ioannes Hemselmans Lovaniensis [Louvain]
Virgo
  Lambertus de Vernulz Novohabeanus [Nieuwpoort or Habay-la-Neuve,
                                                    Belgium]
Virgo
  Andraeas Gall Lovaniensis [Louvain]
Filia Catharinae
  Ioannes Grols Lovaniensis [Louvain]

An examination of the above list of students who participated in the two known presentations of *Henricus Octavus* in 1624 invites several observations pertinent to the staging of academic drama at the University of Louvain.

In the first place, one observes that the principal roles were assigned to out-of-town students who remained at their college during the Christmas holidays. Thus, of the thirty students participating, all but thirteen were from outlying districts of Belgium, Holland, and France—one David Clancy being from Ireland. The thirteen Louvain students presumably assembled at the Porc College for rehearsals during the holidays.

Secondly, the practice of doubling in roles is evidenced by the record of four students, their dual roles, however, being minor ones. It is interesting to note, further, that the Chorus of Exiles consisted of three students, all from Louvain, while the Chorus of English Maidens numbered five students, all of them Louvainists except Vernulaeus' nephew, Lambert de Vernulz. Three student actors had younger brothers in the cast: George and Nicholas Bottinus of Marchienne-au-Pont, Belgium; Cornelius and Louis Vranx, as well as Charles and Robert Schutteput, of Louvain.

Five of these students continued their dramatic experience two years later in *Ottocarus* (1626), their names being listed in the first edition of the play. Francis Staes, who played Heresy in *Henricus*, returned as Senator Waldricus in *Ottocarus*; George Pisroux, Henrican senator, played Bishop Bernard; Jean du Molin, Impiety, played the role of the Austrian legate; Anthony Matthei (Bishop Fisher) became legion commander Milotas; finally Robert Schutteput, who played the role of the much-abused Religion of *Henricus*, advanced to the fiery role of Queen Kunegundis in *Ottocarus*.

APPENDIX C
Chronological List of the Works of Vernulaeus

Gorcomienses sive fidei exilium, tragoedia. Exhibita ludis encoenialibus Lovanii anno 1609 ab alumnis collegii Porcensis. Coloniae, Bern. Gualterus, 1610 [microfilm, St. Mary's U.].

Divus Eustachius sive fidei & patientiae triumphus, tragoedia. Lovanii, Phil. Dormalius, 1612 [microfilm, St. Mary's U.].

Quis inter orbis monarchas potentissimus. Dissertatio politica. Lovanii, Joan. Masius, 1613.

De conceptione & visitatione Mariae, orationes duae. Accedit tertia de affinitate & cognatione eloquentiae cum caeteris scientiis. Lovanii, 1614.

Rhetorum collegii Porcensis inclytae academiae Lovaniensis orationes, sub Nic. Vernulaeo . . . Lovanii, 1614. Lovanii, 1633, 1645, 1649; Coloniae, 1619, 1639, 1663–88 [1663–88 in Newberry]; Antuerpiensis, 1684.

Dissertatio politica de una & diversa religione, constans orationibus X, habita ab eloquentiae candidatis juvenibus in publica artium schola Lovanii sub D. Nic. Vernulaeo. Lovanii, Gerard. Rivius, 1618.

De arte dicendi libri tres; una cum praxi rhetoricae & duobus de inventione libris. Lovanii, Phil. Dormalius, 1619. Lovanii, 1631, 1637, 1667; Ienae, 1631; Norimbergae, 1658.

Disputatio politica de bello, quam . . . sub praesidio Nic. Vernulaei defendet . . . septembris 1619 N. in auditorio rhetoricae Porcensis. Lovanii, 1619.

Disputatio politica, de universa republica, sub praesidio Nic. Vernulaei, proposita a Nicolao Lahodowsky. Lovanii, Phil. Dormalius, 1621.

Oratio de laudibus D. Francisci. Coloniae, 1622. [Delivered at the convent of the Recollects.]

Panegyricus, memoriae & famae Joannis Duns Scoti, doctoris subtilis, dictus & dicatus. Coloniae, 1622. Montibus Hannoncae, 1644.

Theodoricus, rex Italiae, tragoedia. Exhibita ludis remigialibus in collegio Porcensi, nonis octobris, 1622. Lovanii, Henr. Hostenius, 1623. Lovanii, Georg. Lipsius, 1633.

Laus posthuma Buquoi, supremi S. Caesareae majestatis exercitus praefecti, a quinque militibus wallone-belga, italo, germano, hispano, cosacco polono celebrata, stylo Nic. Vernulaei. Coloniae, 1623.

Certamen oratorium inter duos oratores, Francum et Hispanum: utri de ecclesia romana melius meriti sint, Franciae an Hispaniae reges? Accedit tertius pontificius, reges illos ad firmam concordiam, & bellum ecclesiae hostibus inferendum adhortans. Lovanii, Phil. Dormalius, 1624. Coloniae, 1649.

Henricus Octavus, seu schisma anglicanum, tragoedia. Exhibita ludis encaenialibus, Lovanii in collegio Porcensi. Lovanii, Phil. Dormalius, 1624 [Folger, Newberry, Henry Huntington; microfilm, St. Mary's U.].

Certamen oratorium de militari gloria, inter septem milites, hispanum, belgam, germanum, francum, italum, polonum, hungarum. Lovanii, Phil. Dormalius, 1624. Coloniae, 1649.

Institutionum politicarum libri iv, qui omnia civilis doctrinae elementa continent. Lovanii, Phil. Dormalius, 1624. Coloniae, 1628; Lovanii, 1635, 1647 [1647 in Newberry].

Institutionum moralium libri iv, qui omnia ethicae, seu bene vivendi doctrinae elementa continent. Lovanii, Phil. Dormalius, 1625. Lovanii, 1640, 1649; Cura Joannis Weisii, Giessoe, 1668.

Institutionum oeconomicarum libri duo, qui omnia domesticae doctrinae, seu familiae regendae elementa continent. Lovanii, Phil. Dormalius, 1626 [Columbia U.]. Lovanii, 1640, 1649.

Ottocarus Bohemiae rex seu rebellio contra Rudolphum I imperatorem austriacae familiae conditorem tragoedia. Exhibita ludis encoenialibus Lovanii in collegio Porcensi. Lovanii, Phil. Dormalius, 1626.

Academia lovaniensis. Ejus origo, incrementum, forma, magistratus, facultates, privilegia, scholae, collegia, viri illustres, res gestae. Lovanii, Phil. Dormalius, 1627 [Union Theological Seminary]. Lovanii (recognita & aucta per Christianum a Langendonck) 1667 [Newberry, Harvard].

Conradinus et Crispus, tragoediae. Lovanii, Joan. Oliverius, 1628 [microfilm, St. Mary's U.].

Annus austriacus, seu ephemeris historica, continens per singulos anni dies aliquid, quod in serenissima austriaca familia accidit. Lovanii, Phil. Dormalius, 1628 [Harvard].

Dissertatio oratoria de libertate politica, habita a rhetoribus academicis in publica schola artium. Lovanii, Phil. Dormalius, 1628.

Joanna Darcia, vulgo puella Aurelianensis, tragoedia. Lovanii, Phil. Dormalius, 1629.

Dissertationum politicarum stylo oratorio explicatarum decas prima. Lovanii, Phil. Dormalius, 1629. Lovanii, 1646.

Dissertatio oratoria de bello feliciter gerendo, constans orationibus sex, habita publice ab eloquentiae candidatis juvenibus. Lovanii, Phil. Dormalius, 1630.

Orationum sacrarum volumen singulare in festa Deiparae virginis, & aliquot divorum. Lovanii, 1630. Coloniae, 1632; Lovanii, 1635.

Maximus, tragoedia. Lovanii, Phil. Dormalius, 1630.

Tragoediae decem, nunc primum simul editae. Coloniae, Joan. Oliverius & Cor. Coenestenius, 1631 [Contains *Gorcomienses, Eustachius, Theodoricus, Henricus Octavus, Ottocarus, Conradinus, Crispus, Joanna Darcia, Stanislaus, Thomas Cantuariensis.*] [New York Public Library, Folger, U. of Chicago, U. of Michigan; microfilm, St. Mary's U.].

Trophaea Ambrosii Spinolae, supremi exercituum catholici regis in Belgio & Italia ducis, celebrata a sex orationibus, flandro, trans-rhenano, caesareo, brabanto, hispano, italo. Lovanii, Phil. Dormalius, 1631.

Munus parentale piis manibus sereniss. Isabellae clarae Eugeniae, infantis hispaniarum . . . sacrum, & a studiosa juventute collegii Porcensis Lovanii exhibitum. Lovanii, Phil. Dormalius & Georg. Lipsius, 1634. Lovanii, 1634.

Elogia oratoria Alberti Pii, belgar. principis: Isabellae Clarae Eugeniae, Ambrosii Spinolae; Caroli, comites Buquoi; Joannis, comitis Tilli. Accedunt triumphus ob receptam Bredam, & orationes aliquot miscellaneae. Lovanii, Jac. Zegers, 1634 [Harvard]; Coloniae, 1635.

Laudatio funebris aeternae memoriae Isabellae Clarae Eugeniae, infanti hispaniarum, archiduci Austriae . . . dicta Lovanii in aede D. Petri, cum ei solemnibus exequiis academia parentaret. Lovanii, Phil. Dormalius, 1634.

Apologia pro augustissima, serenissima & potentissima gente austriaca, in qua illius magnitudo, imperium, virtus adversus ejus hoc tempore aemulos asseritur. Lovanii, Franc. Simonis & Jac. Zegers, 1635 [Harvard].

Triumphus lovaniensium, ob solutam urbis suae obsidionem, per recessum duorum potentissimorum exercituum, christianissimi Franciae regis, & foederatorum Belgii ordinum. Adjungitur oratio ad studiosam juventutem, cum kal. julii studia resumerentur. Lovanii, Phil. Dormalius, 1635.

Dissertatio oratoria, de causis belli sueco-germanici, inter duos oratores, germanum, & suecum. Lovanii, Phil. Dormalius, 1635. Coloniae, 1641; Amsterdamiensis, 1646.

Dissertatio historica de causis occupatae a Francis Lotharingiae. Lovanii, Jac. Zegers, 1636.

Fritlandus, tragoedia. Lovanii, Justus Coppenius, 1637 [New York Public Library].

Laudatio funebris, augustissimi imp. Ferdinandi II memoriae consecrata, ad Ferdinandum III, imp. Lovanii, Judoc. Coppenius, 1637.

Panegyricus gratulatorius Ferdinando III, Romanorum regi electo, & coronato scriptus. Lovanii, Judoc. Coppenius, 1637.

Dissertatio oratoria de justitia armorum batavicorum adversus catholicum regem principem suum, inter duos oratores, batavum & belgam catholicum. Accedit tertius Cineas Pacificus, qui pacem cum rege ineundam suadet. Lovanii, Jac. Zegers, 1637. Coloniae, 1638, 1643.

Triumphus ob caesos ad Colloam Batavos, a rhetoribus academicis collegii Porcensis celebratus, stylo Nic. Vernulaei. Lovanii, Jac. Zegers, 1638.

De propagatione fidei christianae in Belgio per sanctos ex Hibernia viros, liber. Lovanii, Jac. Zegers, 1639. Lovanii, 1654.

Virtutum augustissimae gentis austriacae libri tres, solis caesarum, regum, principumque austriacorum exemplis adornati; una cum monitis ethicis, politicisque. Lovanii, Jac. Zegers, 1640.

Laudatio funebris serenissimo . . . Ferdinando . . . S. R. E. Cardinali, Belgii & Burgundiae gubernatori dicta in aede D. Petri Lovanii, cum ei academia & civitas parentarent die xxi decemb. 1641. Lovanii, Jac. Zegers, 1641.

Munus parentale sacris manibus sereniss. Ferdinandi . . . sacrum, . . . stylo Nic. Vernulaei. Lovanii, Jac. Zegers, 1641.

Dissertationum politicarum decas secunda. Lovanii, Joan. Vryenborch & Germanus Sassenus, 1646.

Andreae del Vaulx, alias Vallensis, juris canonici professoris, vitae synopsis. Mechliniensis, 1646 [Prefixed to *De Beneficiis* of Andre del Vaulx].

Oratio in funere cl. & ampliss. viri Erycii Puteani . . . habita Lovanii in aede D. Gertrudis die xix septembris 1646. Lovanii, Joan. Vryenborch, 1646.

Imperatorum symbola, praeclaris regum principumque, necnon variorum scriptorum exemplis illustrata, quibus accedit commentarius in Andreae Alciati emblemata, usque ad emblema xv. Omnia nunc primum edita. Lovanii, Judoc. Coppenius, 1650 [U. of Chicago].

Observationum politicarum ex Cornelii Taciti operibus, syntagma. Opus posthumum nunc primo editum. Lovanii, Hieron. Nempaeus, 1651.

Historia austriaca, gentis augustissimae, serenissimae, ac potentissimae archiduces, reges, imperatores, breviter complexa, nunc primum typis edita. Lovanii, Hieron. Nempaeus, 1651.

Epitome historiarum, ab orbe condita ad haec usque tempora, per monarchias iv, deducta; cum supplemento ab anno 1650 Bernardi Heymbachi . . . Adjecta est Cornelii Valerii oratio funebris, Lovanii in exequiis Caroli V imp. nomine universitatis habita. Omnia nunc primum edita. Lovanii, Pet. Sassenus, & Hieron. Nempaeus, 1654.

Tragoediae, in duos tomos distributae. Editio secunda. Priore, aliquot tragoediis, nunc primum in lucem editis, auctior. Additum Bernardi Heymbachi otium itinerarium, in quo natura tragoediae examinatur. Lovanii, Pet. Sassenus & Hieron. Nempaeus, 1656 [Western Reserve, Harvard; microfilm copy, Folger, St. Mary's U.].

BIBLIOGRAPHY

Primary Sources: Manuscripts

Belgium, Brussels. *Archives générales du royaume: Archives of the University of Louvain* [*AUL*].

AUL No. 146. Régistre contenant les actes relatifs à la fondation des collèges erigés par J. Milius 1617–1750. *MS. Folio.*

AUL No. 326. Documents relatifs à la part prise par l'université à la fortification et à la défense de la ville de Louvain. 1506–1744. *Liasse.*

AUL No. 387. Acta facultatis S. *Theologiae* (procès-verbau des réunions de la faculté), 1608–1796: from August 30, 1608, to December 2, 1630. *MS. Folio.*

AUL No. 714. Liber decimus, April 18, 1597, to September 30, 1631, contained in the *Acta facultatis artium. MS. Folio.*

AUL No. 715. Liber undecimus facultatis artium, October 1, 1613, to June 2, 1625. *MS. Folio.*

AUL No. 763. Dossier du procès arbitral entre Corn. Faes, professeur de philosophie, avec ses collègues, et Matthias Rosmer, professeur d'éthique, avec le professeur de rhétorique, au sujet de la préférence à donner aux uns ou aux autres dans les nominations aux bénéfices. *Liasse.*

AUL No. 3517. Comptes de l'économie du Collège Mylius par Nicolas Vernulée: October 1, 1619, to April 16, 1649. *Liasse.*

AUL No. 5061. Ivoix, Ivoy, chapellenie: nomination de Nicolas Vernulée, 1631–32; J. Ballon, 1632; J. de Wipion: contestations du chapitre: 1646. *Liasse.*

Germany, Cologne. *Stadtarchiv Köln, allgemeine Verwaltung der Universität Köln, No. 74. Fünfte Matrikel der Kölner Universität, 1559–1627. MS. Folio.*

Primary Sources: Books

Andreas, Valerius. *Bibliotheca belgica: de Belgis vita scriptisque claris praemissa topographica Belgii totius seu Germaniae inferioris descriptione.* Editio renovata, & tertia parte auctior. Louvain: J. Zegers, 1643.

————. *Fasti academici studii generalis Lovaniensis, id est origo et institutio: rectores, cancellarii, conservatores, doctores & professores, fundatores et benefactores, resque aliquot memorabiles ejusdem universitatis.* Editio iterata accuratior, et altera parte auctior. Louvain: H. Nempaeus, 1650.

Ardennes, Remacle d'. *Palamedes.* Paris: Giles de Gourmont, 1512.

Ave, Antoine d'. *Oratio in funere N. Vernulaei, habita Lovanii in primaria aede sacra beati Petri die 8. januarii MDCXLIX.* Louvain: J. Vryenborch, 1649.

Bellarmine, Robertus. *Conciones habitae Lovanii ante annos circiter quadraginta: nunc consensu auctoris publicatae.* Cologne: J. Crithius, 1615.

Bémont, Charles. *Le premier divorce de Henri VIII, et le schisme d'Angleterre. Chronique latine sur le premier divorce de Henri VIII. Fragment d'une chronique anonyme en latin. Publié avec une introduction, une traduction française et des notes* ("Bibliothèque de l'école des hautes études, sciences historiques et philologiques." Fasc. 221). Paris: Honoré Champion, 1917.

Bolte, Johannes. *Coligny, Gustaf Adolf, Wallenstein: drei zeitgenössische lateinische Dramen von Rhodius, Narssius, Vernulaeus* ("Bibliothek des literarischen Vereins in Stuttgart," 280). Leipzig: Karl W. Hiersemann, 1933.

Bradner, Leicester (ed.). *Musae anglicanae. Anglo-Latin Poetry from 1500–1925.* London: Oxford University Press, 1940.

Brechtanus, Livinus. *Euripus: tragoedia christiana.* 2d ed. Louvain: P. Phalesius & M. Rotarius, 1550.

Burnet, Gilbert. *The History of the Reformation of the Church of England. A new edition carefully revised, and the records collated with the originals by Nicholas Pocock.* 7 vols. (of which IV, V, and VI are documentary records). Oxford: Clarendon Press, 1865.

Calendar of Letters, Despatches, and State Papers relating to the Negotiations between England and Spain, preserved in the Archives at Simancas and elsewhere. Edited by G. A. Bergenroth, Pascual de Gayangos, M. A. S. Hume, and R. Tyler. 11 vols. London: Eyre and Spottiswoode; Longman and Co., 1862–1916.

Calendar of State Papers and Manuscripts relating to English Affairs, existing in the Archives and Collections of Venice, and in other libraries of northern Italy. Edited by Rawdon Brown. 6 vols. London: Longmans, Green and Co., 1864–84.

Calendar of State Papers, Domestic Ser., Elizabeth, Addenda, 1566–1579. Edited by Mary Anne Everett Green. London: Longmans, Green and Co., 1871.

Calendar of State Papers, Ireland. Vol. II, 1574–85. Edited by H. C. Hamilton. 4 vols. London, 1860–90.

Caussinus, Nicolas. *Tragoediae sacrae: Solyma, Nabuchodonosor, Felicitas, Theodoricus, Hermengildus.* Paris: Sebastian Chappelet, 1629.

Cavendish, George. *The Life and Death of Cardinal Wolsey.* Edited for the Early English Text Society by Richard S. Sylvester, original ser., No. 243. London: Oxford University Press, 1959.

Clenardus, Nicolas. *Epistolarum libri duo.* Antwerp: Chr. Plantin. 1566.

A Collection of State Papers Relating to Affairs in the Reign of Queen Elizabeth from 1571–1596. Edited by William Murdin. London: William Bowyer, 1759.

Ehses, Stephan (ed.). *Römische Dokumente zur Geschichte der Ehescheidung Heinrichs VIII. von England, 1527–1534.* Paderborn: F. Schoningh, 1893.

Ellis, Henry (ed.). *Original Letters Illustrative of English History.* 11 vols. in 3 series. London: Harding and Lepard, 1824–46.

Erasmus, Desiderius. *Collectanea adagiorum veterum.* Vol. II of *Desiderii Erasmi Roterodami opera omnia.* 10 vols. Leyden: Peter Vander Aa, 1703–06.

————. *Ten Colloquies of Erasmus*. Edited and translated by Craig Thompson. New York: Liberal Arts Press, 1957.

Foppens, J. F. *Bibliotheca belgica, sive virorum in Belgio vita, scriptisque illustrium catalogus, librorumque nomenclatura. Continens scriptores a clariss. viris Valerio Andrea, Auberto Miraeo, Francisco Swertio, aliisque recensitos usque ad annum MDCLXXX.* 2 vols. Brussels: Per Petrum Foppens, Typographum & Bibliopolam, 1739.

Glapthorne, Henry. *The Tragedy of Albertus Wallenstein, Late Duke of Friedland, and General to the Emperor Ferdinand the Second. The Scene Egers. Acted, with good allowance, at the Globe on the Bankside, by His Majesty's Servants.* London: Thomas Paine, 1639.

Hall, Edward. *The Vnion of the Two Noble and Illustre Famelies of Lancastre & Yorke.* London, 1542, 1548, 1550. Reprinted, London, 1809.

Harpsfield, Nicholas. *The Life and Death of Sir Thomas More, knight, sometymes Lord High Chancellor of England.* Edited for the Early English Text Society by E. V. Hitchcock and R. W. Chambers, original ser., No. 186. London: Oxford University Press, 1932.

————. *A Treatise on the Pretended Divorce between Henry VIII. and Catherine of Aragon.* Edited for the Camden Society by Nicholas Pocock, new ser., No. 21. London: Camden Society, 1878.

Hay, Denys (ed.). *The Anglica Historia* by Polydore Vergil. Edited with a translation and introduction for the Camden Society, Ser. 3, Vol. 74. London: Offices of the Royal Historical Society, 1950.

Heymbach, Bernard. *Otium itinerarium in quo tragoediae natura examinatur.* Appended to *Duos tomos Vernulaei.* 2d ed. Louvain: Sassenus & Nempaeus, 1656.

Knox, T. F. (ed.). *The Letters and Memorials of William Cardinal Allen.* CXXII ("Records of the English Catholics under the Penal Laws," 2). London: D. Nutt, 1882.

Le Grand, Joachim. *Histoire du divorce de Henri VIII, roy d'Angleterre et de Catherine d'Aragon, avec le défense de Sanderus, la réfutation des deux premiers livres de l'histoire de la réformation de M. Burnet, et les preuves.* 3 vols. Paris: Martin, Boudot, Martin, 1688.

Lettenhove, Kervyn de. *Relations politiques des Pays-Bas avec l'Angleterre sous le règne de Philippe II.* 11 vols. Brussels: F. Hayez, 1882–1900.

Letters and Papers, foreign and domestic of the reign of Henry VIII, preserved in the Public Record Office, the British Museum, and elsewhere in England. I–IV., edited by J. S. Brewer, 1862–76; V–XIII, edited by J. Gairdner, 1880–93; XIV–XXI, edited by J. Gairdner and R. H. Brodie, 1894–1910. London: Longmans, Green and Co., 1862–1910.

More, Thomas. *Thomae Mori Angliae ornamenti eximii, lucubrationes, ab innumeris mendis repurgatae.* Basel: F. Episcopius, 1563.

Philicinus, Petrus [Peter Campson]. *Comoedia tragica, quae inscribitur Magdalena evangelica.* Antwerp: J. Steels, 1546.

Pocock, Nicholas (ed.). *The History of the Reformation of the Church of England by Gilbert Burnet.* 7 vols. Oxford: Clarendon Press, 1865.

————. (ed.). *Records of the Reformation. The Divorce, 1527–1533, mostly now for the first time printed from the manuscripts in the British Museum, the Public Record Office, the Venetian Archives.* 2 vols. Oxford: Clarendon Press, 1870.

——. (ed.). *A Treatise on the Pretended Divorce between Henry VIII. and Catherine of Aragon,* by Nicholas Harpsfield. Edited for the Camden Society, new ser., No. 21. London: Camden Society, 1878.

Pole, Reginald Cardinal. *Ad Henricum Octavum Britanniae regem pro ecclesiasticae unitatis defensione, libri quatuor.* Rome: Antonio Blado, 1536.

Roersch, Alphonse (ed.). *Correspondance de Nicolas Clénard.* 3 vols. ("Collection des anciens auteurs belges," new ser., No. 2). Brussels: Palais des académies, 1940–41.

Rogers, Elizabeth F. (ed.). *The Correspondence of Sir Thomas More.* Princeton: Princeton University Press, 1947.

Roper, William. *The Life of Sir Thomas More, Knyght.* Edited for the Early English Text Society by E. V. Hitchcock, original ser., No. 197. London: Oxford University Press, 1935.

Sander, Nicholas. *De origine ac progressu schismatis anglicani, liber.* Cologne: Agrippinae, 1585. Translated with an introduction and notes by David Lewis, *Rise and Growth of the Anglican Schism.* London: Burns & Oates, 1877.

——. . . . *Tres orationes in scholis publicis Lovanii habitae, 14 cal. ianuarii, A.D. 1565.* Antwerp: Joannes Latius, 1566.

——. *De visibili monarchia ecclesiae, libri viii.* Louvain: John Fowler, 1571.

——. *De visibili monarchia ecclesiae, libri viii.* Wurzburg: apud viduam Henrici Aquensis episcopalis typographi, 1592.

Scaliger, J. C. *Poetices libri septem.* Editio secunda, Heidelberg: In Bibliopolio Commeliano, 1617.

Schöpperus, Jacobus. *Ectrachelistis, sive Joannes decollatus, tragoedia nova & sacra.* Cologne: Mart. Gymnicus, 1546.

——. *Euphemus, seu foelicitatus Jacob: actio nova & sacra, descripta historice, item Ovis perdita, parabola evangelica, comice descripta.* Basel: Joannes Oporinus, 1553.

——. *Voluptatis ac virtutis pugna, comoedia tragica.* Cologne: Mart. Gymnicus, 1546.

Selectae PP. Soc. Iesu tragoediae. Antwerp: John Cnobarrus, 1634.

Stapleton, Thomas. *Tres Thomae, seu de S. Thomae Apostoli rebus gestis. De S. Thoma archiepiscopo Cantuariensi & martyre. De Thomae Mori Angliae quondam cancellarii vita.* Douay: Joannes Borgardus, 1588.

Stow, John. *Annales, or a Generall Chronicle of England. Continued and augmented by Edmund Howes to the end of 1631.* London: Richard Meighen, 1631.

Strype, John. *Memorials of Thomas Cranmer.* 3 vols. Oxford: Clarendon Press, 1812.

Thompson, Craig (ed.). *Ten Colloquies of Erasmus.* New York: Liberal Arts Press, 1957.

Vergil, Polydore. *The Anglica Historia.* Edited with a translation and introduction for the Camden Society by Denys Hay, Ser. 3, Vol. 74. London: Offices of the Royal Historical Society, 1950.

Vernulaeus, Nicolaus. *De arte dicendi libri tres una cum praxi rhetoricae. Editio tertia. Ad quam accesserunt topica seu de inventione libri duo.* Louvain: Phil. Dormalius, 1627.

——. *Conradinus et Crispus, tragoediae.* Louvain: J. Oliverius, 1628.

——. *Divus Eustachius, sive fidei & patientiae triumphus, tragoedia.* Louvain: Phil. Dormalius, 1612.

——. *Elogia oratoria.* Louvain: J. Zegers, 1634.

——. *Fritlandus, tragoedia.* Louvain: J. Coppenius, 1637.

——. *Gorcomienses, sive fidei exilium tragoedia. Exhibita ludis encaenialibus Lovanii anno MDCIX ab alumnis collegii Porcensis.* Cologne: Bernard Gualterus, 1610.

——. *Henricus Octavus, seu schisma anglicanum tragoedia. Exhibita ludis encenialibus Lovanii in collegio Porcensi.* Louvain: Philip Dormalius, 1624.

——. *Institutionum politicarum libri iv, qui omnia civilis doctrinae elementa continent.* Louvain: Phil. Dormalius, 1623.

——. *Institutionum politicarum libri iv.* Louvain: J. Vryenborch, 1647.

——. *Jeanne d'Arc, tragédie latine par Nicolas de Vernulz.* Translated by Antoine de Latour. Orléans: H. Herluison, 1880.

——. *Maximus, tragoedia. Rebellio in Gratianum imp. & ejus punitio. Exhibita a studiosis collegii Porcensis ludis encenialibus anno 1630.* Louvain: Phil. Dormalius, 1630.

——. *Ottocarus, Bohemiae rex, seu rebellio contra Rudolphum I. imperatorem austriacae familiae conditorem, tragoedia. Exhibita ludis encenialibus Lovanii in collegio Porcensi.* Louvain: Phil. Dormalius, 1626.

——. *Rhetorum collegii Porcensis inclytae academiae lovaniensis orationes, sub Nic. Vernulaeo.* Editio sexta. Cologne: Iodocus Kalcovius, 1679.

——. *Theodoricus tragoedia. Exhibita ludis remigialibus in collegio Porcensi nonis octobris 1623.* Louvain: H. Hastenius, 1623.

——. *Tragoediae decem, nunc primum simul editae.* Louvain: J. Oliverius & C. Coenestenius, 1631.

——. *Tragoediae, in duos tomos distributae. Editio secunda. Priore aliquot tragoediis nunc primum in lucem editis auctior.* Louvain: P. Sassenus & H. Nempaeus, 1656.

Vita et scripta Nicolai Vernulaei, prefacing Vol. II of *Tragoediae, in duos tomos distributae.* Louvain: P. Sassenus & H. Nempaeus, 1656.

Vocht, Henri de. *Acta Thomae Mori. History of the Reports of his Trial and Death, with an unedited Contemporary Narrative* ("Humanistica Lovaniensia," 7). Louvain: Uystpruyst, 1947.

Wriothesley, Charles. *A Chronicle of England.* Edited for the Camden Society by W. D. Hamilton, new ser., Nos. 11 and 20. 2 vols. London: Camden Society, 1875–77.

Secondary Sources

Allgemeine deutsche Biographie. Edited by R. von Lilienkron and F. X. von Wegele. 56 vols. Leipzig: Duncker & Humblot, 1875–1912.

Attwater, Donald (ed.). *Orbis catholicus.* London: Burns, Oates, and Washbourne, 1938.

Bahlmann, Paul. *Die Erneuerer des antiken Dramas und ihre ersten dramatischen Versuche, 1314–1478. Eine biobliographische Darstellung der Anfänge der modernen Dramendichtung.* Münster: Regensberschen, 1896.

———. *Die lateinischen Dramen von Wimphelings Stylpho bis zur Mitte des sechzehnten Jahrhunderts, 1480–1550. Ein Beitrag zur Literaturgeschichte.* Münster: Regensbergschen, 1893.

Baumgartner, A. *Die lateinische und griechische Literatur der christlichen Völker.* Vol. IV of *Geschichte der Weltliteratur.* Freiburg im Breisgau: Herder & Co., 1925.

Biographie nationale de Belgique. Edited by the Académie Royale de Belgique. 27 vols. Brussels: H. Thiry-Van Bruggenhoudt, 1866–1938.

Blunt, J. H. *The Reformation of the Church of England: its History, Principles, and Results.* 2 vols. London: Longmans, Green and Co., 1896–97.

Boas, F. S. *An Introduction to Stuart Drama.* London: Oxford University Press, 1946.

———. *An Introduction to Tudor Drama.* Oxford: Clarendon Press, 1946.

———. *Thomas Heywood.* London: Williams & Norgate, 1950.

———. *University Drama in the Tudor Age.* Oxford: Clarendon Press, 1914.

Bolte, Johannes. "Vernuläus," *Allgemeine deutsche Biographie,* Vol. XXXIX (1895), cols. 628–32.

Börner, A. *Die lateinische Schülergespräche der Humanisten.* 2 vols. Berlin: J. Harrwitz Nachfolger, 1897–99.

Bradner, Leicester. "The Latin Drama of the Renaissance (1340–1640)," *Studies in the Renaissance,* IV (1957), 31–70.

———. "The Rise of Secular Drama in the Renaissance," *Studies in the Renaissance,* III (1956), 7–22.

Brants, Victor. "Nicolas de Vernulz, publiciste (1583–1649)," in *L'université de Louvain à travers cinq siècles.* Brussels: A. Lesigne, 1927. Pp. 84–97.

Busch, Wilhelm. *England Under the Tudors.* Translated under the supervision of A. H. Johnson, by Alice Todd. London: A. D. Innes & Co., 1895.

Campbell, Lily B. *Tudor Conceptions of History and Tragedy in "A Mirror for Magistrates."* Berkeley: University of California Press, 1936.

The Catholic Encyclopedia. 15 vols. New York: Robert Appleton Company, 1907–12.

Churchill, George R., and Wolfgang Keller. "Die lateinischen Universitäts Dramen in der Zeit der Königin Elisabeth," *Shakespeare Jahrbuch,* XXXIV (1898), 258–64.

Constant, Gustave. "Clément VII et le divorce d'Henri VIII, 1527–1533," in *Mélanges Albert Dufourcq.* Paris: Librairie Plon, 1932. Pp. 145–61.

———. *La réforme en Angleterre.* Vol. I: *Le schisme anglican, Henri VIII, 1509–1547;* Vol. II: *L'introduction de la réforme en Angleterre, Edouard VI, 1547–1553.* Paris: I, Perrin et Cie., 1930; II, Editions "Alsatia," 1939.

Craig, Hardin. *The Enchanted Glass: The Elizabethan Mind in Literature.* Oxford: Basil Blackwell, 1952.

Crane, William G. *Wit and Rhetoric in the Renaissance.* New York: Columbia University Press, 1937.

Creizenach, Wilhelm. *Geschichte des neueren Dramas.* 5 vols. Halle: Max Niemeyer, 1911–23.

Croll, Morris W. "Attic Prose in the Seventeenth Century," *Studies in Philology*, XVIII (April, 1921), 79–128.

——. "Attic Prose: Lipsius, Montaigne, Bacon," in *Schelling Anniversary Papers*. New York, 1923. Pp. 117–50.

——. "Muret and the History of 'Attic' Prose," *PMLA*, XXXIX (June, 1924), 254–309.

Cunliffe, John W. *The Influence of Seneca on Elizabethan Tragedy*. New York: G. E. Stechert, 1925.

Dabney, Lancaster E. *French Dramatic Literature in the Reign of Henry IV*. Austin, Texas: University of Texas Cooperative Society, 1952.

Daxhelet, Etienne. *Adrien Barlandus, humaniste belge, 1486–1538, sa vie, son oeuvre, sa personnalité* ("Humanistica Lovaniensia," 6). Louvain: Uystpruyst, 1938.

Dictionary of National Biography. Edited by Sir Leslie Stephen and Sir Sidney Lee. 22 vols. London: Oxford University Press, since 1917.

Dittrich, Paul. *Plautus und Terenz in Pädagogik und Schulwesen der deutschen Humanisten*. Leipzig, 1915.

Enciclopedia italiana de scienze, lettere, ed arti. 37 vols. Milan: Istituto Giovanni Trecani, 1929–37.

Enciclopedia universal illustrada europeo-americana. 70 vols. Barcelona: Espasa-Calpe, S. A., 1905–30.

Encyclopedia Britannica. Walter Yust (ed.). 24 vols. Chicago: William Benton, 1955.

Essen, Léon van der. *Une institution d'enseignement superieur sous l'ancien régime*. Brussels: Vromant & Co., 1921.

Even, Edward van. *Louvain dans le passé et dans le présent*. Louvain: Auguste Fonteyn, 1895.

Faber, Frédéric. *Histoire du théâtre français en Belgique, depuis son origine jusqu'à nos jours; d'après des documents inédits reposant aux archives générales du royaume*. 5 vols. Brussels: F. J. Olivier, 1878–80.

Fisher, H. A. L. *The History of England from the Accession of Henry VII. to the Death of Henry VIII. (1485–1547)*. London: Longmans, Green and Co., 1924.

Friedmann, Paul. *Anne Boleyn: A Chapter of English History, 1527–1536*. 2 vols. London: Macmillan and Co., 1884.

Froude, J. A. *History of England from the Fall of Wolsey to the Defeat of the Spanish Armada*. 12 vols. London: Longmans, Green and Co., 1870–75.

Fueter, E. *Histoire de l'historiographie moderne*. Translated by E. Jeanmaire. Paris: Félix Alcan, 1914.

Gairdner, J. "New Lights on the Divorce of Henry VIII.," *English Historical Review*, XI (October, 1896), 673–702; XII (January, 1897), 1–16; XII (April, 1897), 237–53.

Gillow, Joseph. *Bibliographical Dictionary of the English Catholics, from the Breach with Rome, in 1534, to the Present Time*. 5 vols. London: Burns & Oates, 1885–1902.

Goettlingius, C. *Commentariolum de Nicolao Vernulaeo Schilleri antecessore in tragoediis viraginis Aurelianensis et Wallenstenii*. Jena: Libraria Braniana, 1862.

Gofflot, L. V. *Le théâtre au collège du moyen age à nos jours*. Paris: Honoré Champion, 1907.

Guilday, Peter. "The English Catholic Refugees at Louvain, 1559–1575," in *Extraits des Mélanges Charles Moeller* (Université de Louvain: Recueil de travaux publiés par les membres des conférences d'histoire et de philologie, fascicules 40–41). Louvain: Bureaux de Recueil, 1914. Pp. 1–15.

——. *The English Catholic Refugees on the Continent 1558–1795* (Université de Louvain: Recueil de travaux publiés par les membres des conférences d'histoire et de philologie, 1e série, 39e fascicule). London: Longmans, Green and Co., 1914.

Hackett, Francis. *Henry the Eighth*. New York: Horace Liveright, 1929.

Harbage, Alfred. "A Census of Anglo-Latin Plays," *PMLA*, LIII (June, (1938), 624–29.

Herford, Charles H. *Studies in the Literary Relations of England and Germany in the Sixteenth Century*. Cambridge, England: Cambridge University Press, 1886.

Herrick, Marvin T. *Tragicomedy, Its Origin and Development in Italy, France, and England* ("Illinois Studies in Language and Literature," Vol. 39). Urbana: University of Illinois Press, 1955.

Hocking, George Drew. *A Study of the* TRAGOEDIAE SACRAE *of Father Caussin, 1583–1651* ("The Johns Hopkins Studies in Renaissance Literatures and Languages," Vol. 44). Baltimore: The Johns Hopkins Press, 1943.

Howell, Wilbur Samuel. *Logic and Rhetoric in England, 1500–1700*. Princeton: Princeton University Press, 1956.

Hughes, Philip. *The Reformation in England*. Vol. I: *The King's Proceedings*. Vol. II: *Religio Depopulata*. Vol. III: *True Religion now Established*. London: Hollis & Carter, 1950–54.

——. *Rome and the Counter-Reformation in England*. London: Burns & Oates, 1944.

Jongh, H. de. *L'ancienne faculté de théologie de Louvain au premier siècle de son existence, 1432–1540*. Edited by R. Roger and F. Chernoviz ("Bureaux de la revue d'histoire ecclésiastique"). Louvain: Pierre Smeesters, 1911.

Kastner, L. W., and H. B. Charlton (eds.). *The Poetical Works of Sir William Alexander, Earl of Stirling. With an Introductory Essay on the Growth of the Senecan Tradition in Renaissance Tragedy*. 2 vols. ("Publications of the University of Manchester, English Ser., Nos. 10, 18). Manchester: University of Manchester, 1921, 1929.

Kristeller, Paul Oskar. *The Classics and Renaissance Thought*. Cambridge, Mass.: Harvard University Press, 1955.

Law, Thomas Graves. "Sanders or Sander, Nicholas." *Dictionary of National Biography*, Vol. XVII, cols. 748–51.

Lebègue, Raymond. "L'humanisme latin de la renaissance," in *Mémorial Marouzeau*. Paris, 1943. Pp. 271–84.

——. *La tragédie religieuse en France. Les débuts*. Paris: Honoré Champion, 1929.

Lechat, Robert, S. J. *Les réfugié anglais dans les Pays-Bas espagnols durant le règne d'Elisabeth, 1558–1603* (Université de Louvain: Recueil de travaux publiés par les membres des conférences d'histoire et de philologie, 1ᵉ série, 38ᵐᵉ fascicule). Louvain: Jules de Meester, 1914.

Lucas, F. L. *Seneca and Elizabethan Tragedy.* Cambridge, England: Cambridge University Press, 1922.

McCabe, William, S.J. "An Introduction to the Jesuit Theatre" (unpublished Ph.D. dissertation, Dept. of English, Cambridge University, England, 1929).

———. "Notes on the St. Omers Theatre," *Philological Quarterly,* XVII (July, 1938), 225–39.

———. "The Play-List of the English College of St. Omers, 1592–1762," *Revue de littérature comparée,* XVII (Avril-Juin, 1937), 355–75.

Mackie, John D. *The Earlier Tudors, 1485–1558.* Vol. VII of the *Oxford History of England.* 14 vols. Edited by G. N. Clark. Oxford: Clarendon Press, 1952.

Massebieau, L. *Les colloques scolaires du seizième siècle et leurs auteurs, 1480–1570.* Paris: J. Bonheur, 1878.

Mattingly, Garrett. *Catherine of Aragon.* Boston: Little, Brown and Co., 1941.

Méril, Edélstand du. *Les origines latines du théâtre moderne.* Leipzig: H. Welter, 1897.

Mitford, J. "Retrospective Review of Vernulaeus' *Henricus Octavus,*" *The Gentleman's Magazine,* XXIII (May, 1845), 501–04.

Müller, Johannes. *Das Jesuitendrama in den Ländern deutschen Zunge vom Anfang (1555) bis zum Hochbarock (1665).* 2 vols. Augsburg: Benno Filser, 1930.

Murarasu, D. *La poésie néolatine et la renaissance des lettres antiques en France, 1500–1549.* Paris: J. Gamber, 1928.

Murray, John Courtney. "Contemporary Orientations of Catholic Thought on Church and State in the Light of History," *Theological Studies,* X (June, 1949), 177–234.

Nève, Félix. *Mémoire historique et littéraire sur le collège des Trois-Langues à l'université de Louvain.* Brussels: M. Hayez, 1856.

———. *La renaissance des lettres et l'essor de l'érudition ancienne en Belgique.* Louvain: Charles Peeters, 1890.

Niceron, J. P. *Mémoires pour servir à l'histoire des hommes illustres dans la république des lettres avec un catalogue raisonné de leurs ouvrages.* 43 vols. Paris: Briasson, 1729–45.

Niemann, Gottfried. *Die Dialogliteratur der Reformationszeit.* Leipzig: R. Voigtlander, 1905.

Nijhoff, W., and M. E. Kronenberg. *Nederlandsche Bibliographie van 1500 tot 1540.* 4 vols. The Hague: Martinus Nijhoff, 1919–53.

Pachtler, G. Michael (ed.). *Ratio studiorum et institutiones scholasticae societatis Jesu per Germaniam olim vigentes collectae concinnatae, dilucidatae.* 4 vols. Berlin: A. Hofman & Co., 1887–94.

Palmer, Ralph Graham. *Seneca's* De Remediis Fortuitorum *and the Elizabethans* ("Publication of the Institute of Elizabethan Studies," No. 1). Chicago: Institute of Elizabethan Studies, 1953.

Paquot, J. N. *Mémoires pour servir à l'histoire littéraire des dix-sept provinces des Pay-Bas, la principauté de Liège et de quelques contrées voisines.* 18 vols. Louvain: Imprimerie académique, 1763–70.

Peerlkamp, Petrus Hofman. *Liber de vita, doctrina, et facultate Nederlandorum qui carmina latina composuerunt.* Editio altera emendata et aucta. Leyden: H. W. Hagenberg, 1843.

Pirenne, Henri. *Histoire de Belgique.* 3d ed. revised. 4 vols. Brussels: H. Lamertin, 1909.

Polain, M. Louis. *Catalogue des livres imprimés au quinzième siècle des bibliothèques de Belgique.* 4 vols. Brussels: Societé des bibliophiles et iconophiles de Belgique, 1932.

Polet, A. *Petrus Nannius, 1500–1557* ("Humanistica Lovaniensia," 5). Louvain: Uystpruyst, 1936.

Pollard, A. F. *Henry VIII.* London: Longmans, Green and Co., 1905.

——. *The History of England, 1547–1603.* Vol. VI of *The Political History of England.* 12 vols. London: Longmans, Green and Co., 1910.

——. *Thomas Cranmer and the English Reformation.* London: G. T. Putnam's Sons, 1927.

——. *Wolsey.* London: Longmans, Green and Co., 1929.

Pollen, J. H. *The English Catholics in the Reign of Queen Elizabeth. A Study of their Politics, Civil Life, and Government, 1558–1580.* London: Longmans, Green and Co., 1920.

——. "Dr. Nicholas Sander," *English Historical Review*, VI (January, 1891), 36–47.

Poncelet, Alfred. *Histoire de la compagnie de Jésus dans les anciens Pays-Bas.* 2 vols. Brussels: M. Hayez, 1927–28.

Reynolds, Ernst E. *Saint John Fisher.* London: Burns & Oates, 1956.

Ribadaneira, Petrus. *Illustrium scriptorum religionis societatis Jesu catalogus.* Antwerp, 1608.

Ribner, Irving. *The English History Play in the Age of Shakespeare.* Princeton: Princeton University Press, 1957.

Roersch, Alphonse. *L'humanisme belge à l'époque de la renaissance.* Brussels: G. Van Oest, 1910.

Rygiel, Stefan. *Puteanus und die Polen.* Berlin: H. Lonys, 1913.

Saunders, Jason Lewis. *Justus Lipsius. The Philosophy of Renaissance Stoicism.* New York: Liberal Arts Press, 1955.

Schrevel, A. C. de. *Histoire du séminaire de Bruges.* 2 vols. Bruges: Louis de Plancke, 1883, 1895.

Simar, Th. *Étude sur Erycius Puteanus, 1574–1646.* Louvain: Bureaux du Recueil, 1909.

Sommervogel, Carlos, Augustin de Backer, and Alois de Backer. *Bibliothèque de la compagnie de Jésus.* 10 vols. Paris: A. Picard et fils, 1890–1909.

Stachel, Paul. *Seneca und das deutsche Renaissancedrama.* Berlin: Mayer & Müller, 1907.

Stone, J. M. *The History of Mary I. Queen of England.* London: E. P. Dutton & Co., 1901.

Stratman, Carl L. "University Drama in Cambridge and Oxford from 1603–1642" (unpublished Ph.D. dissertation, Dept. of English, University of Illinois. Urbana, Illinois, 1947).

Symonds, John Addington. *Renaissance in Italy: The Revival of Learning.* 2d ed. London: Smith, Elder, and Co., 1882.

Tarlier, H. *Dictionnaires des communes, hameaux, chateaux, fermes, hauts fourneaux, charbonnages, etc. du royaume de Belgique.* Brussels: H. Tarlier, 1858.

Taunton, Ethelred L. *Thomas Wolsey, Legate and Reformer.* London: John Lane, 1902.

Tieghem, Paul van. *La littérature latine de la renaissance: étude d'histoire littéraire européenne.* Paris: E. Droz, 1944.

Veech, Thomas McNevin. *Dr. Nicholas Sanders and the English Reformation, 1530–1581* (Université de Louvain: Recueil de travaux publiés par les membres des conférences d'histoire et de philologie, 2ᵉ série, 32ᵐᵉ fascicule). Louvain: Bureaux du Recueil, 1935.

Vetter, Theodor. *Wallenstein in der dramatischen Dichtung des Jahrzehntes seines Todes.* Frankfurt: J. Huber, 1894.

Vocht, Henri de. *History of the Foundation and Rise of the Collegium Trilingue Lovaniense, 1517–1550.* 4 vols. ("Recueil de travaux d'histoire et de philologie"). Louvain: Bureau de Recueil, 1951–55.

——. *Inventaire des archives de l'université de Louvain, 1426–1797, aux archives générales du royaume à Bruxelles.* Louvain: Uystpruyst, 1927.

——. *Jerome de Busleyden, Founder of the Collegium Trilingue, His Life and Writings.* Turnhout: Brepols Press, 1950.

——. "Les jubilés de l'université sous L'Ancien Régime, 1526, 1626, 1726," *L'Université de Louvain à travers cinq siècles.* Études historiques, publiées avec une introduction par Léon van der Essen. Brussels: A. Lesigne, 1927.

——. *Monumenta Humanistica Lovaniensia. Texts and Studies about Louvain Humanists: Erasmus, Vives, Dorpius, Clenardus, Goes, Moringus* ("Humanistica Lovaniensia," 4). Louvain: Uystpruyst, 1934.

——. "Thomas Harding," *English Historical Review,* XXXV (April, 1920), 231–46.

——. "Vernulaeus," *Biographie nationale de Belgique,* Vol. XXVI (1936–37), cols. 676–82.

Wainewright, John B. "Some Letters and Papers of Nicolas Sander, 1562–1580," *Miscellanea XIII* ("Publications of the Catholic Record Society," XXVI, 1–57). London: J. Whitehead & Son, 1926.

Wood, Anthony. *Athenae Oxonienses.* Edited by P. Bliss. 4 vols. 3d ed. London, 1813–20.

Zanta, Leontine. *La renaissance du stoïcisme au XVIᵉ siècle* ("Bibliothèque littéraire de la renaissance," new ser., No. 5). Paris: Edouard Champion, 1914.

INDEX

Abel [Abell], Thomas: 257
Abrahamus tentatus (Schöpperus):
21 n., 22, 22 n.
Achilleis (Luschus): 31
Acts of Supremacy and Uniformity,
1559: 50
Adelphi [*Adelphoe*] (Terence): 18
Adolphus (*Hermenigildus*): 47
Adolphus, Gustavus: 44 n.
Adrian VI, Pope: 240
Aeneid (Vergil): 20, 66, 223, 250
Aesop: 57
Albert (*Wallenstein*, Glapthorne): 45
Albert, Archduke of Austria: 11 n., 25,
25 n., 212
Alcazar, Battle of: 52 n.
Alençon, Duchess of (Margaret of
Navarre): 228–29
Alençon, Duke of: 25, 228
Alexander III, Pope: 39
Alkmaar, Holland: 19 n.
Allen, Don Cameron: xi
Allen, William Cardinal: 51 n., 52, 52 n.,
57
Alpais (*Lambertus*): 46
Ambrose, Bishop of Milan (*Maximus*):
43
Andreas, Valerius: 6 n., 214
Andria (Terence): 18
Angel, *Angelus* (*Henry VIII*): 282, 286
Anglican Schism (*De origine ac pro-
gressu schismatis Anglicani*, 1585, by
Nicholas Sander): genesis of, 55, 56;
circulation of, in manuscript, 55; press
preparation and printing of, 55, 55 n.;
editions of, 54, 54 n., 56, 209; alteration of, 55–56; translations of, 54 n.;
and Lewis translation, 49 n.; sources
of: Vatican and Madrid documents,
54, 57, 57 n., 250, 252, 253; and oral
and written testimony, 56–57, 257;
and their reliability, 59 n.; outline of,
56; analysis of, 59–60; popularity of,
54; influence of, 58; Anne Boleyn in,
60, 219, 241; slander in, 60; Wolsey
in, 60; Catherine in, 230–31; and
origins of schism, 60; and royal divorce, 60; church-state conflict in, 60;
partisan polemics in, 59 n.; accepted
by Roman Catholic authorities, 54–55;

adverse opinions about, 55, 57–58;
verdict of modern historians on, 58–
59, 213; historical accuracy of, xii,
229, 235, 239, 243, 244, 247, 250,
252, 253; historical inaccuracies in,
264, 284; as source of Vernulaeus'
Henricus Octavus (*Henry VIII*), xii,
49 n.; mentioned, 52, 57, 208, 224,
280. SEE ALSO Sander, Nicholas;
Henry VIII
Antwerp: 16 n., 19 n., 22 n., 23 n.
Archilocus (Frachaeus): 21 n.
Ardennes, Remacle d': 17, 17 nn., 18
Arianism: 36, 47
Aristophanes: 18
Aristotle: 211
Arthur, Prince of Wales: 213, 253, 254,
255
Assertio septem sacramentorum (King
Henry VIII): 209
Auction of Philosophers (Lucian): 18
Augustus, Sigismund, King (Poland):
51
Aulularia (Plautus): presented at Lily
and Arras Colleges, 15, 17
Austria: 40, 50
Austrian dynasty, guardian spirit of,
Genius Austriacus (*Fritlandus*): 45
Avalos, Ferrante de (captain of Charles
V): 211
Ave, Antoine d' (student of Vernu-
laeus): 8, 12, 67

Bachusius, Gerald: 18
Bahlmann, Paul: xi, 19 n.
Barlandus, Adrian: Latin teacher at
Porc College, 17; colleague and friend
of Dorp, 17; produces Plautus' *Aulu-
laria* and supplies prologue, 17–18;
composes prologues and epilogues for
Porc classic repertory, 18; and interest
in classics, 19; influences Nannius, 19;
member of Louvain Humanist circle,
18; as producer of classical plays, 22
Baronius: 55
Bath, diocese of: 276
beadles (*pedelli*): 4 n.
Beauchamp Tower: 271
Becket, St. Thomas (*Thomas Cantuari-*